FOUNDATIONS OF AMERICAN EDUCATION: READINGS

Fourth Edition

James A. Johnson
Harold W. Collins
Victor L. Dupuis
John H. Johansen

FOUNDATIONS OF AMERICAN EDUCATION: Readings

FOUNDATIONS OF AMERICAN EDUCATION: Readings

FOURTH EDITION

JAMES A. JOHNSON
Northern Illinois University

HAROLD W. COLLINS
Northern Illinois University

VICTOR L. DUPUIS
Pennsylvania State University

JOHN H. JOHANSEN
Northern Illinois University

Allyn and Bacon, Inc.
Boston London Sydney Toronto

Copyright © 1979, 1975, 1972, and 1969 by
Allyn and Bacon, Inc.,
470 Atlantic Avenue, Boston, Massachusetts 02210.

Library of Congress Cataloging in Publication Data
Main entry under title:

Foundations of American education.

  Includes index.
  1. Education—United States—History—Addresses,
essays, lectures, I. Johnson, James Allen, 1932–
LA212.F6 1979 370′.973   78-31745
ISBN 0-205-06565-1

Printed in the United States of America.

Contents

Preface

This book contains a wealth of resources on a variety of educational topics from an impressive array of contemporary authorities. It can serve as a single book in courses in the foundations of American education. It can also serve as a supplemental reading source with any standard book in educational foundations. However, this book will perhaps best serve as an enrichment source with its companion volume, *An Introduction to the Foundations of American Education*, fourth edition, written by the same authors. We believe that these companion volumes make an ideal set of instructional material for courses in the foundations of American education. We have also prepared a teaching aid, *Resource Booklet and Overhead Transparency Masters for Introduction to the Foundations of American Education*, which can aid in enriching foundation courses and save the instructor precious time. Enrichment audio tapes have also been prepared for instructors' uses.

This new fourth edition of readings is divided into seven parts: Professional Aspects of Teaching; School and Society; Control, Organization, and Support of American Education; Historical Foundations of Education; Philosophical Bases of Education; Structuring Educational Programs; and American Education and the Future.

In selecting the readings for this volume, we drew from a cross-section of the best articles that have appeared in recent professional literature. Some of the selections represent dissenting views and no endorsement of ideas is intended.

There is disagreement concerning what constitutes the foundations of American education. The most common elements include educational philosophy, history, sociology, and psychology. Educational psychology is taught as a separate subject at most teacher-preparing institutions and, therefore, is not dealt with in this book. Four additional areas—professional aspects of teaching, educational administration, school curriculum, and educational futurism—are very important topics but are not usually thought of as foundation areas. It appears logical to the authors that these four additional areas have a rightful place in a foundations of American education readings text. Thus, seven foundation areas commonly found in introductory courses preparing teachers for certification are included.

Part I introduces the reader to various professional aspects of teaching. Part II helps the teacher to see the school in relationship to our society. It also helps him or her to examine the school as a social institution and to understand its relationship to societal problems and issues. Part III is intended to give the teacher a better understanding of some of the current administrative problems faced by American educators. If the teacher is to participate in the administrative decision-making process, he or she needs to understand the historical development of education in America. We hope that the introduction

to educational philosophy presented in Part V will assist the teacher in formulating a philosophy of education and to contemplate basic questions in education. Part VI discusses various aspects of school curriculum. Part VII deals with the future of our educational system.

We are indebted to the many writers and publishers who so generously gave permission for the use of their material in this book. We are also indebted to our colleagues in teacher education programs throughout the United States who helped to evaluate the materials used in this volume.

J.A.J.
H.W.C.
V.L.D.
J.H.J.

FOUNDATIONS OF AMERICAN EDUCATION: Readings

PART I

Professional Aspects of Teaching

The magnitude of the educational enterprise is enormous. Because of its institutional status it directly and indirectly affects a significant segment of the society. Of the 214 million people in the United States, three out of every ten persons are directly involved in the educational process; namely, teachers, students, board members, and administrators. In addition, millions of people are indirectly involved in education-related occupations such as the automotive industry that manufactures school vehicles, the construction trades that build school facilities, and the paper manufacturers and publishing companies that provide textbooks. Among this vast number of education and educational-related employees, classroom teachers represent the basis of the foundation of the educational system.

Two recent trends are contributing to an overall reduction in the magnitude of the educational enterprise. The trend of declining birth rates has prompted most school districts to engage in careful examinations of their local growth projections. Enrollment data from 1965 projected through 1985 for the entire

United States project a decline in public school pupil population for both the elementary schools and the high schools. The second trend is the reduction in the number of persons who will be qualified to teach. Fewer and fewer students are selecting teacher preparation as a career choice. When enrollments begin to increase in the mid-eighties, it is conceivable that teacher shortages in selected areas will be prevalent. The impact of such trends on the professional aspects of teaching is generally uncertain.

It has long been asserted by members of the educational enterprise that anyone who becomes a teacher becomes a member of a profession. On the other hand, there are those who argue that teaching should not be considered a profession in the same light as the long-recognized professions of medicine, law, and the ministry. The opponents do not consider teachers as skilled labor technicians or blue collar workers; however, they do speak of teaching as a category of subprofessionalism, a term as yet undefined. Despite this rhetorical exercise directed at the profession of teaching, there is little doubt that the nature of the teaching profession is rapidly changing.

Teacher concerns have vastly broadened, further contributing to the complexity of the teaching profession. Topics such as teacher supply and demand, teacher salaries, academic freedom, student rights, tenure, professional liability, professional organizations for educators, and teacher unions are typical concerns that were probably not included in former teacher preparation programs. Part I presents a group of articles which are intended to provide an overview of selected dimensions in the work world of teachers. Attention is given to getting a teaching job in a tight job market, rise and fall of teachers' salaries, value of a college diploma, merger possibilities for teacher organizations, ethics from teacher organization viewpoints, and thoughts about the professionalization of teachers.

As a beginning teacher, you realize that a four-year degree does not guarantee employment. Public schools are evaluating prospective candidates much more stringently. In his article, "How to Get a Job in a Tight Job Market," James Galloway offers suggestions related to interviewing, self-analysis, utilization of resource people, and preparation of a resume. In addition, points of consideration for writing letters of application, interview questions to anticipate, and a list of several general suggestions for seeking your first teaching position are provided. Prospective teachers should candidly consider the fact that teaching is not an appropriate career choice for everyone. For those who possess the prerequisites of commitment to education, adequate personal and social skills, and the basic ability to develop the technical skills for successful teaching, the teaching career is excellent. Within the career framework many avenues are provided for teachers to specialize, modify their career orientation,

and/or seek well paying supervisory or administrative positions.

While teachers considered themselves poorly paid for their work, school communities and their respective boards of education were slow in raising teacher salaries. As teacher organizations became increasingly more powerful and militant, particularly during the decade of the sixties, teachers began to demand increased salary and economic fringe benefits. Consequently, boards of education have approved substantial increases in salaries and benefits over the past few years .

Richard A. Musemeche and Sam Adams write about "The Rise and Fall of Teachers' Salaries: A Nine-Region Survey" in the second reading. Salary data are presented according to several geographic regions of the United States. The summary findings suggest that teacher salaries have increased substantially since 1967–68. However, the value of these increases has been almost entirely neutralized in many cases, and in almost half of the states was actually reversed by inflation.

Much discussion has recently emerged regarding the advantages and disadvantages of earning an advanced degree. One side of the argument suggests that in a lessened job market, the bachelor's degree person can be hired for less salary and, therefore, one would further limit the chances of finding employment by earning an advanced degree. Large numbers of educators cling to the historic faith of Americans that education benefits provide for a better life as well as more hard cash. "Value of a College Diploma: Center of Growing Debate" is reprinted from *U.S. News and World Report* for the purpose of providing some enlightenment on this topic. As related to teaching, advanced degrees do mean higher salaries on typical teacher salary schedules. While a somber note to the demand for teachers was presented earlier, when enrollments increase again causing teaching positions to increase, the advanced degree would be worthwhile.

In some districts the climate of the working environment for teachers may be likened strongly to the unionistic climate of the trade unions. In other districts the teachers strive to maintain a more scholarly professional climate likened to that of the traditional professions (lawyers, dentists, doctors). Each teacher must determine the manner in which he or she will contribute to the organizational climate associated with their respective memberships. The potential merger of the two largest teacher organizations, the National Education Association and the American Federation of Teachers, is discussed by Kenneth P. Lubetsky in his article, "Will the NEA and the AFT Ever Merge?" Also related to teacher organizations are selected statements which suggest the ethics base upon which the organizations desire to function. The "Bill of Teacher Rights" is a statement of the National Education Association. The American Federation of Teachers statement is entitled "Bill of Rights."

While the brief mention of some of the effects of a teacher surplus seems to portray a rocky road for the teaching profession, the overall long-term view envisions a stronger profession with better trained, better qualified, and better paid teachers. One of the most perplexing problems for teachers during the past century has been the upgrading of their occupation to a profession. In his article, "Second Thoughts About the Professionalization of Teachers," James Covert proceeds to explore several aspects of the professional model which suggest that teachers ought to review the very basic question of the desirability of becoming a profession. Seemingly, most teacher education institutions have overlooked the difficulties primarily because of the desirable status and prestige that accrue to professionals.

Reading 1

How to Get a Job in a Tight Job Market

James L. Galloway

Prospective teacher graduates for the most part are aware of the current job market and projections of the next few years. To many, it is a traumatic experience to realize that after four years of study and the ambition to teach, one might be thwarted by a recessed market. Today, more and more graduates are discovering that it is increasingly difficult to find and secure a teaching position. This is a far cry from the fluid job market of four to six years ago. There are many reasons for the oversupply. One can point to decreased birth rates, the number of teachers graduating from colleges in the last ten years, and other reasons. In light of these conditions, it behooves graduating teachers to evaluate the market, take an inventory of themselves, and plan an aggressive job campaign.

As beginning teachers, one must realize that a four-year degree does not guarantee employment. The market is overcrowded in many areas and yet there are teaching areas where there are definite shortages. Presently,

there is an oversupply in English, social studies, elementary education, foreign language while definite shortages exist in special education, industrial arts, math and science.

Students planning to become teachers should be aware that usually there are always positions open in practically any field for the top-notch graduate. The average and marginal student may experience difficulty finding a teaching job in the oversupplied areas.

Public schools, because of the situation, have become much more selective in hiring teachers. They are evaluating candidates much more stringently. Prospective teachers are judged on student teaching evaluations, grades, alternate teaching areas, appearance, maturity, motivation, personality, extracurricular activity, and personal recommendations.

In many cases, the teacher who has limited his teaching subject area might find the job market even more limited. Teachers can certainly increase their marketability as teacher candidates in many of the oversupplied areas by increasing the scope of classes they are qualified to teach. In this

Source: James L. Galloway, "How to Get a Job in a Tight Job Market." ASCUS 1977, pp. 14–16. Association for School, College and University Staffing.

regard, a teacher who has majored for example in men's physical education, would have greater employment possibilities if he would have a strong minor such as industrial arts, science, or math. Additional course work during the summer or at night would give one more options in today's and tomorrow's job market.

In the past few years, fewer and fewer school systems have recruited teachers on the campus. Not only are their needs reduced, but they no longer feel that it is necessary to spend the money to send recruiters to campus. In addition, most school systems today are besieged with applications by mail and in person from prospective teachers.

In light of this reduction in campus interviewing, graduating teachers should not solely rely on campus interviews to secure a job. One must use ingenuity, be resourceful, and use every attack possible to find a position. This does not suggest that candidates not take advantage of campus interviews as this is one of the best approaches. A candidate should therefore take as many interviews as possible.

Prior to the job campaign, it is prudent for the candidate to analyze himself. It is important to assess your strengths and weaknesses, to decide on what you want to do, where you want to go, what your personal limitations such as location are, and what alternatives you might want to consider.

The next step would be to take advantage of many of the resources and people who could assist you in finding the *right* job for you. Talk to your placement staff, faculty, friends, school administrators and teachers. They will be quite willing to give you as much assistance as they can offer.

Before engaging in your campaign it will also be necessary for you to collect and secure such forms as credentials, recom-

mendations, and transcripts. Gathering this important and necessary information *early* will eliminate future problems. A note of caution: prepare credentials and supportive data with care. Sloppy, poorly prepared documents can reflect upon you as a person and could possibly mean the difference of whether or not you are hired.

Preparation of a resume is an important task. An effective resume can sell you if told in a concise, attractive format. Before preparing such a resume, you must understand yourself, your potential and aspirations, and prepare such with care and organization. This important document will represent *you* to the potential employer. If you are to mount an extensive job campaign, it would be wise to have your resume printed or offset. An attractive cover and format is an asset. This approach will possibly cost you a considerable amount of money but the funds you spend to seek employment should be considered an investment, not an expense. If you are to expose yourself to a great number of employers, you have to be prepared to spend money on typing of letters, envelopes, stationery, postage, resumes, and follow-up. There are many excellent books and guides to use in preparing a job-winning resume. Many times however, the unusual format, content, and packaging of a resume is the factor that will catch the eye of the employer. Therefore, put some time and effort in its preparation.

Letters of application are equally important in your job search. Prepare a good letter. Write it to sell you as a candidate. It should be an original, typed, single spaced, one-page document addressed to a *specific person* if possible. There are a number of good resource books to which you may refer in formulating your letter of application. You may also consider using the pre-introductory letter prior to an interview and certainly the post interview letter to the individual. Follow-up of this nature is not only courteous, it might be the deciding factor in hiring you over another candidate.

Preparing for the interview, whether it be on campus or at the school site is obviously an important step. Most school systems will require at least two interviews. In preparing for interviews, research the school system as much as possible. Ask yourself such questions as: what is the reputation of the system, what is the assessed evaluation within the system, what has been the history of the community backing the system financially and in other ways, what is the organizational structure of the school, what is the pupil-teacher ratio, what are some of the benefits and services provided in the area of support to the teacher, and many other important considerations. The prospective candidate who does his homework prior to the interview will have a distinct advantage.

The interview itself can be a rewarding, stimulating experience. Candidates should be prepared to answer some of the following types of questions.

- What is your philosophy of education?
- Why did you select teaching as a career goal?
- How would you handle such problems as motivation, discipline, parental concerns?
- Why do you want to teach in our system?

In addition, the interviewer will be attempting to discover what you as a candidate feel about commitment to education, motivation, and above all—you as an individual. Attention should be paid to stressing your strengths and concern should be paid to not being critical of others or placing blame for your record on others. Naturally, appropriate dress, attitude, and grooming are extremely important parts of your overall image.

Follow-up on all interviews and letters of application is a must. Too often candidates fail to adhere to this important aspect of the employment procedure. To sit back and wait for a reply many times eliminates candidates from serious consideration! In today's job market, one *must* be aggressive and follow-up on all contacts. Many times candidates feel that they shouldn't bother the employer after the initial contact. Instead, the candidate should make certain that the employer knows he is interested in a position.

The following is a list of other suggestions which should be considered in preparing to seek your first position:

1. When will you be available for employment?
2. Be geographically flexible and mobile. Restricting yourself to particular geographic regions will restrict your job possibilities. Seeking positions in areas of the country such as California, Denver, Miami, etc., is difficult due to the number of other candidates looking for positions in these regions. Teaching positions in rural areas presently exist because of location in many cases.
3. Try not to restrict yourself to grade level selections, school size, teaching responsibility. Every time you become more selective, the odds will fall accordingly.
4. Develop a portfolio of as much information about you as possible to take with you to interviews. Such items as a resume, biographical sketch, reference letters, transcript, student teaching report, lesson plans, etc., will assist you in selling yourself.
5. Start now to get ready for your campaign. Don't wait until the last minute

and then decide that you need a job. It may be too late.

6. Keep a record of interviews and application letters sent. Follow-up at predetermined time periods on each contract if you do not have a response.

7. Don't panic if you don't have a teaching job by June. More and more, teaching positions are opening in July and August as teachers resign late to accept other positions. *Keep in touch with your placement office* regularly to advise them that you are still actively looking.

8. Keep your placement credentials, resumes, and other information up-to-date. Especially is this true in case of changes in marital status, address, telephone number, and additional education or experience.

9. Avoid too much emphasis upon salary, fringe benefits, or your desire to pursue a graduate program. Your main emphasis should be in obtaining that best position for you.

10. Honor contracts! If you sign a contract, ethically and sometimes legally you are bound to adhere to your decision. Violation of such might jeopardize future job considerations and possibilities.

SOURCES OF JOBS:

Every source possible should be utilized by the prospective teacher. Some of the following are examples:

1. Your best possible source is your Placement Office. Most school systems today recruit their teachers through campus interviews or through the use of vacancy announcements sent to placement offices. Follow-up on job vacancies as soon as possible.

2. Make up a list of all possible systems in which you may have an interest. In addition, devise a list of school systems that would be possibilities after you have exhausted all your primary interest contacts. This would include out-of-the-way employers, small, rural, and other types of employers.

3. Follow newspaper, journal, and other types of advertisements. Contacts of this nature are sometimes very productive.

4. Talk to your advisor, faculty, or chairman to determine if they have any contacts, friends, or leads that you might investigate.

5. Contact Chambers of Commerce for information about school systems in the area.

6. Use of directories listing the contract person in each school system will be a valuable source. Make sure that the directory is current. Addressing an inquiry to a person no longer in a position can sometimes damage your chances.

7. Placing ads yourself in newspapers is not effective for teacher candidates. Often you are besieged by employment agencies, salesmen, peddlers and the like.

8. Private employment agencies normally have a fee attached to placement. Persons registering with these agencies should be cautioned to read the contract thoroughly and understand all phases of the negotiation before signing!

9. The United States Employment Offices is a nationwide network which services professionals and is free of charge.

10. Some off-beat methods sometimes work but should be seriously thought out before doing anything radical. For example, telegrams and telephone calls sometimes will direct attention to you

as a candidate. "Wanted" types of posters in the form of a resume, unusual color, style, format, paper, etc., for application letters and resumes at times are effective.

11. The more letters, interviews, and contacts you make, the better your chances. The law of averages will come into play. So, don't limit yourself. Be prepared to invest time and effort in finding the job you want.

When you are fortunate enough to locate a position and you are in need of a sounding board and listener, your placement officer can be of assistance to you in this decision-making process.

After you have been offered a contract, read it and decide whether you want the job. If you sign the contract, you should advise all other employers of your decision. In addition, notify your Placement Office so that they can take your name off the active list.

These suggestions are possibilities. If they work—great. The job-hunting game is an exciting one if you make it such. It takes time, money, perseverance, action, thought, preparation, and *hard work*. If you are turned down time after time, don't give up. If you adhere to some of the suggestions made in this article, your chances will be enhanced.

The investment you make in seeking a job is small when you consider that you have already invested probably over $10,000 and four years of your time to obtain a degree. Additionally, you have lost about four years earning power. This outline for you as a prospective teacher in a tight job market has attempted to describe what to expect and how to do it in the process of seeking employment.

Reading 2

The Rise and Fall of Teachers' Salaries: A Nine-Region Survey

Richard A. Musemeche and Sam Adams

In 1975–76 the average salary of classroom teachers in the 50 states and the District of Columbia stood at $12,524, according to the National Education Association's Research Division. That represented an increase of $5,101, or 41% over the 1967–68 average. But in terms of buying power it was an improvement of only 1.2%. This figure will startle many observers, because education writers generally assume that collective negotiations and better teacher organization have improved the economic position of teachers notably in recent years, despite rapid inflation and budget difficulties at all governmental levels.

As is usually the case, the average conceals more than it reveals. Some states and some regions have fared much better than others. The accompanying table provides state-by-state comparisons. We have also divided the states into regions for comparison purposes.

We can offer no definitive explanations

Source: Richard A. Musemeche and Sam Adams, "The Rise and Fall of Teachers' Salaries: A Nine-Region Survey." Phi Delta Kappan (February 1977), pp. 479–481. Reprinted with permission.

for the considerable state and regional variations in the teacher salary increases revealed for the nine-year period we studied. However, we checked with observers who are familiar with the factors and events which affect teacher salary levels in several states. We report their observations simply as informed opinion and without attribution, because we think they are worthy of consideration.

New England Region. New England experienced the largest decrease in real income of any of the nine regions studied. The purchasing power of the average teacher dropped 4.8% ($356). Of the six New England states, only Rhode Island and Maine showed gains in real income ($491 and $31 respectively). Teachers in Vermont lost $601, or 9.1%, in real income during this time span.

We sought background information on Vermont and Massachusetts, since both showed substantial declines in teacher purchasing power. A collective bargaining law was passed in Vermont in 1969. It requires school boards to negotiate if petitioned by the teachers. Fringe benefits received by teachers in Vermont include a family health insurance plan. A key reason for the decline appears to be a recent drop in state support of approximately 12% (from 32% of the total cost to 20%) in the past few years.

One possible cause for the failure of teacher salaries in Massachusetts to keep pace with living costs is the fact that the number of school districts in the state has increased. Defying the national trend toward consolidation, Massachusetts has added new school districts, some of which are very small. These districts have tended to hire teachers at the lower end of the pay scale, thus reducing the state average. A second cause is that state support, intended to be in the vicinity of 35%, actually stands near 24%.

In contrast to the regional pattern, Rhode Island teachers experienced a substantial growth in purchasing power. The state's legislature approved a collective bargaining law in 1968; in operation, it appears to have improved teacher salaries. In 1975 there were 13 strikes; in 1976 only one. Besides salary increases, the following fringe benefits have been provided to teachers: family plan dental and health insurance statewide, vision care in one district, and income protection in some systems.

Mideastern Region.   As a group, states comprising the Mideast had the largest increase in real income (6%) of all the regions. The gain for New York's teachers amounted to $930, or 10.8%. Collective bargaining undoubtedly played an important part in the income and fringe benefit gains of New York teachers, where unionism is strong both in New York City and in upstate districts. The Taylor Law (1967), though widely criticized by teacher groups, has been the basis for collective bargaining in nearly every district. The following fringe benefits are found

statewide: dental, health, life, and long-term disability insurance; extra pay for extracurricular activities.

Southeastern Region.   As a group, the southeastern states merely held their own in terms of salaries. However, two of these states, Florida and Louisiana, experienced the largest losses in real income not only for the region but for the nation. Average salaries dropped 12.7% ($920) in Florida and 10.4% ($704) in Louisiana. In percentage terms, the average salary of classroom teachers in Mississippi showed a major increase (19.2%). But the 1967–68 base was very low. Alabama showed a gain in real income of $638, or 11.2%.

Real income decline in Florida has been attributed to several factors. One was loss of sales tax income from the tourist industry as a result of the energy crisis. Although the 1974 legislature passed a law permitting collective bargaining, teachers have not yet benefited notably. School boards generally withheld increases that might have been automatic before passage of the act, waiting for teachers to take the initiative. Once bargaining did take place, boards often resisted successfully, and outcomes tended to be much less than teachers demanded (50% increases).

The Florida Educational Finance Program adopted in 1973 established a new equalization formula. Because the state has not moved toward the full funding of education proposed in this law, a greater burden has fallen on local school districts.

Paradoxically, Louisiana's loss in real income for teachers can be attributed to the fact that the state participates very heavily in financing education. When there is talk of teacher increases, all state civil servants expect similar increases, and the total constitutes a frightening figure, on the order of $100 million. An extension of an existing

Table 1. Comparison of average salary of classroom teachers for 1967–68 and 1975–76 school year by states

Region and State	Average Salary of Classroom Teachers 1967–68 [1]	Average Salary of Classroom Teachers 1975–76 [2]	Dollar Increase	Real Income After Deflating to 1967 Dollars *	Real Income Gain/Loss	Percent
50 States and D.C.	$7,423	$12,524	$ 5,101	$ 7,513	$ 90	+ 1.2%
NEW ENGLAND	7,478	11,873	4,395	7,122	(356)	− 4.8%
Connecticut	7,987	12,628	4,641	7,575	(412)	− 5.2%
Maine	6,150	10,304	4,154	6,181	31	+ 0.5%
Massachusetts	7,650	11,900	4,250	7,139	(511)	− 6.7%
New Hampshire	6,463	10,500	4,037	6,299	(164)	− 2.5%
Rhode Island	7,536	13,381	5,845	8,027	491	+ 6.5%
Vermont	6,585	9,975	3,390	5,984	(601)	− 9.1%
MIDEAST (Inc. D.C.)	8,065	14,259	6,194	8,554	489	+ 6.0%
Delaware	7,718	12,545	4,827	7,525	(193)	− 2.5%
Maryland	7,857	13,705	5,848	8,221	364	+ 4.6%
New Jersey	7,845	13,375	5,530	8,023	178	+ 2.3%
New York [3]	8,638	15,950	7,312	9,568	930	+10.8%
Pennsylvania	7,292	12,350	5,058	7,409	117	+ 1.6%
SOUTHEAST	6,281	10,469	4,188	6,280	(1)	0.0%
Alabama	5,719	10,597	4,878	6,357	638	+11.2%
Arkansas	5,552	9,692	4,140	5,814	262	+ 4.7%
Florida	7,216	10,496	3,280	6,296	(920)	−12.7%
Georgia	6,600	10,846	4,246	6,506	(94)	− 1.4%
Kentucky	6,010	9,770	3,760	5,861	149	− 2.5%
Louisiana	6,758	10,092	3,334	6,054	(704)	−10.4%
Mississippi	4,685	9,314	4,629	5,587	902	+19.2%
North Carolina	6,301	11,002	4,701	6,600	299	+ 4.7%
South Carolina	5,645	9,915	4,270	5,948	303	+ 5.4%
Tennessee	6,000	10,299	4,299	6,178	178	+ 3.0%
Virginia	6,720	11,300	4,580	6,779	59	+ 0.9%
West Virginia	6,093	10,480	4,387	6,287	194	+ 3.2%
GREAT LAKES	7,977	13,202	5,225	7,920	(57)	− 0.7%
Illinois	8,600	13,980	5,380	8,386	(214)	− 2.5%
Indiana	7,925	11,999	4,074	7,198	(727)	− 9.2%
Michigan	8,293	15,540	7,247	9,322	1,029	+12.4%
Ohio	7,353	11,400	4,047	6,839	(514)	− 7.0%
Wisconsin [4]	7,292	12,346	5,054	7,406	114	+ 1.6%
PLAINS	6,717	11,404	4,687	6,841	124	+ 1.8%
Iowa [5]	6,959	11,570	4,611	6,941	(18)	− 0.3%
Kansas [4]	6,507	10,710	4,203	6,425	(82)	− 1.2%
Minnesota	7,465	13,888	6,423	8,331	866	+11.6%
Missouri	6,608	10,490	3,882	6,293	(315)	− 4.8%
Nebraska	6,068	10,017	3,949	6,009	(59)	− 1.0%
North Dakota	5,837	10,063	4,226	6,037	200	+ 3.4%
South Dakota	5,500	9,314	3,814	5,587	87	+ 1.6%

Region and State	Average Salary of Classroom Teachers		Dollar Increase	Real Income After Deflating to 1967 Dollars *	Real Income Gain/Loss	Percent
	1967–68 [1]	1975–76 [2]				
SOUTHWEST	6,632	11,210	4,578	6,725	93	+ 1.4%
Arizona	7,610	12,394	4,784	7,435	(175)	− 2.3%
New Mexico	7,057	11,005	3,948	6,602	(455)	− 6.4%
Oklahoma	6,041	9,600	3,559	5,759	(282)	− 4.7%
Texas	6,576	11,373	4,797	6,822	246	+ 3.7%
ROCKY MTS.	6,674	11,422	4,748	6,852	78	+ 2.7%
Colorado	6,900	12,000	5,100	7,199	299	+ 4.3%
Idaho	6,045	10,206	4,161	6,122	75	+ 1.3%
Montana	6,475	11,205	4,730	6,722	247	+ 3.8%
Utah	6,634	11,360	4,726	6,815	181	+ 2.7%
Wyoming	7,052	11,100	4,048	6,659	(393)	− 5.6%
FAR WEST	8,731	14,669	5,938	8,800	69	+ 0.8%
California [6]	9,035	15,200	6,165	9,118	83	+ 1.0%
Nevada	8,107	13,400	5,293	8,038	(69)	− 0.9%
Oregon	7,667	12,106	4,439	7,262	(405)	− 5.3%
Washington	7,861	13,615	5,754	8,167	306	+ 3.9%
Alaska [7]	9,444	19,880	10,436	11,926	2,482	+26.3%
Hawaii	7,914	15,209	7,295	9,124	1,210	+15.3%

* The Consumer Price Index, with 1967 as base 100, had risen to 1.667 by January 1, 1976. (See *Monthly Labor Review,* January 1, 1976, U.S. Department of Labor.)

1. *Estimates of School Statistics, 1968–69* (Washington, D.C.: National Education Association—Research, 1968), p. 30. All rights reserved.

2. *Estimates of School Statistics, 1975–76* (Washington, D.C.: National Education Association—Research, 1975). All rights reserved.

3. Data reported as median salary.

4. Excludes vocational schools not operated as a part of the regular public school system.

5. Does not include special education teachers for 1975–76.

6. Includes extra pay for coaching, supervising intern teachers, etc., for 1967–68.

7. All dollar amounts for Alaska (1968–69) should be reduced by approximately one-fourth to make the purchasing power of Alaska figures generally more comparable to figures reported for other areas of the U.S.

state tax or a new tax would be necessary to raise such a sum. Laws authorizing new taxes are difficult to pass anywhere, but particularly in Louisiana, where approval requires a favorable vote by two-thirds of both the senate and house.

Higher salaries in Alabama can be attributed to a united effort on the part of teachers, administrators, the Alabama Education Association, and the Alabama School Boards Association. A dedicated fund, the Special Education Trust Fund, was the key source of revenue used for teachers' salaries. Inflation created a surplus in this fund by pushing up sales tax receipts. Also, the state realized greater economic growth than the national average, and this helped finance teacher raises.

The Mississippi Education Association has probably been the single most effective group in raising the salary of Mississippi teachers, we were informed. Between 1967–

68 and 1975–76 the Mississippi legislature granted two $1,000 across-the-board raises (1968 and 1974), and cost-of-living increases have also been granted.

Great Lakes Region.   Among the five states in the Great Lakes Region, Michigan's classroom teachers have fared best. The average salary increased from $8,293 (1967–68) to $15,540 (1975–76), or $7,247. Converted to 1967 dollars, this means that the average pay increased by 12.4%. Michigan has had a strong collective negotiations law for many years and its teacher organizations are very aggressive.

Michigan teachers have not only improved their salaries through collective bargaining, but have negotiated a variety of fringe benefits. Health, dental, and life insurance with full family coverage are common statewide. Michigan has had a high incidence of teacher strikes, and while collective bargaining has aided teachers, it appears to have had a detrimental impact on school programs, cutting away at enrichment, music, art, physical education, and cultural programs. Also, the percentage of the budget allotted to teaching supplies has diminished, being shifted to salaries and fringe benefits.

Over the nine-year period studied, by contrast, Indiana classroom teachers lost 9.2% in buying power, on the average. Indiana has had mandated collective bargaining only since 1973. In that same year, the legislature approved a freeze on property tax levies (*not* rates). The two statutes have opposite effects and have created a dilemma for school boards. Salvation was expected to come from the state, but it has fallen short of appropriating adequate funds. Indiana teachers have obtained some fringe benefits, including a family health insurance plan, life insurance for employees, and an income protection plan. School boards by law cannot pay 100% of these benefits, but many districts have negotiated sizable fringe benefit packages.

Ohio passed a state income tax law in 1971. The initial impact was an increase in revenue and in money from the state to school districts. However, revenue from this tax has not grown as anticipated because of the nationwide economic slowdown. The state's financial picture has deteriorated in the past two years, causing budget cuts of 2 to 3%. Consequently, school districts received less state money than anticipated. Also, Ohio voters have in many instances failed to approve school board referendums during the 1967–76 period.

Plains States Region.   The average teacher's salary in this region increased by $4,687 during the period under study, which, converted to 1967–68 dollars, is a 1.8% increase. Minnesota teachers fared best. The average classroom teacher salary in Minnesota was $13,888 in 1975–76. Deflated to 1967 dollars, that works out to an 11.6% gain in purchasing power. The greatest loss in real income was borne by teachers in Missouri, where the loss was 4.8%.

Our informants attribute Minnesota's salary increases primarily to collective bargaining. Both the Minnesota Education Association and the Minnesota Federation of Teachers have been effective at the bargaining table. Not only were teachers successful in achieving take-home pay increases, but won fringe benefits such as health insurance, life insurance, dental insurance, longterm disability insurance, and additional pay for coaching, sponsorship of clubs, etc. The Minnesota Federation of Teachers represents approximately 25% of the teachers, mainly in the metropolitan areas.

Southwestern Region.   Gains in real income amounted to $93 (1.4%) for classroom teachers in this region. The buying power of the average Texas classroom teacher's salary increased by 3.7%. New Mexico's classroom teachers suffered a 6.4% loss.

Rocky Mountain Region.   This region experienced an increase of 2.7% in real income. All the states gained in real income, except Wyoming, where the average real income of classroom teachers lost 5.6%.

Far Western Region.   The average real income of classroom teachers increased in every state of this region. Oregon and Washington showed the largest dollar increases, $4,439 and $5,754 respectively. An increase of $6,165 for California teachers amounted to a real income gain of 1%.

Noncontiguous States.   Both Alaska and Hawaii reported very substantial dollar increases in teachers' average salaries for the nine-year period. The average salary of a classroom teacher in Alaska went from $9,444 to $19,880, but the real income gain was 26.3%. Hawaii teacher salaries increased by 15.3% in 1967 dollars.

SUMMARY

In 22 of the states studied, teachers lost in real income over the 1967–68—1975–76 period. The loss range was from a high of 12.7% in Florida to a low of .3% in Iowa.

Twenty-nine states showed gains in real income for teachers. The gains ranged from a high of 26.3% in Alaska (followed by Mississippi's 19.2%) to a low of .5% in Maine.

Obviously, salaries have increased substantially since 1967–68. However, the value of these increases has been almost entirely neutralized in many cases and, in almost half of the states, was actually reversed by inflation.

Reading 3

Value of a College Diploma: Center of Growing Debate

At a time when many college graduates are finding it difficult to get a worthwhile job, faith in the value of a degree—intellectual or monetary—is slipping badly.

More and more young people are proclaiming their disdain for a four-year course of study, especially in liberal arts

Junior colleges are packed with students taking two-year vocational courses. So are schools specializing in electronics, secretarial work and mechanical repairs.

Educators themselves concede that the value of a college degree may have been oversold.

In an article entitled "The Declining Value of College Going," in the September issue of *Change* magazine, Profs. Richard Freeman and J. Herbert Hollomon write: "By all relevant measures, the economic status of college graduates is deteriorating, with employment prospects for the young declining exceptionally sharply. In the brief span of about five years, the college job market has gone from a major boom to a major bust." They cite these statistics:

In 1958, only 1 percent of the college graduating class was unemployed. In 1972, it was 9.3 percent—compared with 7.7 percent for high-school graduates of the same age and 5.6 percent of all workers. Of all those with college degrees, fewer than 1 percent were unemployed in 1969. In 1974, it was 2 percent.

Continuing Slide. Bureau of Labor Statistics figures show that, at present, unemployment among all holders of college degrees has risen further—to 2.9 percent. And a College Placement Council survey reported in August that the hiring of college graduates by industry was off this year by 24 percent.

Selling briskly, and soon to appear in paperback, is the recently published book "The Case Against College," by Caroline Bird, a feminist and herself a college lecturer.

The book contains iconoclastic statements such as:

"We may now be systematically damaging 18-year-olds by insisting that their proper place is in college."

"In strictly financial terms, college is the dumbest investment a young man can make."

Source: "Value of a College Diploma: Center of Growing Debate." Reprinted from *U.S. News & World Report* (October 13, 1975), pp. 37–38.

"The most charitable conclusion is probably correct: College has very little, if any, effect on people and things at all."

Such judgments are producing angry denials and counterarguments from educators. Large numbers still retain the historic faith of Americans in education's benefits in providing for a better and happier life as well as more hard cash. They cite arguments to prove that college is still a good way to "get ahead."

They point out that the current 2.9 percent unemployment among holders of college degrees is considerably below the 9.1 percent for high school graduates, the 9.2 percent for the nation's work force as a whole, and 15.2 percent among those who did not graduate from high school.

Also seen are long-range employment trends that favor college graduates.

Department of Labor estimates are that about 20 percent of all jobs in this decade will require a college degree, while only 15.7 percent of the people in the labor force are college graduates now.

More Flexibility.   College educators also make the point that the average American can be expected to change jobs several times in a lifetime—an adjustment easier to make for a person with a broad college education than for one who is narrowly specialized.

In rebuttal, skeptics point out that a growing percentage of graduates are unable to find the kind of jobs for which they prepared themselves.

According to Professors Freeman and Hollomon, the number of college graduates in positions unrelated to their majors in the 1970s was one third among men and two thirds among women, against only 10 percent and 13 percent, respectively, in the early 1960s.

To complaints of this nature, Fred Gehrung, a university relations counselor, replies: "A job unrelated to a major field of study may not be what a graduate expected or initially wanted, but it may nonetheless have career potential." He cites a survey by Southern Illinois University of its 1972 liberal-arts graduates, in which 70 percent reported that their jobs had possible or definite career potential.

Half of those so reporting were persons who had found themselves compelled to take jobs unrelated to their majors.

Professors Freeman and Hollomon themselves suggest the possibility of a brighter picture for the future, writing:

"Perhaps the single most important possible change that could improve the situation of higher education would be the growth of those sectors of the U.S. economy that require larger numbers of trained professional and managerial manpower— due, say, to policies and programs that enhance productivity and technological innovation." They add:

"Paradoxically, a major increase in defense spending would increase the demand for educated people, because defense-related industries employ large numbers of college graduates."

Narrowing Gap.   What seems clear is that the salary differential between college graduates and other Americans is narrowing. Professors Freeman and Hollomon report:

"From 1969, the last good year in the college job market, to 1975, the starting salaries of male graduates in industry, having increased rapidly in the previous decade, dropped sharply, both in real terms and relative to the earnings of other workers. College Placement Council data show a decrease of 23 percent in the real starting pay for men with social science or humanities degrees; a fall of 21 percent in the real pay for beginning mathematics majors; and of 17 percent for beginning electrical engineers with doctorates.

"The ratio of college-graduate to high school-graduate incomes—quite stable since World War II—also dropped in the early 1970s. In 1969, full-time male workers with four years of college earned 53 percent more than male workers with four years of high school; in 1973, 40 percent more."

Defenders of college training do not deny that its relative monetary value has lately been decreasing. But they point out that male workers with four years of college still earn 40 percent more than those with four years of high school, which translates into nearly $300,000 over a lifetime.

While Ms. Bird argues that family status—not education—is the biggest single source of income differences among males, Prof. David Featherman of the University of Wisconsin says:

"We are moving toward a more meritocratic society—with increased returns for educational advancement, and a decrease in the effects of social origins on occupational status and earnings."

Increased cost of college, coupled with decreased financial rewards in many instances, raises the question of the value of college as a long-term financial investment.

Here again, opinions differ. Professors Freeman and Hollomon find that "according to one set of estimates, the return on college investment dropped from 11 to 12 percent in 1969 to 7 to 8 percent in 1974. A decrease of this magnitude is unprecedented."

Ms. Bird, going further, contends that "if a male Princeton-bound high school graduate of 1972 had put the $34,181 his diploma would eventually cost him into a savings bank at 7.5 percent interest compounded daily, he would have at the retirement age of 64 a total of $1,129,200." This, she says would be "$528,200 more than the earnings of a male college graduate and more than five times as much as the $199,000 extra he could expect to earn between 22 and 64 because he was a college . . . graduate."

Replied Jane Bryant Quinn in the *Washington Post:* "It's a neat calculation. But since anyone who skips college won't have any 'foregone income' to bank, the whole exercise becomes a mathematical game rather than an honest evaluation of personal options."

The Intangibles.   Lately the controversy over education's worth has moved beyond its monetary benefits to less-tangible areas. Defenders of liberal-arts college education point out that jobs which require a college degree often carry such nonmonetary benefits as greater stimulation, less fatigue and a cleaner and more healthful environment. Even more important, they say, are a multitude of off-the-job gains for degree holders.

A typical comment comes from Thomas Bonner, president of Union College in Schenectady, N.Y.: "Whoever said life was a matter of bread alone? No educated person would argue seriously that the study of history, literature, art or philosophy is irrelevant to a satisfactory life or the enduring values of a citizen. What of the quality of a graduate's life, the realization of one's own goals, success as a parent or marriage partner, or one's contributions as a citizen?"

Skeptics remain unimpressed by such arguments. Says Ms. Bird: "College doesn't make people intelligent, ambitious, happy, liberal, or quick to learn new things. Colleges can't claim much credit for the learning experiences that really change students while they are there. Jobs, friends, history, and most of all the sheer passage of time have as big an impact as anything even indirectly related to the campus."

How young people themselves are being affected by the arguments and counterarguments in this debate is hard to measure.

In absolute figures, college enrollment this fall is at an all-time high—nearly 4 percent above last year. But the percentage of young people who choose to go to college seems to be declining.

Professors Freeman and Hollomon report that the proportion of 18 to 19-year-old men enrolled in higher education declined from 44 percent in 1969 to 33.4 percent in 1974.

Why the Fall-Off?   The question arising, however, is this: Does the decline result chiefly from the rising cost of college or from disillusionment with higher education?

The growing controversy on the value of going to college could have far-reaching consequences.

Professors Freeman and Hollomon specu-

late that large numbers of young people, for the first time, are likely to obtain less schooling and potentially lower occupational status than their parents.

Ms. Bird advocates shifting money now used to subsidize college education to such alternatives as job apprenticeships and national-service jobs.

In this controversy, one thing is emerging clearly: Americans, in growing numbers, are turning a hard look on the assumption, once taken for granted, that a college degree is the gilt-edged passport to success in life.

Reading 4

Will the NEA and the AFT Ever Merge?

Kenneth P. Lubetsky

The prospective and perhaps inevitable merger of the National Education Association and the American Federation of Teachers is perhaps further away at present than at any time in recent years.

This article will examine the factors present which have prevented the merger that would at once create the single largest union in the United States. To place the issue of merger into proper perspective, I will first report some pertinent descriptive information about the two organizations.

The National Education Association (NEA), by far the larger of the two national teacher organizations, reported its membership as of May 31, 1974, to be 1,467,186.[1] The NEA has local affiliates in all fifty states as well as several overseas chapters. The majority of the NEA's membership is concentrated in rural America.

Historically, the NEA has presented itself as an association of professionals, as opposed to a trade union. Only within the last fifteen years has the NEA endorsed and

Source: Kenneth P. Lubetsky, "Will the NEA and the AFT Ever Merge?" The Educational Forum (March 1977), pp. 309–316. Reprinted with permission.

sanctioned strikes by its local affiliates, as well as the right of all teachers collectively to bargain with their employers. As an "association of professionals," the NEA traditionally refrained from participating to any significant extent in the arena of professional politics on either the local or national fronts.

The NEA was formally affiliated with one segment of organized labor, the American Federation of State, County, and Municipal Employees (AFSCME), a member union of the AFL-CIO. They joined together to form the Coalition of American Public Employees (CAPE). This alliance will be analyzed in greater depth in a later section of this article.

The American Federation of Teachers (AFT) has local affiliates in most major states as well as several overseas chapters. As of May 31, 1974, the AFT reported its membership to be 414,854.[2] Officials of the AFT are quick to point out that, although in the number of total dues-paying members the AFT is indeed dwarfed by the NEA, the AFT does, in fact, represent more teachers in collective bargaining negotiations than does the NEA.[3]

The majority of the AFT's membership is concentrated in urban America. AFT locals represent the teachers in New York City, Boston, Baltimore, Philadelphia, Cleveland, Gary, Chicago, and Detroit, for example. The AFT is directly affiliated with organized labor as a member union of the AFL-CIO. Albert Shanker, president of the AFT, is a vice president of the AFL-CIO and sits on its thirty-five member executive council.

The issue of merger between the NEA and the AFT is certainly not a new one. It has existed perhaps as long as the two respective organizations, and parallels their separate histories. On any number of occasions, individuals within the two organizations have addressed themselves either formally or informally to the merger issue. In his text, *Teachers and Power: The Story of the American Federation of Teachers,* Robert J. Braun recalls that, in March of 1920, when the NEA had been criticized by the AFT for allowing itself to be dominated by and primarily concerned with the affairs of school superintendents, thereby relegating the rank-and-file teacher within the association to a secondary status, the NEA entered into a wide-scale, multi-faceted, anti-AFT publicity campaign. Braun tells us, "Up to that point, many AFT officers, as many do now, had hoped that the two organizations might someday merge, with the AFT working for teacher-welfare programs while the NEA developed professional-improvement strategy. Not only was that dream destroyed, but also the AFT itself was practically destroyed by the torrent of anti-union rhetoric provided by NEA members and supporters." [4]

Within the framework cast by the histories of the nation's two national teacher organizations, the overtures to merge have been diminished by the approximately eight hundred collective bargaining elections into which both sides have participated as witting and perhaps overzealous opponents. These elections, it should be noted, have increased significantly within the past decade as more and more state legislatures have passed collective bargaining statutes. The increased level of hostility which has pervaded any superficial attempts at merger between the NEA and the AFT over the years has closely paralleled the increased frequency of these collective bargaining elections.

The first serious attempt to merge the NEA and the AFT in recent times occurred in 1968, upon the election of David Selden as president of the American Federation of Teachers. Selden had built his campaign for the AFT presidency upon his pledge to initiate merger negotiations with the NEA. George Fisher, newly elected president of the National Education Association, also advocated the commencement of merger talks between the two organizations. Events not directly under the control of the two respective leaders, however, undermined this effort to commence merger negotiations. While attempting to make the negotiating postures of their respective organizations more flexible, both Selden and Fisher alienated segments of their executive boards. As a result, their positions within their organizations were eroded. Merger talks were never seriously entered into, and representatives of the NEA and the AFT were not to sit down at the same table to negotiate until October 1973. [5]

During this five-year interval, several mergers of NEA and AFT local affiliates were successfully forged, despite the inability of both parent organizations to reach even the most basic accord. In 1970, the NEA's local affiliate in Los Angeles merged with the AFT's local affiliate to form the United Teachers of Los Angeles (UTLA). Since the merger, the UTLA has succeeded in:

1. Winning agreement to a master contract (due in part to a four-week strike supported jointly by the NEA and the AFT).
2. Opening a drive for a collective bargaining law for all of the state's public em-

ployees; converting of the California Teachers Association to a pro-collective bargaining posture.

3. Amending the teachers' pension law, permitting credit for unused sick leave.[6]

In 1972, the NEA's and the AFT's local affiliates in New Orleans merged to form the United Teachers of New Orleans (UTNO). Since the merger in New Orleans, UTNO has succeeded in:

1. Electing a pro-teacher swing-vote to the New Orleans school board.
2. Electing a UTNO member to the State Teachers Retirement System Board.
3. Winning the school board's agreement to hold a collective bargaining election, despite the absence of a state collective bargaining law.[7]

The only merger between NEA and AFT affiliates at the state level occurred in 1972 in New York State. In New York State, the NEA's affiliate, the New York State Teachers Association (NYSTA), and the AFT's affiliate, the United Teachers of New York (UTNY), merged to form the New York State United Teachers (NYSUT). At the time of the merger, the combined memberships of the two state organizations totaled approximately 177,000. At present, NYSUT's membership is in excess of 217,000. After the statewide merger was forged in New York, NYSUT has succeeded in:

1. Gaining improved benefits in the non-contributory retirement system, and having these benefits made permanent.
2. Reducing the probationary period for tenure from five years to three years.
3. Eliminating the legislative hearing from the negotiations law.[8]

The merged organization in New York was to have been the prototype for any future merger between the NEA and the AFT. This has not become a reality. NEA officials pointed to the many pro-AFT decisions reached by NYSUT's Representative Assembly at its first three conventions as proof that the intent of the AFT was to "force" its policies upon the NEA if the two organizations merge. Within the last year, however, the New York State United Teachers voted formally to terminate its affiliation with the National Education Association, thereby ending the only merger of the NEA and AFT affiliates at the state level.

In spite of the fears of merger, which permeated a large part of the NEA's executive board, the backdrop of successful mergers of NEA and AFT local affiliates in strategic locations across the country, coupled with the increasingly high number of attacks upon public education and teachers by the mass media, made the issue of a national merger of the nation's two major teacher organizations once again appear to be a distinct possibility. The potential political influence of a merged organization, through its campaign contributions to pro-education legislators, as well as its massive lobbying potential, would be unparalleled in American history. This prospect made the idea of a merger all the more alluring.

In June of 1973, Selden, still AFT president, received a phone call from NEA past president Donald Morrison. Morrison informed Selden that the NEA Executive Committee would vote to open merger discussions if the committee could be convinced that the long-standing dispute between the two organizations with regard to the issue of mandatory affiliation with the AFL-CIO could be satisfactorily resolved. Selden informed Morrison that there were several ways that this most touchy and potentially explosive of issues might be resolved.[9]

Four merger negotiating sessions were held between October 1973 and February 1974. Selden stated: "Although the tone of the first meeting was formal it was nevertheless friendly. The negotiations in each succeeding meeting, however, became more rigid and unfriendly." [10]

The NEA opened by stating its basic conditions as laid down by its Representative Assembly—no AFL-CIO affiliation, secret ballot election of officers, and quotas for racial and other minorities on official bodies. At the following meeting the AFT presented its own position paper rejecting the NEA conditions and calling attention to other problems which it felt should be solved. Although there were clarifying questions by both sides, there was no discussion of substance at either of the first two meetings. [11]

Prior to the convening of the third negotiating session in December 1973, the AFT Executive Council formally requested the resignation of its president, David Selden. Albert Shanker, Selden's old friend and fellow AFT organizer over a decade earlier, felt that Selden was wrongly willing to sacrifice or compromise the AFT's staunch position on mandatory AFL-CIO affiliation in order to forge a merger. Shanker accused Selden of unilaterally altering the AFT's negotiating posture with regard to this issue. Shanker chose this opportunity to announce formally his intention to pursue the office of AFT president at the AFT's 1974 Convention in Toronto.

The majority of the then twenty-member AFT Executive Council shared Shanker's great disappointment and dissatisfaction with Selden's willingness to compromise the issue of AFL-CIO affiliation and gave Shanker their support in this internal dispute. Selden was left operating as a mere figurehead.

The NEA became aware of the internal strife within the ranks of the AFT negotiating team and responded by altering its negotiating posture accordingly. NEA leaders became convinced that Shanker was the true spokesman for the AFT and his position with regard to the issue of AFL-CIO affiliation appeared to be unalterable. Negotia-

tions took a definite turn for the worse after the AFT Executive Council's resignation request.

Selden voluntarily absented himself from the third negotiating session in order to avoid encumbering the meeting with an AFT internal problem. Although there was discussion of issues at the third meeting, no compromise proposal was made by either side. [12]

At the fourth meeting in February, the AFT proposed compromises on the AFL-CIO question. Any NEA member (who was not also an AFT member) could, at the time of merger, direct that none of his dues would be used to pay AFL-CIO per capita dues, and a timetable for phasing in affiliation over a period of years would be worked out. [13] Selden recalled that, "it was apparent that the NEA negotiators had come to the meeting determined to break-off the discussions, and the AFT proposals were brusquely rejected without offer of counter proposals." [14] No attempt was made by either side following the break-off to resume negotiations.

At this point it is appropriate to specify and examine the four items which seem to be the stumbling blocks preventing a merger of the NEA and the AFT.

The primary obstacle to merger between the two organizations is, and has been, the issue of affiliation with the AFL-CIO.

As mentioned previously, the AFT is directly affiliated with the AFL-CIO. The AFT considers itself to be within the mainstream of organized labor. The AFT has approached the issue of AFL-CIO affiliation at the merger negotiations table with a very firm posture. AFT leaders have, by tradition, steadfastly held their ground on this issue. Selden's initial offer of compromise at the fourth NEA-AFT negotiating session broke with this tradition. Since Selden's formal defeat as president of the AFT in August 1974, the AFT, under newly elected President Albert Shanker (Shanker amassed approximately 87 percent of the votes cast by the delegates at the August 1974 AFT Convention in Toronto) has returned to its more rigid stance of prior years. Shanker has hinted that he might consider some form of an "opt-out" clause as a possible solution to the current NEA-AFT dilemma.

The NEA has just as steadfastly set forth and reaffirmed its own bargaining position: no AFL-CIO affiliation. For those in high level leadership positions in the NEA who still choose to view the association as as independent force comprised of "professionals," the thought of a compromise on the issue of AFL-CIO affiliation has remained totally unacceptable. The NEA has thought of itself as being more progressive than George Meany's AFL-CIO. NEA leaders have long feared being swallowed-up by the giant labor leader and his massive organization of unions. They fear, as well, that Albert Shanker will become the spokesman for any merged organization within the AFL-CIO.

The NEA complicated the question of AFL-CIO affiliation by joining into an alliance with the American Federation of State, County, and Municipal Employees (AFSCME), an AFL-CIO member union. By entering into an alliance with the NEA, the AFSCME gave credence to the NEA leaders' claims that they need not affiliate with the AFL-CIO in order to enjoy the benefits of an affiliation with organized labor.

AFT leaders openly questioned the sincerity of NEA leaders who, on the one hand, rejected an alliance with organized labor through affiliation with the AFL-CIO, but, on the other hand, entered into an alliance with an AFL-CIO member union.

In response to the threat posed by the Coalition of American Public Employees (NEA plus AFSCME) to the AFL-CIO, the federation convened on November 6, 1974, a founding convention of its newly fashioned Public Employee Department. The federation's Public Employee Department is made up of AFL-CIO affiliates representing more than two million workers employed by federal, state, and local governments and by the U.S. Postal Service. At the founding convention, AFL-CIO President Meany pledged the complete cooperation of all AFL-CIO affiliates, including the AFSCME.[15]

Among the founding unions granted this charter were: the State, County, and Municipal Employees; the AFT; the Transport Workers; and the School Administrators and Supervisors Organizing Committee.[16]

The mission of this formidable new department within the AFL-CIO is to develop an area where organized labor has been slow to move while preventing the further expansion of CAPE.

Whether these moves and counter-moves on the part of the NEA and the AFL-CIO have further complicated the resolution of this primary stumbling block remains to be seen. However, the American Federation of State, County, and Municipal Employees has terminated its membership in the AFL-CIO Department of Public Employees. It is anticipated that these actions will serve to further expand the schism which exists between the two national teacher organizations.

The second obstacle to merger is one the author believes will be difficult, if not impossible, to isolate from all of the areas of disagreement between the NEA and the AFT, namely, Albert Shanker himself. The fact that Shanker's ascent from his position as an AFT organizer to his present status as a major figure in the field of organized labor has been accomplished in such a relatively short period of time might tend to lend credence to the contention of some NEA leaders that he is a political opportunist interested primarily in amassing power. These same NEA leaders, however, choose to ignore Shanker's long record of commitment to organized labor, its principles, and to the many causes labor has seen fit to champion. That Shanker's ascent may have been facilitated by the high level of competence which his supporters claim he brings to each task he undertakes is also overlooked. That it may have been a symptom of our times that allowed for so rapid an ascent is also not considered by Shanker's detractors. Nevertheless, Shanker continues to be described by his "enemies" as power hungry, self-seeking, and uncompromising. These descriptions may not be based upon factual evidence and documentation, but a number of people in the teacher-union movement perceive these criticisms to be true. In an effort to discredit Shanker, some NEA leaders have expressed the feeling that, were he to be removed from the scene, both the NEA and the AFT would be able to reach a compromise accord on the issue of AFL-CIO affiliation. If such an accord were realized, it is contended, the remaining lesser points of disagreement could easily be resolved.

The reality of the situation appears to be that Albert Shanker will not abandon that which he has for so many years strived— one unified organization of teachers within the mainstream of the labor movement. Any merger agreement will have to be forged in his presence and predicated upon this tenet.

NEA and AFT leaders tend to agree that the remaining two items which must be considered as obstacles to merger might be satisfactorily resolved if both sides were to agree to a solution on the issue of AFL-CIO affiliation.

The NEA supports the employment of quota systems in order to guarantee adequate representation to racial and other minority group members on NEA committees. The NEA Representative Assembly has, by resolve, endorsed the employment of "affirmative action" programs as they apply to other areas in our society as well.

The AFT has rejected this technique of insuring adequate minority group representation. It has chosen, instead, to endorse the strict employment of a merit system. That is to say, the person most qualified for a given position should receive that position, regardless of race or sex.

Both teacher organizations have attacked the other as employing a racist philosophy. Although these two different philosophies appear to be irreconcilable, a compromise will have to be reached on this point as well if there is to be an NEA-AFT merger enacted.

The final point of disagreement between the two organizations concerns itself with the method by which the duly elected delegates of the two organizations cast their votes at their respective representative assemblies when electing officers.

The NEA has endorsed and employed the secret ballot method of casting votes at its convention, believing all delegates should have their right to anonymity protected.

The AFT has endorsed and employed the roll call method of casting votes at its convention, believing, as delegates are elected representatives of AFT members, their votes should be recorded and published for their constituents' scrutiny.

This issue, too, will have to be subjected to some form of a compromise if teacher-unity is to be a reality.

Since the NEA formally broke-off merger talks with the AFT in February 1974, both sides have moved progressively further apart. At its 1973 Convention in Portland, Oregon, the NEA Representative Assembly ratified New Business Item 52, a reaffirmation of the NEA's position with regard to AFL-CIO affiliation. At its 1974 Convention in Chicago, the NEA's Representative Assembly first defeated attempts by delegates to re-open for consideration N.B.I. 52, and subsequently, in strong and unwavering terms, once again set forth its own position on AFL-CIO affiliation in the form of several additional new business items.

The AFT has, with the election of Albert

Shanker as its president, embarked on a path directed to develop and organize those areas that have heretofore been neglected: college and university personnel; the South, where the AFT previously disaffiliated (with Shanker's enthusiastic and active support) a number of segregated locals; and California and other states that have new collective bargaining laws.

The NEA, as well, has embarked upon the path of expansion. These respective paths continue to cross, and both organizations continue to spend hundreds of thousands of dollars on collective bargaining elections.

James Harris, past NEA president (he was elected on an anti-merger platform at the 1973 convention) has said: "There is no purpose even in sitting down unless the AFT agrees to accept the NEA's three pre-conditions in advance. The three are:

1. no affiliation with any labor organization except CAPE;
2. quotas for minorities in hiring and elections;
3. secrecy in voting at the Representative Assembly." [17]

AFT President Shanker has responded by stating: "Teachers won't accept pre-conditions from school boards, and there's no reason for them to accept pre-conditions from other teachers before negotiations even begin." [18]

In summation, a merger of the NEA and the AFT is further away at present than at any time in recent years. While the NEA president and AFT president remain firm in their respective bargaining positions, the collective bargaining "wars" go on, teacher against teacher, as millions of teacher hours and hundreds of thousands of dollars that might be used to advance the cause of education in America continue to be wasted.

What are the prospects for the future? It is highly unlikely that the AFT will be able to close the vast gap which now exists between its membership and the NEA's. This, however, may not be necessary, for the AFT now has perhaps the most effective, if not most well-liked teacher leader in America today as its president. It is equally unlikely that the NEA will benefit significantly from its membership in CAPE. The newly formed AFL-CIO Public Employee Department will probably see to this.

What is likely is that as economic conditions and working conditions for teachers across America get progressively worse, the two organizations will be forced into an alliance to better combat their common enemies. When the respective hierarchies of these two organizations will perceive this time to be remains the unanswered question.

NOTES

1. "NEA Membership Hits Record High," *NEA Reporter* 13 (October 1974): 3.
2. "Union Membership at Record High," *American Teacher*, September 1974, p. 13.
3. Robert J. Braun, *Teachers and Power: The Story of the American Federation of Teachers* (New York: Simon and Schuster, 1972), p. 245.
4. Ibid.
5. Ibid.
6. Teacher-Unity, National Coalition for Teacher Unity (Washington, D.C., 1974).
7. Ibid.
8. Ibid.
9. American Federation of Teachers Officers' Reports to AFT Convention (President's Report), 1974.
10. Ibid.
11. Ibid.
12. Ibid.
13. Ibid.
14. Ibid.
15. James M. Shevis, "Twenty-four Unions Establish Public Employee Department," *AFL-CIO News*, November 1974, p. 1.
16. Ibid.
17. Teacher-Unity, National Coalition for Teacher Unity (Washington, D.C., 1974).
18. Ibid.

Reading 5

Bill of Teacher Rights

National Education Association

PREAMBLE

We, the teachers of the United States of America, aware that a free society is dependent upon the education afforded its citizens, affirm the right to freely pursue truth and knowledge.

As an individual, the teacher is entitled to such fundamental rights as dignity, privacy, and respect.

As a citizen, the teacher is entitled to such basic constitutional rights as freedom of religion, speech, assembly, association and political action, and equal protection of the law.

In order to develop and preserve respect for the worth and dignity of man, to provide a climate in which actions develop as a consequence of rational thought, and to insure intellectual freedom, we further affirm that teachers must be free to contribute fully to an educational environment which secures the freedom to teach and the freedom to learn.

Believing that certain rights of teachers

Source: National Education Association, "Bill of Teacher Rights," National Education Association: Washington, D.C. Used by permission.

derived from these fundamental freedoms must be universally recognized and respected, we proclaim this Bill of Teacher Rights.

ARTICLE I—RIGHTS AS A PROFESSIONAL

As a member of the teaching profession, the individual teacher has the right:

Section 1.   To be licensed under professional and ethical standards established, maintained, and enforced by the profession.

Section 2.   To maintain and improve professional competence.

Section 3.   To exercise professional judgment in presenting, interpreting, and criticizing information and ideas, including controversial issues.

Section 4.   To influence effectively the formulation of policies and procedures which affect one's professional services, including curriculum, teaching materials, methods of instruction, and school-community relations.

Section 5.   To exercise professional judgment in the use of teaching methods and materials appropriate to the needs, interests, capacities, and the linguistic and cultural background of each student.

Section 6. To safeguard information obtained in the course of professional service.

Section 7. To work in an atmosphere conducive to learning, including the use of reasonable means to preserve the learning environment and to protect the health and safety of students, oneself, and others.

Section 8. To express publicly views on matters affecting education.

Section 9. To attend and address a governing body and be afforded access to its minutes when official action may affect one's professional concerns.

ARTICLE II—RIGHTS AS AN EMPLOYEE

As an employee, the individual teacher has the right:

Section 1. To seek and be fairly considered for any position commensurate with one's qualifications.

Section 2. To retain employment following entrance into the profession in the absence of a showing of just cause for dismissal or nonrenewal through fair and impartial proceedings.

Section 3. To be fully informed, in writing, of rules, regulations, terms, and conditions affecting one's employment.

Section 4. To have conditions of employment in which health, security, and property are adequately protected.

Section 5. To influence effectively the development and application of evaluation procedures.

Section 6. To have access to writtten evaluations, to have documents placed in one's personnel file to rebut derogatory information and to have removed false or unfair material through a clearly defined process.

Section 7. To be free from arbitrary, capricious, or discriminatory actions affecting the terms and conditions of employment.

Section 8. To be advised promptly in writing of the specific reasons for any actions which might affect one's employment.

Section 9. To be afforded due process through the fair and impartial hearing of grievances, including binding arbitration as a means of resolving disputes.

Section 10. To be free from interference to form, join, or assist employee organizations, to negotiate collectively through representatives of one's own choosing, and to engage in other concerted activities for the purpose of professional negotiations or other mutual aid or protection.

Section 11. To withdraw services collectively when reasonable procedures to resolve impasse have been exhausted.

ARTICLE III—RIGHTS AS AN ORGANIZATION

As an individual member of an employee organization, the teacher has the right:

Section 1. To acquire membership in employee organizations based upon reasonable standards equally applied.

Section 2. To have equal opportunity to participate freely in the affairs and governance of the organization.

Section 3. To have freedom of expression, both within and outside the organization.

Section 4. To vote for organization officers, either directly or through delegate bodies, in fair elections.

Section 5. To stand for and hold office subject only to fair qualifications uniformly applied.

Section 6. To be fairly represented by the organization in all matters.

Section 7. To be provided periodic reports of the affairs and conduct of business of the organization.

Section 8. To be provided detailed and accurate financial records, audited and reported at least annually.

Section 9. To be free from arbitrary disciplinary action or threat of such action by the organization.

Section 10. To be afforded due process by the organization in a disciplinary action.

Reading 6

Bill of Rights

American Federation of Teachers

The teacher is entitled to a life of dignity equal to the high standard of service that is justly demanded of that profession. Therefore, we hold these truths to be self-evident:

I. Teachers have the right to think freely and to express themselves openly and without fear. This includes the right to hold views contrary to the majority.

II. They shall be entitled to the free exercise of their religion. No restraint shall be put upon them in the manner, time or place of their worship.

III. They shall have the right to take part in social, civil, and political affairs. They shall have the right, outside the classroom, to participate in political campaigns and to hold office. They may assemble peaceably and may petition any government agency, including their employers, for a redress of grievances. They shall have the same freedom in all things as other citizens.

IV. The right of teachers to live in places of their own choosing, to be free of restraints in their mode of living and the use of their leisure time shall not be abridged.

V. Teaching is a profession, the right to practice which is not subject to the surrender of other human rights. No one shall be deprived of professional status, or the right to practice it, or the practice thereof in any particular position, without due process of law.

VI. The right of teachers to be secure in their jobs, free from political influence or public clamor, shall be established by law. The right to teach after qualification in the manner prescribed by law, is a property right, based upon the inalienable rights of life, liberty, and the pursuit of happiness.

VII. In all cases affecting the teacher's employment or professional status a full hearing by an impartial tribunal shall be afforded with the right to full judicial review. No teacher shall be deprived of employment or professional status but for specific causes established by law having a clear relation to the competence or qualification to teach proved by the weight of the evidence. In all such cases the teacher shall enjoy the right to a speedy and public trial, to be informed of the nature and cause of the accusation;

Source: American Federation of Teachers, *Bill of Rights.* Washington, D.C.: American Federation of Teachers. Used by permission.

to be confronted with the accusing witnesses, to subpoena witnesses and papers, and the assistance of counsel. No teacher shall be called upon to answer any charge affecting his employment or professional status but upon probable cause, supported by oath or affirmation.

VIII. It shall be the duty of the employer to provide culturally adequate salaries, security in illness and adequate retirement income. The teacher has the right to such a salary as will: (a) Afford a family standard of living comparable to that enjoyed by other professional people in the community (b) To make possible freely chosen professional study (c) Afford the opportunity for leisure and recreation common to our heritage.

IX. No teacher shall be required under penalty of reduction of salary to pursue studies beyond those required to obtain professional status. After serving a reasonable probationary period a teacher shall be entitled to permanent tenure terminable only for just cause. They shall be free as in other professions in the use of their own time. They shall not be required to perform extracurricular work against their will or without added compensation.

X. To equip people for modern life requires the most advanced educational methods. Therefore, the teacher is entitled to good classrooms, adequate teaching materials, teachable class size and administrative protection and assistance in maintaining discipline.

XI. These rights are based upon the proposition that the culture of a people can rise only as its teachers improve. A teaching force accorded the highest possible professional dignity is the surest guarantee that blessings of liberty will be preserved. Therefore, the possession of these rights imposes the challenge to be worthy of their enjoyment.

XII. Since teachers must be free in order to teach freedom, the right to be members of organizations of their own choosing must be guaranteed. In all matters pertaining to their salaries and working conditions they shall be entitled to bargain collectively through representatives of their own choosing. They are entitled to have the schools administered by superintendents, boards or committees which function in a democratic manner.

Reading 7

Second Thoughts About the Professionalization of Teachers

James R. Covert

One of the most perplexing problems for teachers during the past century has been the upgrading of their occupation to a profession. While it is generally conceded that the various professional ranks engaged in "higher education" are professional, those lesser teachers hired in "lower education" must still fulfill a few more vital criteria before they are granted the esteem and prestige that professionals enjoy. Some skeptics point out however, that even when teachers fulfill all of these enumerated criteria, they will still not be thought of as professionals because that title is granted only to a few traditional occupations by society. Though this latter statement may have some validity, we must not revert to accepting the contemporary connotations and definitions assigned to professions. There must be some difference between a professional hockey player, a professional union organizer, and a professional surgeon. Unless we can agree on certain definite criteria to distinguish the

Source: James R. Covert, "Second Thoughts About the Professionalization of Teachers." *The Educational Forum* vol. 39, no. 2 (January 1975), pp. 149–153. Reprinted with permission.

accepted professions from those aspiring to professional status, all is lost. We might as well await the conferring of the honor by the society.

As society changes it becomes increasingly difficult to separate the traditional, established professions from their aspiring counterparts. Many of the distinguishing features which used to separate professions from crafts have become less distinct in the past decade. The notion of a professional private practice for doctors and lawyers and a public practice for teachers and social workers is no longer important with lawyers working in large partnerships and doctors joining to form clinics and even participating in socialized medicine. Such incompatible ideas as autonomous professionals working in bureaucracies, joining unions or associations, and even striking are no longer seen as incongruous. While the traditional professions have redefined what being professional means, aspiring occupations have made little headway in gaining professional standing, in spite of constant efforts in that direction. Social work has made its program more rigorous by introducing social science. Teachers have doubled their number of years of college training from two to four. Nurses have raised their requirements for admittance into the training program and have made acceptance into the occupation conditional on passing a rigorous standardized test. Following each of these exercises they have proclaimed themselves as more professional and sought public recognition as a full-fledged profession.

For those occupations that aspire to professional status and prestige, this can be a very frustrating experience. They often feel a "sense of calling" to their chosen "profession" and can demonstrate, in large measure, the fulfillment of the two basic criteria of the established professions. That is, they can provide empirical evidence: "(1) that social function is the primary reference point for guiding their activity or work and (2) they possess at this point in time, a specialized knowledge and means for verifying claims to knowledge that enable them to perform this function with an economy unique to that individual or group."[1]

While arguments continue to rage about the social function that is unique to education, the optimists can gain considerable support for the notion that socialization into the ongoing culture is their social function and pessimists can claim organized and essential baby sitting as their social function. The claim to a specific body of knowledge has also been a thorny problem for education. There may be an unexpected source of relief for this dilemma as we review the diverse nature of the bodies of knowledge possessed by the traditional professions. Medicine and law have always found it difficult to retain some definite and unique body of knowledge and are continually being forced to introduce interdisciplinary modes of information gathering and knowledge verification to educate their professionals. We are seeing, for instance, a new movement toward producing more general practitioners in medicine who must have an even wider-range of ability, drawn from a greater variety of disciplines.

The issues raised here are vital to the definition of a profession. Such things as changing social definitions, selection, education and entry requirements, a unique social function, and a specialized body of knowledge all play an important part in identifying those occupations designated as professions. I would like to explore certain aspects of the professional model that do not frequently appear in the literature and suggest that teachers review the very basic question of the desirability of becoming a profession.

FOUR BASIC QUESTIONS

There is one issue that is becoming increasingly important to the established professions which hinges upon the very professional claim of a unique service performed by experts in their field. With the increasing number of malpractice suits brought against people in all professions, it might give teachers reason to pause and consider that which might readily be considered malpractice, should the profession firmly establish an area of competence. The list might be staggering as well as frightening. There has been no case tried, to my knowledge, where a teacher has been charged with malpractice as opposed to incompetence or improper supervision in a particular situation. In most cases the courts have been very careful to not attribute any special expertness or superior powers to a teacher. As a matter of fact, they have ruled that a teacher was no more responsible than any common man acting in a similar situation.[2]

This argument is not to be misconstrued as a reason for teachers not to pursue the professional promised land; it is rather to serve as a warning flag hoisted by the established professions. When teachers begin to strike for benefits other than wages, it seems likely they are claiming that there are certain benefits to be gained from instituting such practices as class size, special education classes, and increased per pupil expenditures. The school, being a part of a pragmatic pluralistic society, is likely to expect increased returns in the form of increments of learning. If a profession fails to deliver what it professes, or actually inflicts some harm on the client, then they may leave themselves open to charges of malpractice. If, as in other professions, educators were to define explicitly what constitutes standards of teaching performance and the duties to be performed by a competent teacher in this professional capacity, the possibility of inflicting "emotional damage" would become immense. For instance, is reprimanding a child in front of his peers not conducive to at least temporary emotional damage and perhaps a permanent emotional disability? Another case of malpractice might involve the "graduation" of an illiterate passed through the grades for compassionate reasons. A second point arises concerning the description of a competent teacher. Professions, through their rigorous selection and demanding educational programs, certify that all graduates are competent to perform the minimal professional service. This faith in the preparation of professionals is the result of a long history of tight controls exercised by the professionals themselves, building mutual trust within the profession and faith from the general public. It is not necessary for professionals to advertise because all are competent, nor is it likely that any professional will speak disparagingly of his colleagues because all are aware of the certification program and its safeguards against allowing incompetents to practice.[3]

Teacher education institutions, however, have not enjoyed this same degree of professional control nor public faith and trust. In most instances, teachers have been mass produced in response to crisis situations and professional control was not of major concern. With the advent of mass education nearly everyone has experienced some public education, and familiarity has not only bred contempt but an assumed understanding of what constitutes good teaching. This notion of a common understanding of education has been encouraged by public ownership of schools and a vast social institution that offers an open invitation to the public to visit and inspect their schools. Many argue that in a democratic society the schools should be shaped by the pressures of a pluralistic society, but the point remains that the openness of the public school system and its lay control does not lead to the development of a traditional profession.

Educational experts have provided only limited assistance in the solution of this problem. While there are extensive lists of criteria and competencies of good teachers, there is no consensus on this point.[4] Once again the problem of quality control rears its ugly head. Unless an adequate description of what constitutes a competent teacher can be agreed upon, the control mechanism of the traditional professional model will fail to function.

The third argument involves the superior-subordinate relationship of the traditional professions. In all established professions the client comes to the professional in ignorance of the special information which the professional possesses and professes. The client may bring certain information about the particular circumstances of his predicament, but he comes with complete faith that the professional will act beneficially on his behalf. This necessitates a superior-subordinate relationship, and, as a matter of fact, the professional must maintain this situation in order to retain his professional status. In a strictly professional situation the client is at the mercy of the professional, and their continued relationship depends upon the maintenance of these role relationships.

Most teachers would reject this drastic kind of superior-subordinate relationship. While many speak of maintaining a certain degree of social distance, they would flatly reject the notion that learning takes place primarily in school and mostly under the supervision of a teacher. Children come to school with vast amounts of varied knowledge which teachers may try to build on or try to "unlearn." Most teachers assume that education is an ongoing process which takes place both inside and outside of school and continues throughout our lifetime. There can be no monopoly on knowledge, which raises the question of how teaching may best be executed.

There is a vocal group of educators that suggests teachers should be guides and reference persons assisting students in pursuing their own interests rather than acting in the traditional superior-subordinate mode.[5] While there is no overwhelming majority that would support this position, it is sizeable enough to pose a reasonable doubt about the superior-subordinate relationship that the professional must establish and encourage.

The final point has been hinted at in the previous section and is the most damaging of all arguments put forward. In order for a profession to maintain its superior-subordinate relationship, it is essential for the occupation to remain shrouded in secrecy. It should be obvious that education is the antithesis of this position. The very nature of education is a sharing of information. Withholding information for the purpose of exercising power should be a foreign concept to education.

The traditional profession is built on a rigorous selection system and a stringent socializing program which insures that those people who are chosen do not allow their professional knowledge to become public knowledge. If wills and deeds were written in language that lay people could understand, the need for the lawyer would be greatly diminished. If the clergy performed their services in anyone's home and did not invoke some special knowledge of a spiritual being, their clients would soon lose the faith that perpetuates their position. The more the professions are exposed to public scrutiny, the less professional they become and their previous advantage is eroded away. Professions are built on knowledge not common to all people, and the more the mystery is removed from the profession, the more each person feels competent in performing the professional function.

It can be seen that this latter position is diametrically opposed to the purpose of education. It is the function of a teacher to explain to the student and assist him in understanding and knowing, not only all that the teacher knows, but more. The best teachers will be those that encourage and facilitate their students learning more than they ever knew themselves. This cannot be accomplished by withholding information and maintaining the advantage of mysterious knowledge. The teacher must be giving of knowledge, and the occupation must be built on the idea of shared information.[6]

As can be seen from this discussion, there are some real difficulties when the aspiring public occupations seek to adopt the model of the traditional professions. However, most teacher education institutions seek to adopt the traditional professional model and have overlooked the difficulties outlined here primarily because of the desirable status and prestige that accrue to professionals. Even the more recently initiated programs of teacher education retain the professional title in certain parts of their program or as a title for their entire program, constructed on the unexamined traditional professional model.

From the evidence presented in this article it might seem to be a more profitable venture for teachers to explore the changing models of the traditional professions to examine how the theoretical model has been altered in practice. It would appear that the traditional professions are becoming more like the public professions. If we could curb our aspirations toward an *outmoded* model, we might find that they are trying to emulate us. At least we should become less paranoid about the prestige and status accorded to our occupation and get on with the business of establishing an optimal learning climate for all students.

NOTES

1. Frank H. Blackington and Robert S. Patterson, *Schools, Society and the Professional Educator* (New York: Holt, Rinehart and Winston, 1968), p. 21.
2. By common man it is meant that teachers are required to exercise only that degree of care in the management and supervision of pupils that might reasonably be expected of any prudent person in the same or similar circumstances. Johnson devotes one paragraph to explaining incompetence, but a chapter to exploring tort liability. See George M. Johnson, *Education Law* (East Lansing, Mich.: Michigan State University Press, 1969), p. 41.
3. Howard Becker in his construction of the ideal professional model makes these points in greater detail. See Howard S. Becker, "The Nature of a Profession," *Education for the Professions*, Sixty-first Yearbook of the National Society for the Study of Education, Part II (Chicago: Chicago Press, 1962), p. 30.
4. For explication of this point refer to Harry S. Broudy "Criteria for the Professional Preparation of Teachers," *Journal of Teacher Education* 16 (December 1965): 408–15.
5. Such authors as John Holt, William Glasser, Carl Rogers, and George Dennison are exemplars of this position.
6. It might be argued that there are mysteries of knowing that are kept secret until a certain level of learning has been attained. That is, only the initiated can properly understand sophisticated concepts. This presupposes a certain sequential way of knowing which ignores some of the more esoteric modes such as insight, intuition, and revelation. Furthermore, it forces us into a sequential, lock-step arrangement of teaching which may be seriously questioned.

PART II

School and Society

Advancing technology and changes in standards of living and social structure have all contributed to the complexity of the American society. Within this complex picture, the school looms today as one of the more stable institutions with which youth come in contact. The stability within this institution is the teacher. If the teacher is to understand his or her role within the educational system, the teacher must be knowledgeable of the societal pressures for educational change. Yet, it is this societal complexity that has led to a national unrest with the educational system. Part II helps the prospective teacher gain some insight into the sources of social problems and their relationships to the school, and understand the school's role within society.

There are the problems of socialization and the young, yet concern for self and development of individuals. All cultures have societal needs, yet we attribute more advanced cultures with societal concerns for individuality in family life customs, religious practices, and a capacity for fostering personal individuality. There are the changing models of expectation for the socialization of ethnic and social minorities.

This society has moved away from the "melting pot" theory and has attempted to embrace a posture of cultural pluralism. What kind of significant change this means for the school has yet to be encountered.

Changes in the American family have been taking place at an alarming rate and the primary recipients of these changes have been the children. Urie Bronfenbrenner has labelled these family changes as disturbing in that the family is the key social unit in our society. In examining these changes, he analyzes the social fabric of the family and discusses the causes of changes and their effect on youth.

The movement toward cultural pluralism has spawned multitudinous efforts in bicultural/multicultural education. Milton J. Gold discusses what he calls pressure points which may thwart multicultural efforts in education. Focusing on cultural, political, and social pressure points, he builds a case for a commonality of respect for all people in their interactions with societal diversity.

Youth in the age bracket of 15 to 24 years comprise approximately one-fifth of our population. Until the recent drop in birth rates is felt nationally, jobs for youth will continue as a persistent social problem. Robert Havighurst addresses this problem in an historical perspective and offers some temporary solutions. The solutions he offers have the potential for tremendous import upon the schools.

It is somewhat paradoxical that one of the biggest minority problems this nation faces is that associated with a majority group— women. Despite a variety of federal attempts to end all forms of discriminatory practices in educational institutions, it was not until 1972 that Title IX assured the end of sex discrimination in educational programs. Bernice Sandler discusses the federal government's role in correcting sex discrimination in education and the policies to be followed in meeting Title IX requirements.

The social problems of youth offer serious concern for the school and, in particular, have a broadening effect on school programs. Because of the changing nature and expectations of responsibility for the social problems of learners, schools have had to provide programs that attempt to curb or alleviate the problems of youth culture. Lee Edson discusses the smoking problems of youth and describes how schools have attacked this problem from a health perspective. *U.S. News & World Report* offers some frightening statistics on the use of alcohol and marijuana and their effects on school youth. Birch Bayh speaks to the issues associated with school violence and vandalism. Although these three articles present somewhat of a dismal picture of our youth culture, it is apparent that the schools are responding to what society is asking of them.

Peter Schrag discusses a delicate issue for the schools in his essay on gay teachers. How these teachers are treated within the institution offers serious constitutional concerns for society. This is not an issue

over which the school can stand by idly while others make decisions as to the danger or lack of danger attributed to individuals with differing social preferences.

Child abuse outside the school and the increase of adolescent suicide have serious implications for school programming. N. D. Colucci examines the child abuse issue and describes the role of the teacher when confronted with this problem in the learning environment. The teacher is alerted to the variety of outside help that is available when this type of problem occurs. Donald Smith presents some shocking statistics on youth suicide and discusses the teacher's role in identifying and dealing with the problems. There is no doubt that teacher sensitivity and alertness to the problem are crucial if the school is to have any impact on reducing the potential for adolescent suicide and child abuse.

Title IV, the Indian Education Act of 1972, has helped Indian Education with much of the same impact felt by the early elementary and secondary education acts. Leona Foerster and Dale Little Soldier describe early childhood programs for Native Americans. Stressing the importance of family and an understanding of that relationship, they describe meaningful efforts in southwestern United States. I.G.E. activities are explained programatically with these early childhood efforts for Native Americans.

The social problems faced by the nations of the world are complex and varied. Millions of people suffer from hunger or malnutrition. At the same time, the population of the world steadily increases, further compounding the problem. Can education solve this problem as well as other world problems? All nations face the difficulty of adjusting to a world community. The relative smallness of the world created by effective communication and rapid transportation creates a greater need for international cooperation. It is obvious that the American teacher and the American school cannot remain aloof from what is happening internationally.

Along this line, Section II concludes with two selections on international education.

The Hechingers discuss the relative effectiveness of schools in other nations in comparison with the United States, and Bel Kaufman offers a fresh peek at education in the Soviet Union.

Reading 8

The Disturbing Changes in the American Family

Urie Bronfenbrenner

Americans like to talk a lot about "progress," "improving the quality of life," and "meeting the challenges of tomorrow." All these depend on our ability to raise today's children well. Yet, when our nation more than ever needs a public-spirited and enlightened young, and when the best new research points to the critical role of the family, our nation pays little attention to the family as a key social unit, and there are mounting indications that the American family as we know it is falling apart. What has happened in the United States since the 1950s really adds up to a rapid and radical change in American family life. And the consequences for the young, and for society as a whole, are approaching the calamitous.

There was a kind of family stability in the late 1940s and early 1950s. In the past 25 years, however, the change has been dramatic. From roughly 10 percent of all homes having a third or fourth adult living under the family roof in 1950, the percent-

Source: Urie Bronfenbrenner, "The Disturbing Changes in the American Family." *The Education Digest* (February 1977), pp. 22–25. Reprinted with permission from *Search*, the journal of scholarly research of the State University of New York, Fall 1976.

age has dropped to half that. Today the figure is 4 percent. This leaves Mom and Dad. But Mom is increasingly not home. In 1975 for the first time a majority—54 percent—of American mothers with school-age children—ages 6 to 17—held jobs outside the home; and 39 percent of mothers of children under six were working, more than three times as many as in 1948. As for mothers with children under three, nearly one in three is working. All this has had a major impact on American child-rearing.

Parents have been leaving the home not only to work; they have increasingly been disappearing. The number of children under 18 living with only one parent—*now one out of six*—has almost doubled in the past 25 years. And the change has been most rapid for children under six. In 1974, 13 percent of all infants under *three*—nearly one million babies—lived with one parent. Main contributors to the rise of one-parent homes are divorces, illegitimate births, and desertions.

There has also been a sharp decline in the amount of attention that one or both parents give to affectionate child-raising even when the children and adults are not separated by school or work. With demands of a job that sometimes claims evening hours and weekends, with increasing time spent commuting and caring for cars, with entertaining and social visits as well as meetings and community obligations, parents spend less time working, playing, reading, and talking with their children. More and more children come home to an empty house. In some homes a child spends more evenings with a passive, uninterested baby-sitter than with a participating parent.

An increasing number of parents enrol their children in day-care centers—enrolment doubled from 1965 to 1975—and then preschools. And they sit them in front of television. Experts estimate that children under six spend an average 50 hours a week watching TV. By the time the average American youngster graduates from high school, he has spent more hours watching TV than in any other activity except sleeping.

And we are paying a price for this growing inattention, even hostility, to our children. Accidents among children appear to be increasing. Child abuse by parents has become a national problem. Nor should all the blame fall on the parents themselves. It is not only the parents of children who are neglecting them; society does so, too. And, in many ways, the crux of the problem is not the battered child but the battered parent who exists in a society exerting pressures which may undermine the role of parents and the functions of parenthood.

What has replaced the parents, relatives, neighbors, and other caring adults? Three things primarily: television, peer groups (same-age cliques or gangs), and loneliness. Today, children at all age levels show greater dependency on their age-mates than they did 10 years ago. And increasing numbers of lonely "latch-key children" are growing up with almost no care at all, often running away to join colonies of other solitary juveniles and to experiment with drugs,

crime, sex, religious cults, and the sheer restless busy-ness of Kerouac-like movement over the American landscape. These children contribute more than their proportion to the ranks of young persons who have reading problems, are dropouts, use drugs, and become juvenile delinquents.

What is not often recognized is that the tearing of the social fabric which so many people feel around them is largely a result of deteriorating family life and declining care for our children. Look at what has been happening to America's youth.

The first consequence is that many of them die at birth or soon after. America, the richest and the most scientifically and medically advanced country in the world, is seventeenth among nations in combating infant mortality. Crime in America is increasingly a youth problem. According to FBI data, the increase of crime by children in the past 15 years is three times that of adults over the same period. At the present rate, one of every nine teenagers can be expected to appear in court before age 18. In some areas, school vandalism has become as American as apple pie, soft drinks, and aspirin. The suicide rate for young people aged 15 to 19 has more than tripled in less than 20 years. The self-destructiveness of our children has become a serious problem.

Well known by now is the decline in academic capability among the nation's young in the last 15 years. Teachers are alarmed by their students' growing inability to write decently, their refusal to be rigorous in their work, and their inability to use common sense reasoning about everyday adult affairs of life. In addition, the alienation, anti-social behavior, and disorientation of the young have made an ever-larger minority of them unemployable, without training or self-discipline. Yet investigations have demonstrated that it is not so much the schools that determine academic achievement or character as a student's family life and the conditions undergirding a strong life within the family: employment, health services, work schedules, child care, neighbors who care, and the like.

What are we as a nation to do? I think there are three main causes of the change in family life. So perhaps our remedies need to take three paths.

THREE CAUSES OF CHANGE

One cause is our attitudes. America has temporarily lost its balance. Today, what matters most for many people is their own growth and happiness, their own self-fulfillment. We seem to be sunk in individualism. We want so much to "make it" for ourselves that we have almost stopped being a caring society that cares for others. We seem to be hesitant about making a commitment to anyone or anything, including our own flesh and blood.

To be sure, individualism has helped bring about extraordinary solo efforts by many Americans. But we have entered a period of history when we need to put other, neglected values on the scale, too. We have many other traditions in the American past: our social welfare schemes, our great public education system, our way of helping our neighbors—or foreign peoples— in times of catastrophe, our outstanding volunteer organizations, our scholarships and other help for the poor but able, our quickness in extending friendship and care to strangers. Like individualism, they too are American traits; and we should draw on them also. It's a matter of more balanced attitudes.

The healthy growth of each child requires a commitment of love, care, and attention from someone. Neighbors, day-care leaders, and school teachers can help, but most of the enduring, irrational involvement and in-

timate activities must come from parents. No one else can care so much or so continually. We need to get out of ourselves and into the lives of our children more than we do.

A second cause is our socio-technical structure—the network of work schemes, social dances, travel patterns, telephones, and other social patterns and apparatus that conduce us to separate and fragment rather than come together. We need to reshape parts of this structure to meet new needs of today's parents and children.

We often refuse to try little experiments in human affairs to see if our society can be more harmonious, and our children happier. Little things, like more part-time work schemes to allow mothers, students, and fathers to have more flexible schedules for greater human contact, seem so difficult. Our welfare system is a disaster, actively abetting the dissolution of our families. Do we re-design it? No, we prefer to muddle through, despite the staggering cost in human lives. The United States can no longer afford to be methodical, precise, pragmatic, and research-oriented solely in its scientific technological advances and continue to be so sloppy, neglectful, cautious, and fatalistic in its social programs.

Last, our national rules and policy are a cause of family trouble. The United States is now the only industrialized nation that does not insure health care or a minimum income for every family with young children, and the only one that has not yet established a program of child-care services for working mothers. In our taxes, our plane fares, our government welfare policies, we pay close atention to individual privileges but little attention to family rates or policies that would help build more cohesive families. We are "far out" not only in some of our individual behavior; among the advanced nations of the world, the United States is "far out" in its national permissiveness toward individuals and its neglect of the upbringing of its children.

Obviously, we cannot go back to the family life of an earlier age—nor should we wish to, given some of the old-time family's inequalities and authoritarian practices. But we can design and put into practice new attitudes and structures appropriate for our time. None of the hopes of returning to decency and fundamental values after Vietnam

and Watergate should be more dear than that of a renewed concentration on the proper care, instruction, guidance, and values of America's young people and the families in which they are raised.

The bodies, minds, and emotional health of our children demand it. And the ability of our country to cope with its awesome future demands it.

Reading 9

Pressure Points in Multicultural Education

Milton J. Gold

In essence, multiculturalism equates with the respect shown to the varied cultures and ethnic groups which have built the United States and which continue today to contribute to its richness and diversity. At first glance, such a statement may appear to be obvious and easy to achieve. It becomes less so when we recognize that many Americans perceive our culture as homogeneous rather than pluralistic. Our schools, among other institutions, have long operated on the assumption that there is a single American culture.

The contrary concept of pluralism is winning increasing acceptance, but much remains to be done if respect and acceptance are to be accorded to all the peoples who have contributed diverse cultures to the American scene. We must be aware of the numerous points at which conflict and confrontation may emerge because they can frustrate efforts to implement a culturally pluralistic policy in school and society.

Source: Milton J. Gold, "Pressure Points in Multicultural Education." In Praise of Diversity: A Resource Book for Multicultural Education (Teacher Corps, Association of Teacher Educators: Washington, D.C.), 1977, pp. 18–26. Reprinted with permission.

Some of these pressure points are cultural, some political, some social in nature.

CULTURAL PRESSURE POINTS

1. Basic obstacles to the recognition of American pluralism are (a) the failure to recognize that the United States is not a homogeneous country and (b) the continuing misperception of the United States as an Anglo-Saxon country. England was the "mother country," the source of the new country's language, the home of most of the new settlers up to the middle of the 19th century, and the origin of initially adopted political institutions. Yet, even in Colonial days, the influence of American Indians and immigrants from Europe and Africa was felt as new political institutions were forged, as new religions were introduced, as the language was subtly altered, and as new ways of living developed.

New needs of a different country, new technology and the unprecedented transplantation of peoples from all over the globe produced in the 19th and 20th centuries still greater changes. These transformations built a new culture different from both its Anglo-Saxon and non-Anglo-Saxon origins. And because continuity is a yearning need for all people, these transformations were accompanied by the maintenance, parallel with the common culture, of numerous sub-cultures—ethnic, racial and religious in origin and nature.

A consequence of this misperception of the United States as a white Anglo-Saxon Protestant country is the illusion of the superiority of Anglo-Saxon elements in the culture and of the inferiority of all others—a sense that what is British and Protestant is native and natural, and that what is not is foreign and unnatural. In a sense, the dominant culture regards descendants of Anglo-Saxon immigrants as the hosts and all others only as guests in this country, sometimes welcome, sometimes not welcome. What can the schools do, what can the country as a whole do, to correct this misperception and to establish a true cultural equality of all groups in the United States?

2. Conventionally, intergroup education programs have placed their emphasis on the attitude of the white, middle-class teacher toward minority group children and their parents. This effort is desirable but not sufficient in itself. It is also of prime importance that minorities understand the values, behavior and culture of the majority culture. While we are eager to preserve the values of diversity, we also share in a common life, participate in a common economy, are involved with the same political, social, educational, and cultural institutions, and make use of the same public and health services.

It is important, too, that minorities understand and value each other. To do less is to invite a Balkanization of the diverse cultural groups within the country, to construct a new Tower of Babel. Too frequently minorities are arrayed against each other, fighting over the same inadequate jobs, housing and social services. Members of different minority groups must recognize the common interests and legitimate aspirations of each other.

3. Maintenance of each group's mother tongue is still another pressure point. Many individuals as immigrants have been willing to give up use of their native language in the process of acculturation—of adopting a new country, its new ways and its language, for reasons of social adjustment and economic progress. Others have clung tenaciously to their language, seeing in it the primary carrier of a culture which they prize.

Prior to mass migration from Eastern and Southern Europe from 1880 to 1914, instruction in languages other than English was not uncommon in public schools attended by large numbers of immigrant children. In the period of great immigration, however, pressures toward "Americanization" mounted and English was mandated as the only language of instruction in many states and cities.

Concern with educational underachievement in the past decade has prompted development in schools of bilingual programs with two objectives: to enable a non-English-speaking child to learn in his parent language until he has mastered English, and to encourage the maintenance of the parent language and culture. Court decisions in the 1970s have gone beyond the mere encouragement of such programs and have mandated instruction in other languages in schools where there are concentrations of children who do not understand English. A corollary is the effort to help English-speaking students develop bilingualism and biculturalism vis-à-vis a neighborhood culture.

Pressures mount as misunderstandings arise concerning (a) handicapping the non-English-speaking child by slowing his progress in English, which is necessary for educational and economic achievement; (b) encouraging "un-Americanism"—that is, loyalty to another language and culture; and (c) using bilingualism as a screen to cover neglect of learning English. Judging the merits of introducing or maintaining bilingual programs is complicated because concerns other than the children's educational progress are intruded.

On one side there is the fear that loss of the mother tongue may accentuate the generation gap in the families of newcomers. On the other side is the fear that maintenance of the mother tongue will accentuate nationalist pride and will widen the gulf between minorities and the dominant culture.

Unsympathetic persons may view bilingual programs as a sign that the minority is getting too many "favors." Sometimes objections are expressed on "patriotic" grounds: "We had to learn English; why don't they?" Yet there is little disagreement over the fact that ability to speak English is an important part of the fight for jobs in a restricted job market.

A significant counterpart of bilingualism is bidialecticalism. Linguists have established the fact that Black English is not to be viewed as ungrammatical or inferior English, but that it reflects the features of an independent dialect with its own grammatical structures and variations in vocabulary. Teachers who reject regional or ethnic dialects are seen by their students as rejecting them as persons, as rejecting their culture, or, in the popular phrase, as "putting them down." Teachers need to recognize the value of local dialects as the proper medium for communication in certain contexts, while helping students acquire standard American English for contacts with the broader culture.

It is the position of this article that bilingualism has a legitimacy both for the student who cannot yet function in English and for the student who is proficient in English but who wishes to preserve his linguistic and cultural heritage. However, a concurrent goal must be the establishment of competence in standard American English for economic adjustment, for educational achievement, and for communication in the broader social and political sphere.

4. Efforts to make education multicultural frequently put their emphasis on the past—on contributions already made by an ethnic group as a whole or by its celebrities, on its history in the country of origin. Certainly, knowledge of the past is necessary and desirable, but major attention must also be given to the contributions that now are being made and *can* be made by individuals of each group as their potential for enriching the American scene is recognized.

For example, one contribution that might be made and gratefully accepted lies in the more humanistic orientation that many ethnic minorities express in their daily living. The stress placed by American Indians on cooperation rather than competition—and interest in winning only if winning is not accomplished at another's expense—is one instance. Attitudes of many European and Oriental cultures toward older people, loyalty to the family, respect for nature in an ecological and also a religious sense: all of these represent contributions that can strengthen our country if the majority will pay heed to and respect the minorities.

The general theme is simple. Diversity offers a richer potential than does uniformity. By resisting pressures to conform and by working actively to maintain pluralism, we enrich our daily lives—in the variety of people we encounter, the cultures that enhance our society, the life-style we express, the foods we eat, the customs we observe, the leisure we enjoy, the sense of fellowship with an international community.

POLITICAL PRESSURE POINTS

1. Integration of schools and housing continues to be a major pressure point in the United States. Despite legislative action, discrimination and segregation persist in education, housing, employment, and social organizations whose impact may be economic as well as social. Some ethnic groups desire to maintain ethnic enclaves as a way of preserving their cultural identity and traditions, and they resist the entrance of newcomers who are seeking to break out of poor housing in slum conditions.

It is no accident that busing has become a major issue in public education. Busing *per se* has had a long and honorable history in American education, making it possible to transport children from remote areas to schools offering richer programs and wider personal contacts. Obviously, objections to busing are not on the issue of transportation or of neighborhood schools but on implementation of a national policy of school integration as decreed by the courts.

Opposition to school integration, as to integrated housing, arises from two quarters—from those with a positive purpose of maintaining the cultural identity of their neighborhood, but also from those with less worthy fears and prejudices, from negative stereotypes of the newcomers, especially if they are visibly different, non-white. It is necessary to distinguish the negative element of prejudice from the positive element of cultural identity.

It also is necessary to face openly those points at which pressure is brought upon oneself. There are many who advocate integration for others in remote places, but not when they themselves are affected. Parents who send their own children to private schools must be sensitive about advocating integration in the South Boston public schools. Similarly, suburbanites are on weak ground in criticizing city folk who oppose

integrated housing, for example, in the Forest Hills section of New York City.

This article does not presume to offer any magic solution of integration problems. Like the purpose of this volume as a whole, our goal here is to help build a basis for constructive study of issues that should not be avoided or swept under the rug in a pluralistic society.

2. These issues arise because ethnicity is a powerful factor in our lives, and it is necessary to understand that ethnicity can be a force for good or evil. Ethnicity (the sense of identification with a group of people who are tied together by common geographical origin, language, religion, traditions, customs and history—or some combination of these elements) gives the individual a sense of identity, of belonging, a cultural rootedness. It also can foster petty chauvinism and prejudice against other groups. Education is a key to the constructive use of ethnicity.

3. The concern over chauvinism (excessive pride in and allegiance to a cultural subgroup) leads to a perceived conflict between ethnicity and nationhood. Is the nation stronger if it aims at total assimilation of diverse groups and eventual development of a homogeneous culture? Or is it stronger if it encourages diversity while maintaining a common core that includes participation in political institutions, language, history, national traditions—while encouraging the maintenance of language, social institutions, and traditions of the subcultures?

The position of this article is that homogenization has been tried and does not work. Whether differentiation is forced upon a group as a result of prejudice, or whether individuals choose of their own free will to express their uniqueness, we have abundant evidence that membership in ethnic societies, eating ethnic foods, praying in ethnic houses of worship, living in ethnic neighborhoods will continue—and will continue in varying degrees as individuals choose different ways of expressing both their ethnic origin and their human individuality. Moreover, if it were possible to melt all cultures down to a homogeneous blend, there would be a tragic loss of the cultural contributions that come from maintaining the unique cultural contributions of the many different component parts.

However, this differentiation has not only a significance for the individual or for the particular ethnic group; it has meaning also for the larger American society. The argument in favor of cultural pluralism is an argument for heterogeneity. This is the conviction that in maintaining differences we create a richer reservoir of human potential than we do by forcing all groups into a single cultural mold. By continuing to draw on the strengths that come from a multiplicity of sources—American Indian, Black, European, and Asian, for example—we utilize the best that all humankind has been able to develop in human values and thought, the arts, sciences, farming, industry, and recreation. However, an overarching principle remains—that we retain the distinctiveness of these cultures without enforcing or encouraging isolation; that we implement our nation's motto, e *pluribus unum*—out of many, *one*.

4. A parallel to legal efforts to enforce integration is the current "affirmative action" program of governments in trying to ensure more equitable treatment of non-white minorities and women in employment and education. This effort has run afoul of those groups which interpret affirmative action as the imposition of a quota system, a new form of the "numerus clausus" in European countries which at one time were used to restrict the opportunities of Jews in education and the professions.

Various values come into conflict here— the desire to compensate for disadvantages encountered by minorities in a competitive scheme; the desire to provide equal opportunity for equally qualified persons regardless of group identification; the desire to treat individuals as individuals and not as members of a group; the desire to use merit as a single criterion; the desire to define merit in a non-discriminatory way.

This conflict of values—of Right vs. Right —has become particularly apparent in education. In recent years, non-white minorities have begun to find places at last on school and college faculties. More lately, worsening economic conditions have forced reductions in educational staffs in many places. The principles of seniority and tenure have as a result come into conflict with the policy of minority employment because the "last hired, first fired" principle affects most seriously the minority groups which previously held few academic positions.

Right vs. wrong decisions are not always easy to make, but right vs. right choices are difficult indeed. These choices should not be made on the basis of simplistic arguments or slogans but rather on commitments to policies one affirms. Each person has to make his or her own choice and commitment.

5. Both the integration and affirmative action issues raise questions because of the uneven legitimization of minority groups in recent years. When 140,000,000 Americans viewed Alex Haley's *Roots* on television in the winter of 1977, they saw remarkable evidence of a new acceptance of Black people and their culture by the media.

One swallow does not make a summer. Blacks continue to be portrayed via demeaning stereotypes, and other ethnic groups in the United States have yet to achieve even the limited recognition exemplified by *Roots*. Television and other media continue to ridicule or disparage Hispanics, Indians, Italians, Poles, and other groups. Negative stereotypes continue to abound.

Nor is the problem limited to the entertainment media. Members of minority groups continue to attest to uneven treatment by authors and publishers of school textbooks and by Federal and state governments in the application of integration and affirmative action programs as they affect education, housing, welfare, and employment.

In these cases, persons believing in fairness must themselves exert pressure. Not only must they seek fair treatment for their own group but they cannot rest content so long as any group is maligned in the media or in popular folklore, legend or "comedy."

6. Schools do not operate in a vacuum but in a complex social context. An important part of the context is economic. Poverty keeps more people "in their place" than do racism and discrimination. Relationships among ethnic groups at the bottom of the economic ladder reflect a sad history of fighting over the crumbs left by longer established groups.

Culturally different people are not poor because of their ethnicity; they are poor because of limited opportunity to seek careers other than those in stereotyped and poorly-paid occupations. Schools have an opportunity to do something to improve the economic position of ethnic minorities. For example, they should be helping young people learn about careers for which their parents were not prepared or from which they were excluded. As yet another example, schools should underline the economic as well as the cultural significance of standard English, as indicated in our earlier discussion of bilingualism and bidialecticalism.

Schools aiming at a truly multicultural society have to take note of economic factors and social attitudes which affect the lives of their students. Yet they must recognize the pressures that build when the school tries to express values that are denied by the community. Positive multiculturalism within the school can have little effect unless it is part of a total commitment in the society—in the nation, in the state, in the neighborhood.

What part does the school play in affecting community and national attitudes and behavior? Does the school have a responsibility—does it have the resources?—to help build a social context which will make its educational efforts succeed by supporting its goals? These are considerations to which every worker in the educational vineyard must address himself.

SOCIAL PRESSURE POINTS

1. There is little question that ethnic, racial, and religious prejudices continue to exist despite a greater openness within the larger society. Archie Bunker is a popular figure on television not only because he is a comic character but also, unfortunately, because he reflects the prejudices of many of his viewers.

It is partly to combat prejudice and partly to foster a positive view of pluralism that this volume has been prepared. Recent achievements of minorities and public expressions of increased tolerance should not obscure our awareness of persisting prejudice, discrimination, and racism.

2. Liberalized immigration laws have enabled many new immigrants to enter the country since 1965. Most of them come from countries which were discriminated against in post-World War I legislation—from Southern and Eastern Europe, the Far East, Latin America, and the Caribbean Islands.

Sometimes they represent different economic, social, and cultural backgrounds than do earlier immigrants from the same countries. They experience the problems that all other immigrants encountered. The need continues to assist and understand them; the opportunity exists to utilize the resources they bring if we are wise enough to recognize them.

IN CONCLUSION

The final word in this article echoes our initial statement. *Respect* is the theme. The purpose of this volume is to help build respect, based on understanding, for the roots of all children—respect *for all,* for both the "stars" and the plain people who never are listed in *Who's Who.*

Reading 10
More Youth than Jobs

Robert J. Havighurst

According to the conventional wisdom young people take a major solid step into adult identity by getting and holding a stable job. There are almost no other alternatives for boys. And girls are more and more achieving their initial adult identity through a job rather than through marriage.

If at any period in history boys in their late teens or early twenties have difficulty finding jobs, this is generally taken as a serious social and personal problem, predictive of alienation or political disturbances, and also of delinquency.

Since the numbers of young people reaching the age of eighteen amounted to four million for the first time in 1972 and will continue at this high level until 1979 after which there will be a rather sharp drop, it was to be expected that they might experience more difficulty getting into the adult labor force than their older siblings who reached their twenties during the 1960s when they were in smaller age cohorts.

Source: Robert J. Havighurst, "More Youth than Jobs." The Center Magazine (May–June 1976) pp. 16–19. Reprinted with permission from The Center Magazine, a publication of the Center for the Study of Democratic Institutions, Santa Barbara, California.

This situation was worsened by the severe economic recession which came soon after 1972. The result is that in 1975–76 we have the highest rates of youth unemployment since the Depression decade of the 1930s, and possibly the current level of youth unemployment is greater than it was in the mid-1930s.

The relevant population facts are in table 1. Even in the best of economic conditions, the United States would have a problem of youth unemployment during the 1970s due to the temporary very large birth cohorts of the 1950s. In 1975 we have forty-one million young people between the ages of fifteen and twenty-four, compared with only twenty-two million in 1960. This group is about twice as large as the age group from fifty-five to sixty-five who are moving out of the labor force during this decade. In 1980 the situation will be equally difficult, with forty-one million in the fifteen through twenty-four age group. After that, this age group will decrease in size, due to the relatively low birthrates since 1965. Thus the youth unemployment problem is critical for the next ten years, and may require temporary measures for this emergency period.

Table 1.   Youth and the working force, 1960–2000

Age Group	Number in Millions					
	1960	**1970**	**1975**	**1980**	**1985**	**2000**
15–19	13.3	19.3	20.9	20.0	17.6	20.9 (est.)
20–24	10.8	17.2	19.3	21.2	20.3	19.8 (est.)
25–64	83.2	90.2	97.0	105.9	115.5	135.8
Total Population	179	205	217	225	236	264 (est.)
Ratio:						
15–19/25–64	.16	.21	.22	.19	.15	.15
20–24/25–64	.13	.19	.20	.20	.17	.15

Source: U.S. Bureau of the Census. *Current Population Reports* Series P-25. No. 480. April 1972. Table 7, p. 17.
Assumptions: Fertility Rate at 2.110 (replacement level). Immigration 400,000 per year. Slight decrease in mortality.

The table shows that the ratio of the fifteen through twenty-four age group to the twenty-five through sixty-four age group is about 50 percent higher for the period from 1970 to 1980 than it was in 1960.

The unemployment figures for young people have received less public attention recently than the unemployment levels of the twenty-five through sixty-four group, the men and women who have major responsibility for family support. However, the "official" unemployment data published by the Bureau of Labor Statistics state that the unemployment rate of youth (defined as the sixteen through nineteen age group) is three times as high as the rate for the total labor force. Furthermore, the actual unemployment rate of young people may be overestimated or underestimated by the B.L.S. numbers because so many young people seek work only in the summer, and they spend a considerable amount of time looking for work, which marks them as "unemployed" at those times. On the other hand, many young people (and older ones as well) simply give up the search for work because they are convinced that it is useless to try

to find a job. They do not register at an employment service office and therefore are not counted as unemployed. In any case, the B.L.S. figures for 1973 showed the "unemployed" sixteen- through nineteen-year-olds to be 30 percent of the total unemployed group of all ages.

Unemployed young people are most numerous among the economically disadvantaged minority groups, especially the black and the Spanish origin groups. The official unemployment statistics are especially ambiguous for these groups. For example, the Chicago Urban League, early in 1975, estimated that about 50 percent of all black youth in Chicago aged sixteen through nineteen were unemployed.

The problem is now clearly visible and our society is worried; but no major solutions have been tried.

It seems clear that the conventional employers—private and public—cannot give work to all the youth in the age range sixteen through twenty-five who want it. The American economy simply does not have places for them and will not have places even if the indices of economic activity get back to "normal." We cannot hope for a "natural solution" before 1985, when the age cohort born in 1961 will be twenty-four years of age, and will be followed by smaller cohorts, all with less than four million members.

There have been several quantitative analyses of this problem. It was pointed out by Kenneth Keniston in 1970. The Panel on Youth of the President's Science Advisory Council gave the problem wide publicity in 1973–74. The 1975 *Yearbook on Youth,* published by the National Society for the Study of Education, gave major attention to it. The problem has been aired, but no constructive solutions have been established.

For obvious reasons, the public high school and community college have taken on a kind of custodial function for young people beyond the legal age of compulsory school attendance. No doubt a good many young people now attending senior high school or the first two years of college would have quit school and gone to full-time work if there had been jobs for them. Since 1970 the situation has somewhat stabilized, with 80 percent of an age cohort "graduating" from high school, 50 percent entering a post-secondary institution, and 25 percent completing a four-year college program.

The mid-1970s see the great majority of youth as politically quiet and oriented toward their own personal careers, in contrast to the general unrest of the mid-1960s. For example, the National Association of Secondary School Principals in 1974 published a report entitled *The Mood of American Youth: 1974,* based on a survey of a national sample of high school students made by the Gilbert Youth Research Corporation. Asked whether the high school is doing a good job of educating the respondent, 77 percent said "yes." Asked about their plans for the time after they leave high school, 47 percent said they would go to a two- or four-year college, and 12 percent to a vocational training school. Asked "to what degree does your high school give a good college preparatory program?" 18 percent said "very well," 45 percent said "adequately," 14 percent said "not very well or inadequately," and 23 percent said "no opinion."

Practically all high-school students think that they should have some kind of employment. Only 8 percent said that high school students should not work or seek work, and 92 percent said they should be employed at least part time. The favorite work program was a part-time, year-round job, favored by 84 percent of the high school students. Thus there is a wide gap between what high school students want in terms of employment and the actual employment facts for youth.

At this time, the next move is in the hands of the educators and the legislators. They have perhaps six types of solution from which to choose. These can be described as having either an economic or a humanistic emphasis. Also, they vary in the extent to which they depend on the public educational system for leadership and administration.

There are two possible time perspectives —one is focused on the next five years—the 1976–80 period—the other is focused on the next twenty-five years—the 1976–2000 period.

For the 1976–1980 perspective, the emphasis is on helping young people to grow in maturity and socio-economic competence while many of them are waiting to get into a stable and satisfactory occupational and family-centered career pattern. This perspective is based on the reasonable assumption that the American economy will make a strong and stable recovery, and that the labor force will absorb the products of the 1950–60 baby boom fairly easily after 1980, when the oncoming young adult cohorts will be smaller.

For the 1976–2000 perspective, the emphasis is on helping young people understand the basic socio-economic and value changes of American society which are now taking place, and to find their places, not only as workers and parents, but also as citizens of a society that is preparing itself for the twenty-first century. This perspective will require more attention to a high school and college curriculum which emphasizes problems of social values, social structure, and technology in a world which must solve its problems of population control, energy production, and conservation of essential minerals and chemicals so as to create a stable equilibrium for the twenty-first century.

The following description of "models" illustrate the various alternatives that seem to be available.

1. A National Service Corps providing useful employment outside the private economy for about two million youths aged eighteen through twenty-four each year. If they were paid perhaps two thousand dollars a year for the socially valuable work they perform, the cost of the program would be about $4.5 billion a year. The Congress will probably pass a bill to establish this kind of program within a year. This is reminiscent of the program of the National Youth Administration during the late 1930s. It might be administered through state youth authorities, which would have to be created in most of the states, there being only a few now in existence.

2. A Community Service Corps carried on through community colleges and senior high schools, and administered by education agencies on a county or a city basis. This is an alternative to a National Service Corps, and would be administered by existing educational agencies. This would be most feasible in the big cities and in certain counties which have a county community college. Rural counties could work it out through the county school superintendent and the high school and community-college directors in the county. Also, most big cities have such projects going on a small basis for youth who are out of school and out of work. These agencies could be brought together into some form of mobilization of resources for youth.

3. A program of action learning in senior high schools and community colleges, tied to the curriculum and providing graduation credit together with modest payment for students from low-income families. This differs from the preceding model mainly in the amount of emphasis on work for pay, as distinguished from emphasis on a variety of service activities where the service motive takes priority over the money-earning motive.

4. A program of "apprenticeship" in local business and industry. Employers—both private and public—would be asked to organize cadres of young workers to do useful jobs which do not reduce the employment of mature workers. This might be difficult to establish, though the present work-study programs in many cities could perhaps be expanded somewhat. However, these programs are generally geared to the needs of the employer to recruit new workers, and they have very little elasticity as far as numbers are concerned.

5. Youth Communes. Though this might be controversial, it would be possible to establish a number of subsistence-oriented communes on the edges of cities where young people could grow most of their food, keep a few cows and chickens, and perhaps draw simple clothing and food rations from a public supply-station. There would be a number of controversial issues: How much adult supervision? How about coeducational communes? What kind of political ideologies might be encouraged or tolerated?

6. An *Education for the Future* program at senior high school and college levels for which selected students are given a cost-of-living stipend, while the majority are not subsidized. This has more of a humanistic than economic emphasis. It stresses a curriculum development that might catch on and become a central part of the liberal education of the sixteen- to twenty-year-olds of the next quarter-century. Since it is aimed at all alert and intellectually able youth, regardless of their economic status, it should include a cost-of-living stipend for youth of low-income families, analogous to the Basic Educational Opportunity Grants which have been paid to college students from low-income families in recent years. The aim would be to help produce a socially sensitive and sophisticated group of college graduates who are prepared by their school and college studies to take a lead in fashioning the society of the year 2000, a society which will be prepared to meet the problems of human life on this planet in the twenty-first century.

This program might well begin in the senior year of high school, which needs curriculum options to make it come alive to the more ambitious students. The National Association of Secondary School Principals has called for optional courses in the twelfth grade to relieve what it calls the boredom of the one-track senior year program that prevails in most high schools. In its December, 1975, *Curriculum Report*, the N.A.S.S.P. describes how a number of senior high schools are opening up the senior year curriculum, in cooperation with colleges which give college credit for certain courses. Some of them are simply basic college freshman courses for which the high-school senior gets college credit upon passing an examination. Others are experimental courses in which high school teachers and some of their students move into new areas where the main considerations are changing social values, problems of the relation of man to the natural environment, and problems of the relations between the developed and the underdeveloped parts of the world.

Possibly progress could be made with this kind of program through a joint curriculum commission funded by the National Endowment for the Humanities and the National Science Foundation.

The contemporary youth crisis calls for leadership and action by educators working at the high school and college levels. However, they will have to think and act outside of their accustomed routines. Youth need practical, maturity-promoting experience in the adult world, together with vision and perspective on the future of the society for which they will soon become responsible.

Reading 11

Title IX: Antisexism's Big Legal Stick

Bernice Sandler

Until very recently, sex discrimination in schools was largely unnoticed, unchallenged, and unchecked. All educational institutions could legally discriminate against females as students, staff, and faculty.

The 92nd Congress (1971–72), in a little-noticed legislative explosion, articulated a national policy to end sex discrimination on the campus. Title VIII of the Civil Rights Act of 1964 was amended to cover employment in *all* educational institutions whether or not they receive federal monies. The Equal Pay Act was amended to cover all administrative, executive, and professional employees, including faculty. Titles VII and VIII of the Public Health Service were amended to prohibit sex discrimination in admissions to all federally assisted programs that train health professionals; the U.S. Commission on Civil Rights was given jurisdiction over sex discrimination; and last, but certainly not least, the Congress enacted Title IX of the Education Amendments Act

Source: Bernice Sandler, "Title IX: Antisexism's Big Legal Stick." *American Education* vol. 13 no. 4 (Washington: U.S. Department of Health, Education, and Welfare) (May 1977), pp. 6–9.

of 1972 to forbid sex discrimination against students and employees in federally assisted education programs.

There was virtually no opposition to the passage of these laws by either the education community or the public at large. Sex discrimination, once only a philosophical or moral issue, is now a legal issue as well.

The key provision in Title IX reads: "No person in the United States shall, on the basis of sex, be excluded from participation in, be denied the benefits of, or be subjected to discrimination under any education program or activity receiving federal financial assistance."

Title IX covers virtually all areas of student life: admissions, financial aid, health services, sports, testing, differential rules and regulations, and the like. Title IX is patterned after Title VI of the Civil Rights Act of 1964, which prohibits discrimination in *all* federally assisted programs on the basis of race, color, and national origin. However, Title IX is narrower in that it covers only federally assisted education programs rather than *all* federally assisted programs; on the other hand, Title IX is broader in that it covers both students and employees, whereas Title VI is in most instances restricted to coverage of students.

Both Title VI and Title IX are enforced by the Office of Civil Rights of the U.S. Department of Health, Education, and Welfare. Individuals and organizations can challenge any discriminatory policy or practice by writing a letter of complaint to the Secretary of HEW. They may file on their own behalf or on behalf of someone else or a group. Complaints can be filed on a class-action basis, with or without specific aggrieved individuals being named. If discrimination is found, the statute requires that the government first attempt to resolve the problem through informed conciliation and persuasion.

The legal sanctions for noncompliance are identical for Titles VI and IX: The government may delay or terminate awards, or debar institutions from eligibility for future awards. Although a formal administrative hearing is required before funds can be cut off or before the institution can be debarred from future aid, no hearing is required for HEW to delay awards. Such delays in awards can occur while HEW informally "negotiates" with an institution to bring about compliance. HEW can also request the Department of Justice to bring suit in the event of noncompliance.

Since Title IX is patterned after Title VI, precedents developed under Title VI are likely to be applied to Title IX. Individuals may have a private right to sue institutions that allegedly discriminate. Therefore, it may be possible for individuals and organizations to bypass HEW and go directly into court, thus avoiding long delays.

Which Institutions Are Covered?

Any educational institution, public or private, which receives federal monies by way of a grant, loan, or contract (other than a contract of insurance or guaranty) is required to comply with Title IX. Schools at all levels are covered, preschools to graduate schools alike.

The statute exempts military schools only when the primary purpose is to train individuals for the military services. An institution controlled by religious organizations is exempt only to the extent that the antidiscrimination provisions of Title IX are not consistent with the religious tenets of the organization; thus discrimination on the basis of custom or convenience is prohibited.

Title IX exempts admissions to private undergraduate institutions, preschools, elementary, and secondary schools (other than vocational schools), and single-sex public undergraduate institutions. Although exempt from the admissions requirements of Title IX, these schools are not exempt from the obligation to treat students in a nondiscriminatory manner in all areas other than admissions. Thus a private undergraduate school, by virtue of its admissions exemption, could legally hold down the number of women it allows to attend. However, having admitted students of both sexes (in whatever proportion), it cannot discriminate after admission on the basis of sex.

The statute was amended in 1974 to exempt the membership practices of social fraternities and sororities at the postsecondary level, the Boy Scouts, Girl Scouts, Campfire Girls, Y.W.C.A., Y.M.C.A., and certain voluntary youth service organizations.

What Constitutes Discrimination?

One of the problems encountered under Title IX and other civil-rights laws is the answer to the question What constitutes discrimination? Policies and practices that clearly and specifically apply to one sex are generally easy to assess as discriminatory.

Admissions quotas for women, for example, or rules that require dormitory residence for women but not for men, are overtly discriminatory and a violation of Title IX. Other examples of overt discrimination are:

* requiring different courses for males and females;
* allowing boys but not girls to be crossing guards;
* sponsoring a summer science camp for male students only;
* awarding academic credit to males, but not to females, who participate in interscholastic athletics;
* providing an after-school bus for boys who participate in after-school athletics but making girls walk or provide their own transportation;
* prohibiting women from use of athletic facilities or equipment unless a male signs up for them;
* requiring higher grades for admission from women than from men.

While many of these rules and practices are often "explained" on the basis of supposed "differences" between males and females, they are nonetheless discriminatory and violate Title IX.

The indirect forms of discrimination are far harder to identify and correct. Many of the principles developed in the courts under the Constitution and civil-rights laws are used as precedents in assessing sex discrimination in education. For example, for some time, the intent to discriminate has been considered largely irrelevant in determining whether a specific policy or practice is discriminatory. In a landmark decision (*Griggs* v. *Duke Power Co.*) the Supreme Court noted that the intent of a policy is not what counts; it is the effect of the policy or practice that is important. Any policy or practice that is fair on its face but has a disproportionate effect on a protected class (that is, women and minorities), and cannot be justified by business necessity, is discriminatory. While the Griggs decision occurred in connection with employment discrimination, the same principle has been utilized by the courts in other civil-rights issues, and is being applied to sex discrimination in education. Indeed, this principle enunciated by Chief Justice Warren Burger, who wrote the opinion for the unanimous court, is likely to be the touchstone in evaluating the more subtle forms of discrimination against women in education.

Thus at the college level, nepotism rules prohibiting the employment of spouses might well be considered a violation to Title IX because women are more likely to be the spouses kept out of work. Similarly, women's groups are claiming that restrictions on part-time attendance or on part-time financial aid might be a violation of Title IX because women are more likely, due to child-rearing responsibilities, to need to attend school on a part-time basis. Although part-time policies are ostensibly neutral, they often have a disproportionate effect on restricting opportunities for women.

Another example of policies which at first glance seem neutral and fair would be that of giving preference in admission to a non-athletic program or activity to persons who have participated in interscholastic or intercollegiate athletics. Such experience is often viewed as evidence of being "well-rounded" or "competitive." However, because athletic opportunities have been severely limited for females at most institutions, participation in athletics as a criterion for admission or financial aid is heavily biased, even though it seems to be neutral on its face.

The Title IX Regulation

The Title IX regulation, which went into effect on July 21, 1975, details the impact of

Title IX on students and employees: recruiting, admissions, financial aid, differential rules or regulations, housing rules and facilities, physical education and athletics, health care and insurance, student employment opportunities, extracurricular activities, counseling and testing, single-sex courses and programs, graduation requirements, vocational-education programs.

The employment section of the regulation covers all conditions of employment including part-time employment, maternity leave, and fringe benefits. In general, the employment provisions are similar to those of other nondiscrimination laws and regulations. Women's groups are highly critical of the regulation for being too weak. Some education administrators and some representatives of male athletic interests are highly critical of the regulations for being too strong. Others are simply confused.

Some highlights from the regulation follow:

• In general, the regulation does not require or forbid institutions from taking affirmative action when there is a limited participation by one sex without a specific finding of discrimination. Institutions that have previously discriminated are required to take "remedial action" to overcome the effects of past discrimination.

• The regulation required all recipients (including state departments of education that receive federal aid) to have done a self-evaluation study by July 21, 1976. In thus examining their policies and practices for sex bias, many institutions have discovered numerous examples of inadvertent discrimination.

Institutions must also set up a grievance procedure for student and employee complaints concerning sex discrimination. However, there is no requirement forcing people to use the grievance procedure; persons can

file a complaint directly with HEW without using the grievance procedure.

Additionally, institutions must appoint one person to be in charge of Title IX activities. Employees, students, and parents of elementary and secondary students must also be notified that the institution has a nondiscriminatory policy.

• Although some schools are exempt from coverage with regard to admissions, all schools must treat their students without discrimination on the basis of sex. This includes course offerings; extracurricular activities, including student organizations and competitive athletics; all benefits, services, and financial aid; and facilities and housing. In all of these, the institutions cannot provide different aid, benefits, or services, or provide them in a different manner, or have different rules and regulations on the basis of sex. In other words, schools cannot use sex as a category to classify students.

A school that wants to "protect" its students by requiring only women students to sign in and out would have to apply the same rule for both sexes. Girls could not be required to take a course in home economics unless boys were required to take it; nor could girls be excluded from courses in industrial arts. Similarly women college students could not be excluded from a criminology course because it involved working with male prisoners. Title IX does *not* tell an institution *what* it should do, only that whatever the institution does, it does the same for both sexes.

• In general, financial aid, including scholarships, loans, grants-in-aid, work-study programs, and fellowships cannot be restricted to one sex, nor can criteria be different for each sex.

Thus, offering a woman a loan and giving a comparably qualified male a fellowship would be a violation. Denying or limiting financial aid to married women (while not similarly denying such aid to married men), or offering financial aid to married women and married men on a different basis would also be illegal. At some institutions, financial-aid committees have automatically assumed that a married woman needs less assistance because her husband will support her, while a married man needs more assistance because he is the "head of the household." While this assumption may be correct in some instances, it is obviously not correct in all instances. Policies such as these which are based on assumptions about women or girls as a group are likely to come under question. Individuals must be considered on the basis of their individual capabilities and qualifications, and not on the basis of characteristics attributed to the group.

Single-sex scholarships that are established by a will, bequest, or trust are nevertheless allowed; however, institutions with such scholarships must follow a complicated pooling procedure to ensure that there is no sex discrimination in awarding financial aid. As a result of that procedure, institutions in some instances may have to provide additional funds to "match" the single-sex restricted awards.

- The regulation prohibits discrimination in counseling and guidance. If a school finds that a class is disproportionately female (or male) it must make sure that it's not a result of sex bias stemming from counseling or testing. Counselors encouraging girls to take one course (such as home economics) while encouraging boys to take another (such as industrial arts) are in violation of Title IX.

Schools cannot use separate tests or other materials which permit different treatment, unless the different materials cover the same occupation and interest and the use of the different materials is shown to be essential to remove sex bias. Thus, using the old forms of the Strong Vocational Interest Blank with its separate blue and pink forms is prohibited, but materials encouraging women to consider engineering would be allowed.

Institutions are required to develop an internal procedure to insure that their materials are not sex biased.

- Institutions cannot treat students differently in terms of actual or potential marital or parental status, nor can they ask marital status for admission purposes. If an institution wants to include all married students it could do so, but it could not exclude only married females while it allowed married males to attend. Again, Title IX doesn't tell what to do, it only says that whatever is done must be fair.

A school must treat pregnancy-related disabilities in the same way it treats any other temporary disability in medical plans, or benefit policies it offers to students. Pregnancy must be treated as a justification for leave if the student's physician considers it necessary. A student cannot be required to have a physician's note certifying her ability to stay in school unless the institution requires a physician's certification for students with other conditions.

Title IX permits institutions to maintain separate living facilities for each sex, although housing for students of both sexes on the whole must be comparable in quantity, quality, and cost to the student. Housing regulations cannot be different for each sex.

It is illegal therefore to charge both sexes the same housing fee but to provide maid service only to male students, or to provide different security provisions, such as guards or locks, to only one sex.

Title IX does not require integrated locker

rooms, bathrooms, or co-educational housing. However, a school could not use lack of facilities or housing as an artificial excuse to exclude or limit participation by women. Some facilities might have to be reallocated, partitions might have to be built, and some facilities might have to be shared on an alternating basis.

What About Single Sex Organizations and Programs?

With few exceptions, programs operated by institutions cannot provide different benefits or services, or treat students differently on the basis of sex. However, programs aimed at women need not be abolished, although some modifications may be needed.

- Women's Studies Courses: All such courses must be open to both sexes. The courses, when open to both sexes, do not violate Title IX.
- Continuing-Education Programs: Programs and services which are aimed at persons continuing their education must be open to both sexes.
- Programs Aimed at Improving the Status of Women: Remedial programs and services provided by the institution and aimed at special groups (such as older women who have been out of school and out of the work force for a number of years) may continue, provided that men who wish to participate are not excluded.
- Campus Committees on the Status of Women: Such committees do not violate Title IX. However, membership cannot be restricted on the basis of sex. Having a predominantly female committee would also not violate Title IX if the members had been chosen on some basis other than sex (such as their ability to contribute constructively to the committee's activities).

Title IX covers the activities and programs of education institutions which receive federal funds. Unless it falls under one of the exemptions listed earlier, any organization which receives "significant assistance" from such institutions—even if the program is not operated by them—cannot discriminate on the basis of sex in any way, including membership, programs, services, or benefits. Organizations which operate off campus without significant assistance from institutions (and which do not receive direct federal funding) are not covered by Title IX.

- Business and Professional Fraternities, Sororities, and Societies: When the organization receives significant assistance from the institution, its membership must be open to both sexes. Similarly, its programs, services, and benefits must be offered without discrimination on the basis of sex.
- Women's Organizations, such as women's honorary societies, Mortar Board, Association of Women Students: When these groups receive significant assistance from the institution, their membership must be open to both sexes. However, the purpose of such groups (for example, to develop leadership in women) does not violate Title IX. Males who subscribe to the general purpose of the organization and wish to join cannot be denied membership because of their sex. (Programs, services, and benefits must also be offered to both sexes.) In practice, few males are likely to join, and those that do are likely to be sympathetic to the aims of the group. The situation is somewhat analogous to that of a campus chapter of NAACP, a group which aims to better the status of blacks, and allows whites to join.
- Women's Centers: Campus women's centers, whether operated by an institution or by students with assistance from

the institution, can continue without changing their purpose (to improve the status of women). However, their membership, programs, and services must be open to both sexes. A great many centers already allow men to use their services and to participate in their programs.

Employment of Students

Employment of students is covered by other legislation as well as by Title IX. Jobs within an institution as well as those handled by a student-placement service cannot be limited to one sex, nor can there be differences in pay or conditions of employment based on sex. Thus, women dormitory managers must be paid the same as men dormitory managers. Women students cannot be excluded from night jobs or grounds-maintenance jobs on the basis of sex.

Athletics and Physical Education

Apart from the pressures of the organized male athletic hierarchy that finds it difficult to give a woman a sporting chance, the sports issue is one of the most complex to deal with. More than most areas of our education system, athletics and physical education reflect the essence of our most stereotyped cultural norms: men are "supposed" to be strong and aggressive and women are "supposed" to be weak and passive. Women and girls have generally not been encouraged to participate in physical activities partly because the traits associated with athletic excellence such as achievement, self-confidence, leadership, and strength, are often seen as being in "contradiction" with the expected role females are "supposed" to play.

Another difficulty in dealing with the sports issue is that the legal precedents are far from clear. In almost all other areas of discrimination, the precedents developing out of race discrimination cases can readily and easily be applied to sex discrimination. Because of the general physical differences between men and women, the principles developed in other discrimination areas do not easily apply to athletic issues, particularly in the area of competitive sports, where the issue of single-sex teams and integrated teams is one that is hardly solved by the regulation. "Separate-but-equal," which is a discredited theory in terms of civil rights, may have some limited validity when applied to the athletics issue.

Generally, schools cannot discriminate in interscholastic, intercollegiate, club, or intramural athletics. Schools can offer separate teams for males and females when team selection is based on competitive skill or in contact sports, such as boxing, wrestling, rugby, football, and basketball. In noncontact sports, if a school has only one team and it is single sex, the other sex must be allowed to try out for it if their overall athletic opportunities have been previously limited. In contrast, a single-sex team in contact sports can remain single sex; the school does not have to let persons of the other sex try out. Thus, an all-male football team can remain all male. However, schools in general must provide overall equal opportunities in athletics for both sexes. A school could not, for example, offer only contact sports for men and have no program for women.

Among the factors HEW will assess in determining whether or not equal opportunity in athletics exists are the following:

- whether the selection of sports and levels of competition "effectively accommodate the interests and abilities" of students of both sexes;
- equipment and supplies;
- scheduling of games and practice times;

- travel and per diem allowances;
- provision of locker rooms, space for practice, and other facilities;
- assignment and compensation of coaches;
- opportunity to receive coaching and academic tutoring;
- provision of medical and training facilities and services; and
- publicity.

Equal funding is not required, although HEW "may consider the failure to provide necessary funds" in assessing equal opportunity.

There is a three-year transition period for high schools and colleges to comply with the physical-education and athletic requirement (July 21, 1978); elementary schools were given a one-year transition period (July 21, 1976). The transition period is not a grace period or waiting time.

Certainly upgrading women's athletics will cost money. Unless there is an influx of new money from contributions, which is not likely, the money will have to come from somewhere else. One means would be reducing the amount that is currently being spent on men's sports. It is not unusual, for example, for the budget for men's athletics to be 100 or even 1,000 times greater than the budget for women's athletics. Higher education in general is retrenching, and it may well be that male athletic programs may also have to retrench. Male athletic programs, of which nine out of ten run at a deficit, have been highly subsidized at the expense of women's programs.

The sports issue will be an interesting one to watch since it is drawing support not only from women and girls, mothers and daughters, but also from fathers and brothers—all of whom have an interest in seeing that athletic programs do not discriminate against their daughters and sisters.

Women and those allied with them in their battle for equal opportunity have come around to believing that the hand that rocks the cradle can indeed rock the boat.

Reading 12

Schools Attack the Smoking Problem

Lee Edson

In a California classroom in full view of an audience of parents and teachers, a ten-year-old girl lies on a makeshift operating table, her eyes closed. As the "surgeon," also ten years old, flashes his scalpel preparing to make an incision, he pauses. Then he looks at the audience and explains that the "patient" is suffering from lung cancer which could have been prevented. At this point the patient sits up on the operating table, and, with a self-conscious giggle, produces a poster that reads: "If you smoke, stop: if you don't smoke, don't start."

In another classroom 2,000 miles away in Albany, New York, another ten-year-old youngster sets up a movie projector, dims the lights, and flashes a homemade film on a screen. The filmstrip shows what looks like Martian invaders voraciously tearing apart and then eating a rubbery grey mass. The show's youthful producer explains that the material is really our lung tissue and that the inhalation of cigarette smoke produces dangerous elements that can destroy the lung

Source: Lee Edson, "Schools Attack the Smoking Problem." *American Education* vol. 9 no. 1 (January–February 1973).

function and cause premature death. The moral, once again: Don't induce air pollution into your lungs. Don't smoke.

And so it goes. In classroom after classroom across the Nation, such hard-hitting presentations by elementary school youngsters have become an important part of a unique educational program sponsored by the National Clearinghouse for Smoking and Health, an arm of the U.S. Department of Health, Education, and Welfare. The Clearinghouse was created in 1965 to monitor world research on smoking and smoking practice and to carry on a national effort against it. Under the leadership of behavioral psychologist and director Daniel Horn, and Roy Davis, chief of the Community Program Development Branch, the smoking and health program in the schools has grown into a potent educational force. Not only is it in the forefront of the current fight against the health hazards of smoking, but it is also demonstrating how an innovative idea can revitalize health education and help lay a foundation for bringing about desirable changes in behavior in later years.

"For years," says Davis, "health education was an orphan of the elementary school curriculum. It was generally on teeth brushing and personal hygiene, and dispensed in a 'thou shalt not' fashion. Now we're seeing a new awareness of the fact that health is not only related to personal well-being, but also to a person's harmonious association with the environment and society."

The results of this approach have been striking. From an original seed study in the San Francisco Bay Area, the health and smoking program has extended in four years into more than 40 school districts across the country, and the organizers of the program figure on doubling that number in another few years. Hundreds of inquiries and letters of support have been received from teachers and interested observers, not only in the United States but from countries as far away as Australia. And, while before-and-after statistics are not yet available, especially on a long-term basis, preliminary evidence indicates a noticeable decline in the use of cigarettes among teenagers who have been exposed to the total program as compared to a group without such exposure.

The idea of using elementary school health education as a vehicle for focusing on the dangers of smoking and for laying the groundwork for wise health behavior is not new. But the practical and innovative approach used today really began in the early 1960s, when Richard L. Foster, then superintendent of schools in Daly City, a suburb of San Francisco, became interested in overhauling the health education program of his district, which he found appallingly ineffective. In Daly City, for instance, health education was taught for one hour on Friday afternoon just before the children went home for the weekend. Impact, understandably, was minimal.

The Daly City situation, Foster felt, was typical of other school districts. Traditional approaches to the teaching of health involved over-reliance on preaching and didactics (good and evil sermonizing), on delineation of the health laws, and on concepts that students found obscure or dull. As an example, it was obvious that warning children of an early death from smoking had little or no effect on them. "Death is so distant to children it has little reality to them, especially when they see adults smoking and apparently living to ripe old ages," says Foster.

Could the educational process be made more effective by other methods? To seek answers, he involved Helen Delafield, the school district nurse who was also developing new ideas in health education. Out of this professional union there emerged a new approach to working with classroom teachers in the development of an exciting new health curriculum. If teachers are given the right kind of training and assistance, then they can motivate and help the boys and girls in the classes to make good decisions for themselves—not only about such things as smoking, but about many other matters affecting their lives. Moreover, they can make these decisions in the face of contradictory messages and pressures.

To implement these ideas, Mrs. Delafield sought out a cooperative school in the district, and with the help of the teachers of several fifth-grade classes, she asked the pupils what they knew about the different parts of the body to determine at what point to start the educational program. Their ignorance, she learned, was profound. For instance, in the case of the heart, the youngsters seemed to know only that it was shaped like a valentine and that it beat. The children were then asked to think up interesting questions about the heart. They responded eagerly. The questions came tumbling out: Why is the blood red? What makes it flow? What causes heart attacks? Eventually 22 questions were selected from the outpouring and posted on the bulletin board. Next, a large diagram of the heart and its vessels was outlined on the floor, the parts were identified, and, by means of a piece of red yarn, the students proceeded to trace the movement of a drop of blood passing through the circulatory system. Says Foster: "The children loved to do it. And why not? In learning about the heart they were learning about themselves."

After drawing the portrait of the normal heart and its workings, the team of teacher and nurse went on to develop activities to help children learn about the various things that can go wrong with the heart and the blood vessels: arteriosclerosis, heart attack, stroke, and other disorders. Most of the emphasis was placed on the prevention of disease—how poor diet may cause problems for the heart, and the effects of drugs, cigarettes, and alcohol, and the need for exercise. The same general procedures were carried out with the respiratory and nervous systems at other grade levels. The net result was the creation of an educational model or unit for each of several major body systems. Each unit was intended for introduction at a different grade level: lungs in the fifth grade, heart in the sixth grade, and the more advanced brain and nervous system in the seventh grade.

At the same time, teacher-training courses were set up in the use of the models. "What we had," recalls Foster, "was a model for teaching health that 2,500 students showed could be duplicated throughout the educational system." Follow-up with some would work. Teachers and pupils were excited and pleased. As one student put it, "It was real fun and I learned a lot." To involve the community, invitations were later extended to parents and other community leaders to monitor courses and see what the schools were doing.

In the meanwhile the Surgeon General's famous 1964 report on cigarette smoking, which showed that, among other things, the death rate for smokers is 70 percent higher

than for nonsmokers and 100 percent higher for men who begin smoking early in life, was making itself felt throughout the country and simultaneously offering a new focal point for teaching health in the schools. The National Clearinghouse for Smoking and Health took on the job of looking into the traditional methods of health teaching in the hope of streamlining it to create greater impact on youngsters.

Roy Davis, charged with bringing the cause to the schools, visited his friend Foster in California and learned firsthand of the Daly City work. Davis immediately saw in it a vehicle for carrying out part of his mandate on antismoking education and he obtained Federal funding of the program in order to broaden its scope. The project started in San Ramon in 1966 and then moved to Berkeley in 1969. The Berkeley Project, as it was first known in educational circles, became the pilot project of the Nation's smoking and health effort in the elementary schools. Teams of teachers, principals, and curriculum-support personnel from nine other school districts were the first to receive intensive training and material support in this experimental program. After training, the teams returned to their home districts to launch the curriculum in selected classrooms and eventually to conduct training for other teachers of their grade level in their district. In 1972, six of these districts became regional training centers responsible for spreading the model to other districts within their State and for introducing the training into potential centers in other States.

At the regional training center located in a suburb of Albany, New York, known as Delmar, a visitor will meet Frederick C. Burdick, principal of the Bethlehem Junior High School who recently completed his first year as director of the center. Here 52 fifth-grade teachers and their principals, along with nurses and other health education personnel from ten school districts in New York, Massachusetts, and Maine, are in the first week of a two-week session, sharing the experience of learning how to battle one of mankind's most entrenched bad habits by means of a broad-based health education program.

The wall is covered with colorful and gay slogans, signs, and cartoons, developed by the teams and spelling out subtle information and concepts about smoking and the respiratory system. A teacher wanders about the room wearing a smock on which has been drawn a picture of the lung. From time to time teachers pause to examine it. Teams gathered in small groups are cutting pages from magazines, pasting pictures of anatomical detail on cardboard, and making filmstrips. Everyone works rapidly and with a spirit of *gemütlichkeit* and enthusiasm which one sees only in highly motivated classrooms. A wide variety of educational materials and devices are scattered about the room.

The program opens with a discussion of why the lung system should be studied in terms of the goals of the overall project and how it can be successfully introduced into the classroom. The remaining time is divided so as to cover everything from air pollution to mouth-to-mouth resuscitation. After presentations by resource people, such as prominent physicians and surgeons, the teachers split up into teams to develop skits designed to show how they would handle a subject in their classrooms. The teams actually enter into competition with one another, and winners are noisily cheered. Movies, slides, and shadow shows also play a role in the program.

The highlight of the session comes when lungs of animals are brought from the local slaughterhouse to be cut open by the teachers and observed. After awhile the table looks like a butcher's block. One teacher is amazed to discover that a lung

actually contains sacs which fill with air. Another teacher is gripped by the reality of seeing tissue in full bloody color. There is a lineup in front of the microscope to examine the lung cells. "I guess we get excited about the same things as the kids," a teacher admits.

During the two-week session each team reviews and selects approximately $2,000 worth of materials—including books, pamphlets, filmstrips, audiotapes, charts, and models—and thus armed, returns home to carry on the work and to incorporate the program, which runs eight to ten weeks, into the general curriculum. The Delmar training staff later visits the teachers who have undergone the training to see how their individual programs are progressing. This year Burdick is repeating the whole procedure for sixth-grade teams from the same school districts and next year will do the same for the seventh-grade teachers. Eventually, if the overall strategy is accomplished, each of these districts will become a training center for its neigboring districts. The program is so highly thought of that in New York the State Department of Education is supporting Delmar's Bethlehem Training Center at the $70,000 level.

Since its establishment, the National Clearinghouse has surveyed thousands of teenagers to monitor their changing smoking knowledge and practice and the impact of the program on their attitude toward school, themselves, and society. One of the more striking findings is that the children in the program exercise a compelling, sometimes chilling, effect on their parents; a reversal of what usually happens between parent and child over smoking behavior. As one mother put it, "Every time I picked up a cigarette my child bugged me. I finally felt so self-conscious I quit."

A double victory occurred in the case of one 12-year-old youngster who would sneak off to the bathroom and turn on the fan while he surreptitiously lit up and puffed away. After a brief stint in the Delmar program he quit entirely and then started to work on his smoking parents. At one time his mother punished him for throwing away her cigarettes. But he persisted until she eventually stopped smoking.

Teachers are also affected by the highly charged antismoking youngsters, sometimes in ways they hardly expected. In one class where the teacher was a heavy smoker who was trying to cut down, the students brought in a gravestone, set it up in front of the teacher's desk and marked on it the teacher's life expectancy based on age. Each time the teacher admitted to lighting up (outside of the class, of course) a class representative reduced the life expectancy figure by a few minutes (the biological cost of a single cigarette) as a grim reminder of a life being willfully shortened.

To those involved in the program, even more gratifying than the youngsters' efforts on behalf of parents and teachers, is the impact the program has on the children themselves. This reaches beyond simply obtaining, as often happens, their fervent declaration "never to smoke," to subtler spinoffs on their general behavioral development. In one followup study, for instance, a youngster who had been diffident about his school work and had never shown independent initiative suddenly startled his teachers by handing in a long and well-done study of drugs and their usage in South and North America. In another case a girl became so enthusiastic when a doctor explained the heart to her class that she later phoned to compliment him on the good job he had done. Another student, a slow learner, asked to be transferred to a special reading class so he could read more quickly the materials about the human body that were available to him.

The Clearinghouse role does not stop at the elementary school level. As Federal gad-

fly on the issue of smoking and youth, Davis feels it is important to continue to look for innovative approaches to curtail (or better, stamp out) smoking at the junior and senior high school levels and even in colleges. In the higher levels, of course, a new set of problems arises, mainly because students may have already started smoking and because peer pressures become greater. Surveys show that youngsters often tend to start exploring smoking in the upper elementary grades and that if a regular smoking habit takes hold, it is likely to do so about the eighth and ninth grades.

As an indicator of the formidable extent of the problem, a recent national survey of youth smoking habits shows an increase of regular smoking between 1968 and 1972 for both sexes—a 4 percent jump for boys, and 3.5 percent for girls, particularly girls in the 15–16 age group. About four million youngsters in the 12–18 group smoke on a regular basis in the United States. Even though in the last two years this rise seems to have stopped for boys and slowed down for girls, it has been estimated that about a million youths start smoking each year. The effect of this trend, as well as that of family smoking patterns in general, constitutes a continuing menace to antismoking progress in the schools.

Toward reducing these statistics, the Clearinghouse experts have looked into a variety of educational approaches designed to discourage teenage smoking and to reinforce whatever gains can be made in the preadolescent levels. The most effective approach to getting the antismoking message across was once thought to be a "contemporary" approach, as it is known, in which the immediate disadvantages of cigarette smoking are emphasized. These include cost, shortness of breath (bad for sports), and in the case of girls, bad breath, stained fingers, and nut brown teeth. The many variables involved in the cigarette habit have prevented general acceptance of this approach as a working method.

Today the most promising approaches appear to be those in which youngsters themselves run their own antismoking campaigns in school settings. The adolescent, after all, is shifting from the family, shaping his own destiny, and therefore is proud of his own decisions. As an example, one young group that included some smokers started up an ad agency to develop antismoking slogans and did such an effective job that the smokers among them followed their own advice and cut out the habit.

Finally the antismoking message has to penetrate the entire community, and Davis and his group have made strides in this respect. Not only do parents become involved in the elementary school programs, but various organizations such as the American Cancer Society, American Heart Association, and the National Tuberculosis and Respiratory Diseases Association have provided support with materials, with resource personnel and even with direct funds. The Clearinghouse also does its best to develop programs that present to the next generation an image of a nonsmoker who is as sophisticated, urbane, and altogether charming as anyone with a cigarette in his hand.

Alcohol and Marijuana Spreading Menace Among Teen-Agers

Use of alcohol and marijuana by teen-agers—and even preteens—is reaching epidemic proportions, and authorities are quick to admit that they have no sure-fire solutions.

The problem cuts across economic, cultural and racial lines. From coast to coast, it infects schools in small towns and wealthy suburbs, as well as in inner-city ghettos. And what's more, the age of those involved is becoming younger and younger.

There's one hopeful sign: Educators and police generally agree that hard drugs are less plentiful around schools now than a few years ago. LSD seems to be out of favor, cocaine is too expensive, heroin use has declined.

Yet over all, these authorities say, the drug problem for schools is bigger than it has ever been, primarily because of major increases in consumption of alcohol and smoking of marijuana.

A recent study for the National Institute on Drug Abuse found that among 14- and 15-year-olds, use of marijuana more than doubled between 1972 and 1974 until now at least 1 in 5 children in that age group smokes pot.

Another authoritative study, sponsored by the U.S. Public Health Service in California's San Mateo County, shows that more than half of all students in grades 9 through 12 in that county consume alcoholic beverages at least 10 times a year. More than one-fourth drink at least 50 times a year.

"Serious Epidemic." "Alcohol is now our No. 1 drug," says Dr. Ruth Rich, health educational specialist for the Los Angeles City schools.

Ken Graham, assistant principal at Hillsdale High School in San Mateo County, says that "any time you have 50 percent or more of the population using a drug like alcohol, you have a serious epidemic."

Nor, in Mr. Graham's view, is the epidemic confined to any group. "Increased use of alcohol and marijuana," he says, "seems to have little relationship with either poverty or affluence. We find wealthy parents with children having drug and alcohol problems, and we find poor parents in the ghetto with the same problems. It has nothing to do with money or race."

Source: "Alcohol and Marijuana Spreading Menace Among Teen-Agers." Reprinted from *U.S. News & World Report* (November 24, 1975).

Also of urgent concern to authorities is the extreme youth of some of the alcohol users.

The San Mateo study found that among seventh graders, roughly 1 in 12 drank 50 or more times a year. In Charlotte, N.C., a similar survey showed about 6 percent of the seventh graders drank either daily or at least several times each week.

A 13-year-old in Fairfax, Va., told his father he was dropping a girl friend "because she's a drunk." The boy said the girl regularly brought miniature bottles of liquor to school and drank them during the day.

"In all our treatment programs the age is lowering," notes John McDonald, director of State support programs for the Texas Commission on Alcoholism. "There have been some under age 10 admitted to State hospitals."

Teen Alcoholics. A study of drinking in New York City high schools concludes that not only are youths starting to drink at an earlier age, but those who start imbibing before the seventh grade become more frequent and heavier drinkers than those who begin later. Says Ross Fishman, director of training and education for the New York City affiliate of the National Council on Alcoholism, who helped conduct the study: "Kids can be drinking long enough to become teen-age alcoholics."

Many obviously do. In Los Angeles County, 25 chapters of Alcoholics Anonymous are composed solely of teen-agers and 75 other chapters in the county have some teen-age members.

One young Houston woman, now 18, says she began drinking when she was 9 and quit, as an alcoholic, at age 15.

Many States have lowered the legal drinking age in recent years—usually from 21 to 18. Some are now having second thoughts. Massachusetts, for one, expects to raise the age to 19 next year. A spokesman for the Alcoholism Division of the Massachusetts Department of Public Health comments:

"The 18-year-old did not show the maturity to handle drinking responsibly and was buying alcoholic beverages for much younger persons. If we are going to let kids drink we should also expose them to the responsibility of drinking."

Don Moody, principal at Hempstead Senior High School in Dubuque, Ia., says: "We have seen a tremendous increase in drinking problems since the age was lowered. Beer and hard liquor are readily available to young kids through friends of a drinking age. It's a rather common thing to have to remove kids from school activities because they are drunk."

At many schools, drinking isn't confined to after-school functions. In fact, the "drinking lunch" no longer is the preserve of white-collar executives. The kids are joining in.

San Francisco authorities say some children inject rum and vodka into the oranges and grapefruits that they bring in their lunch pails. In New York, it's jugs of whisky sours brought from home. And in the Detroit suburbs it could be beer bought at carry-outs during the lunch hour.

"There is definitely more drinking on campus today than in 1968," says Lilian Blackford, a biostatistician who supervises San Mateo County's drug survey. "The gardeners and janitors get a particularly good idea by the phenomenal increase of discarded bottles and cans."

The headmaster of a private preparatory school in the Washington, D.C., area declares: "Any headmaster or principal who says he doesn't have an alcohol problem is either an out-and-out liar or so out of touch that he should be in some other line of work."

Lethal Drink. The shift from hard drugs to liquor has been marked, authorities say, by a rise in "polydrug" abuse—the combination of a drug or drugs with alcohol.

"It's a serious problem nationwide," says Thomas Kirkpatrick, executive director of the Illinois Dangerous Drug Commission. "They use alcohol as a substitute for drugs or in combination with drugs, but in both cases for the same purpose, which is to get high."

Alcohol and "downers," which can be barbiturates, sedatives or tranquilizers, act as depressants on the central nervous system. When used together, they intensify the effects of each other and can cause coma or death.

In Des Moines, Ia., Loren Zimmerman of the police narcotics squad says that it has become popular at teen-age parties to have punch bowls full of wine, vodka and an assortment of "downers." The result: a series of punch-bowl overdoses.

"I picked up a seventh grader recently for intoxication and he was really out of it," recounts Lew Case, police chief in Rolling Meadows, Ill., a Chicago suburb. "What makes it worse is that they play a game—something like spin the bottle—where they toss a bunch of pills into a hat and pull one out and swallow it. When they do this we don't know what to treat them for if they get into trouble with the drug."

Counselors, school officials and physicians almost universally lament what they describe as parental indifference to the spread of alcohol among youngsters. Such unconcern, they say, can be both dangerous to the children and inhibiting to attempts by the schools to remedy the problems.

Says one principal: "Drinking is a much more difficult problem to handle than drugs. How can you send a kid home to explain that he is being disciplined for drinking, when he may have to tell that to parents who are having their second drink before dinner?"

Robert Owens, vice principal of the high school in Palmdale, Calif., a town of 8,511, voices a complaint heard over and over from educators:

"So far this year I've suspended three or four kids for drunkenness. But usually when parents are brought in they say, 'Thank God, it wasn't drugs.' "

Dr. John C. Heffelfinger of Coldwater, Mich., who helped spearhead a drug-prevention program in his rural area, comments: "Alcohol and marijuana are most used by our teens, and I don't know any community that does not have these problems. But I think our biggest problems are parents and television. We've become an alcoholic society, so it's going to be used and abused because it's our standard way of living."

Parental attitudes can be inconsistent, in the view of a Miami, Fla., medical expert. Dr. Robert A. Ladner, adjunct professor of psychology at the University of Miami School of Medicine, says parents often dismiss alcohol problems as "indiscretions," and appear less upset with drug abuse when the drugs are the prescription type they use themselves.

But the doctor adds: "If it's glue, the parents are freaking out—calling the kids junkies, trying to get the kids into a drug program. In terms of teen-age culture, they'd rather see them legislate solvents off the market than cigarettes or alcohol."

What Youngsters Think. It is not only parents who view alcohol as less dangerous than most drugs. Many youngsters do, too. Dene Stamas, who is director of alcoholism treatment and rehabilitation at Riveredge Psychiatric Hospital in Forest Park, Ill., is one who disagrees. Says Mr. Stamas:

"In many respects, alcohol is much more dangerous. Withdrawal is more difficult. It potentiates drugs. It is so easy to get, and discipline is difficult because so many adults use alcohol."

Sharing Mr. Stamas's concern is Lionel Lazowick, chief of the Eden Alcoholism Clinic in San Leandro, Calif., who maintains that "if alcohol were invented and brought before the Federal Food and Drug Administration tomorrow, it would be banned outright as too dangerous for human consumption."

J. Irvin Nichols, administrator of the office of substance abuse services in the Michigan Department of Public Health, narrows the comparisons to alcohol and marijuana, saying:

"There's substantially more drinking than pot smoking and there's little question that alcohol is the more dangerous drug. I think that there was a period when persons were so concerned about pot and other drugs that they overlooked the teen-age use and abuse of alcohol. This is where people in authority and the general population are now realizing we've been lax."

There are indications that for young people marijuana and alcohol go hand in hand. The San Mateo surveys in particular show that students who drink also tend to use marijuana heavily.

Subject to age restrictions, alcohol can be sold legally in most areas. The sale of marijuana is illegal everywhere in the U.S. Thus, in dealing with marijuana, the emphasis by police and educators usually is on the sellers, rather than the users.

A "White Paper on Drug Abuse," prepared for President Ford by the Domestic Council Drug Abuse Task Force and released in October, notes that "a great deal of controversy exists about marijuana policy." The White Paper calls marijuana the most widely used but "least serious" of all illicit drugs. Its recommendation: enforcement efforts and treatment facilities for drugs other than marijuana should be given priority.

"Senior and junior high school students of today cannot remember a time when marijuana was not commonly accepted and used, at least experimentally, by a sizable proportion of the youthful population," says Mrs. Blackford of the San Mateo project. "Limited use of marijuana may not be condoned by parents, but use is so widespread that it would be difficult for a young person to even consider it out of the ordinary."

In Montgomery County, Md., an affluent suburban area adjacent to Washington, D.C., hearings are being conducted simultaneously on measures that would return the legal age for wine and beer to 21 from 18, and would make legal the private possession of less than one ounce of marijuana. "What these bills say," declared one critic, "is: 'Hey kids, we politicians are thinking about taking away the beer and wine we gave you a couple of years ago and giving you pot instead.' "

Extreme youth is a problem with drugs as well as with alcohol. In Cedar Rapids, Ia., for example, Capt. Ralph Myers of the police youth bureau says the age of the average juvenile drug offender is now 13 years. "The 12- and 13-year-olds are using marijuana more than beer—though they use that, too—because pot is easier to obtain," says Captain Myers.

What to Do. Is drug education the answer? In the views of those working with young people it depends on what kind. Some believe the more sophisticated teens become about drugs the less they fear them.

Increasingly, schools are moving to programs that emphasize mental health and away from those that focused on the chemical aspects of drugs, which "just helped students be better consumers," says Donna Steuver, of the Houston independent school district.

Denny McGuire of the Charlotte Drug Education Center observes: "Drug educators have gone through three phases of evolution. The first started with scare tactics. Scare the hell out of them. If they smoked a marijuana cigarette they'd be an addict and go out and create mayhem on the streets.

"Then it was the straight nonevaluative education. The idea was to give kids a string of facts so they might be able to make a straight decision. That didn't work. You can see it didn't for adults with the number of people who still drink and smoke.

"Now it's humanistic. We don't go into the schools with a one-shot deal."

In dealing with drug sellers, Superior Court Judge Hugh D. Sosebee of Forsyth, Ga., exemplifies those who favor a hard-line approach.

Last spring, 18 young people in Forsyth were indicted and convicted for trafficking in illicit drugs ranging from marijuana to cocaine. Included were the sons of a city councilman, city clerk, bank president, county coroner and nephew of a State legislator. Judge Sosebee sentenced them to prison for from three to more than six years.

Despite a mixed public reaction, Judge Sosebee says he doesn't regret the tough sentencing. "From all indications," he says, "it's gotten good results. It has slowed drug traffic down.

"Records show throughout the history of this country that certainty of punishment will bring good results."

Many who are active in drug-control programs say that too often young people fail to understand that drugs aren't necessary for "the good life."

Bill Davis, of Boniface Community Action, Inc., in Detroit, tells this story to illustrate the point: "I worked in a prison in Ohio in the 1960s, and I encountered a kid who'd been selling tea and oregano as marijuana— for $15 a baggie. He had no complaints from users, but was caught and jailed for fraud. So I think a lot of this is just kids psyching themselves up to be high—which suggests there are certainly alternatives to drugs if we could just convince kids of this."

—Copyright 1975 U.S. News & World Report, Inc.

Reading 14

Seeking Solutions to School Violence and Vandalism

Birch Bayh

During the six years I served as chairman of the Senate Subcommittee To Investigate Juvenile Delinquency we conducted numerous hearings and received testimony from more than 500 witnesses on a variety of topics, including the extent and cause of drug abuse, runaway youths, school dropouts, the confinement of juveniles in detention facilities, and the most promising programs for reducing the alarming rate of juvenile delinquency. The legislation enacted to deal with these problems is the Juvenile Justice and Delinquency Prevention Act. This act is designed to prevent young people from entering our failing juvenile system and to assist communities in creating more sensible and economic approaches for youngsters already in the system. It makes possible for the first time a coordinated effort by federal, state, and local governments along with private groups to address the problems and causes of crime and delinquency among our youth.

In the course of our work on this legisla-

Source: Birch Bayh, "Seeking Solutions to School Violence and Vandalism." *Phi Delta Kappan* (January 1978), pp. 299–302.

tion I became increasingly concerned with reports from educators and others over the rising level of violence and vandalism in the nation's public school system. Because many of the underlying problems of delinquency, as well as their prevention and control, are intimately connected with the nature and quality of the school experience, it became apparent that, to the extent that our schools were being subjected to an increasing trend of violence and vandalism, they would necessarily become a factor in the escalating rate of juvenile crime and delinquency. No effort to prevent delinquency could ignore the tremendous impact of such a development. Therefore the subcommittee began an indepth investigation to determine both the extent of these problems and possible programs to improve the situation. We conducted a nationwide survey of 757 school systems enrolling approximately half of the public elementary and secondary students in the country. In addition, the subcommittee corresponded with numerous school security directors, requesting their assistance. While the primary purpose of this initial survey was to gauge the extent and trend of violence, vandalism, and related problems, it also produced a considerable number of recommendations concerning the prevention and deterrence of school crime. In April, 1975, the subcommittee released a preliminary report on the stage of our study that focused on the trends and extent of these problems: *Our Nation's Schools—A Report Card: 'A' in School Violence and Vandalism.*

Following the release of the report, I introduced the Juvenile Delinquency in the Schools Act as an amendment of the Juvenile Justice and Delinquency Prevention Act. We also urged the Office of Juvenile Justice and Delinquency Prevention, under the authority provided by the school- and education-related sections of the Juvenile Justice Act, to explore ways in which the federal government might help reduce the growing problems of violence and vandalism. The subcommittee initiated a series of meetings and correspondence with more than 70 prominent educational, governmental, and private organizations that have a particular interest and expertise in the solution to these problems. We also held a series of public hearings with more than 30 witnesses, including teachers, administrators, students, parents, counselors, school security directors, superintendents, and several education research groups. In July, 1976, the chairman released two volumes developed by the subcommittee over the course of the investigation.

These two documents, *Nature, Extent, and Cost of School Violence and Vandalism* and *School Violence and Vandalism: Models and Strategies for Change,* contain more than 1,600 pages of testimony and articles concerning the nature of violence and vandalism in our schools and the various programs that can be useful in reducing these problems.*

Only a decade ago violence and vandalism in schools were considered troublesome but hardly critical problems. Virtually every school in America had experienced an occasional fight or a broken window. Such occurrences had long been viewed as more or less a fixture of school life. Recently, however, the situation has changed. What was once regarded as an unfortunate but tolerable fact of life for teachers and students has become a source of growing concern and even alarm for many members of the education community. Our investigation has found these concerns to be well founded; acts of violence and vandalism are indeed occurring with more frequency and intensity than in the past. In some schools, in fact, the problems have escalated to a degree that makes the already difficult tasks of education nearly impossible.

In a growing number of schools across the country, administrators, parents, teachers, and students are being confronted with a new and frightening factor in education. As the president of the American Federation of Teachers, Albert Shanker, told the subcommittee at its initial hearing:

Many authorities on education have written books on the importance of producing an effective learning environment in the schools by introducing more effective methods of teaching. None of them, however, seems to understand the shocking fact that the learning environment in thousands upon thousands of schools is filled with violence and danger. Violent crime has entered the schoolhouse, and the teachers and students are learning some bitter lessons.

James A. Harris, president of the National Education Association at the time of the subcommittee's first hearing on this topic, expressed the concern of his organization:

---

*This material is summarized in the subcommittee's final report: *Challenge for the Third Century: Educa-*

tion in a Safe Environment—Final Report on the Nature and Prevention of School Violence and Vandalism, 1977, 102 pp. Order from the U.S. Government Printing Office, Washington, D.C. 20402. Price: $1.25.

Incidents of physical assault have increased dramatically; vandalism and destruction of property are even more awesome; and many schools are required to tax already strained resources to meet exorbitant costs of school insurance.

In addition to the membership of these two nationwide teacher organizations, many principals who bear the responsibility for the daily operation of our schools have viewed this trend with growing concern. Owen Kiernan, executive secretary of the National Association of Secondary School Principals, told the subcommittee:

Ten years ago, in the secondary schools of this nation, violence and vandalism were remote problems. Occasionally we would have a so-called "blackboard jungle school," but this was quite unique. This is no longer the case.

The collective concerns of such prominent education organizations are, of course, a persuasive measure of the growing dimensions of the problem of crime in schools. But perhaps the words of students and teachers who occupy our classrooms every day constitute the most compelling testimony. A teacher from a large metropolitan high school related her experience to the subcommittee:

The past few years have seen violence and vandalism become an almost daily occurrence on school grounds. Students and school personnel have become numbed to these acts; a subdued anger, frustration, and acquiescence seems to pervade the system.

Two students, one from a large city and one from a suburb, summed up their views of the situation in this way:

Robert—If you saw these people you would be shocked.
Kevin—You would be surprised. You would not believe that some of the things could happen. You see somebody walking down the hall with a cane. If you unscrew the top and pull it out,

it is a type of dagger. You would not believe something like that could go on in school, but it does.

It should be made clear, of course, that not every elementary and secondary school in the country is staggering under a crime wave of violence and vandalism. However, while many school systems are able to operate on a relatively satisfactory basis, there is abundant evidence that a significant and growing number of schools in urban, suburban, and rural areas are confronting serious levels of violence and vandalism.

I should emphasize that this is not a problem found exclusively in large cities or in less affluent school districts. Schools voicing concern over the escalating rates of violence and vandalism along with the often attendant problems of weapons, drugs, and rampant absenteeism can be found in any city, suburb, or town, irrespective of geographic location or per-capita income. Simply put, while not every school suffers from serious violence and vandalism, no school can afford to adopt the smug attitude that "it can't happen here." Unfortunately, it can and has been happening in far too many schools.

The costs of vandalism prevention and repair can result in significant and sometimes staggering strains on education budgets. Los Angeles spent more than $7 million on these efforts in 1974–75, at a time when the school system was already facing a $40 million deficit. The Chicago school system suffered $3.5 million in property loss in 1974, to which can be added $3.2 million for school security programs and $3 million for guards necessitated by violence and vandalism. On a national level, the National Association of School Security Directors estimates that school vandalism diverts more than $590 million from annual education budgets. This sum exceeds the total amount spent on school textbooks in 1972.

Obviously, these are serious problems. But

I believe that we can solve them through careful analysis of their nature and through construction of various solutions that are compatible with an educational atmosphere. We must, however, keep several points in mind.

Initially, we must recognize that the solution to crime in the schools does not lie solely within the schools. Numerous factors totally beyond the school's control have a significant impact. As was extensively explored throughout our hearings, problems involving home environment, severe unemployment among young people, and a lack of adequate recreational activities all have tremendous influence on youth, yet the school's ability to deal directly with them is obviously minimal.

We should also be aware that promises to resolve violence and vandalism in schools defined only in terms of legislative enactments, whether on the federal, state, or local level, create false hopes, because of the nature of these problems, the diversity of their origins, and the intricacies of human behavior. I believe that the principal ingredient in successful efforts to reduce violence and vandalism is not more money or more laws but the active involvement of the education community in a range of thoughtful and balanced programs.

In order to stimulate this process of involvement, the subcommittee prepared and issued a report, *Challenge for America's Third Century: Education in a Safe Environment,* which outlined the kinds of locally based programs we found that could help prevent and reduce school violence and vandalism. These approaches are *not* based on the premise that we should confront these problems by turning our schools into armed fortresses. Instead, they are educationally oriented strategies that can succeed in enriching the classroom environment and creating the kind of atmosphere in which education can best take place.

Among the integral steps in a positive approach to these problems are:

- community education and optional alternative education programs;
- codes of rights and responsibilities;
- curriculum reform;
- police/school/community liaison arrangements;
- inservice and preservice teacher preparation courses;
- school security programs;
- counseling and guidance strategies;
- architectural and design techniques;
- student and parental involvement programs;
- various alternatives to suspension.

While it is of course impossible within the limitations of this article to provide an in-depth explanation of each of these strategies, I would like to describe two of them briefly.

Our studies show that a significant number of incidents of violence and vandalism can be traced to young school-aged intruders who are not currently attending school because they are truant, suspended, or have dropped out completely. One way to reduce the intruder problem, in addition to programs to reduce truancy and dropouts, would be to insure that suspension policies are helping to provide proper discipline in school and are not detracting from it by needlessly creating potential school intruders.

In some schools violation of ordinary student rules against such behavior as smoking or tardiness is punished by suspension. Suspension should be reserved for more serious violations. While students who pose a serious danger to persons or property obviously should be quickly removed from schools, our studies show that many teachers and principals feel they should have other alternatives in disciplining youngsters for ordinary day-to-day offenses than putting them out on the streets. Among useful alternatives are "cool-off" rooms, behavior contracts, and additional counseling strategies. These can be used to keep order at the same time we keep kids in schools.

Our study of vandalism also indicates that much of this destructive activity occurs in the late afternoon, in the evening, or on weekends when the school buildings are empty. Community education programs that expand the active use of the school plant can help prevent vandalism and turn a "target of opportunity" into a more valued community resource.

As mentioned above, I am convinced that the most important element in the prevention of school violence and vandalism is the active involvement of the entire education community in local efforts to accomplish this goal. Our report can be an important stimulus to this involvement along the lines of the positive programs discussed throughout our hearings and studies.

In closing, let me emphasize that I do not agree with the apostles of gloom and despair who tell us that we are poised on the brink of a declining era in American education, marked only by the burnt out hopes of an institution that tried to do too much. The spirit and sense of purpose and the willingness to strive and the desire to accomplish that were the hallmarks of the American educational effort over our first 200 years are alive and flourishing in schools across our country today. As we enter the third century we are obviously facing grave problems in American education, but we have in the past confronted such challenges and have succeeded in producing a public education system with a breadth and depth unmatched in the history of the world. Indeed, it seems that the very strengths of the system are forged through the experience of overcoming numerous obstacles. Today we face yet another challenge, but, while there may be reason for concern, there is no need for discouragement. Anyone who has worked closely with the education community cannot fail to be impressed with the vitality and confidence of the students, teachers, administrators, and parents confronting and successfully overcoming the problems of violence and vandalism. With the cooperation and commitment of all elements of the education community, I am confident that we can succeed in exchanging the adversity and strife so harmful to education in our schools for the diversity and debate so necessary for learning.

Reading 15

Are "Gay" Teachers Dangerous?

by Peter Schrag

Over the years schools have employed racists, sexists, religious fundamentalists, atheists, Communists, Birchers, vegetarians, smokers, alcoholics, and thousands of others professing something or belonging to some category to which segments of the community have objected. Some preach in the classroom that which they practice outside, and some practice it in the classroom; most do neither. As each of these instances arises, those who object most vehemently manage to define their favorite vices in such ways as to make each one distinct from all other categories of belief, preference, or idiosyncracy and to render them exceptions to those things they would generally protect under "civil liberties."

Questions like this always conceal others: Will my child be molested physically, emotionally, or intellectually? What subtle powers do certain (or all) teachers possess to influence or corrupt my child's attitudes, morals, and behavior? What subjects, ideas, and questions are proper matters for discussion among children and adolescents? Un-

Source: Peter Schrag, "Are 'Gay' Teachers Dangerous?" Saturday Review (November 12, 1977), pp. 53–54. Reprinted with permission.

fortunately, as posed, they never provide the one piece of information necessary for a conclusive answer: Are the people in question—in this case the two "self-professed" homosexuals—capable and sensitive teachers? If the information were provided, the question would answer itself. If the same question were asked about the illiterates, sadists, deadbeats, charlatans, and bigots who now teach in our schools and who are being hired every day, the purge would last for a generation.

To return to the question. There is no evidence—none—that homosexuals molest children any more than heterosexuals do; if anything, the research on sexual behavior and child molesters—most of it poor because the definitions are uncertain—suggests the reverse. Young girls run at least as much risk of being molested by heterosexual males as boys do from gay males. (It should be pointed out, incidentally, that females, gay or straight, rarely molest anyone; in this society at least, pedophilia seems to be an almost exclusively male pastime.) In a book called Sex Offenders (Harper & Row, 1965), for example, Paul H. Gebhard, John H. Gagnon, and their colleagues point out that males convicted of homosexual acts with boys "also show a relative predisposition toward heterosexual offenses with girls under sixteen. In brief, most of them are interested sexually in young people." The research also indicates that while the average age of boys seduced or molested by homosexuals is around fifteen—an age when the "victim" is often thought to be a collaborator than merely an innocent victim of perverted affection—the girls who are molested in heterosexual acts are usually preadolescents, many of them no more than six or seven years old and therefore genuine victims of the straight people who prey on them. If one were to count the thousands of unreported cases of incest—those in which fathers, stepfathers, uncles, and brothers molest their daughters, nieces, and sisters—the disproportion would be staggering.

None of this may reassure Name Withheld, who seems to be more concerned with "attitudes" than with outright physical tampering. Yet here again, the mere "profession" of homosexuality is a label that doesn't tell anything. If the concern is with mannerisms or modes of dress or personal habits, then another purge will be necessary to rid the schools of the nose pickers, lapel grabbers, leg and bust fetishists, and fanny patters—not to mention the physical and psychological sadists—who inhabit the classroom. If the concern is with the unlikely possibility that the teachers in question will verbally promote their sexual preferences, the chances are at least even that they will do for homsexuality what many teachers of English have done for *Mill on the Floss, Julius Caesar,* and the poetry of Longfellow.

In any case, there appears to be evidence that an individual's sexual identity is fairly well formed by the time he or she is five or six years old, and no evidence that children or adolescents have been converted by their homosexual teachers. (There is, of course, always the possibility that anything treated with so much hysteria by the official community will, for that reason alone, become a subject of fascination or experimentation for a rebellious adolescent.)

The issue, as always, is not what the teacher is or what he does in his private life but what he does on the job. The National Education Association (NEA), the country's largest organization of teachers and a group that has never been accused of political or social radicalism, takes the position that homosexuals should be allowed to teach. "We're not in favor of child-molesting," an NEA official told a reporter recently, "but assuming one's sex life is one's own private business, we consider that refusing to employ homosexuals simply on that basis is an act of discrimination." In the last few years a number of cities and the federal civil service have prohibited employment discrimination against homosexuals. As more communities discover that gay teachers are no more prone to abuse their students than straight teachers, and that when they do, the abuse is much more likely to be rooted in hostility or stupidity than in homosexuality, the question of gays in the classroom may look as quaint as the prohibition of the Twenties against women teachers who smoked or kept late hours. The question then was not homo or hetero, but whether the person who entered the classroom could have any sexual feelings at all.

Reading 16

The Schools and the Problem of Child Abuse and Neglect

N. D. Colucci, Jr.

Child abuse and neglect is not new to the United States. Most of us have either read about or encountered first-hand an incident of a child being abused or neglected by his parents or legal guardians. While these incidents may have stirred some emotion within us, they were usually dismissed as not serious enough to be labelled a "social problem." This perception has been fundamentally altered, however, by the publication over the past several years of research findings which suggest that the mistreatment of children is much more widespread than we had expected. Experts now predict that anywhere from 60,000 to 500,000 children suffer cruel and abusive treatment each year. Moreover, experts are now characterizing child abuse as a "disease," one believed to be the largest killer of children in America today.[1]

How Is Child Abuse and Neglect Defined?

Child abuse and neglect usually conjures up an image of a physically battered and distraught child who is at the mercy of un-caring and malicious adults. This image is accurate but misleading in that it does not tell the whole story. Too quickly do we identify the apparent victims of physical mistreatment while overlooking those children whose scars are of an emotional rather than a physical nature. Consequently, today's experts do not restrict their diagnoses to physical symptoms, nor will they accept definitions which ignore psychological and emotional injury. This position is reflected in both state and national legislation aimed at marshalling our energies and resources so that this debilitating disease can be eradicated.

According to Public Law 93-247 signed into law on January 31, 1974 by the President, child abuse and neglect is any "physical or mental injury, sexual abuse, negligent treatment or maltreatment of a child under the age of eighteen by a person who is responsible for the child's welfare under circumstances which indicate that the child's

Source: N. D. Colucci, Jr., "The Schools and the Problem of Child Abuse and Neglect." *Contemporary Education*, vol. 48, no. 2 (Winter 1977), pp. 98–100. Reprinted with the permission of the author and Indiana State University.

health or welfare is harmed or threatened." [2]

Dr. Barton D. Schmitt, a pediatric consultant to the National Center for the Prevention and Treatment of Child Abuse and Neglect, has identified specific categories of abuse and neglect which help to clarify the intent of PL 93-247. These include physical abuse, nutritional deprivation, drug abuse, medical care neglect, sexual abuse, emotional abuse, severe hygiene neglect, and educational neglect. [3]

What Does the Research Tell Us?

Examination of the literature on child abuse and neglect indicates that we actually know very little about this problem. Of the research done to date, David Gil's comprehensive national survey published in *Violence Against Children* and Ray Helfer and C. Henry Kempe's *The Battered Child* are the most widely quoted and praised. The profile of characterisitcs presented in this section is based on these studies.

Incidence of Child Abuse.   Experts admit that we really do not know how many children are victims of child abuse and neglect. Helfer and Kempe, two pioneers in this field, report that between 250 and 300 cases per million population are recorded in our larger cities each year. [4] But these figures may be only the tip of the iceberg since they represent only reported incidences. Some authorities predict that for each reported case there are a minimum of 25 actual cases. [5]

Characteristics of the Abuser and Abused. Child abuse and neglect is inflicted upon both boys and girls, infants and adolescents. Boys outnumber girls below the age of 12. Girls outnumber boys above the age of 12.

Seventy-five percent are over two years of age, but nearly half are over six. Nearly one-fifth are teenagers, the majority of whom are girls. [6]

All racial and ethnic groups experience abuse and neglect. There is, however, an over-representation of nonwhite children. For every 100,000 white children about seven cases are reported. The corresponding figure for nonwhites is 21. [7]

Thirty percent of the children live in homes without a father or father substitute. This figure is higher for Negro and Puerto Rican children. [8]

The educational level of the child abuser is very low for both men and women. Less than 20 percent are high school graduates. [9]

The occupational status of these individuals corresponds to their low educational status. The majority fall into the unskilled or semi-skilled areas. Moreover, almost half are unemployed part of the year. Forty percent of the families rely totally on public assistance, and 60 percent of the families receive public assistance during part or all the year. [10]

Children who are abused once will more than likely be abused again. Siblings of currently abused children are often previous victims. [11]

Ninety percent of all reported physical injuries are not serious enough to leave lasting physical effects. About 5 percent cause permanent damage, while 4 percent are fatal. Most of the injuries take the form of bruises, welts, abrasions and lacerations. Bone fractures account for about 15 percent of all injuries. [12]

Is It a School Problem?

Child abuse and neglect may not originate inside the schoolhouse, but it often finds its way there. Once inside, it must be dealt with as quickly and as effectively as possible.

The schools are a logical place to detect and report cases of abuse and neglect. Compulsory attendance laws and local truancy personnel enable teachers and school officials to keep close watch on children. Research suggests, however, that these tools have been used neither effectively nor consistently.[13]

Three problems stand out. First, school districts do not take the time to formulate working policies and procedures. It is estimated, for example, that less than 5 percent have done so.[14] Secondly, when policies are enacted, teachers are not informed by the central office of their existence; if they are informed, they are not adequately helped to interpret them. Thirdly, little or no training is provided to teachers on how to handle and report incidents of abuse and neglect.

What Should Teachers Look For?

Teachers can make a significant contribution to the resolution of this problem by becoming alert observers and by making it a point to report their observations. Failure to report is the major obstacle to providing protective services to abused children. Once diagnosed, cases of abuse should be reported immediately to the appropriate authority.[15]

Teachers should look for these behaviors and outward appearances: the over aggressive child, the disruptive or destructive child, the passive child, the frequently absent or late child, the dirty or unkempt child, the tired or undernourished child, the physically scarred or beaten child, the inadequately dressed child, and the child who comes to school early and leaves late.

What Steps Should Schools Take?

The school cannot deal with this problem independently of other social institutions in the community. Its primary function is to help detect and then to report to the appropriate child protection agency the incident recorded. Kay Drews, a recognized expert in the field, suggests that any operating procedure should include the following:

1. Special training programs for teachers to enable them to recognize suspected cases of physical abuse.
2. Specific instructions given to the teacher to report all suspected cases to a stated individual in her school.
3. The child should be seen by the school physician who would examine the child, interview the parents and report the case to the proper agency.
4. The school must then communicate its information to the agency and develop a cooperative therapeutic plan.
5. A follow-through system should be established by the school to make certain that the case was handled properly and the therapeutic plan is working.[16]

What Help Are We Receiving From the Federal Government?

With passage of the Child Abuse Prevention and Treatment Act (PL 93–247), Congress committed some 60 million dollars to the development of strategies aimed at solving the child abuse and neglect problem. To get things moving, the National Center on Child Abuse and Neglect was created. Its purpose is to identify and select programs submitted by states and public and private agencies which show promise of effectively dealing with the causes and consequences of abuse and neglect. At the time of this writing, the

Center had already reviewed over 525 research and demonstration applications and over seventy contract proposals. Many of these have been funded. It is anticipated that these efforts will make a significant impact in the fight to protect the lives of defenseless children throughout the nation.[17]

Needed: A Campaign to Educate the Public

It is now apparent that no one agency or institution will be able to solve this problem. Indeed, its solution is nowhere in sight. But we have made some progress, and we will continue to do so as long as dedicated professionals and concerned citizens respond to the cries of the injured. To do less is to feed the cycle of the abused becoming the abuser. Consequently, we need to do even more in the way of educating the public as well as those practicing professionals who have contact with the young about the nature and consequences of this disease.

NOTES

1. Bert Shanas, "Child Abuse: A Killer Teachers Can Help Control," *Phi Delta Kappan*, March, 1975, p. 479.
2. Frank Ferro, "Protecting Children: The National Center on Child Abuse and Neglect," *Childhood Education*, November/December, 1975, p. 63.
3. Barton D. Schmitt, "What Teachers Need to Know About Child Abuse and Neglect," *Childhood Education*, November/December, 1975, p. 58.
4. Henry C. Kempe, and Ray E. Helfer, *Helping the Battered Child and His Family* (Philadelphia: J. B. Lippincott Company, 1972), p. xiii.
5. Shanas, op. cit., p. 479.
6. David G. Gil, *Violence Against Children* (Cambridge: Harvard University Press, 1970), p. 104.
7. Ibid., p. 106.
8. Ibid., pp. 108–9.
9. Ibid., pp. 110–111.
10. Ibid., p. 111.
11. Ibid., p. 114.
12. Ibid., pp. 118–19.
13. Annette Lynch, "Child Abuse in the School-Age Population," *The Journal of School Health*, March, 1975, p. 148.
14. Ibid., p. 141.
15. Ibid.
16. Kay Drews, "The Child and the School." In *Helping the Battered Child and His Family*, p. 122.
17. Ferro, op. cit., p. 63.

Reading 17

Adolescent Suicide: A Problem for Teachers?

Donald F. Smith

> If I ever commit suicide, I'll leave my school schedule behind as a suicide note.
> The teen suicide rate is shocking.
>
> —White House Conference on Children, 1970

Case 1. After a very intense relationship that ended in unwanted pregnancy, an adolescent female decided to take her life. Alienated from her family, peers, teachers, and school, she slashed her wrists with a razor. The attempt would have proven fatal had not her parents arrived home and rushed her to a hospital.

Classification and rating:

Suicide Gesture
Lethality: Low
Intent: High
Method: Cut wrists
Mitigating Circumstances: High
Certainty: ?

Case 2. After receiving a letter of rejection from a prestigious Eastern university, a male high school student bid goodnight to his girl friend, drove to a deserted road, and shot himself. Several hours later, police found him slumped over the steering wheel of his car and took him to a local hospital, where he was pronounced dead.

Classification and rating:

Suicide
Lethality: High
Intent: High
Mitigating Circumstances: High
Certainty: 100%

Case 3. An impressionable adolescent female became incoherent from intoxicating beverages given to her by a male companion. Surprised by her mother while losing her virginity, the girl could only reply with sobs of "I'm going to kill myself." Later, after thinking more clearly of the event, she rationalized the act into an allegation of rape.

Classification and rating:

Suicide Ideas
Lethality: Low
Intent: Low
Mitigating Circumstances: High
Certainty: ?[1]

Source: Donald F. Smith, "Adolescent Suicide: A Problem for Teachers?" *Phi Delta Kappan*, vol. 57, no. 8 (April 1976), pp. 539–42. Reprinted with permission.

PROBLEM AND DEFINITION

Psychiatrists and other social professionals are increasingly concerned with the recent upsurge in suicide among adolescents. Of the 25,000 Americans who commit suicide each year, more than 6.6% are adolescents and young adults aged 15 to 19.[2] There will be 20 times this number of suicide attempts. Experts recognize depression, lack of ambition, lack of goals, and a rise in alcoholic consumption as danger signs among teen-agers. Suicide has been among the leading causes of death in the past decade. Among teen-agers and young adults, it has moved from fourth to second place. Only accidents cause more deaths among adolescents.

In fact, self-destruction among young people in the U.S. has been rising sharply over the past quarter of a century, from 1,958 cases in 1951 to 2,319 in 1961 and 5,548 in 1971. Experts in suicidology claim that from 70,000 to 80,000 young people will attempt suicide this year; 3,500 to 4,000 will be successful. The actual number of suicide attempts will really never be known. The fact that there is no uniform legal requirement for reporting suggests that many suicides or attempts go unreported. Said one psychiatrist of a family who lost their son, "I wrote 'heart attack' on the death certificate to protect the family."

Male students are three times more likely than females to commit suicide. Although no satisfactory explanation of this phenomenon has been offered, clinical psychologists at the Los Angeles Institute for the Study of Self-Destructive Behavior—the nation's first suicide prevention center—suggest that society's less tolerant attitude toward emotional expression and failure among males, coupled with the postwar baby boom and the ensuing fierce competition in schools and in the job market, have contributed to the higher suicide rate among males.

The above reasons seldom apply to girls, because, until recently, schools and parents have not expected as much of them. However, adolescent females often have a special need for intense relationships, which is usually fulfilled by a romance. If the romance fails and the girl is left with an unwanted pregnancy, she can become alienated from friends and from her own family. In cases of suicide in both boys and girls, "chronic social isolation and a striking lack of involvement with either peers or teachers were prominent features."[3]

Suicide rates among blacks are also high and expected to be even higher, according to Dr. Charles Prudhomme, a psychiatrist who is predicting a rash of black adolescent suicides because of school and job reversals. The progress of the sixties is dwindling, he claims, and many blacks will not be able to handle the loss.

Suicide among American Indians—at least five times the national average—is a national disgrace. Most of these suicides occur among adolescents and young adults. The reasons range from poverty, unemployment, and geographic isolation to the conflict between reservation society values and those of mainstream America. All of these may be symptoms of a deeper problem: living in a hostile environment. The adolescent Indian seeking identity, adult autonomy, and an independent role in society is faced with a bewildering set of conflicts. Emotional conflict enters the Indian child's world early; he may be sent to a government boarding school far removed from the supportive role of the reservation and tribal culture. Conflict continues to grow in the Indian youth as he chooses whether to remain on the reservation or enter the white man's world. If he should choose mainstream America, the average Indian finds himself in a blind alley, working at menial jobs. Frustrated and unable to assert himself, he may turn to heavy drinking and ultimately self-destruction.[4]

The reason for increased suicide among

nonwhites is a provocative question. The rate is higher at a much earlier age than among whites, whose rates keep rising steadily until age 60. The consensus among minority psychiatrists is that a white person does not realize until middle age that he may not reach goals he has set for himself; he then must accept his limitations or resign himself to a life of quiet desperation. Such depression occurs earlier among nonwhites as they see doors that will be permanently closed to them.

METHODS

The methods used in suicide attempts indicate that males aged 15–19 tend to favor more violent means, such as firearms and hanging; females, on the other hand, use poisoning first and firearms second. Pamela Cantor, a Boston University psychologist, believes that when boys decide to kill themselves they really want to die. Their motives are strong and their methods correspondingly tend to be failure-proof.[5] The tendency of males to use firearms may be due to greater availability of and familiarity with guns, while the females' use of sleeping pills and other drugs that take time to work may indicate a latent desire for rescue.

Another method that requires further exploration and research is subintentional self-destruction among youth. This classification refers to ill-defined deaths and practices which lead toward death; it includes death-risking activities such as not following medical advice and abuse of drugs and food, as well as inattention to life-threatening situations, such as walking too close to the edge of a cliff or highway and taking unusual chances when driving an automobile.[6] An adolescent undergoing severe emotional turmoil and unable to cope with psychological and sociological stress can attract friends or peers by showing that he has enough guts to take a chance.

THEORIES OF SUICIDE

Sigmund Freud and Karl Menninger located possible explanations or theories of suicide in the unconscious,[7] but Emile Durkheim, a nineteenth-century sociologist, believed that society alone was responsible for the suicidal personality. He classified three types of suicidal personalities which were a response to a social situation: the egoistic, altruistic, and anomie suicides.[8]

The egoistic suicide is the "loner" who is not integrated into society, the individual who feels the cards are stacked against him. Feeling alienated from society, with weak religious and family ties, the individual is a prime candidate for egoistic suicide.

Type two, altruistic suicide, occurs when the individual has overidentified with a group to the extent that he is willing to sacrifice himself to advance or preserve the group's goal. In the adolescent world, as teachers are well aware, group pressures on the adolescent are extremely strong and particularly difficult to resist. During the youth turmoil at the height of the Vietnam war, a youth burned himself to death on the steps of the Pentagon as a symbolic protest of America's young peoples' opposition to the war.

Anomie suicide is the result of sudden and unexpected changes in one's personal or social life that create confusion and alienation. The accelerated pace of social life with its corresponding value conflicts between generations and the changing position of youth and its subculture are areas that may cause serious mental illness resulting in excessive use of drugs, alcoholism, or suicide.

All of these theories—whether they find the causes of suicide in the unconscious or in society—agree on the main point: They all see the individual's actions resulting from forces over which he has little or no control.

Recent contributions to understanding suicide range from social-psychological to sociocultural explanations. The social-psychological theory sees self-destruction as a result of high personal ambition, keen rivalry, and the discrepancy between opportunity and meager results with resulting disappointment, guilt, and depression. The sociocultural theory takes into account a person's life-style and his adaptive capability. A longitudinal study being carried out at Johns Hopkins University may offer the most promising hope for identifying suicide-prone individuals. The study involves identifying personality types who may be prone to self-destruction, thereby providing an opportunity for treatment.

Suicide Today

Studies of adolescents hospitalized for suicide attempts point to school adjustment as one of the variables related to self-destruction. School performance was almost uniformly poor in these study groups. Poor grades, truancy, and discipline problems were evident among students dropping out of school at the time of hospitalization.[9] It is interesting to note that a disproportionate number of suicides occur in the spring, when school problems often come to a head.

Dr. Joseph Teicher, a director of child/adolescent psychiatric services on the West Coast, suggests that many factors contribute to a teen-ager's decision to die. Teicher's studies indicate that the five years preceding the suicide attempt are marked by personal, medical, social, and family difficulties.[10] In 1972 the most prevalent underlying cause of the suicide attempts studied was the loss of a parent or close relative early in the adolescent's life, a loss that left him alone in his endeavor to cope with the stresses and anxieties of growing up. Death, divorce, and separation of parents, in that order, were the most frequent causes of suicide. Un-

wanted step-parents and constant family conflicts, coupled with poverty and poor peer relationships, combined to overwhelm the suicidal youth.

Dr. Teicher recommends that adolescents be hospitalized if suicide is attempted; they should be placed in a special ward where other adolescent patients can offer them support, warmth, and understanding. Young people need this assistance because they are shaken, insecure, anxious, depressed, guilty, and apprehensive because of the despair and anger they have caused. A therapist can also assist the youth in understanding the precipitating events, such as parental refusal to use the family car, a broken romance, or a feeling that no one cares. The therapist helps the youth cope with the conflict and open his channels of communication with family and peers. He also offers continued support so that the individual does not feel lonely and isolated. This contact should be maintained from first meeting to final rehabilitation.

SOLUTIONS

Teacher's Role Suicides rarely occur without warning, and teachers should be aware of distress signals, including both direct and indirect verbal signals. Direct signals—"You'll be sorry when I'm dead" or "I'm going to kill myself"—or indirect ones—"That won't matter where I'm going" —should not be allowed to pass unnoticed. The Center for Studies of Suicide Prevention has developed a concise and comprehensive list of "distress signals." This list of behavior changes should alert the sensitive teacher to the possibility of suicide:

- a dramatic shift in the quality of school-work
- social behavior changes, including excessive use of drugs or alcohol

- changes in daily behavior and living patterns, such as extreme fatigue, boredom, decreased appetite, preoccupation, and inability to concentrate
- open signs of mental illness, such as delusions and hallucinations
- giving away prized possessions
- truancy [11]

In addition to the above list, studies have turned up symptoms that may assist school personnel in noticing potential adolescent suicides:

- A distress signal. The adolescent through verbal and nonverbal communication is saying, "Notice me. I need help badly."
- An attempt to manipulate another. An adolescent girl takes an overdose of pills to persuade her boy friend to come back to her.
- A reaction to rejection. Adolescents whose parents reject them may act out wishes of their parents and attempt suicide.
- A result of overwhelming shame or guilt. To avoid an extremely painful situation, a young person may attempt suicide. Situations that seem relatively unimportant to the student's teachers could be painful to the student. These range from unwanted pregnancies to inability to get an A on a test, turn in a paper, or deal with a particular teacher or peer relationship.
- An attempt to punish another. The youth is saying, usually to his parents, "You'll be sorry when I'm gone."
- A manifestation of mental disorder. In a severely disturbed, mentally ill condition, the child or adolescent may hear inner voices commanding him to kill himself. [12]

Crisis Intervention   In addition to recognizing potential serious problems, teachers can put the adolescent in touch with agencies and specialists. At no time should a teacher act as a therapist, although he could provide a source of emotional support once the youth is in therapy.

The suicide prevention movement is based on the theoretical foundations of crisis intervention formulated during the 1950s and put into practice in the sixties. Suicide was seen as the ultimate crisis, and efforts were made to train crisis workers to effectively identify and handle suicidal persons. The 1960s saw extensive testing and refinement of crisis intervention; hotlines at universities and other centers are the direct result of this pioneering research and experimentation in the development of crisis intervention techniques.

"Postvention" is a program that attempts to prevent further suicides by dealing with the effects on survivors, family, friends, and classmates. Authorities in suicidology urge schools to recognize the need for special help directed at siblings and children of suicides. At the school level, suicides should be handled in a constructive way. Open discussion of the subject among classmates should benefit them by allowing them to share their sense of loss, guilt, and bewilderment. Such frank and open discussion, with students encouraged to suggest alternatives, should help dispel myths surrounding suicide.

Another program that has grown rapidly in the last few years is the "crisis hotline." At both the high school and college levels, these hotlines are telephone stations manned by students who have been screened psychologically and trained to handle emergency calls. The student's job is to listen and, in serious cases, to refer callers to the appropriate counselor, clergyman, psychologist, or psychiatrist. The students, like the teachers above, do not act as therapists, since the wrong advice could be catastrophic.

·*Special Training for Teachers as "Gate-keepers"* The educational process for "gatekeepers"—social workers, nurses, physicians, clergy, those most likely to hear suicide hints and to be in a position to act—must be extended to teachers. The teacher is in a most strategic position to identify and help the potential suicide. The theory and study of suicide should be included in a teacher's course of study. In addition to knowledge of the sources of emotional and interpersonal disturbances, teachers might also receive instruction in interviewing and counseling so that they could relate more effectively to the suicidal person and his family. They should learn about community services and techniques of referral. Along with theoretical training, they might participate actively in a suicide prevention center or other community agency. This would insure the development of a cadre in education that would recognize suicidal youngsters and help prevent loss of life.

For youth today, the deaths of Janis Joplin and Jimi Hendrix are reminders that suicide in America is a hushed-up and unpleasant subject to discuss. Teachers must attempt to help make suicide understandable. By providing opportunities to discuss it in the classroom, teachers may be able to alert adolescents and their parents to the danger signals of suicide.

One of the challenges of the seventies for educators is to be aware that most adolescent suicidal gestures are unconscious cries for help in solving some problem that appears urgent and hopeless. A. Alvarez reminds us that the suicide is' not born, but rather is shaped by one's environment. In the case of the adolescent, education is a most important part of that environment.[13]

NOTES

1. Harvey L. Resnik and Berkley Hawthorne, eds., *Suicide Prevention in the Seventies.* National Institute of Mental Health (Washington, D.C.: U.S. Government Printing Office, 1973), pp. 7–12.
2. U.S. Department of Health, Education, and Welfare, *Suicide in the United States: 1950–1975* (Washington, D.C.: U.S. Government Printing Office, 1975).
3. Susan A. Winickoff and Harvey L. Resnik, "Student Suicide," *Today's Education*, April, 1971, p. 32.
4. Larry Dizmang, "Adolescent Suicide at an Indian Reservation," *American Journal of Orthopsychiatry*, vol. 44, pp. 43–49.
5. Pamela Cantor, "Adolescent Suicide," *Time*, January 3, 1972, p. 57.
6. Norman Tabachnik, M.D., "Subintentioned Self-Destruction in Teen-agers," *Psychiatric Opinion*, July, 1975, pp. 21–26.
7. Edwin S. Schneider, ed., "Sigmund Freud on Suicide," *Essays on Suicide* (New York: Science House, 1967); Karl Menninger, *Man Against Himself* (New York: Harcourt Brace, 1938).
8. Emile Durkheim, *Suicide: A Sociological Study* (Glencoe, Ill.: Free Press, 1951).
9. J. T. Barter, M.D., et al., "Adolescent Suicide Attempts," *General Psychiatry,* vol. 19, 1968, p. 524.
10. Joseph Teicher, "Portrait of a Teen-age Suicide," *Science News,* December 30, 1972, p. 42.
11. Ibid.
12. Ibid.
13. A. Alvarez, *The Savage God* (New York: Random House, 1972).

Reading 18

Trends in Early Childhood Education for Native American Pupils

Leona M. Foerster and Dale Little Soldier

Many promising trends in early childhood education for American Indian children have surfaced during this decade. Some of these trends are characteristic of early childhood education generally. Others relate specifically to programs for Native Americans. All seem noteworthy and represent a breakthrough for pupils who, for a variety of reasons, have fared poorly in the educational institutions of this nation and whose prognosis for success in school has, in the past, been dismal indeed.

Perhaps the prime trend has been the inclusion of many more Indian pupils in early childhood programs than in the past. Part of this increase, no doubt, is due to the expansion of Head Start programs on and off reservations. In addition, the trend nationally is toward state-supported kindergartens for all pupils. Parents appear to be more receptive to enrolling their children in preschool programs. The programs may be more attractive, and parents may perceive something

Source: Leona M. Foerster and Dale Little Soldier, "Trends in Early Childhood Education for Native American Pupils." *Educational Leadership* (February 1977), pp. 373–78.

of the impact of the early years on future success in school and in society. For a variety of reasons, early childhood education for Native American pupils is on the increase. This trend in itself might not be too important. However, when it is linked with a discussion of certain promising practices that are to be found within many of these programs, the reader may perceive something of the really exciting things that are occurring for young Native Americans.

Role of the Parents

The Indian Education Act of 1972 (P.L. 92–318, Title IV) has done for Indian education what the Elementary and Secondary Education Act of 1965 has accomplished for the overall student population of this country (Demmert, 1976). Part B of this Act encourages the support of community-based early childhood programs and thus stimulates the involvement of Indian parents and their communities in the education of their young children. The participation of Indian parents in the educative process is one of the most promising trends on the horizon and is an impetus which has long been needed.

In addition, involvement of Indian parents in educational programs has been increased through Indian advisory boards that are formed at local and state levels so that input from parents may be channelled and utilized in building relevant programs (Foerster and Little Soldier, 1975). These boards play a vital role in assessing the special needs of Indian pupils and may help with the writing of proposals for federal monies to meet these needs under the provisions of the Johnson-O'Malley Act of 1932 or Title IV. The advisory boards may help select textbooks and develop curricula on the local or state level as well as serve to monitor programs once they are implemented.

One of the most exciting and potentially far-reaching trends in Indian education is the thrust toward parent-based early childhood education for children under three (Demmert, 1976). Head Start and kindergarten programs may come too late to prevent the dropping out of school of Indian youngsters that begins at about the fourth grade when pupils move from a more child-centered curriculum to a subject-matter orientation. Children who begin school lacking the prerequisite experiences and skills needed for success tend to fall further behind the longer they stay in school.

Parents are the child's first and best teachers. Programs which enable parents to gain understanding of how to work with their young children and to promote optimal growth can make an important contribution. It is difficult to speculate about the possible impact of such programs on the future school achievement of pupils. However, these programs offer the potential of dramatically reducing the dropout rate of Indian pupils particularly at the elementary and junior high levels and greatly increasing the school achievement of these youngsters.

Curriculum Bolsters Self-Image

Another noteworthy trend is visible in the area of curriculum. Many Indian pupils have suffered from a very poor self-image. Often the school curriculum does little to correct this image. In fact, it may contribute to the problem. Curriculum projects that take into account the unique heritage of Indian pupils and that promote pride are under way in many parts of the country. Much of this curricular reform is the result of pressures from Indian people themselves to provide something better for their children than what they themselves experienced in school (Tsanusdi, 1976).

It should be noted that the Bureau of Indian Affairs kindergarten curriculum guide reflects a bilingual-bicultural approach (U.S. Department of the Interior, 1970). The kindergarten is viewed as the bridge between home and school. Attention is given to building upon the strengths that the child brings to school including the richness of culture, language, and history which are part of the Native American heritage. Cultural differences are viewed as just that—differences, not deficiencies.

Learning centers, which frequently abound in early childhood classrooms, currently may offer a more culturally relevant setting for Indian pupils. For example, the home living center may include kitchen utensils and dishes that are familiar to the child. Dolls may look more like Indian infants than "palefaces." The dress-up corner can include bustles, headdresses, jewelry, and the like which the children are used to. Rather than puzzles, pictures, and games that reflect things unfamiliar to pupils, the visitor to the early childhood classroom may find rodeo lotto games, pictures of dwellings and scenery found on the reservation, and other materials, many of which are teacher-constructed and with which young children can identify immediately and feel comfortable. Cooking experiences may include fry bread, Indian tacos, and mutton stew.

Churchman, Herman, and Hall (1975) have reported the development of a culturally relevant preschool curriculum for Indian pupils living in the greater Los Angeles area. The curriculum was designed by the Tribal American Consulting Corporation (TACC) and based on at least two premises. The first of these was that children will learn best in a culturally relevant context. Thus learning materials were developed to demonstrate the richness of tribal history, values, and culture. The curriculum was to be implemented employing the traditional Indian communal interaction pattern wherein individuals work cooperatively and share the products of their labor.

The second premise that guided this curriculum development project was that preschool experiences should perpare the Indian child for success in school. Referring to the work of Bruner, Kagan, and White, the authors cited above stress the need for competence before the age of five in such basic skills as language, problem solving, coping, perception, and coordination to enable the child to interact positively with the environment. Thus the curriculum materials were designed to tap children's culture and heritage while developing basic skills and promoting growth of a positive self-concept.

Curriculum building efforts were quite complex due to the fact that many tribal groups are represented in the Los Angeles area. Nevertheless, the TACC cultural curriculum for Indian preschools appears to have made some excellent advances in meeting needs of the culturally diverse Indian population in this area.

Great Strides Are Made

Additional noteworthy curriculum projects can also be cited. The Wisconsin Native American Language and Culture project was set up under Title IV of the Indian Education Act (Roth, 1976). The major thrust of the project was to preserve the languages of the five Wisconsin tribes (Chippewa, Oneida, Menominee, Potawatomi, and Winnebago) by establishing written systems for these languages, developing reference and teaching materials for them, and finally teaching these languages and cultures in the schools. Wisconsin Indians who are native speakers of these languages were hired and trained as language teachers and consultants. Linguists were employed to help develop instructional and reference materials. As a result, in Wisconsin Indian pupils beginning with Head Start may have the opportunity to become literate in their native language, to learn more about their heritage, and to develop a deep sense of prideful identity.

In North Dakota, the American Indian Curricula Development Program, a subsidiary group of the United Tribes of North Dakota Development Corporation, has been involved in a social studies curriculum and teacher training package that is culturally relevant for children in grades K-12 (Gray, 1973). The curriculum includes text material, supplementary booklets, overhead transparencies, slide-tape programs, cassette tapes, and a comprehensive teacher's manual. It is an attempt to provide relevance in curriculum for the more than 18,000 Indians living on or near the four United Tribes reservations.

That there is a need for the project is not open to question. Not only has the average family income on these reservations been dreadfully low and unemployment extremely high, but additional problems such as high drop-out rate of pupils, below par academic achievement of those who remain in school, and an alarming teenage suicide rate have indicated the need for changes in the education of Indian students. It is hoped that the curriculum relevance provided by the project will encourage greater pupil interest in school, motivation to remain and achieve at a higher level, a more positive self-concept, pride, and a sense of identity.

North Dakota is not the only state which has made strides in serving the educational needs of Native Americans. Curriculum projects have surfaced in most states which have an identifiable Indian population such as Alaska, Montana, Idaho, Washington, California, Arizona, Nevada, Oklahoma, and New Mexico. Most of these projects have goals similar to those of the North Dakota program cited above. In addition to helping Indian pupils learn about their culture, heritage, and language, many of these programs provide opportunities for non-Indians to gain more accurate perceptions of Indian peoples and their important contributions to the nation as well as to combat the stereotyped images perpetuated in the media.

No discussion of curriculum would be complete without reference to the many projects under way on the Navajo reservation. The Rough Rock Demonstration School has developed a myriad of culturally relevant curriculum materials for Navajo pupils. In 1966, this school was established as a community controlled school, a Bureau of Indian Affairs (BIA) contract school, and has served since then as a model for other schools on the reservation. The Navajo Nation, through its Division of Education, has promoted educational change on the reservation from early childhood education to adult education.

The Navajo Area Language Arts Project (NALAP) has helped with the problems of teaching English to the many Navajo children who enter school speaking Navajo as their prime or sole language (U.S. Department of the Interior, 1973). A Navajo Social Studies Curriculum project has been completed that provides a culture-based social studies curriculum for beginners through eighth-graders. These materials are designed to demonstrate the many contributions the

Indian has made to this nation, to provide insight into his or her relationship to other cultures, and to enable each pupil to find a rightful place in society.

Needs in Special Education

The increase in special services for exceptional Indian pupils is a trend that is worthy of some discussion too. In 1972, a survey of pupils enrolled in BIA schools indicated that a total of 19,540 students was in need of special educational services but that only 3,715 were receiving such services (U.S. Department of the Interior, 1973). Since that time, important gains have been made in attempting to meet these needs. For example, the Pine Ridge Agency in South Dakota (Aberdeen Area) was the first agency in the Bureau of Indian Affairs to have a full-time special education coordinator at the agency level and a special education teacher at each of the agency's eight schools. A special education instructional materials center located at the Porcupine School provides the agency area with materials to help meet the special needs of the agency's children.

The Navajo Nation has responded to the needs of its special children, too. Of the more than 60,000 Navajo pupils enrolled in school, it was estimated that 30 percent required some type of special education service (Murphy, 1974). Navajo parents, tribal leaders, community persons, and educators have exhibited increased awareness of and concern for the needs of special children. As a result, these needs are being partially met, although there remains much work to be done to provide services for all who could profit from them.

The St. Michaels Association for Special Education located at St. Michaels, Arizona, on the reservation opened in September 1970, and was the first school to offer comprehensive educational, social, and medical services for handicapped Navajo children beginning with age 1½ (Murphy, 1974). The Chinle Valley School for Exceptional Children at Chinle, Arizona, opened in August 1973 and was designed to serve trainable children ranging in age from five to fifteen years.

At the Greasewood Boarding School, also on the Navajo reservation, pupils in grades 1–8 participate in Resource Centers funded under Title I and designed to correct specific language disabilities and promote progress in academic skills (Ramey, Sileo, and Zongolowicz, 1975). The program at Greasewood has a three-fold thrust. The language development component fosters the acquisition of language skills including listening, oral and written language, articulation, reading skills development, and reading comprehension. The conceptual development component deals with number concepts, reasoning, classification skills, and general information. The developmental motor skills component encompasses the range of skills involved in gross motor development, sensorimotor integration, and perceptual motor skills. The program is individualized, objectives are stated behaviorally, and daily logs are maintained for each pupil.

The trend toward earlier diagnosis of needs of exceptional children is a healthy one. The continued growth of special programs for Indian pupils should result in halting the dreadful waste of human resources that has occurred in the past when such services were either nonexistent for these children or came too late to prevent the maladjustment of pupils, damage to self-esteem, and early retreat from the educational institution.

IGE and Open Education

Two additional trends will be discussed here. These two trends are interrelated. One is the move to provide greater individualiza-tion of instruction; the other is a thrust toward open education.

Individually Guided Education (IGE) is a refreshingly new approach to education that has come about as a result of research by the Wisconsin Research and Development Center for Cognitive Learning and other educational agencies (U.S. Department of the Interior, 1973). The Institute for the Development of Educational Activities (|I|D|E|A|), established by the Charles F. Kettering Foundation in 1965, has been instrumental in the national expansion of this program.

IGE schools include the Acomita Day School on the Acoma reservation 60 miles west of Albuquerque, New Mexico, and two other schools at Jemez and Zia in the Albuquerque area (U.S. Department of the Interior, 1973). Pupils have a great deal of physical freedom within these IGE schools. The schools are ungraded and cut across at least two age groups. Work is contracted for and each student draws an assignment from a "contract board." Pupils are responsible for completing their own work. Progress reports are prepared periodically and shared with parents in conferences.

In addition, open education appears to offer a viable alternative to traditional education for many Indian pupils (Foerster and Little Soldier, 1974). Schools for Native American pupils using this approach include the Concho Indian School located near El Reno, Oklahoma, the Rocky Boy Elementary School in Montana, and the Finlayson School in Sault Ste. Marie, Michigan. The latter school includes a preschool program for children ranging in age from 3½ years to 6 years. Preacademic skills are fostered in an open setting which allows pupils to manipulate materials and learn by discovery.

The open classroom setting may provide a better psychological fit for many Indian pupils. Traditional Indian values such as sharing and personal freedom are fostered in this type of classroom context (Foerster and Little Soldier, 1974). In addition, the greater flexibility in the use of time and the permissiveness characteristic of the open classroom may blend much more effectively with the child-rearing practices of many Native Americans. The informal education of the home should be the basis for planning the formal early learning experiences of pupils in school. The open setting may provide greater opportunities for the teacher of young Native American pupils to utilize the strengths these children bring to school with them.

For this discussion of promising trends in early childhood education for Indian pupils the authors have selected only certain highlights. Parents and their involvement were noted as were certain curriculum projects, programs for exceptional children, and experiments with individualization and open education. Whether these trends should persist and flourish or wither should be based upon data gathered through exacting research efforts. Until such data are available, however, educators must continue to move in directions that they intuitively feel are positive ones. Much has been accomplished in early childhood education "Native American style." But new challenges continually appear on the horizon to be dealt with as effectively and efficiently as possible by knowledgeable and dedicated educators of these pupils.

REFERENCES

David Churchman, Joan Herman, and Teresa Hall. "To Know Both Worlds." *Journal of American Indian Education* 14: 7–12; May 1975.

William G. Demmert, Jr. "Indian Education: Where and Whither?" *American Education* 12: 6–9; August/September 1976.

Leona M. Foerster and Dale Little Solder. "Open Education and Native American Values." *Educational Leadership* 32(1): 41–45; October 1974.

Leona M. Foerster and Dale Little Solder. "What's New and Good in Indian Education Today?" *Educational Leadership* 33(3): 192–98; December 1975.

Farnum Gray. "Breakthrough in North Dakota." *Learning* 26:53–58; January 1973.

Elizabeth A. Murphy. "The Classroom: Meeting the Needs of the Culturally Different Child—The Navajo Nation." *Exceptional Children* 40: 601–608; May 1974.

Joseph H. Ramey, Thomas W. Sileo, and Zongolowicz. "Resource Centers for Children with Learning Disabilities." *Journal of American Indian Education* 14:13–20; May 1975.

Edith Brill Roth. "Lato: Lats—Hunting in the Indian Languages." *American Education* 12: 6–9; August/September 1976.

Tlanuwa Tsanusdi. "Native American Children—Values of the Past May Be Keys to a Brighter Future." *Dimensions* 4: 65–69, 77; March 1976.

U.S. Department of the Interior. *A Kindergarten Curriculum Guide for Indian Children.* Curriculum Bulletin No. 5. Washington, D.C.: Bureau of Indian Affairs, 1970.

U.S. Department of the Interior. *Indian Education Steps to Progress in the 70's.* Washington, D.C.: Bureau of Indian Affairs, 1973.

Reading 19

Are Schools Better in Other Countries?

Grace Hechinger
Fred M. Hechinger

All attempts to compare educational achievements are fraught with danger. What seems like success in one community may leave judges elsewhere, under different conditions, entirely unimpressed. Expectations and standards are culture-bound. And so, it is an act of considerable courage when academic researchers try to assess and compare the educational achievements, not of the schools of one city to those of schools in another city, but between literally thousands of children, teachers, and schools in 22 nations.

Yet, that is precisely what the International Association for the Evaluation of Educational Achievement (IEA) has attempted. Based in Stockholm and financed by foundations and agencies of governments, including the U.S. Office of Education, the research agency has surveyed educational achievement in science, literature, and reading comprehension. The nations taking part in the studies were Australia, Belgium, Chile, England, Finland, France, West Ger-

many, Hungary, India, Iran, Ireland, Israel, Italy, Japan, the Netherlands, New Zealand, Poland, Romania, Scotland, Sweden, Thailand, and the United States.

Masses of data were collected in this, the biggest international education survey ever attempted. Some 258,000 students and 50,000 teachers in 9,700 schools participated —taking or administering tests, answering questions in interviews, or filling out questionnaires. Millions of items of information have been collected at a cost of $5 million. In addition to the volumes to be published on each of the subject areas, data banks in Chicago, Melbourne, New York, Stockholm, Tokyo, and one at Stanford University in California will store all the information for future use by researchers and scholars all over the world.

While the experts are still sorting out the facts and debating possible conclusions, the temptation is to ask: "Who's ahead? Is it true that Johnny can't read, and is Hans reading any better? And what about the charges made by American sociologists that school really doesn't matter or doesn't work?"

Torsten Husen, the chairman of the IEA

Source: Grace Hechinger and Fred M. Hechinger, "Are Schools Better in Other Countries?" *American Education* 10, no. 1 (January–February 1974).

and a professor of education at the University of Stockholm, was well aware that the horse-race aspects of the study would most intrigue the press and the public. He recalls what he considers "the fiasco of 1964," when the IEA disclosed the findings of its first international survey—one relating to achievement in mathematics. The only part of the report to get any attention was that which showed that Japan was ahead of everybody or, in more parochial terms, "beat the United States."

Professor Husen considers this a simple-minded approach to complex problems. It ignores differences in the national, cultural, and social environments and priorities. It brushes aside such questions as: What proportion of the children actually go to school? What is expected of pupils in other areas of study? And what are the yardsticks of achievements in different countries?

"Our intention," says Professor Husen, "has been to avoid any sort of intellectual Olympics." The aim was rather to find answers that might be useful in reviewing, charting, or changing educational policies.

For the United States, any international comparison of educational achievement raises the enormously important question of whether the basic philosophy and the guiding principles of mass education really work —not just in theory, but in comparison with other nations.

Universal education in America has long been an article of faith. To generations of immigrants the promise of the land of unlimited opportunity was virtually synonymous with free access to free schools. There was no sorting out at age 10 or 11, as in Britain, Germany, and many other countries, of those who would or would not pursue an academically oriented course which, in turn, determined the child's future life and career. Education, universal and egalitarian, was, in Horace Mann's optimistic forecast, the cornerstone of a free, open, prosperous society.

Dream or reality? Conservative critics of American education have never fully accepted this egalitarian approach. They warned that this undifferentiated access to the public schools for all comers penalizes the gifted by lowering the level of achievement to a mediocre common denominator. They felt, as did Britain's Tories in the face of proposals for expanded educational opportunities, that more means worse.

When the high financial cost of educating everybody is considered in addition to such philosophical and ideological doubts, the question of how well the United States compares with other nations assumes an importance quite different from that of intellectual Olympics.

One of the study's crucial findings therefore is that, in reading comprehension, the top 9 or 10 percent of the American high school seniors performed better than the similar elite groups of all the other nations. This is clearly significant, particularly when it is viewed against the fact that many of the other countries in the sample remain highly selective—or restrictive. In other words, the cream of talent in the United States does as well as or better than the able students in educationally less egalitarian or more elitist countries.

"It is actually the selective system that pays a price in lost talent and social dislocation," says Professor Husen. To prove his point, he showed that in West Germany, which screens out "non-academic" children roughly at age 10, the top-achieving group among high school seniors also showed the "highest index of social bias." This means that these most successful students came almost exclusively from the privileged classes. At age 18, only 1 percent of children from lower-class (unskilled or semi-skilled workers') homes were found in German schools, compared with 14 percent in American schools.

In science, the American top group of high school seniors, it must be conceded finished in only seventh place—not as spectacular a performance as that of the reading comprehension lead, but still a respectable performance. (The reason may well be that, compared with many European counterparts, American schools are quite lax in the amount of science required of their students. It is a laxity that has been frequently criticized most persuasively by James B. Conant, who tried in his high school reform proposals to stiffen the science requirements for the upper 15 percent of gifted students.)

The important and undeniable conclusion to be drawn from the IEA study is that mass education, American-style, while in no way hurting the academic achievement of the most talented young people, assures a constant infusion of new blood into the academic elite. This is crucial to any effort to keep society fluid and to allow rich and poor, workers' and professional people's children, long-term Americans and recent immigrants to rise to the top.

Such an open society does, of course, pay a price in terms of the total standing in any international competition. For example, in an assessment of the entire senior class, rather than just the top nine percent, the United States dropped from top rank to only 12th place. While such a "poor" showing may alarm all uninformed observers and may give rise to the charge that Johnny can't read, a realistic look should lead to quite a different conclusion.

The United States, which graduates by far the highest proportion—75 percent—of its school-age youths from high school, should quite naturally be expected to score near the bottom in a comparison with nations which, at that level, have already eliminated large numbers—in some instances, the majority—from their academic schools, and thus from the competition. While these American youngsters, by remaining in school, may bring the United States' total achievement scores down, at the same time they benefit from the additional years of education. In other words, their inclusion in the international test scores may superficially hurt the "image" of the United States, but far more important is the fact that the additional educational opportunities they enjoy will not only help their own future careers but give to their country a much better pool of educated manpower. (This is precisely the reason why Professor Husen warned against the abuse of the IEA findings by those who turn the comparative studies into scholastic Olympics.)

Closely related to the IEA's findings is an issue that is currently arousing intense debate and controversy in the United States and abroad—the relationship between schooling and subsequent success and status in society. For example, the Stockholm report appears to challenge the widely publicized theories of the Harvard research team headed by Christopher Jencks which holds that schools have failed to reduce social and economic inequality.

The IEA survey admittedly did not concern itself directly with children's future income; but by clearly showing that open access to schooling allows children from poor and disadvantaged homes to rise to the level of the academic elite, it offers persuasive evidence that education does open the doors to economic success as well. And while the schools may not have achieved as much on that score as might have been wished, they have clearly done better in the United States than elsewhere.

At the same time, the IEA survey appears to confirm the claim—first published by James Coleman in 1966—that in the total pattern of achievement, home background is more important than anything the schools have so far been able to contribute. But Professor Husen nevertheless stresses that the schools do make a substantial difference and that there is a direct correlation between concentrated study and success. Or, as one of the Stockholm researchers puts it: "Get them and stretch them"—open access and hard work is the winning combination.

Here, an item of some slight mystery enters the findings. An analysis of the schools' greater success in teaching science—which the Stockholm researchers call a "school-oriented" subject—than in teaching "home-oriented" reading raises questions about the educators' capacity to adapt their teaching methods and attitudes to children's needs. "The schools," says the report, "appear to do little to mobilize their resources for the improvement of reading beyond the early years."

The very fact that there is a clearly defined difference in the schools' success with "home-oriented" subjects—that is, those in which Coleman's theory is found to hold to a remarkable degree—and those "school-oriented" areas in which most of the work is being done by teachers, with the home making only a minimal contribution, suggests that educators could do a better all-around job if they reordered their own priorities. Or, to put it differently, the "mysteries" that make children learn science, mathematics, and other school-oriented subjects with relatively more success than they do home-oriented subjects could undoubtedly be more effectively identified and applied to the latter subjects as well.

That this is more than a wishful hypothesis is suggested by another IEA finding—confirmation of the charge made by women's liberation that girls are being traditionally and chronically shortchanged by the schools. Thus, the study found that, vir-

tually without exception (and those exceptions were found to occur only in a few highly specialized schools), girls lag behind boys in interest and performance in science. The clue to the reason for that discrepancy is in the discovery that the gap grows wider the longer girls attend all-girl schools, where the teachers clearly act on the assumption that girls ought not to be bothered with such boy-oriented subjects. When girls attend coeducational schools, the study found, the gap narrows significantly.

It therefore seems evident that, whether the accepted doctrine is one of the "home-oriented" or the "boy-oriented" subject, the cause for low achievement is in large part to be sought in the schools—and society's—lack of determination to overcome learning problems.

The IEA research ventured on the most slippery ground when it tried to get a reading not only of students' achievements but also of their attitudes. Such efforts, whether by way of questionnaire or interview, tend to be devalued by the fact that teachers and pupils everywhere usually know how to outguess their questioners, and to come up with the answers they feel are expected of them.

Too many subtle factors affect attitudes to allow them to be easily reduced to charts. For example, a surprising finding was that Swedish pupils scored rather high on "dislike" of school. (The U.S. sample, contrary to widespread American complaint, scored on the positive, "liking school" side of the chart.) A visit to a typical suburban school near Stockholm offered a reason for this attitude on the part of Swedish students. The facilities were superb—all-carpeted classrooms, super-modern laboratories, extensive student activities and meeting rooms, the latest in cafeteria equipment. But it was also evident that the students' activities and behavior were rigidly supervised and monitored. In contrast to American-style freedom enjoyed by Swedish youngsters only when they were outside the school, the academic atmosphere was stiff and regimented, and it seemed hardly surprising that such a discrepancy would lead to a relative dislike for school.

In other areas, however, the question of likes and dislikes did point to enough international agreement to make the answers useful and relevant to educational planners everywhere. Fourteen-year-olds in all countries, regardless of class or socio-economic background, prefer humor, adventure, mysteries, sports, and romance in their reading. Upper secondary school students tend to read current events, history, and travel, as well as adventure and humor. (Incidentally, American students were more interested in symbolic meanings than were young people from any other countries.)

"The best students in most countries," the study found, "enjoy reading humor and comic strips in newspapers as well as folklore"—surely a blow to the more conventional, not to say stuffy, pedagogues.

"The implications of the IEA literature study are vast," concludes the report. "If teachers and schools can persuade students to see stories and think of them as their teachers do, the schools might not be so ineffective as some have suggested. A new look at the goals of schools and what schools *can* do could lead to a serious consideration of the curriculum in literature and mother tongue studies as a whole."

In summary, the virtue of the IEA studies is that they shatter much of the parochialism of both the conservative and the radical critics of American public education. The international comparisons provide a more rational perspective. The most vocal challengers of American public education, in keeping with the prevailing mood of self-criticism, make their judgments from an essentially provincial point of view. While they are entirely justified in exposing those policies and attitudes which have discriminated against the poor and against the minorities, they have tended to characterize such deficiencies as peculiarly American sins. A look at the schools of other industrialized nations—such as Germany, England and France, where stratification is still far more rigid—places the American achievement, with all its shortcomings, in a different light.

It is precisely because the IEA study has no preconceived notions about ideas which have long become articles of faith with American public school leaders that its findings tend to be reassuring. And central to those findings are two key points which have long been paramount with American public education philosophers: Schools *do* matter in keeping society fluid, and more *can* be better.*

* Readers wishing further information about the IEA survey should write to Teachers College, Columbia University, 120th Street and Morningside Heights, N.Y., N.Y. 10027.

Reading 20

Here's to Children Everywhere!

Bel Kaufman

I am sitting in the large auditorium of the Union of Soviet Writers in Moscow, watching a Russian play adapted from my book, *Up the Down Staircase*. Although the cast had disbanded for the summer, they have returned to give this one performance in June of 1977 in honor of my visit. I find myself as moved as is the rest of the audience by the young, miniskirted teacher and her boisterous pupils, one with face sooted to portray a black student, one with face painted brown to denote a Puerto Rican; for in spite of certain excesses and distortions, what shines through is the glowing feeling of affection, of deep caring.

"Happy families are all alike," so opens Tolstoi's *Anna Karenina:* "every unhappy family is unhappy in its own way." Good teachers, I think, whatever their country or language, are all alike in their dedication to their profession and commitment to the young. I speak not as an expert or as a political or social commentator; my impres-

sions are limited to my personal observations on two separate visits to the Soviet Union. In the spring of 1968, shortly after *Up the Down Staircase* was translated into Russian, I was invited there to spend my royalty rubles, which were many; for the book—although it describes a typically American school—enjoyed wide popularity in that country, perhaps because neither bureaucracy nor love for children is alien to the Russian people. In May and June of 1977, I was invited again, as a guest of the Union of Soviet Writers, and because I speak fluent Russian, when I visited schools and camps I was able to talk with teachers, school administrators, librarians—above all, with the children.

A teacher in whose home in Moscow I dined told me of her first semester in school when, in the middle of a class in which her pupils were diligently writing compositions, the director of the school entered, looked around, approached her desk, and leaned down to whisper in her ear, "Irina Mikhailovna, you will never be a teacher!"

Shocked, she went to see him after class: "What was wrong? My children were writing quietly."

Source: Bel Kaufman, "Here's To Children Everywhere!" *Today's Education* (February/March 1978). Washington, D.C.: National Education Association, pp. 21–29.

"Ah, yes," the director replied, "but when children write, the teacher does not look out of the window; she looks at her children—with affection."

This may seem as farfetched to us Americans as the scene I myself witnessed: the teacher arrived in her classroom on that particular morning resplendent in a velvet dress, her hair carefully coiffed. "Children," she said to the astonished class, her voice trembling with emotion, "today we begin to read our great Russian poet Pushkin."

I doubt that any American teacher would dress in a cocktail gown to introduce the poetry of Robert Frost to her class, but it's the *feeling* of this teacher we recognize; it's the *feeling* of the director we understand.

The affection of Russians for their children is evident everyplace, in private homes and public places as well as in schools, where attention is lavished upon them from early infancy in public nurseries throughout the rest of their schooling. Children are treasured—especially after the devastation of war, the scars of which have been passed down unto the third generation. At a matinee performance of the ballet *Spartacus* in Leningrad, during the battle scene of Romans killing slaves, I heard a little girl sitting in front of me in a pink starched dress with matching ribbon bows in her hair ask her mother in a frightened whisper, "Are they Germans?"

The Soviet people are personally involved with children—their own and those of others. One day on the street in Kiev I saw several people berating a mother who was dragging her crying child by the hand. "Why are they interfering?" I asked my companion.

"It's not interfering," she replied, "it's *caring*."

Even authors of children's books make personal contact with their readers; it is customary for them to travel periodically from city to city, often covering vast distances, to address their small readers, answer their questions, and hear their suggestions. Children's books are beautifully illustrated and cost mere kopeks. Russians are avid readers; new books are sold out immediately and are then passed, like precious heirlooms, from hand to hand.

It starts early, this love of books, from the first grade, when the seven year olds officially begin their education with seriousness, high expectations, and flowers for teacher.

A visit is arranged for me to School No. 752 on the outskirts of Moscow. I am met by the director of the school, a warm, motherly woman, and by the teacher of second grade—her replica. Though school is practically over for the summer, one class of eight year olds is awaiting me. The children wear red kerchiefs around their necks and a look of solemn expectancy on their scrubbed little faces. As we enter, they rise. I comment on this formality. "It's not formality," the director replies, "it's politeness."

I chat with the children: the impishly grinning boy, the shy girl with huge, eloquent eyes, the two identical boys, smug in their twinship. How come I speak Russian? they ask. "I've been in Moscow three whole days!" I reply. After a puzzled second or two, they laugh. Our laughter breaks the ice.

The children read for me. They tell me about their class projects: on the importance of milk and on how it's bad to be fat. One little girl arises to recite a poem and freezes: she has forgotten the first line. The class sits with bated breath; the teacher's lips tremble; no one says a word. Suddenly the child's face lights up—she remembers! The class exhales in relief as she smoothly gallops through the poem. The teacher's broad Russian face beams.

I ask what they want to be when they grow up. A small boy gets up: "When I was young. . . ." (Giggles from the others.) "I mean, when I was younger, I wanted to be an animal trainer."

"And now?"

"Now"—he frowns with the weight of this decision—"now, engineer on a ship."

Another child plans to be an inventor; the teacher whispers to me that his father is a noted inventor of fuels. Still another confides that her ambition is to work on high floors of buildings.

They ask questions in turn: What do American children like to play? We discuss children's games. "Here, too!" they nod happily. They, too, play jacks—only with small pebbles. They, too, jump rope—only to Russian rhymes. They, too, build campfires where they cook not marshmallows but potatoes.

They are curious: "Are there any zoos in America?"

"Are there many Indians in New York?"

"What is Disneyland like?"

Before I leave, a small boy rises on tiptoe to pin on my lapel a *znachok,* one of the little emblems Russians are fond of, and a girl hands me a bunch of flowers that had been patiently wilting in her warm fist. Another child rattles off an obviously rehearsed speech about friendship between our two countries and the hope that there should be no more wars. He gives me a tiny toy airplane "for safe flight home."

Later we go on a tour of the school, which because of its location near the woods, is being converted to a summer camp for children of working parents. In some rooms, cots are already lined up against the blackboards, and conference tables are set up "for chess and discussions"; in others, remnants of the school year are evident. Everything is neat and spotless; I notice that the desks have been freshly shellacked. "For the examinations," explains the director. This—like the velvet dress—I understand.

Later still, in the director's office, over the customary refreshments (all business meetings are held around a table laden with food and drink), I learn that recently there has been greater emphasis on the individual de-

velopment of each child, that math teachers are now equipped with computers to grade papers, that teachers' hours in school vary, depending on the subject, and that their salaries range between 250 and 350 rubles a month (a ruble is about $1.30). Though that is not much, I am reminded that rent is negligible, that medical and other services are free, and that teachers get one month's paid vacation. The cherry preserves served with the tea are delicious. "Who made this?" I ask, licking my spoon.

"I did," the director says, smiling.

I had requested to meet students of high school age, so on June 1, 1977—a day proclaimed as Children's Day—more than 10 teenage youngsters from four different school districts, accompanied by two teachers and a librarian, are assembled for me in the House of Books, a huge children's library in Moscow. Some are Young Pioneers, similar to our Scouts; some are Komsomoltze, members of the Young Communist League. Everyone seems to belong to something.

Shy at first, they gradually relax. Hands begin to go up, tentatively, then eagerly as questions and answers fly back and forth.

"What is the favorite subject of American students?"

"Lunch," I reply.

"Here, too!" Laughter unites us.

"How many days a week do American children go to school?"

"Five."

They groan in unison. "We go six!" But justice triumphs: they have three months of summer vacation to our two.

Their ambitions are sophisticated: economist, pianist, teacher of small children, psychologist (a new subject for them, a new profession).

I learn that from the ages of 12 to 14 all are required to take up certain skills—carpentry, dressmaking, automotive mechanics, cooking—in order to learn the values of manual work. Should they not pass their examinations for college or professional school, all of which are free, each is sure of a job.

"How do American children spend their summers?" they ask.

My answer is self-conscious: "If their parents have money, they travel or go to camps and resorts; or if they can, they get summer jobs."

"Otherwise?"

"Otherwise, they—they hang around. Of course," I add, "we have some camps that are free—like yours."

Since physical culture is emphasized in Soviet schools, the children ask about American sports; to my surprise I have to explain baseball to them.

They are eager to know everything about our schools: hours, exams, marking system. Their own marks range from 5, the highest, down in numerically diminishing merit. They are especially interested in the relationship between American students and teachers. "Informal," I say. "Very informal. Sometimes too informal." This appeals to them.

"What books do American children read? Do they like poetry? Do they know our Soviet writers?"

I shake my head. "You seem to know more about English and American writers." It is true: they are familiar with Shakespeare, Hemingway, Poe, Ray Bradbury (instead of "science fiction," they call it "fantasy," a gentler word). But they know only those books available in translation. No one, not even the teachers or librarian, had ever heard of *A Tale of Two Cities,* though they all knew *Oliver Twist* and *David Copperfield.*

"Why don't American children read more?" Aye, there's the rub. I indicate some of our social problems reflected in schools. I mention the language problem of minority groups, rebelliousness against authority, the number of hours usurped by TV. I point out a recent statistic: American children spend

as many hours in front of TV as in school. They gasp, incredulous. I ask how many have TV sets at home. All raise their hands. They have only three channels, mostly cultural and educational, with no commercials, of course, and children are allowed to watch only certain programs.

I want to know what they don't like about their schools, what improvements they would suggest. They are hesitant—after all, a couple of their teachers are silently present—but a few courageous souls volunteer information that might have come from any of our American students:

"Too much homework!"

"Two or three hours a day!"

"Sometimes more. . . ."

"Well," adds a judicious voice, "but it's *necessary!*"

"Also, we wish we could express our opinions more, instead of the teacher *telling* us!"

(*Here, too!* I say to myself, recalling a student of mine who had written, "Teachers are too dictoral and don't let me self-express.")

I ask the teachers for their comments. "No complaints," says one, smiling.

The other, a white-haired man standing tall behind a row of youngsters, says, "I am a history teacher, retiring after 30 years in the classroom." He places one hand gently on the braided blond hair of a girl sitting in front of him and embraces the others with his eyes, "These are my children," he says with pride.

Some of the students express a wish to correspond with American students. I eagerly agree, suggesting that they leave their names and addresses with me. A teacher speaks up, "It's better to send these letters to their schools." The children, however, stand their ground; they want the letters to come to their homes. At the end of our session, which lasts more than three hours, several come up to me and shyly thrust into my hand slips of paper with their names and addresses in beautiful, painstaking handwriting.

Before I leave, they present me with flowers and chocolates. I ask what message they want me to take back to students in New York. A skinny boy with a fierce crew haircut jumps up and says sternly, "Tell them not to watch so much TV and to be more serious!"

Impressed as I was, I wondered how representative those youngsters were. Perhaps they had been carefully selected for me, the meetings with them specially structured? As if in reply, something totally unstructured occurred one Saturday morning while I was having breakfast in my hotel room. I turned the TV on to what appeared to be a children's poetry program. A modest, soft-spoken young man briefly introduced each child by name, age, and grade in school, and mentioned the name of the poet and the title of the poem about to be recited. The children, some as young as seven or eight, the oldest in their early teens, stood up in turn and recited from memory poems by well-known Russian poets—recited with the lilting cadence, careful enunciation, and emotional expression so typically Russian. Most of the time, the camera dwelt lovingly on the audience of children, on their uplifted, rapt faces.

With a momentary pang I recalled the usual TV programs offered American children: the strident cartoons, the violence and vulgarity. Little wonder Russian children grow up loving poetry.

It starts early, the poetry and indoctrination. I brought home from one of the schools a syllabus in literature published in Moscow for the 1976–77 school year. It covers grades 4 through 10, the equivalent of ages 10 through 15.

From the very first, moral issues are stressed. In the lower grades, triumph of good over evil is emphasized; in higher grades, more advanced concepts of ethics,

but always with a strong political slant and always permeated by love of their native land and Communist morality. Since there are no discipline problems, teachers can teach, but ideology is spelled out for them in the syllabus. Each teacher is required to have a thorough knowledge of Lenin and literature. Lessons are accompanied by supplementary reading and memorization of poetry at home. Parents and librarians are involved in guiding the reading of the students, and at least once a month, literary discussions of books read outside of school are held. In higher classes, oral and written work is emphasized, and films are available in conjunction with the study of literature.

Obviously, only politically acceptable books are chosen. They start with fairy tales and fables; very early, children become acquainted with their great poets like Pushkin, with their classic authors like Tolstoi, and with the humor and satire of Chekhov and Gogol. Gradually, more complicated works of these authors and of others are studied, as well as foreign literature in translation: Balzac, Brecht, Neruda, among others. In each book, moral responsibility to society is unequivocally stressed.

The strong stand against religion is made explicit. The following is a paragraph from the syllabus which I have translated verbatim:

Literature, especially Soviet literature, offers the greatest opportunity for antireligious training of students, showing how belief in God morally deforms man, deprives him of his will and confidence in his own strength, makes him weak and defenseless. The teacher's task is to bring out this aspect in literature.

However greatly we may disagree with this emphasis on political and antireligious indoctrination and partisan selection of books, the scope and depth in the study of literature and the level of appreciation described in this syllabus would do credit to our American college courses.

Many questions remain unasked and unanswered. Whether or not the syllabus is faithfully followed I do not know. Much of our own planning looks good on paper, too. Yet it is obvious to me that Soviet children are motivated to learn; they see the necessity for school. They conform, since they are exposed to fewer divergent views than are our students.

Not only is the school involved with the home, the library, the community, the whole society (some schools are "wards" of shops or factories), but the school molds and develops character. Each year standards of character to be met are strictly defined. Attitudes toward learning, social responsibility, self-discipline, obedience—these are inculcated early through outside projects such as service to the community and through proj-

ects within the school: students' cleaning and repairing school property, older students' helping younger ones, group competition where the honor of the whole group is at stake, and peer pressures to uphold approved standards of conduct. There is no permissiveness and no neglect. Unlike many of our angry, rebellious, and alienated children, those I met appeared cheerful, friendly, and respectful; affectionate toward their teachers, eager to work, ready to laugh.

My last day in Moscow. I am at a farewell luncheon given for me by members of the Writers Union and editors of Soviet magazines. My hosts propose the customary toasts: to each person at the table, to abstractions such as peace and friendship, and—the toast I hear most often in the USSR—"To the children of all countries."

I drink to that.

PART III

Control, Organization, and Support of American Education

All three levels of government, federal, state, and local, have important roles to play in the control, organization, and support of education in the United States. The United States Constitution makes no specific references to education; however, the Tenth Amendment provides that "the powers not delegated to the United States by the Constitution, nor prohibited to it by the States, are reserved to the States respectively or to the people." Therefore, public education is a legal function of the respective states. The states have their own constitutional provisions for education, and legislatively most of them have delegated power to local school districts to operate public schools.

Historically, local school districts had great latitude in operating their own schools in the fashion they desired. In recent years, however, both the state and federal governments have played a much stronger role. This change has resulted from a number of factors, among them being federal court decisions, state and federal legislative mandates, increased community pluralism, and student rights. The article by Lee H. Hansen, "Political Reformation in Local School Districts," explores briefly many of the reasons for the erosion of the power of local school districts. One of the reasons, exclusive of the judiciary, has been the increased political power of teachers exercised at the local, state, and federal levels by their professional organizations. The article by James Browne, "Power Politics for Teachers, Modern Style," explains the political role that professional teacher organizations have developed over the years, and the impact these organizations have had on the control of education.

The role of the judiciary has been significant in recent years in altering the balance of federal, state, and local control of American education. Education in the United States must be conducted in accordance with the provisions of the United States Constitution, specifically those having to do with guaranteed individual rights. The interpretations of the First and Fourteenth Amendments by the United States Supreme Court have had decided effects on the control and operation of education at the local level. The Fourteenth Amendment reads in part: "No State shall make or reinforce any law which shall abrogate the privileges or immunities of citizens of the United States; nor shall any State deprive any persons of life, liberty, or property without due process of law; nor deny to any person within its jurisdiction the equal protection of the laws." The First Amendment, "Congress shall make no law respecting an establishment of religion nor prohibiting the free exercise thereof," has been made applicable to education within the several states by the Fourteenth Amendment.

A most significant application of the Fourteenth Amendment to education in this century was the 1954 decision of the United States Supreme Court in *Brown* v. *Board of Education of Topeka*. The decision referred to de jure segregation (ordained by law) and basically stated that racial discrimination in the public schools is unconstitutional. The Court said, in effect, that in education the separate but equal doctrine has no place and that separate but equal facilities are inherently unequal. Since that decision, many other decisions dealing with segregation have been made by lower courts with respect to both de jure and de facto (resulting from population patterns) segregation. The *Brown* decision is representative of one significant role of the federal government in the control of education—that of assuring that the rights of individual citizens as expressed in the United States Constitution are not denied to them.

Since the *Brown* v. *Board of Education of Topeka* (1954) case, much effort has been put forth to accomplish desegregation. In many instances, desegregation has been accomplished, frequently accompanied by strife.

It has been charged that desegregation frequently results in resegregation; that is, as whites leave a desegregated school, that school then becomes predominantly black again, and is, in effect, again segregated. Robert Wegmann's article, "White Flight and School Resegregation: Some Hypotheses," challenges the concept that racism is a major factor and provides a critical analysis including other potential reasons for the racial changes that occur following desegregation. Busing frequently is used to bring about desegregation. Most often such busing is strongly opposed. The article by Roger Williams, "What Louisville Has Taught Us About Busing," presents evidence that metropolitan area-wide busing can work. Williams is optimistic that busing "can produce better results than anyone dared predict."

While the school-related issues dealing with white flight and busing have drawn much attention from the media, a host of other concepts including public aid to religious schools, women and equality, and the general guarantee of Fourteenth Amendment rights to all children have been litigated in school-related court cases. In the article, "Public Aid to Religious Schools: What the Supreme Court Said—And Didn't Say," M. Chester Nolte attempts to show that "no definitive answer has yet been found to the dilemma of helping parochial schools while remaining within the bounds of the Constitution . . ." In the article, "Women, Equality, and the Public High School," Bea Mayes develops the premise that the high school, as a gatekeeper in the institutional web of our country, is in a position to shape the expectations and choices of the students. George H. Schauer develops his article, "Guaranteeing 14th Amendment Rights to All Children," from the actual language of the Amendment.

The support of education in the United States is closely related to the control and organization of education. All three levels of government contribute to that support. Historically, financial support came predominantly from local sources, namely the property tax. Nationwide, currently local sources contribute approximately 48 percent, state sources about 44 percent, and federal sources approximately 8 percent. There are, however, wide variances among states. The overall trend in the past few years has been to increase state support. This trend has been in harmony with the recommendations of many recent studies and court rulings in the area of school finance, which, in essence, are directed toward achieving equal educational opportunity.

A landmark case, *Serrano* v. *Priest* (1971), dealt with whether or not the California public school financing system, with its substantial dependence on local property taxes, violated the Fourteenth Amendment. The Court held that the heavy reliance on unequal local property taxes "makes the quality of a child's education a function of the wealth of his parents and neighbors." Other state courts made similar rulings. However, the United States Supreme Court, hearing a similar case originating in Texas (*San Antonio Independent School District* v. *Rodriguez*, 1973) overturned the lower court and thus reaffirmed the local property tax as a basis for school financing. Nevertheless, many states have made financial legislative enactments based on the principles identified in *Serrano* v. *Priest* (1971). John Pincus, in his article, "The Serrano Case: Policy for Education or for Public Finance?" clarifies the issues related to the case and discusses solutions currently being tested or debated in respect to equitable systems of school financing.

As was indicated earlier, education is legally a function of the states. Much legislation is created at the state level that impacts education. The role of teachers in legislative political activity is presented in Browne's article, mentioned earlier. Other groups are also quite active politically and influence legislation. Some of these groups include: farm organizations, trade unions, church groups, taxpayer's federations, business and professional associations, patriotic groups, and many others. These various groups both compete and collaborate with one another as legislation is sponsored and makes its way through the political arena and becomes law. Educational legislation, as well as other types, is generated in this political milieu.

In the last few years there has been an increased level of dissatisfaction expressed with education. Public education has been referred to as a disaster. One result of this attitude has been legislation enacted in many states calling for accountability. The public is asking for an accounting of educational results and their costs. The article by James Hayes et al., "Yes, But What Are We Accountable For?" discusses the confusion which has been spread by the varying ways in which accountability has been implemented in school districts and states across the country.

The control, organization, and support of American education are intertwined not only with one another, but with our political processes. As our society has changed, so has our educational system.

Reading 21

Political Reformation in Local Districts

Lee H. Hansen

A superintendent starting for work on a crisp, sunny autumn day in 1966 could hardly have imagined that just a decade later his school district would be in political disarray. Although the seeds were already being sown then, he could hardly have guessed that political change would come so traumatically. Indeed, if the 1960s are to be called the decade of curriculum reform, then the 1970s must be called the decade of political reformation in American education.

Yet there is some danger in labeling the seventies this way, for it suggests that politics is a new phenomenon for local school districts. On the contrary, the educational process in local school districts has always been a political process, particularly if we define *politics* as the art of collecting, controlling, and using that power which determines an organization's values, policies, and decisions.

Source: Lee H. Hansen, "Political Reformation in Local Districts." *Educational Leadership* vol. 34, no. 2 (November 1976), pp. 90–94. Reprinted with permission of the Association for Supervision and Curriculum Development and Lee H. Hansen. Copyright © 1976 by the Association for Supervision and Curriculum Development.

Back in 1966 the superintendent *was* political. He practiced the art of collecting, controlling, and using power. However, in 1966 everything was going his way. Community power structures were relatively stable and dominant; homogeneous coalitions of support were easy for the superintendent to assemble and maintain; resources and enrollment—the raw materials of education were expanding; and the mission was simple and attainable. Most important of all, a basic trust and faith existed in education and in educators. These factors combined to give the superintendent and his administrative staff a large and stable power base from which to impose their will on the local school district.

Redistribution of Power

By 1976 considerable erosion of the power base of many local school superintendents had occurred. The paragraphs which follow suggest why and where these shifts in power have occurred and what lies ahead politically for local school districts. But first, what happened to the power base controlled by the administrative staff? Why and where did it get redistributed?

State and Federal Prerogatives Clearly there has been an erosion of local school district power by state prerogatives and federal inducements. Many states have adopted cost controls, negative aid formulas, educational standards, or mandated accountability programs. Some states will have some combination of two or more of these programs. Each program constrains a local district in some way from exercising prerogatives it formerly had.

Meanwhile, the federal government has also been active. The courts have spoken to desegregation and student rights, constraining many local school districts from previous practices. The U.S. Office of Education has provided support to many local school districts through categorical grants for educationally disadvantaged children, innovation, instructional materials, in-service education, and special educational services. Being categorized, however, these resources have tended to support certain decisions and constrain others in local school districts.

Community Pluralism A second factor eroding the administrative power base is growing community pluralism. The homogeneous middle class community power structure of 1966 is now marked only by its absence. Rapid shifts in personal values during the past ten years, as well as the emerging "self-help" attitude of political activism, have produced a complex patchwork of small independent community groups, each lobbying with a besieged board of education for what it values. These groups have been produced by events such as:

• Ideological splits such as liberal/conservative or intellectual/anti-intellectual;
• Demands for enfranchisement by such groups as blacks, chicanos, and women;
• Geographical schisms within a school district;
• Ideological groups lobbying for the elderly, the preschool child, the open classroom, alternatives, back to the basics, and the child with special educational needs.

While these groups obviously have overlapping memberships and constituencies, they have not yet in most communities formed the political coalitions that would begin to lend some stability to the situation. The cacophonous demands and competitive struggles of these groups for resources are difficult for the superintendent and his or her staff to control and manage. Hence, there is a further erosion of administrative power.

Teacher Militancy Teachers have not only organized; they have unionized. Through the process of negotiation and grievance they have begun to strip the superintendents and their staffs of one "management" right after another. As teacher unions have matured, they have come to realize that instructional decisions and "working condition" decisions cannot be clearly distinguished. Any decision that impacts on a teacher in any way is seemingly fair game for the negotiating or grievance processes. With this attitude, teachers have done much to wrest control for instructional decision making from the administration. The superintendent's power is further eroded.

Student Rights A final contribution to the shift of political power away from administration has been the student rights movement. Court decisions and new laws have regulated the power that administrators have over students. Such developments as due process mechanisms, the student's bill of rights, search and seizure constraints, and control over student records have placed limitations on the prerogatives of superintendents and their staffs, regulating their authority and eroding their power.

All of these factors have contributed over the past decade to shifts in the available political power within many local school districts. But, it might be asked, what factors have triggered these basic shifts in power?

New Imperative

A variety of factors has contributed to the redistribution of power over the past decade.

Expanding Role of the School   First, in the face of a series of crises, society has made and continues to make new demands on education. The school is seen as an easily accessible institution for helping society cope with its problems. Thus, in the past decade, social engineers, reformers, and advocates have tried to use the schools as a vehicle to cope with segregation; human relations; the environmental crisis; vandalism; smoking and cancer; drugs; sexual naïveté and immorality; population control; and early childhood care—to name but a few problem areas.

Since the school is perceived as a useful tool in combating these social ills (whether it really is or not is beside the point), it is: (a) more valuable to society, (b) commands a larger share of resources and societal power, and (c) is more interesting to a variety of people in society who collect and control that power.

In short, schools are no longer perceived as innocent and benign institutions. They are perceived as useful and hence powerful tools for helping society cope with its problems. They are a renewed source of power for power brokers.

Fiscal Woes   A second factor contributing to the redistribution of power is the shift in the locus of financing local school district operations. In the face of inflation and teachers' economic gains, local school administrators have looked upon the interjection of state and federal tax money with eager relief. Somehow the burden on property taxes needed to be lessened.

But resources are power, and as the state and federal governments have injected more and more money into local operations, they have begun to exercise more and more influence over local school district policy decisions.

Broken Promises   The failure of educators to deliver on their promises during the 1960s has also contributed to the power shift. Professional educators promised much during the 1960s—everything from basic educational reform and individualized instruction to the eradication of social and economic injustice. We had the answers. All we needed were the dollars, and we got the dollars in unprecedented amounts.

But somehow we had miscalculated and we could not deliver. Now, a decade later, schools are still kept pretty much as they were 20 years ago and the professional educators, including superintendents and their administrative staffs, have lost face, influence, and power.

Changing Values   As fundamental values have shifted in our society, basic institutions and their supporting values have come under attack. Schools have not escaped this assault. As an example, resources in local school districts have been traditionally allocated on the basis of social utility: the greatest good for the greatest number.

Under this unstated rubric, disproportionate educational resources were provided to average and above average students. Students with handicaps or special educational needs were given only token support relative to the educational needs they exhibited.

Today that is no longer true in many local school districts. Under the threat of legal redress or legislative mandate, local school districts have been forced to distribute resources more equitably. Social utility has been replaced by individual justice; the burden of proof rests increasingly with the school to demonstrate that a "good faith" effort has been made to educate each student, whatever the individual's needs and whatever the expense.

This kind of shift constrains a superintendent's power, for no longer can he or she as easily move resources around to build a support base among the influential power structures of the community.

Summarizing the argument to this point, I have suggested that a considerable shift in the distribution of political power has occurred and is continuing to occur in many local school districts. The big losers in this power shift have been educational administrators. Unfortunately this often traumatic shift in power is creating an unstable management environment at the very point in time when stability is important.

Districts Need Political Stability

Many school systems, but particularly larger school systems, face problems that are unprecedented in magnitude and complexity. Few people will deny that court imposed integration; political accountability; curriculum control and reform; deficit spending and the resource squeeze of inflation; and declining enrollments are large, complex problems that are often interrelated. However, these problems are made more acute by the political instability of the school district.

Many local school districts are moving steadily toward continuous crisis conditions, not because the problems just mentioned are insolvable, but because the unstable political environment within which these problems are embedded precludes any effective movement toward solution.

The growing crises of many local school districts will deepen so long as power is relatively equitably distributed among a number of adversary groups and interests, unless and until those groups and interests learn the skills of coalition formation: compromise, trade-offs, and consensus seeking. At the present time this is not happening.

Future Directions

The growing crisis in the local school has led some soothsayers to predict the demise of this institution. However, there is little to be gained from predicting such a fate for the public schools. Public school systems are proving to be more resilient institutions than many critics would have predicted. Rather than speculate about the ultimate outcome of this political reformation of the 1970s, let's predict some future trends that may influence the political fate of school districts.

Superintendents Become Political The charismatic superintendent will reemerge in a new form as a strong force in some local school districts. Such individuals, however, will not manage by the strength of their commanding personalities alone, but through a repertoire of sophisticated political and interpersonal skills as well. They will possess: (a) expertise in communication skills, (b) an ability to use information to manage public opinion, (c) adeptness at using the informal influence structure, and (d) the ability to create an atmosphere characterized by perceived openness and trust.

In short, such an individual will be an accomplished politician first and an educator second. His or her primary task as superintendent will not be to provide instructional leadership, but rather political leadership. Like some large city mayors, this person will have the almost singular responsibility of forging and maintaining a dominant political coalition to support school system decision making. To accomplish this feat, the person will be equipped with a far more sophisticated repertoire of skills than many administrators presently possess.

Administrative Alliance Grows   Over the next several years school administrators below the level of superintendent, that is, directors, principals, coordinators, and supervisors, will seriously reexamine their positions in the local district power equation. As boards of education take on new roles, often as adversaries of administrators, the concept of administrators as extensions of board authority becomes more tenuous.

Administrators as a group or groups will reach out during the rest of this decade to form new alliances with other influence groups. In particular, where their interests overlap, administrative groups and teachers unions will work more closely together. This will be true particularly on issues involving curriculum and instruction, where current interventio   by parents and other lay people are perceived by .ducators as compromising professional decision-making prerogatives.

General Instruction Suffers   The general quality of instruction will decline during the rest of the decade. At the same time, the quality of instruction will improve for children who have handicaps or special educational needs. This will occur because a shrinking resource base in local districts will be more equitably (if more thinly) spread out to reach more students.

Pluralistic Alternatives Increase   As local communities grow increasingly pluralistic, more educational alternatives will be introduced as a strategy for accommodating

pluralism. Specifically, these alternatives will be designed to quiet the political right and left in education. Along with open classrooms, Montessori classrooms, and high schools without walls for the political left will come fundamental programs, "back to basics" programs, and educational academies to silence the curriculum concerns of the extreme right.

Unfortunately, many of these alternatives will be under-financed, and over-ballyhooed, thus further contributing to the decline in the overall quality of instruction. They will also fail to contribute much to political stability, as individual groups vie for increasingly scarce resources to maintain their particular alternative.

Budget Cuts Foreseen   As enrollments decline, considerable political pressure will be exerted to reduce budgets accordingly. Some school districts will react to the political dilemmas of contraction in a closed, dysfunctional manner. A mentality of distrust and hopelessness will pervade local district decision making during this period.

Rather than careful, long-range planning to reduce the scope of the district's educational mission, many decisions to reduce spending will be expedient and momentarily pleasing; others will come only after an emotional tug of war among opposing political forces.

Increasingly, administrators will be denied the necessary flexibility in allocating resources, since a district reduces resources more quickly than it reduces the scope of its mission.

The picture I have painted here may not be a particularly encouraging one for some educators. However, it is a picture of growing political awareness and maturity in an institution that has lived through some fairly fundamental power shifts and has not witnessed the last of political turmoil and change.

Reading 22

Power Politics for Teachers, Modern Style

James Browne

Charles Wheatley, lobbyist for the Maryland State Teachers Association, stood tensely before a House committee, his arms waving, his voice rising in near panic, as he pleaded with committee members not to amend a bill that would bring huge benefits to his organization." [1] Wheatley's complaint—that a filibuster over Baltimore subway legislation in the state senate would push his teacher agency-shop bill back into committee—proved correct. Wheatley must wait at least one more year.

Three weeks earlier, in the dining room of the NEA's Washington, D.C., headquarters, a National Education Association official convened a meeting of lobbyists who make up the leadership of the Committee for Full Funding of Education Programs. Committee members, who represent a wide array of education interest groups, have met regularly since the Nixon administration took office in January, 1969. Their function: to align themselves and their constituents on behalf of favorable congressional appropriations.

Source: James Browne, "Power Politics for Teachers, Modern Style," *Phi Delta Kappan* vol. 58, no. 2 (October 1976), pp. 158–164. Reprinted with permission.

At the same time, the South Carolina Education Association marked its first year as part of a different mix of organizations: the Citizens' Coalition for Equal School Financing. Linked with such statewide groups as the League of Women Voters, the Farm Bureau, the American Association of University Women, and the American Friends Service Committee, the SCEA assumes that more equitable financing will mean more funds statewide for teachers.

Three months earlier and 2,800 miles away, Vice President James Ballard of the American Federation of Teachers testified against the concept of school-site budgeting as a device to reform management.[2] For years Ballard had tried to streamline San Francisco school managers in his own way, but he felt compelled to protest something that might diminish union power where it thrives: downtown at the school board.

In March of this year, in the state headquarters of the Ohio Education Association, the Ohio version of a nationwide Labor Coalition Clearinghouse, organized without the help of the AFL-CIO's Committee on Political Education (COPE), denied Presidential candidate Henry Jackson's bid for an "all or nothing" endorsement. Spokesmen for the OEA, the United Auto Workers, the Communication Workers of America, Graphic Arts International, the Union of Electrical Workers, and the American Federation of State, County, and Municipal Employees (AFSCME) instead split their endorsement between candidates Morris Udall and Jimmy Carter. The OEA and others reportedly intended to support Jackson—until they "suspected the Jackson camp was being pressured by the leadership of the more conservative AFL-CIO. . . ."[3] A similar coalition of NEA local affiliates and labor unions was instrumental in the historic defeat of Governor George Wallace in Florida by Carter, and political action of this kind by AFT and NEA personnel nationally brought more than 200 teachers to New York City as Democratic convention delegates.

These five incidents reflect goals of teacher politics in the mid-seventies: collective bargaining legislation, one-third federal funding of public education nationally, more state-level funding, influence in local decision making, and power brokering within the Democratic party. Collective bargaining legislation is the mother's milk of all teacher power activities, and for at least four years it has dominated the thinking of most teacher organizations.

Teachers as Public Employees

Rapid growth in the ranks of organized teachers is part of burgeoning political action throughout the public sector. "Teacher power" is a subset of the post-World War II phenomenon of bigness in America: growing corporate power and size, growing universities, growing local and state bureaucracies, growing demands for equality, and growing management/labor schisms in the public sector. Not only have NEA and AFT memberships swelled dramatically in the

last decade, but comparable growth was registered by the American Federation of State, County and Municipal Employees, AFL-CIO, which has risen in 10 years from seventeenth in size nationally among unions to fifth, with 750,000 members. Post-war public education reform which reduced the number of school districts from about 100,000 to 16,000 contributed to the cause of bigness by providing new critical masses of teacher voters for teacher organizers of the seventies. So too did the U.S. Supreme Court's 1962 *Baker* v. *Carr* decision, which initiated reapportionment of all state legislatures on a "one man—one vote" principle.

Most public sector employees find themselves caught up in changing social and political settings; their self-image and behavior change accordingly. In the words of one teacher politician:

Teachers tend to reflect to a remarkable degree the thoughts and moods of their home community. This is because teachers are chosen by school boards who are highly sensitive to the thoughts of their constituents. Boards tend to hire teachers who fit the community mold.[4]

For the 4,000 districts in the nation that have 300 or fewer students enrolled—and most of these in one schoolhouse—community molds don't often change quickly. In big districts and cities, on the other hand, greater anonymity and greater bureaucratization seem to discourage molds and encourage collective action.

The localized, pluralistic basis of American public education, and politics generally, has produced a huge and ever-changing mosaic of collective bargaining practice and legislation in all 50 states. And wherever they are—with a few exceptions—teacher organizations' political action concentrates on improving their bargaining positions.

Major exceptions occur in the South. Georgia allows local firemen to bargain collectively, but not teachers, whose large local and state associations do not appear intent on expanding the law to include them. North Carolina outlaws public sector bargaining—period, making it unwise to attempt political action on its behalf.

Many school districts in states without laws authorizing collective bargaining respond to organized teacher pressure with grievance procedures and other attempts at improved management/labor relations. Some in suburban or urban areas respond with localized collective bargaining agreements. NEA affiliates in Virginia, for example, have local agreements covering about 30% of the state's 58,000 teachers. School boards, in search of something to regulate management/teacher conflict, signed these contracts even though the Virginia attorney general had ruled them unenforceable and even though Governor Mills Godwin is suing suburban Arlington County in order to ask the Virginia Supreme Court to declare local bargaining illegal. (Godwin acknowledged that the legislature probably wouldn't do the job. Lobbyist disclosure records showed that the Virginia Education Association in 1975 logged $30,000 in lobbying expenses on behalf of a bargaining bill.)

The Spectrum of Teacher Politics

A sampling of teacher organization activities in diverse political cultures around the country reveals a wide spectrum of political action and organization on the part of state and local teacher groups—ranging from ineffective to tough and mature.

New Mexico   About 70% of the state's 14,000 public school teachers are members of the NEA state affiliate, down a few percentage points from five years ago. AFT activity is negligible. As in other sparsely populated Rocky Mountain states, political leadership in New Mexico is generally hostile to the idea of public sector collective bargaining. Interested teachers therefore concentrate on securing more tax dollars. Two years ago, a well-orchestrated campaign by determined teachers, legislators, and Governor Jerry Apodaca brought a measure of statewide equalization into the state's school finance laws.[5] Local districts now receive state allocations based in part on the number of degrees held by their teachers—a built-in incentive for school boards to hire, keep, and further train highly qualified staff. State levels of school funding are among the highest in the country.

Texas   Texans in 1975 and 1976 ran annual state surpluses of about $2 billion and rarely discussed the possibility of public sector collective bargaining. Unification in 1975 of Texas State Teachers Association and NEA memberships could upset the status quo soon. Administrators warn that they will withdraw their affiliation with the TSTA if ever there occurs a "teacher strike in Texas sanctioned by TSTA-NEA."

Arkansas   Organized teachers, as well as AFSCME's local and state members, are particularly strong in Little Rock and Pulaski County. Like their Alabama teacher colleagues, they sought collective bargaining legislation in 1975 and failed. Their move was dampened by an unpopular strike by Pine Bluff firemen, whose action brought some firings as well as National Guard emergency replacements. Unrest on the part of teachers in the urban areas created an internal leadership crisis in the 22,000-member Arkansas Education Association. Most of its administrators quit, thereby removing constraints on its own militancy. Teachers voted to unify with the NEA, and the newly elected AEA president was given a leave of absence from his Jonesboro school system to assume full-time AEA political leadership. (The AFT has no local affiliate in Arkansas and two other states.)

Alabama   Alabama has the highest level of political action of a statewide teacher organization in the South, with the possible exception of "non-South" Florida. By early 1975, leaders of the 36,000-member Alabama Education Association, representing nearly 100% of the state's classroom teachers, sensed strong support among legislators for a collective bargaining law. Association priorities are decided in its annual Delegate Assembly meeting, however. Meeting in early March, 1975, delegates unexpectedly rejected by a hair-thin margin the notion of support for collective bargaining legislation. The Alabama NEA affiliate, like several others in the country, includes administrators in its ranks, and the administrators' negative votes tailored the setting for organized teacher political action to administrators' interests, but only for a year. Association leadership left little to chance in 1976, and a pro-bargaining resolution sailed through the Delegate Assembly. But there was no longer a sense of substantial legislative support for a bill, and a splinter group of Alabama teachers had organized to oppose the idea. A constitutional change by Alabama voters had, in addition, injected an unknown into the arena of teacher politics. The tradition of an elected state commissioner of education was gone. In its place was a state commissioner appointed by a State Board of Education, and the first incumbent commissioner under the new constitution is the former executive director of the Alabama School Administrators Association, who sees the state department's role primarily as service to locally controlled school systems.

Nevada   In 1974 the Nevada State Education Association repeated its political action

on behalf of Mike O'Callaghan, a popular governor running for reelection. But the NSEA within a few months lost its leader— influential lobbyist and friend of the governor Dick Morgan—to the Oklahoma Education Association. (Interstate movement of sharp political leadership is increasingly common among NEA state affiliates.) Association political committees endorsed and funded only those legislative and statewide candidates who pledged more money for education. One school district—Clark County's—has about half of Nevada's voters. The key issue in 1975, however, was not money but amendments to a 1969 collective bargaining law which permitted binding arbitration of local public sector disputes. The state supreme court angered important legislators by upholding a Clark County (Las Vegas) judge's 1973 decision that a binding arbitration settlement could cover class size and other broad "policy" considerations. The NSEA strongly supported the lower court judge's successful 1974 race for Congress, but the association could not defeat moves by local government and school district lobbies to narrow "scope of bargaining" definitions. NSEA leaders lost three previously bargained issues: class size, student discipline, and teacher transfer policy.

California   The Golden State will this year and next be the scene of nationally important "teacher power" developments. A broad 1975 collective bargaining law covering the state's 200,000 teachers has set the stage for statewide competition for members between the wealthy, legislatively powerful California Teachers Association and AFT organizers.

The CTA charges its 112,000 members $105 annually, among the highest dues among NEA state affiliates. Its political action arm spent $327,000 as 1974 campaign donations on behalf of the negotiations law, school finance legislation, teacher pensions, and in securing "adequate" due process rights for teachers in dismissal actions. The outlay included $25,000 contributions to the successful campaigns of Governor Jerry Brown, Lieutenant Governor (and ex-AFT teacher) Melvin Dymally, Secretary of State (and ex-school board member) March Fong Eu, and Treasurer Jesse Unruh, plus donations (ranging from $250 to $10,450) to campaigns of more than 50 of the 80 incumbent assemblymen.[6] The statewide candidate who apparently did not receive $25,000 for his campaign was Ken Cory, state controller, who "began his political career in 1963 as a staff consultant to the Assembly Education Committee."[7] The CTA, when local pressures require, also contributes small sums (usually $250 and $500) to help pro-teacher candidates in local school board races.

With the exception of San Francisco, California's major cities are not "union towns." About 16,000 of the 24,000 teachers in quasi-suburban Los Angeles belong to the United Teachers of Los Angeles, a hybrid that mixes NEA members and AFT members in a 3–1 ratio. The UTLA, following the unprecedented merger, refused five years ago to pay dues to a much more conservative CTA, but did send its NEA members' dues on to Washington. This began the series of internal NEA actions which ended in 1975 with a nationwide NEA policy mandating "unification" (automatic dues payment to all three levels of NEA governance), with state affiliates transmitting local funds to Washington. The AFT has always done it this way.

The CTA is undergoing internal change with the retirement of its long-time executive director, a former suburban school district superintendent. The replacement, Ralph Flynn, has been groomed by the CTA and NEA, who took him from his San Francisco association post, brought him to Washington as an NEA executive, and then placed him for a short time as executive director of the nationwide NEA-AFSCME Coalition of American Public Employees (CAPE).

Connecticut   Here, in the state with the highest average personal income in the nation, NEA and AFT state affiliates actively compete for members. Both have strong leadership. The AFT is anchored chiefly in the Middletown and Hartford urban areas and the Connecticut Education Association enjoys a 4–1 statewide membership advantage. CEA Executive Director Tom Mondani is an ex-legislator whose association devotes most of its time to negotiating for local affiliates. Municipalities this year defeated the two organizations' lobbying efforts to extend 1975's "last-best-offer" impasse procedures—enacted on behalf of municipal employees last year—to collective bargaining for teachers. The state's law remains essentially "anti-collective bargaining," due to an uncommon impasse procedure which lets local boards secure antistrike injunctions without court hearings. Connecticut towns voted 17–7 to oppose, successfully, the transplanting of municipal workers' procedures to teachers, pointing out that Connecticut school boards, who negotiate with teachers, could not speak for the municipalities, which must pass on final budgets. This anomaly of "fiscal dependence" of local school boards affects about 20% of the nation's school systems and annually frustrates teacher organization attempts at political action in those jurisdictions.

Illinois   Public sector employees in this big urban state have failed since 1945 to secure even a skeletal collective bargaining statute. As in most states without such a law, negotiations, grievance procedures, and a variety of de facto bargaining occur locally without the benefit of legislative support. Teacher organizations and other public employee lobbies supported at least eight major bargaining bills last year. None passed, despite concentrated letter writing, phone calling, and name calling, reinforced by occasional demonstrations at the state capitol.

Disagreement on controversial provisions like agency shop and the right to strike divided some of the proponents, but probably more important was State Senator Richard M. Daley's determination to block a negotiations bill. His father's patronage-dominated Chicago negotiates with the 20,000-member Chicago Teachers Union in its own fashion. Leaders of the 60,000-member NEA state affiliate and the Illinois AFT envy their counterparts in Michigan, New York, Massachusetts, and Pennsylvania, where the big-city AFT locals of Detroit, New York City, Boston, and Philadelphia operate under statewide ground rules developed partly with the help of teacher organizations.

Michigan   Perhaps no large state is so chronically immersed in political and social conflict as is Michigan, and political action in public education matters reflects the cleavages. Michigan is the ancestral home of the "negative check-off" policy recently adopted nationally by the NEA, whereby $5 is withheld from members' paychecks for political action unless a teacher specifically objects. The Michigan Education Association enjoys an 80,000 membership, an $8 million annual budget, and a staff of 125 or more. Terry Herndon, who moved from the NEA to Michigan as the Michigan Education Association's executive director in 1969, returned to Washington three years ago as the NEA's "reform" executive director. Herndon is a negotiations expert.

The MEA's president from Herndon days, John Ryor, was elected to a two-year term as NEA president in 1975. (Until last year, NEA presidents had served only one-year terms.) The temporary closeness of the NEA presidency and executive director mutes, at

least for awhile, AFT jibes that the association doesn't know where its policy is.

Unlike the Michigan Federation of Teachers (AFT/AFL-CIO), the MEA enjoys close ties with Republican Governor William Milliken, dating back to Milliken's days as an MEA-endorsed state senator and lieutenant governor. The political relationship became even warmer in 1972 when MEA contributed manpower and "about a quarter-million dollars" in support of Milliken's successful school finance reform initiative.[8] AFT political action deals mostly with the politics of Detroit, where its 11,000 members teach in perhaps the most politicized and fractionated climate of any major city in the United States. Detroit's labor politics are dominated by the nation's most politically influential international union, the non-AFL-CIO United Auto Workers. The UAW's political ties with NEA state affiliates and other members of a nationwide labor coalition produced, among other things, a dramatic early primary victory for Presidential aspirant Jimmy Carter over Governor George Wallace in Florida and a victory by the narrowest possible margin for Carter over Morris Udall in Michigan.

Minnesota   Fulton B. Klinderfuss, chairman of the Independent Minnesota Political Action Committee for Education (IMPACE), addressed a political action training session for NEA affiliates earlier this year and reported the belief of the state chairman of the Minnesota Republican Party that Minnesota teachers were "the most powerful and sophisticated influence currently on the scene in the Minnesota State Legislature." Klinderfuss went on to caution his enthusiastic audience, however:

We are not in the business to buy politicians, because those who are for sale are not worth the price. But because of our size and resources we are expected to be on hand when good men and women in both political parties seek office and afford them every possible opportunity to run a good campaign.[9]

IMPACE is to the Minnesota Education Association as statewide political action arms are to NEA state affiliates in 47 states, although the acronym tends to vary with the state. But there is something about the political climate of Minnesota that accepts public sector political action generally. The state has a comprehensive collective bargaining law that provides organizational security to local bargaining organizations. It seems to have an endless line of able candidates for major state and federal elected offices, all of them with close ties to well-organized, generally well-staffed teacher organizations at local and state levels. U.S. Senator Hubert Humphrey (himself an AFT member), vice-presidential candidate Walter "Fritz" Mondale, former State Senator Albert Quie (spokesman for education among congressional Republicans), former U.S. Senator Eugene McCarthy, Minnesota House of Representatives Speaker Martin Sabo, and a host of others are closely identified with organized teachers, whose principal statewide agent, the 39,000-member MEA, was in 1974 the second largest "contributor of campaign funds to candidates for state offices and the legislature." IMPACE, like its counterparts in other states, makes contributions but does not lobby; the MEA lobbies, but does not contribute to war chests. Michigan's negative check-off has not yet been used. Rather, IMPACE volunteers visit teachers personally and solicit political donations, usually of $10 or less. Republicans apparently get a large share of IMPACE-collected funds. Minnesota's AFT locals, whose political ties are reportedly strong with the Democratic governor, compete aggressively and closely with the MEA in the state's major cities and dominate several locals in suburbs and in the northern iron

range. The commonality of interests among teacher organizations and legislators is perhaps stronger in Minnesota than in any other state, with the possible exception of Oregon.

New Jersey   Within the past eight years, the New Jersey Education Association increased its membership from 59,000 to 85,000, and now represents approximately 90% of the state's K–12 teacher population. The state's urban ghettos, wealthy suburbs, and conservative rural communities are divided among more than 600 school districts committed to a tradition of local control and weak state legislatures. The NJEA's struggle for membership with AFT locals, following passage of collective bargaining legislation, was not always successful;[10] but usually it was, befitting a state association well funded ($5 million annual budget) and staffed by shrewd political strategists. In its long history of political struggle in the state capital, the NJEA's most significant victory was probably its 1973 defeat of Carl Marburger's nomination by Republican Governor William Cahill for a second term as commissioner of education. A veteran of Detroit school warfare, the liberal Marburger was originally selected by Cahill's predecessor, Democrat Richard Hughes, and moved vigorously in three controversial directions: to achieve elements of racial balance in some recalcitrant districts, to exert state authority over districts otherwise found incompetent, and to resist rapidly growing NJEA statewide influence. Public education leaders from both sides of the management/labor fence waited nationwide for the results of a test of strength between the governor's influence and the opposition of a host of local powers. Marburger's nomination was defeated by a one-vote margin, following what may well be the most intensive eleventh-hour political campaign ever conducted by a statewide teacher organization.

The Goals of Teacher Power

On occasion state-level NEA and AFT leaders will carefully lower their sights and aim at each other, thereby expending limited resources on jurisdictional conflicts. New York offers the most important instance of this rivalry, and in the state of New York NEA influence has been virtually wiped out, with only Buffalo remaining as a center of NEA strength. Florida is witnessing another NEA setback, this time at the hands of both the AFT and an "independent" group that wants neither affiliation. But the clear trend in the United States today is for political action to concentrate on issues of members' economic benefits, organization security, and public policies that impinge on classroom teaching. Collective bargaining laws deal with all three.

Where bargaining is not an announced goal, as in New Mexico and Texas, most teachers in most states are not strongly organized. Where a first stab at a statute is in prospect, as in Alabama and Arkansas, major internal leadership struggles materialize. Where threats to a satisfactory power status quo emerge, as in Nevada and New Jersey, state teacher organizations defend their turf. Where collective bargaining ground rules and jurisdictional warfare are old hat, as in Minnesota and Michigan, political action works to guarantee legislative and gubernatorial support. Where negotiations laws appear defective, as in Connecticut, allies in the legislature are importuned to finely tune favorable amendments. States with broad new laws, such as California, must seek massive organizing support from NEA and AFT headquarters in Washington to help win local exclusive representation rights.

Teachers as Legislators

Teacher organizations moving to improve their own security and collective bargaining rights for their members need not rely only on lobbying activity and campaign contributions to help clear paths to policy makers. A direct path is for unions, associations, and their allies to elect teachers to state legislatures. By 1975 more than 400 educators were serving as legislators, not counting dozens of others who left their jobs to become legislators. The National Council of State Education Associations estimates that three-fourths of legislator educators are public school teachers.[11] Alaska and Missouri are the only states reporting no teacher legislators; Minnesota reports 16 classroom teachers in its legislature; Montana, Ohio, and Indiana, 12 each; Oregon and Rhode Island, 11 each. Staff members of NEA state affiliates served as teacher legislators in 1975 in eight states: Georgia, Louisiana, Maine, Oklahoma, Oregon, Pennsylvania, South Carolina, and Tennessee. Not all teacher legislators are friendly to teacher lobbies, however, and a few are overtly hostile.

Local Teacher Politics

No estimate is available of the number of teachers serving on local school boards, either their own or somebody else's. Legal problems related to conflict of interest frequently emerge when teachers run for local or state office, especially when an educator is elected to a post that pays a salary and retirement.

Lobbying where collective bargaining

laws operate poses serious problems for public officials, who on the one hand must negotiate contracts and on the other hand deal with occasional demands that the ground rules for bargaining be changed. This end-run technique can obtain benefits from a local or state legislature that would not otherwise be granted at the bargaining table.[12] Teacher activists argue that comparable opportunity exists for their foes to pass punitive state legislation which preempts local policies to which teacher lobbyists may have devoted years of costly attention.

Teacher organization presidents tend to perform local lobbying chores, leaving the state-level job to professionals. Local lobbyists therefore tend to be employees of those officials they lobby. In addition, teacher groups allied with other AFSCME locals or AFL-CIO local labor councils can call upon powerful lobbying allies in many situations.

The Federal Setting

NEA affiliates dominate state-level political activities of teacher organizations everywhere except in Florida and New York. The AFT, on the other hand, is "at home" in Washington, D.C., where a Congress long controlled by Democrats views public education as a subject for social legislation. Education bills in Congress are offered not by education committees, as they are in the states, but by the Committee on Education and Labor of the House of Representatives and the Committee on Labor and Public Welfare of the Senate. And when the AFT's state affiliates do achieve recognition in state capitals, more often than not it is because of their alliance with influential AFL-CIO state and local labor councils.

AFT ties with the AFL-CIO are strong, notably in the person of AFT President Al Shanker. To a great extent, they account for the fact that the NEA's original idea of a totally new national public sector collective bargaining law lost to the AFL-CIO's drive to extend existing private sector legislation —the National Labor Relations Act—to local and state employees. Private sector and public sector collective bargaining assumptions often clash, however. National AFL-CIO officials are ideologically committed, for example, to oppose any restriction on the right to strike. Public sector employees at local and state levels, on the other hand, cannot talk about strike action as freely as their colleagues in the private sector. Some endorse legislation that would outlaw strikes but mandate or permit local boards to settle impasses through compulsory arbitration. The AFL-CIO this year attempted to bring discussion and action on such differences into a Public Employees Department, to help local and state affiliates organize and survive. But AFSCME, the key link in the department, soon quarreled with the department's ancestry, money demands, and objectives—and either quit or was expelled. AFSCME is street-wise, headed politically by a brilliant, aggressive president, Jerry Wurf, and administratively by Jack Conway, Common Cause's former executive director. The AFT is also headed by a brilliant, aggressive strategist, and its locals compete for local dues with members of the NEA, with whom AFSCME (AFL-CIO) is politically allied at the national level. The course of teacher power in the United States might well be influenced, therefore, by an AFSCME (now enrolling 750,000 members) linked to the NEA through CAPE and to the AFT through COPE.

The AFT's stated commitment to broad social causes outside the professional educator's experience fortunately covers the political territory of most of its members: the racially and socially divided big cities of the northeastern United States. Problems of urban America tend also to be the priority concerns of congressional and presidential

Democrats, whose linkages with the AFT tend to be through local, state, and national AFL-CIO labor councils.

AFT classroom teachers (K–12) now number 420,000, up 100% from 1970. The national organization spends about $9 million annually. Members pay $28 a year (plus local dues); $1.20 of this goes for individual AFL-CIO membership, 36 cents into a teacher defense fund, $3 for a teacher strike fund, about 50 cents to finance AFL-CIO public employee organizing efforts, and $1.20 to state federations. The rest finances the AFT's national headquarters. Each local must affiliate with the appropriate local and state AFL-CIO labor council. The AFT maintains two or three dozen national organizers, a small headquarters bureaucracy, and various educational and lobbying activities.

The AFT has set up its own branch of the national AFL-CIO's Committee on Public Education (COPE) and has allocated $90,000 for COPE activities. It would like to produce as much as a million dollars for AFT-COPE political action this year, based on $10 per capita COPE contributions nationally, $3 going for AFT-COPE, and the rest for local and state races. Its prime 1974 target was to help AFL-CIO forces reelect Senator Birch Bayh. Its legislative coordinator, Greg Humphrey, served as the 1975 president of the coalition of public school Washington lobbyists called the Full-Funding Committee.

The NEA has about 1.3 million classroom teacher members (K–12). Its $49 million national budget funds a bureaucracy that includes 290 professionals. (Ironically, the bulk of its support employees are organized by the Communications Workers of America, AFL-CIO.) It spends large sums—more than $2 million last year—for teachers' legal defense and is developing a computer system which will retrieve master contract items for use by local chapters.

The NEA activity with perhaps the greatest political clout is a rapidly developing "UniServ" network of regional organizers formed and financed cooperatively by local and state affiliates and coordinated nationally.

NEA governance mechanisms are far more complex than the AFT's: State affiliates are the basic voting blocs in the governing Representative Assembly (9,000 members), where "ethnic minority" quotas of 20% are enforced. The assembly selects an Executive Committee, which hires the NEA executive director.

Fifteen officials representing state affiliates and two from "ethnic minorities" constitute the NEA Political Action Committee (NEA-PAC) steering committee, whose hardest task is to decide on partisan endorsements. These endorsements can mean both cash and precinct help from organized teachers. Circumstances increasingly move the NEA away from its party-neutral history: Republicans control only 13 of the 50 governorships and only two of these—Michigan and Ohio—are large states. Democrats control both houses in 37 states, the Republicans only four (all of them small). The 49-state network of NEA political action committees deals infrequently with Republican leadership; and the national ties also are weak. But NEA members—middle-class teachers and a number of administrators—are themselves bipartisan. A confidential poll of the membership of the NEA showed that 43% of its members are Democrats and 30% Republicans. A full 26% state no party affiliation.[18] Important headquarters staff members also enjoy strong Republican ties to the Congress.

NEA-sponsored political action since 1972 has been well publicized: timely and expensive support for Senator Claiborne Pell, money and doorbell-ringers for Senator John Durkin in the special New Hampshire race, and a solid track record of helping finance 280 (out of 310 candidates supported) winners in 1974 congressional races.

Democratic victories in those races spurred the NEA and the AFT, along with a host of other public sector employee groups, to press for a federal collective bargaining law which would force heretofore recalcitrant states and municipalities to bargain with their employees, more than two million of whom are teachers. The political climate for passage in early 1976 was good, and those who feared teacher power took an apocalyptic view of pro-labor activities in House and Senate committees. Ralph de Toledano, for instance, labeled moves for such legislation as possible steps toward "an intimidated Congress and a manipulated President" and an NEA that "would indeed be the most powerful force in the United States." [14]

Hostile Public Opinion

The year 1975 proved costly to organized public sector employees: A record number of teacher strikes, an insolvent New York City, a police-struck San Francisco, massive layoffs, local wage settlements, and a host of local and state budget crises shaped public opinion and changed minds of congressmen otherwise loyal to organized labor. These nationally exerted pressures eliminated any short-term prospect of a federal public sector bargaining law. Negotiators for school boards and municipalities quickly sensed rising public concern over new taxes and government expenditures. Smaller wage settlements everywhere in 1976 reflected public opinion, and "teacher power" found itself blocked in Congress and on the economic home front as well.

National League of Cities v. Usery

It took the U.S. Supreme Court—in a watershed decision on federal/state relations—to deliver a body blow to political action of teacher organizations seeking federal collective bargaining legislation. Teachers, whether they consider themselves professionals or not, are employees of state and local governments, and a 1974 lawsuit instituted by the National League of Cities, 19 states, the National Governors Conference, and several local governments asked the High Court to void a 1974 federal statute applying federal wage-and-hour requirements to state and local personnel practices. (The statute in question was based in part on a 1968 Supreme Court decision which the 1976 Court majority said was wrong.) The vote was 5–4 on behalf of state "sovereignty."

The decision—*National League of Cities* v. *Usery*—came 18 months after Chief Justice Warren Burger had first issued a temporary order delaying implementation of the 1974 statute. Leaders of the AFT, NEA, AFSCME, and other public sector unions realized early that the decision might well be 5–4, but they didn't know which way the Court majority would lean. Furthermore, in early 1975 the strong possibility of a federal bargaining statute made the court threat less important, somehow. But the combination of losing a chance at a bargaining statute politically and "permanent" denial of a statute by the Supreme Court left organized teacher leadership in Washington totally frustrated and angry by late 1976. The Court's implied denial of federal interstate commerce authority to regulate public employee working conditions is even more significant for American education politics than was the 1973 Supreme Court decision (*Rodriguez* v. *San Antonio Independent School District et al.*) on school finance reform, also settled by a 5–4 vote.

One slim ray of hope remains at the federal level; it emanates from the fact that a state's "sovereignty"—however superior it is to federal interstate commerce powers—is vulnerable to federal money. As long as local schools and state agencies accept federal support, the NEA and AFT argument goes, a requirement that they allow their employees to bargain collectively can be a condition of their getting federal dollars. If this strategy leads to yet another Supreme Court decision, the case of sovereignty versus bribery should yield some interesting law.

Also victimized by the *Usery* decision are elected state officials, notably legislators, who must bear the brunt of teacher political action aimed at new or improved state bargaining laws. Although more than two dozen states have collective bargaining statutes of some kind, none matches the provisions in the proposed federal measure, which would have applied private sector bargaining procedures to the public sector through extension of the National Labor Relations Act. Blocked politically and judicially from securing a federal statute, the NEA and AFT must now hammer away incessantly at state lawmakers. NEA President Ryor said in July, after hearing of the High Court's action, that approximately $500,000 for federal-level lobbying expenses on behalf of a federal bill would probably be diverted to state-level political arenas. The AFT's Shanker, whose constituents tend to be city dwellers tied closely to congressional Democratic politics, acknowledged the need for state laws, but correctly predicted that "for many states this will be impossible for years to come." [15]

NOTES

1. *Washington Post,* April 9, 1976.
2. "Bulletin on the San Francisco Public Schools Commission," San Francisco Center for Public Education, February 20, 1976.
3. *Washington Post,* March 20, 1976.
4. Lieutenant Governor Wayne G. Sanstead of North Dakota, "From the Classroom and into Politics," *State Government,* Winter, 1975, p. 15.
5. Jo Ann Krueger, "The Politics of School Finance: New Mexico Passes a State Funding Formula," *Journal of Education Finance,* Summer, 1975.
6. *California Journal,* February 1975, p. 65.
7. *California Journal,* January, 1976, p. 17.
8. Interview, January 9, 1973, reported in *State Policy Making for Public Schools of Michigan,* one of 12 state case studies in the Educational Governance Project, Ohio State University, Roald Campbell and Tim Mazoni, eds., June, 1974, p. 67.
9. Minnesota Education Association *Advocate,* January 23, 1976.
10. Donald J. Noone, *Teachers vs. School Board* (New Brunswick, N.J.: Rutgers University, 1970). A case study of the struggle for exclusive representation between NEA and AFT local affiliates, won by the latter.
11. *Educators Serving in State Legislatures* (Washington, D.C.: National Council of State Education Associations, 1975), p. 79.
12. *The Role of Politics in Local Labor Relations* (Washington, D.C.: Labor Management Relations Service, 1973), pp. 7, 8.
13. *New York Times,* June 29, 1976.
14. Ralph de Toledano, *Let Our Cities Burn* (New Rochelle, N.Y.: Arlington House, 1975), p. 79.
15. *Chronicle of Higher Education,* July 6, 1976.

Reading 23

White Flight and School Resegregation: Some Hypotheses

Robert G. Wegmann

As the recent debate between James Coleman and his critics has made clear,* desegregated schools exist within a multitude of
contexts, and each of these contexts influences what does or does not happen in the
school. There is an ongoing process of suburbanization which surely would have occurred if there were no racial minorities, but
which in fact disproportionately involves
the white middle class. There has been a
major downturn in white birthrates which
is now causing, in most school districts, a
loss of white enrollment quite unconnected
with desegregation. Longitudinal studies of
school desegregation are complicated by
the fact that school attendance areas and
school district boundaries change over time.
Comparisons with city census data can be

* James Coleman, "Racial Segregation in the Schools:
New Research with New Policy Implications," Phi
Delta Kappan, October, 1975, pp. 75–78; Robert
Green and Thomas Pettigrew, "Urban Desegregation
and White Flight: A Response to Coleman," Phi
Delta Kappan, February, 1976, pp. 399–402.
Source: Robert G. Wegmann, "White Flight and
School Resegregation: Some Hypotheses." Phi Delta
Kappan vol. 58, no. 5 (January 1977), pp. 389–393. Re-
printed with permission.

difficult because many school systems have
boundaries not conterminous with city
boundaries. Further, there are minority
groups other than blacks in most school
systems. Some authors add these other minority students to the white population
when analyzing white flight, others do not.
Despite these problems, the available research on white withdrawal from desegregated schools does reveal some reasonably
clear patterns.

Two Initial Distinctions

Before examining these patterns, however,
it is particularly important to note the degree to which issues of race and class are
consistently confounded when studying
school resegregation. Blacks and most other
minority groups are, of course, disproportionately poor. The poor do not do well in
school, and schools where the poor are
concentrated are no more attractive to
minority-group parents (especially middle-
class minority parents) than they are to
white parents. The schools in communities
such as Richmond, Virginia, are reported to

be experiencing "black flight" as they become increasingly black and poor; they are just as unattractive to the black middle class as to the white middle class. Similarly, some 10,000 black students in Washington, D.C., are in private schools. What is often called "white flight" is, in fact, a class phenomenon as well as a racial phenomenon.

Further, it is useful to make a distinction between withdrawal and nonentrance. The phrase "white flight" tends to suggest that white students were attending a school, the school was integrated, and then white students found this undesirable and left. In fact, reported drops in white attendance in the first year of school desegregation really refer to students who never showed up at all. It wasn't that they experienced desegregation and found it undesirable; rather, they declined to try the experience in the first place. Some of this decline in white enrollment may consist of students who formerly attended a given school; but part may also consist of students who, in the absence of school integration, would have moved into a neighborhood but now have not done so.

In addition to nonentrance into the neighborhood served by a particular set of schools (elementary and secondary), there is also the issue of nonentrance into a particular school. Schools are particularly susceptible to nonentrance, not only because there are private and parochial alternatives but because the transition from elementary school to junior high, and from junior high to senior high (each school often serving a wider attendance area and having a different reputation and racial composition), repeatedly presents parents and students with the decision to enter or not enter.

Issues of Quality, Safety, and Status

Surprisingly, little research seems to be available on the motives that lead parents to avoid desegregated schools. Such discussions as are found center on three areas: parental perceptions of school quality, parental perceptions of student safety in the desegregated school, and parental concerns about social status. In view of the very limited data, however, any conclusions about the relative importance of these concerns (or their actual impact on the decision to withdraw from a desegregated school) must remain very tentative.

Neil Sullivan, the superintendent of schools who presided over the desegregation of the Berkeley (California) public schools, describes the main fears of white parents when school desegregation is proposed as fear for their children's safety and fear that educational quality will be lost. Concerns about educational quality do seem widespread; national polls show that a fourth of the public believes that the test scores of white students decline sharply in desegregated schools. Although such declines do *not* generally occur, the quality of research in this area leaves much to be desired.

Parental perceptions of student safety may also be involved in decisions to reject desegregated schooling. Black and white students bring differing perceptions of each other to the desegregated school. They may exhibit different behavior patterns and ways of handling conflict and hostility. Rumors can fly as latent parental fears are triggered by incidents which would otherwise be ignored. In some cases, of course, inner-city schools in our major cities are *not* safe, and physical attacks, shakedowns, and threats are real occurrences. What seems to be involved in some of these situations is the fact that, though desegregated, these schools are not truly integrated. Though black and white students are physically present in the same school, the degree of friendship, understanding, and community can be very slow.

Finally, just as some individuals do not wish to live in a neighborhood with members of a group whose social status they view as below their own, some parents who do not have specific concerns about educational quality or safety as such may still object to having their children attend school with students from a lower social class. Desegregation generally brings not only an influx of black children into the white child's environment, but also an influx of lower-class children into a middle-class environment.

Although parental concerns about educational quality, safety, and status may be present no matter how the desegregated situation comes about, the available evidence suggests considerable differences in the likelihood of a school's resegregating and the process by which this may occur, depending on whether the racial mix in the school is a reflection of the neighborhood served by the school or whether some level of government has intervened to bring about school desegregation quite apart from the situation in the surrounding neighborhood. The resulting racial and class conflicts as well as patterns of flight and nonentrance (should these occur) can work themselves out in markedly different ways.

I. NEIGHBORHOODS AND SCHOOLS IN RACIAL TRANSITION

Atlanta has been judicially cited as having a great deal of white flight from its school system, so much as to render further attempts at integration futile. The system, once majority white, was 69% minority by 1970. The minority population of the city as a whole, however, also went from 38% minority in 1960 to 52% in 1970. (It is routinely the case that the proportion black in a city's school system is well ahead of the proportion black in the general population.) Hence the change in the racial make-up of Atlanta's public schools took place within the context of a general change in the racial make-up of the entire city (witness the fact, for example, that Atlanta now has a black mayor). Indeed, all of Coleman's findings as he *initially* presented them must be considered to have happened within the context of the changing neighborhoods of large central cities, since a check by the *New York Times* revealed that there was no court-ordered busing, redistricting, or other "forced" integration in any of the 19 cities initially studied.

These changes in central-city racial balance are of considerable magnitude. According to the U.S. Commission on Civil Rights, enrollment in the 100 largest school districts (which have half of the nation's black pupils) dropped by 280,000 students between 1970 and 1972. Since there was a gain of 146,000 black students during this same period, the data suggest a very considerable loss of white students. Some of this loss, of course, can be attributed to a drop in the white birthrate and to other factors. Nonetheless, it is clear that whites with children are disproportionately likely to live in suburban areas. According to the U.S. Census Bureau, 60.1% of the white population (age 18 and over) of metropolitan areas lived in the suburbs in 1974; but 66.6% of the school-age whites (ages 5 to 17) were to be found in suburbs. Note that this is the opposite of what one might expect, since the poor are more likely to live in the city, and are also more likely to have large families. Of course, this situation need not be totally attributed to problems with schools; suburbanization would no doubt be going on if there were no racial minorities in the U.S., and suburbs hold special attractions for families with school-age children for other reasons. The data suggest, however, that schools do play a part.

The most obvious fact about the neighborhood context of school racial proportions is the very high degree of residential segregation that characterizes every U.S. city; there are only a few stable interracial neighborhoods in American cities. Some of this segregation is due, of course, to differences in income level, but rather convincing data show that economic factors account for only a small part of the concentration of blacks in the central city. According to the Census Bureau, blacks constituted only 5% of suburban populations in both 1970 and 1974, despite the fact that a majority of metropolitan residents now live in the suburbs rather than the central city.

Thus while it is important to understand how the process of school and neighborhood resegration proceeds, it is initially necessary to point out that one fundamental fact cannot be ignored: Given constant density, a growing minority population staying within the central city will inevitably produce an increasing number of segregated neighborhoods and segregated schools.

Interracial neighborhoods are commonly found on the fringes of the black ghetto. What is striking as one reviews studies of the process of racial transition in these areas is the degree to which white *nonentrance* is much more involved than white flight as such. This is not to deny that some individuals move from racially changing neighborhoods specifically to avoid an interracial setting. The fundamental pattern, however, seems to be one of blacks moving short distances into racially mixed neighborhoods, while whites fail to compete with them for the available housing. One study in Milwaukee found that only 4% of a sample of black movers selected housing more than 10 blocks beyond the original ghetto neighborhood. At the same time, beyond 30% black occupancy, the number of new white housing purchases fell off sharply. Other data indicate that this is a common pattern;

neighborhood racial change apparently is less a matter of invasion than of retreat. So long as blacks seek to occupy housing on the fringes of the ghetto while whites avoid it, racial change is inevitable. Such neighborhoods then go through a transition from a white to a black housing market.

The School and Neighborhood Change

The research on the school's role in the process of neighborhood change is sketchy, but suggests much. A study in Milwaukee found that in interracial neighborhoods the proportion of blacks within the school is consistently higher than the proportion of blacks within the school attendance area. And schools, like double beds, enforce a certain intimacy. One can ignore a neighbor down the street; it is harder to ignore someone sitting beside you in the classroom. The school, moreover, is a social institution which serves as the focal point for much community interaction.

Parents, students, and schools may or may not be ready for racial integration. To the extent that they are unprepared and fearful of racial change, the schools can become a focus of discontent. And the schools are, indeed, often unprepared and fearful of racial change. A study of riots and disruptions in public schools indicates that such disruptions are most likely to occur in schools with 6–25% minority population and lacking an integrated faculty—precisely the situation found in most urban schools as the neighborhoods they serve begin the process of racial transition.

The available research suggests that school and neighborhood have a reciprocal relationship, with the school seemingly more sensitive to racial transition. To consider what is happening to the racial make-up of the urban school outside the context of the racial make-up of its school attendance area and the changing racial proportions of the entire school district is to risk serious misunderstanding.

Any consideration of the "tipping point" controversy might most profitably occur within this framework. Various authors, including myself, have referred to a point where white departures accelerate or at least become irreversible, leading shortly to a neighborhood or school's becoming all black. References to this concept can be found in several school desegregation suits. A careful examination of racial change in Milwaukee's schools over the eight years for which data exist convinces me that, though there are occasional "surges" of white departures in individual schools in changing neighborhoods, the more common phenomenon seems to be a relatively steady pattern of black entrance combined with white departure and/or nonentrance. Schools do not "tip" by themselves. They resegregate because there is a growing black population which has to go *somewhere,* and which is being steered by a dual housing market to transitional neighborhoods; simultaneously, white buyers avoid these same neighborhoods, anticipating that they and the schools which serve them will shortly be resegregating. Thus it now seems to me that tipping is not a particularly useful concept to describe the changing racial proportions of schools, because it ignores the contexts within which resegregation takes place and tends to imply that there is no such thing as stable integration—which is not true.

Class Levels and Neighborhood Change

One additional variable which may be closely related to school resegregation is the social-class level of the white population in the changing neighborhood. One study in Detroit found that the moving-order of white households is markedly affected by family income, with the more prosperous families moving first; racial attitudes were irrelevant. Indeed, the disorders which have sometimes accompanied court-ordered busing seem to be concentrated in working- and lower-class areas, perhaps because these groups are more prone to physical expressions of their frustrations, and perhaps because, unlike the middle class, they cannot easily afford to move quietly away.

Taken as a whole, the research evidence indicates rather strongly that, so long as inmigration and natural increase provide a growing minority population, it is most unlikely that the process of school "desegregation" in these changing neighborhoods around the fringes of the inner city will be anything but a temporary situation. Without government intervention to provide a stable level of integration in these schools, and simultaneously to provide adequate, safe, and desirable living opportunities for minority citizens in areas other than those immediately surrounding the inner city, the process of resegregation cannot but continue. In some cases (such as Inglewood, California), this process has passed the boundary of the central city and is continuing on into the suburbs.

II. SCHOOL DESEGREGATION BY GOVERNMENTAL ACTION

The second broad type of school desegregation develops when the local school board, the executive branch of either federal or state government, or the courts intervene to bring about the desegregation of previously segregated schools. In the South this has occasionally meant changing from a dual to a unitary—but still neighborhood—school system, particularly in small towns. In many Southern towns of any size, however, as in many Northern areas, segregated neighborhoods are large enough so that students must be transported if school desegregation is to be accomplished.

School resegregation may or may not occur in such situations. White Plains, New York, which began busing students to desegregate its schools in 1964, did a follow-up study in 1970. White students were doing as well or better academically than before integration, black students were doing better, and there had been no white flight. Pasadena, California, on the other hand, recently completed a four-year follow-up study of its experience with school desegregation. Achievement levels of students throughout the district have dropped significantly. Simultaneously, white enrollment has declined precipitously, from 18,000 in 1969 to 11,000 in 1973. Although much of this wide variation in the consequences of school desegregation may be attributable to the particular characteristics of individual cities and school districts, there do seem to be some general patterns.

Racial Proportion and Class Effects

Studies dating back to the period immediately after the 1954 *Brown* decision indicate that resistance to desegregation is closely related to the proportion of black students in the schools. Just as resistance to school desegregation seems to mount as the proportion of black students increases, so apparently does the likelihood of some white withdrawal. There was less than a 1% additional decline in white enrollment after busing began in the 18%-black Kalamazoo (Michigan) school system, but an additional 4.7% decline in white enrollment in the 38%-black Pontiac school system. A similar relationship between the proportion of blacks and white flight in Mississippi has been reported, with particularly heavy withdrawal from majority-black schools. In Nashville the number of whites in one school declined from 560 to 268 when busing to a 40%-black inner-city school began; the white decline in a similar school was only 15% when students were to be bused to a school which was 20% black. (There was an additional factor, however; the former students were to be bused through high school, while the latter were to be bused only for one year.) In a major research project in Florida, the proportion of whites withdrawing to private schools was found to have a 30% black "threshold" beyond which white withdrawal increased, as well as a close connection to white family income.

The impact of the proportion of blacks on white withdrawal may not be only a matter of the proportion itself, but also of the difference in social-class level between black and white students. Memphis, Tennessee, and Jackson, Mississippi, for instance, are often cited as particularly striking examples of white withdrawal from desegregated schooling. Shortly after the Memphis busing order, white enrollment in public schools fell by 20,000, while the number in private schools rose by 14,000. Memphis lost 46% of its white public school students between 1970 and 1973. What is striking about white withdrawal from public schools in Memphis is that it occurred in a situation where the black school population was both large (54% even in 1968) and unusually poor. According to 1970 census data, 35.7% of black families in Memphis were below the poverty line, compared with only 5.7% of the nonblack families. By one estimate, Memphis is second among the major cities of the nation in poverty, with 80% of it found in the black ghetto.

A similar example can be found in the case of Jackson, Mississippi. The Jackson school system, 55% white before mid-year desegregation, lost 9,000 whites and dropped to 40% upon desegregation; 1,500 additional whites left in the following year, dropping the proportion of whites to 36%. Half of all the white pupils in Jackson now attend private schools. Here again is a combination of high proportion black and extreme poverty. According to recent census data, 27.3% of the black population in Jackson are high school graduates, compared to 77.5% of the nonblack population; and 40.3% of the black families are below the poverty line, compared to only 6.3% of the nonblack families.

Just as the social-class level of minority students involved in school integration may be important in determining the presence and extent of racial instability, so may the social-class level of the white students. One study of white withdrawal to private schooling in the Charlotte-Mecklenburg (North Carolina) school district found that income alone explained 54% of white abandonment of the public schools after integration. Thirteen new private schools have opened in Charlotte-Mecklenburg since the 1969 desegregation order. The Florida study already mentioned found that rejection rates for white students assigned to schools more than 30% black were 4% for low-income students, 7% for middle income, and 17% for high income. It is important to note that though such losses did not represent a very high percentage of the public school population (only 3.6% overall), they can deprive the public schools of a disproportionate number of students from the most affluent part of the community.

The available data suggest, then, that the proportion and social-class level of minority students, the social-class level of the white students, and the cost and availability of schooling alternatives are among the variables which may have a significant relationship to whether or how much white withdrawal may be expected to occur if there is government intervention to desegregate formerly segregated public schools.

III. CONCLUDING COMMENTS

The relationship of one aspect of desegregated schooling to white withdrawal has not, so far as I know, been formally investigated, yet it seems to me to be at the heart of the whole issue: To what extent is the racially mixed school truly integrated? Are the students merely physically co-present, or are they relating to one another in an environment of mutual understanding and respect?

Anyone who has spent any time in racially mixed schools, especially high schools, knows that students in these schools can be as distant from each other as if they were on separate planets. Blacks sit in one part of the cafeteria, whites in another; ditto in classrooms, assemblies, athletic events. Some social events may even be held separately. Indeed, there is evidence that school desegregation may actually *increase* feelings of racial identity. And yet, although a number of studies have investigated interracial attitudes in desegregated schools, the literature contains few reports of programs which foster interracial cooperation and understanding. Yet it should be obvious that schools were never organized to help people understand each other, and there is no evidence that bringing students from different racial, class, and neighborhood backgrounds into them will automatically lead to understanding, appreciation, and friendship. Though some good studies have been done on the relationships among interracial friendship, self-esteem, and academic accomplishment, almost nothing is available that could serve as a blueprint for the school administrator trying to decide what to do tomorrow in order to overcome the racial, class, and cultural gulfs that are so frequently a part of racially mixed education. The answer to this dilemma may contain the key not only to the control of white flight but to the survival of our national commitment to school integration.

Summary and Conclusions

The issue of white withdrawal from desegregated schools is an unusually complex one, and the research done to date has not been equal to the task of explaining all that is involved. Trying to understand this complicated phenomenon is much like trying to put together a giant, confusing jigsaw puzzle with many of the pieces missing. For almost every pattern there seems to be a contrary instance. The available research is characterized by many data gaps, unanswered questions, and unverified assumptions. Nonetheless, the following tentative conclusions seem justified:

1. Whites do not necessarily withdraw from desegregated schools. Some schools maintain a high level of integration for years, some change slowly, and some resegregate very rapidly. Others may experience some white withdrawal followed by stability, or even by white reentrance.

2. Racially mixed schools located in areas bordering the inner city present some markedly different patterns of resegregation from schools located in school districts which have experienced districtwide desegregation. It is important not to extrapolate from the one situation to the other.

3. In situations where there has been no governmental action to bring about desegregation, white withdrawal seems to be linked more than anything else to the underlying demographic consequences of increased minority population growth. This growth takes place primarily in neighborhoods located on the edge of the inner city, as area after area "turns" from black to white. The schools "turn" more quickly than the area generally, and play a significant role in making this process relatively rapid and apparently irreversible. Stable school integration seems to be a necessary if not sufficient precondition for stable neighborhood integration.

4. Decisions on where to purchase a home or where to send one's children to school are made not only on the basis of the present situation but on estimates of what is likely to happen in the future. The belief that presently integrated schools and neighborhoods will shortly resegregate is a major barrier to attracting whites to integrated settings.

5. Little formal research has been done on the motivations behind white withdrawal from desegregated schooling. Worries about the quality of education, student safety, and social-status differences may be among the chief causes. To the extent that this is true, it could be expected that, other things being equal, school integration would more likely be stable and successful when combined with programs of educational improvement, in settings where concerns about safety are adequately met, and when programs of which parents can be proud are featured.

6. School desegregation ordinarily creates situations which have the potential for both racial and class conflict. The degree of white withdrawal to be expected when there is governmental intervention to desegregate schools may vary, depending on the proportion of minority students who are being as-

signed to a given school and on the social-class gap between the minority and white students.

7. White withdrawal from desegregated schooling has widely varying costs in different settings. Moving to a nearby segregated suburb, moving outside a county school district, attending a parochial school, attending a private school, transferring to a segregated public school within the same system, or leaving the state are examples of options which may or may not be present in a given situation. Each of these options, if available, will have different costs for different families, just as families will have varying abilities to meet these costs. So long as school desegregation is feared (or experienced) as painful, threatening, or undesirable, it can be expected that the number of families fleeing the desegregated school will be proportionate to these costs and to their ability to pay these costs.

8. Although there is a certain degree of racial mixing in many public schools, there may also be a notable lack of cross-racial friendship, understanding, and acceptance. Superintendents in desegregated districts tend to describe racial relations as "calm" or characterized by few "incidents." Few claim that they have attained anything like genuine community, nor is there much indication that extensive efforts are being made toward this end.

Some Policy Implications

Given the incomplete nature of research on white withdrawal from desegregated schools, policy implications are perhaps better stated as personal opinion rather than as "proven" by the available research. The suggestions given below are so offered.

1. A thorough, national study of school desegregation is needed. Scattered case studies and sketchy national data are not enough. Unless the public schools of this country are going to continue to contribute heavily to the development of two societies, one white and one black, neither understanding nor trusting the other, white withdrawal from desegregated schools needs to be better understood—and avoided. It is significant that the available research is found in journals of law, political science, economics, education, geography, sociology, psychology, and urban affairs. Any such study would have to be a significantly interdisciplinary effort.

2. Although it may be true that government intervention to desegregate schools has in some instances precipitated white withdrawal, it is equally true that the lack of any positive government intervention in the so-called "changing neighborhoods" surrounding the inner city has been responsible for continuous and ongoing resegregation. In discussing problems of school desegregation in major metropolitan areas, it is desirable to separate the discussion of what to do about inner-city schools from the special problems of resegregating schools on the fringes of the ghetto. If the steady growth of the ghetto is to be arrested, it must be done in these areas. A comprehensive approach to fostering racially stable and integrated neighborhoods and schools would go a long way toward removing the present connection in the minds of many Americans between school desegregation and eventual resegregation.

3. Finally, there is a great need to emphasize the *quality* of school integration and to develop and communicate practical approaches to overcome the cultural and class barriers between the

races. The available evidence does not suggest that, if one can just get black and white students into the same building, the rest will take care of itself. It will not. School integration worthy of the name will only come about as the result of conscious, deliberate effort.

Reading 24

What Louisville Has Taught Us About Busing

Roger M. Williams

Nestled in a curve of the Ohio River, Louisville enjoys a reputation for bourbon whiskey, horse racing, and the gentlemanly life that supposedly accompanies them. In reality, Louisville is a pleasant but not very distinctive manufacturing town where urban blacks and suburban whites find jobs in large plants run by a number of industrial giants. It is also a unique racial testing ground—the only major city to undergo metropolitan-area-wide busing for the purpose of school desegregation.

Louisville has been carrying out "metro" busing since the fall of 1975, at first angrily and under the glare of national publicity, now resignedly and almost in private. While busing has continued to fester as an American social problem, few of its critics have bothered to look closely at the one city where it has been operating on the broadest scale. From Louisville's trauma-turned-success, from its lack of preparation and initial failures of nerve as well as from its ultimate determination to make the unworkable

work, comes a lesson in how even the most disruptive form of busing can produce better results than anyone dared predict.

The lesson bears many practical applications. Unless the U.S. Supreme Court unexpectedly declares busing unconstitutional, the school buses will continue to roll, most provocatively between black cities and white suburbs. Over the next two years, at least a dozen major cities face the start of "massive, forced" busing, as opponents like to call it.

Louisville and surrounding Jefferson County share little but location and economic interests. Louisville has grown up at a confluence of American cultures, a bridge length from Indiana and within easy reach of both the East and the Deep South. In racial attitudes, it has been basically border-state: slow to grant blacks their rights, but not intransigent. Although Jefferson County recently has been developed with tract houses and shopping centers, the values of rural Kentucky still prevail. Thousands of "country" whites have moved into the Louisville area in the past few decades to work at the industrial plants. Those who originally settled in Louisville proper soon moved out into

Source: Roger M. Williams, "What Louisville Has Taught Us About Busing." *Saturday Review* (April 10, 1977), pp. 6–10, 51. Reprinted with permission.

"the county" to avoid what they regarded as the black domination, if not ruin, of city life. By 1975, the student population of Louisville's public schools was 54 percent black, compared with 4 percent in Jefferson County.

In applying cross-district busing to Louisville, the U.S. Sixth District Court of Appeals, in Cincinnati, reached for a remedy that the Supreme Court already had rejected for Detroit and Richmond. It did so because it found in Louisville a pattern of interdistrict actions that had the effect of maintaining segregated schools.

On July 30, 1975, a federal district court, implementing the appellate court's decision, ordered the city and county to desegregate their schools jointly by transporting students across the lines dividing the respective districts. Under the court order, about one-sixth of the two districts' 121,000 students would be bused in order to achieve an enrollment that would be 12 to 40 percent black in every school. To strike such a balance, blacks would have to be bused for eight or nine of their school years; whites, for one or two.

Complicating the situation was the fact that only four months earlier Kentucky had ordered the two school systems to merge. The city system had pressed for merger because it was sinking ever deeper into debt; the county had resisted because merger would mean diluting the county's traditionally structured educational program as well as absorbing unwanted blacks and urban problems.

On the evening of September 5, 1975, the second day of the new school year, Jefferson County exploded with anti-busing emotions. At one suburban high school, a mob of 2,500 almost overwhelmed a contingent of county police; at another, a somewhat smaller mob broke into a bus compound and heavily damaged about 30 of the hated yellow symbols of "forced" busing. Some

50 persons were injured and nearby store windows were smashed before the police, reinforced by 1,000 National Guardsmen, gained control of the situation. Louisville found itself abruptly face-to-face with a community crisis—and with a violently racist image to rival that of Birmingham and Boston.

Although that degree of violence was never again approached in Louisville, the city remained in deep trouble throughout the fall of 1975. Anti-busing forces had seized the initiative, and some 30 organizations of Jefferson County whites demonstrated relentlessly against the court-ordered plan. They were joined by a large number of provocateurs; local groups such as the paramilitary Christian Posse Comitatus and the Ku Klux Klan; and such outsiders as the American Nazi Party, the John Birch Society, and distant elements of the Klan. Together they mounted a boycott of the schools and harassed those merchants and other businessmen who were not outspoken in their opposition to busing.

Louisville labor unions took the leadership of the anti-busing movement. Thousands of white rank-and-filers at such plants as General Electric, Ford, and International Harvester joined in the demonstrations and raised money—from union treasuries, it was later charged—for the cause. Almost every sizable union in the area joined in. Louisville's union ranks reportedly are laced with Klan members. Members or not, the workers seem to share many of the Klan's attitudes. A veteran observer of the union scene describes the typical Jefferson County rank-and-filer as "second-generation rural, not necessarily a red-neck but determined to stop things like busing from happening to him and his."

Louisville's business establishment at first was lulled by the Supreme Court's Detroit decision and later cowed by two-bit intimidation from the anti-busers. Business leaders let busing begin without preparing for the problems that were certain to follow. Then when retailers suffered broken windows and boycotts, they responded with a series of increasingly weak public statements that ended with a declaration of opposition to busing. Banks, major manufacturers, and other businesses exercised none of the leverage that is always at their disposal.

General Electric and Ford were particularly ineffective. Although large numbers of their white employees stayed away from work to protest the onset of busing, resulting in substantial losses in production, the plant managements took at most mild disciplinary action and avoided the busing issue entirely. The respective corporate headquarters did not intervene to help solve their Louisville problems, apparently for fear of alienating consumers.

Only the level-headedness and resolve of others in Louisville kept the city and its desegregation plan from being overwhelmed by the anti-busing pressures. Mayor Harvey I. Sloane banned downtown demonstrations, rode school buses in the tense days following the riots, and consistently called for peaceful compliance with the court order. The city and county police forces, although heavily white in composition, acted with professional impartiality to protect black students and to safeguard school property. County cops proved willing to arrest their unruly white neighbors, and local courts proved willing to punish them.

Despite his generally conservative record and his personal views, federal district judge James F. Gordon steadfastly carried out the appellate court's ruling that Louisville and Jefferson County had to share the burdens of desegregation. Blacks have long shown an extraordinary tolerance of white-racist oratory and activities, and they did so in Louisville. While whites carried "Nigger, Go Home" signs and threw missiles at buses carrying black children, black parents and teen-agers declined to retaliate. Young blacks even ignored a provocative gesture by the Christian Posse Comitatus, which at the height of the tension drove a procession of slogan-covered cars through the heart of the city's black West End.

While white students were prominent among the mobs that raised hell in the first days of busing, they soon left most of the violence and loud protests to parents and what a law-enforcement official describes as "hoodlums looking to take cheap shots at blacks and cops." There was little violence inside schools or on school grounds, and nobody was seriously hurt in the student confrontations that did occur. In general, Louisville again showed that young people left to themselves can accommodate social change better than their parents can.

Since the bitter fall of 1975, Louisville and Jefferson County have made remarkable progress toward full and peaceful implementation of the desegregation plan. They have done so without the massive disruptions predicted by opponents of busing. Despite a continuing boycott by antibusing organizations, school attendance quickly recovered from its initial drop-off; after only five weeks of classes it was up to 85 percent, and it has been nearly normal ever since. An increasing number of white students are volunteering to be bused for more than the required number of years so they don't have to leave schools they've come to like.

Statistics do show an increase in the number of racial incidents and student suspensions since busing began; the most significant recent flare-up involved fighting at several high schools, with the police called in to restore order at one of them. However, in two years no schools have had to be closed, even briefly, because of racial unrest. Some school officials acknowledge privately that the statistics on incidents are of questionable validity, and J. C. Cantrell, deputy superintendent of instruction, says that overall there is less of a discipline problem this school year than last.

Thus far there is no solid evidence of what has happened to the educational process—that is, whether students are learning more or learning less. Among independent observers interviewed, a majority expressed the belief that blacks' grades have improved slightly while whites' have changed little, if at all. Cantrell says the schools are "not able to do as much good teaching in an atmosphere conducive to learning"—a reference to disciplinary problems caused principally by black students—but adds, "We don't feel we've lost too much in the quality of education."

Especially significant is the fact that "white flight," dreaded in all cities under court-ordered busing and a depressing reality in many of them, is not a particular problem in Louisville. Both school districts were losing students well before merger, and busing has not accelerated the trend alarmingly. An obvious reason is that to avoid a "metro" desegregation plan, whites would have to move clear out of the county, far from jobs and friends, and few seem willing to do that. And unlike Memphis, which is now known ironically as the private school capital of the world, Louisville has experienced only a modest increase in the number of "segregation academies," all-white private schools hastily established in the aftermath of court-ordered busing.

Emerging from the confusion caused by the hurry-up merger, the school administration has developed a number of innovative programs to smooth the transition to a fully desegregated system. The school board recently approved plans to improve and expand a so-called alternative school system that had become little more than an 8:30–3:00 warehouse for its heavily black population of alleged misbehavers. Alternative schools at various levels will now offer vocational training and "transition classes"

aimed at helping their students reenter the regular system.

The most heartening single development has been the activity of a grass-roots discussion group, called Community for Educational Excellence, whose purpose is to talk over frankly the fears and problems of school desegregation. Forty members strong, the group includes officials of outspoken anti-busing organizations as well as representatives of the NAACP and Urban League. At the first meeting or two, the sides exchanged strong words, but they reached agreement on the overriding need—as their official statement put it—"to begin to resolve our differences and to work to find a peaceful means to achieve the best possible education" for local students. Says participant Robert DePrez, an International Harvester millwright who is an official of two national anti-busing organizations: "We're all looking for better ways to educate children, and if busing stopped tomorrow we'd still have to deal with the poor schools we have here."

The grass-roots group is important, too, because it was sponsored by the county's chief executive, Todd Hollenbach, who had played a mostly negative role in earlier stages of the busing controversy. A sure sign of the extent to which busing has been publicly accepted is that with only one exception, none of the candidates for office, not even those who came out of the anti-busing movement, is expected to make it a major issue in this year's local elections.

Demonstrations against busing have become sporadic and wholly peaceful. Local anti-busing groups have quietly disassociated themselves from the Christian Posse Comitatus and other zealots of the far Right. Jack Shore, former head of the powerful United Labor Against Busing, says that while he still believes busing "someday will be turned around," he no longer thinks demonstrations will accomplish that end. United

Labor Against Busing is now relying on lobbying and legal action, including a constitutional amendment.

Many problems remain for the new Jefferson County school district. These include an overly generous policy toward student transfers, which thwarts the purposes of desegregation; the demise of interscholastic sports at some high schools; a chronic inability to meet the special needs of troubled black students; and an impending loss of federal funds to aid the desegregation process, funds that may not be replaced by the predominantly conservative school board. The eight-member board currently includes only one black, but others may be added in upcoming elections that will increase its membership to twelve. The school administration remains burdened with an inordinate number of high titled and high salaried subalterns—promoted by both districts in a pre-merger spree—and with an uninspiring, budget-oriented superintendent.

At a Washington meeting last year, some 30 civil rights attorneys, policy analysts, and community leaders discussed the state of American race relations. The director of the Southern Regional Council, Peter Petkas, who attended the meeting, recalls: "Not more than six or seven of the group spoke positively about school desegregation, let alone busing, and all of them were white professional people. The blacks and Chicanos took the attitude that desegregation is no longer a top priority."

While that may be ironic as well as disturbing news to advocates of school desegregation, it is not likely to slow desegregation efforts or to make busing a less controversial issue. American society must finish righting a century of racial wrongs, and the public schools should play a key role in the process. If racial balance in schools is desirable, busing remains the only sure means of producing it. "Magnet" schools will draw middle-class, well-motivated blacks, but not poor blacks; integrated residential neighborhoods, which would permit integrated neighborhood schools, may be the ultimate solution, but they are somewhere in the future.

Busing is here today, and Louisville's cross-district plan can fairly be considered its severest test. That such a plan has been carried out, amid fading public protests and normal school activity, is cause for modest optimism about the future of American race relations and education.

Public Aid to Religious Schools: What the Supreme Court Said—and Didn't Say

M. Chester Nolte

Will the recent U.S. Supreme Court decision —*Wolman* v. *Walter*—on state aid to parochial schools divert needed money from the public schools to private, religious schools? Perhaps—the answer probably depends on your state legislature.

Under the pressure of deadlines, some reporters and editorial writers, noting that the high court, in its *Wolman* ruling, had upheld four parts of Ohio's parochiaid law and struck down two parts, gave the impression that the final tally was parochiaiders 4, separationists 2. The situation was complicated further when both sides immediately claimed victory: Parochiaiders on the grounds that four kinds of state aid to nonpublic schools now are permitted; Separationists claiming they had won at least a moral victory if not indeed all the marbles. The problem, of course, is that John Q. Public quickly became confused on what the Supreme Court had ruled, and it appears that this understandable confusion also may afflict school people.

The issue of state aid to church-supported schools is complex to say the least. For 30 years, the Supreme Court has attempted to come up with fair and workable guidelines for parochial schools. As the pendulum of legislative opinion swung from side to side, the court vacillated from allowing states to provide textbooks and busing (using what now is called the "child benefit" theory) over to complete blockage of any form of state aid to parochial schools as simply "too entangling." It is understandable, then, that school people may have a hard time understanding why in this most recent case the Supreme Court allowed four kinds of state aid to parochial schools but knocked down two others. Even some of the justices agree that the matter is confusing. Wrote Justice Powell in this case: "Our decisions in this troubled area draw lines that often seem arbitrary." The dazed school person can only question in reply: "If even the Supreme Court justices don't quite know what they're doing, how can school districts be consis-

Source: M. Chester Nolte, "Public Aid to Religious Schools: What the Supreme Court Said—And Didn't Say." *American School Board Journal* vol. 165, no. 1 (January 1978), pp. 35, 45. Reprinted with permission from the American School Board Journal, January 1978. Copyright 1978, National School Boards Association. All rights reserved.

tent in providing tax moneys for private and parochial schools?"

In the course of its gyrations, however, the high court has made some discernible progress in deciding just how far a state may go in providing financial aid to parochial schools. The yardstick is now a test composed of three questions: (1) Does the law in question meet a valid secular (as opposed to religious) purpose? (2) Does the law either advance or inhibit religion? (3) Does the law create an excessive governmental entanglement with religion?

It was this three-way test that the Court applied to the Ohio law that originally permitted half a dozen kinds of state financial assistance to 720 nonpublic schools in that state. While the three-question yardstick represents an improvement in deciding which state plans are acceptable, the *Wolman* decision still divided the justices.

At one extreme was Justice Brennan, who said that the entire Ohio statute is unconstitutional. At the other extreme were Chief Justice Berger and Justices White and Rehnquist, who declared *all six* forms of aid to be constitutional. In between were Justice Stevens, who opposed everything but the law's health services provision; Marshall, who supported only the section providing diagnostic services; Powell, who liked everything except equipment loans for parochial schools; and Blackmun and Stewart, who upheld four provisions and disapproved of two.

Let's look at the first yardstick question: *Does the law in question meet a valid secular purpose?* Over the years, the Supreme Court has recognized that parochial schools serve an important secular purpose in teaching citizens nonreligious subjects such as reading, writing, English, and arithmetic. So long as religious entanglement has been avoided, the court has tried to support nonpublic schools for performing this important state service. Using this logic, the court approved Ohio's law in four areas: (1) loaning of textbooks to parochial schools; (2) administering standardized tests to parochial school students; (3) helping with the treatment of speech and hearing problems, and (4) taking care of students' dental needs. These are all "secular" objectives, for which tax moneys may legally be used, the court ruled.

Two forms of state aid, however, were knocked down: (1) spending state money for instructional materials and equipment, and (2) permitting parochial school students to take field trips to museums and other points of interest at public expense. Not enough justices felt these provisions were worth the risk of possible entanglement, and some justices even argued that it would advance religion in some form if these provisions were allowed to stand. But this rationale is difficult to follow. It requires a certain amount of tolerance to understand why the court okayed textbooks lent to students in parochial schools and then turned around and insisted that supplying instructional materials and equipment would violate the Constitution. Perhaps the court will clear up this confusion in cases yet to be decided.

The court's second yardstick question relates to whether parochial schools will be hindered or advanced by a given state law. *Does the law either advance or inhibit religion?* is the question. It is easy enough for well-intentioned individuals to split hairs over this one. In all six provisions of Ohio state aid law, the justices conceded they were "just supposing" situations in which state aid might help nonpublic schools to transmit "ideological views" to pupils. Basing its decision on previous cases decided in the past seven years, the Supreme Court said the state may provide nonpublic school pupils with books, standardized testing and scoring, diagnostic services, and therapeutic and remedial services—all without offending the Constitution by "advancing" religion. But the state may *not* provide instructional materials, equipment or field trip services without advancing the interests of the religious supporters of the schools in question. (See what I mean about hair-splitting?)

The third yardstick question posed by the court: *Does the law promote an excessive entanglement of the government with religion?* In earlier cases, the court struck down some forms of state aid to parochial schools on the grounds that an unfeasibly extensive degree of auditing would be required to make sure that none of the state money was used for religious, rather than secular, purposes. The state, understandably, is interested in seeing that state money given directly or indirectly to parochial schools (or public schools, for that matter) is used for the purposes intended by the legislature. Apparently, the high court reasoned in *Wolman* that some provisions of the Ohio law (those upheld) were simple enough to monitor or important enough to be worth the effort entailed in monitoring, while others (those struck down) would entail auditing so extensive as to amount to an entanglement with religion.

The new ruling will help some states seeking to aid church-related schools, hinder others, and in most states will make little immediate difference at all. In states such as Ohio and Pennsylvania, where the legislatures tend to be sympathetic to those parents who wish alternative educations for their children, the ruling could mean that millions of dollars of services soon will become available to parochial school children.

Clearly, no definitive answer has yet been found to the dilemma of helping parochial schools while remaining within the bounds of the Constitution, and the Supreme Court has not assumed it issued one in *Wolman*. Saying that Ohio may loan a textbook but not a science kit to a child in a parochial school seems a murky position at best. Furthermore, such a ruling seems to discriminate against one of the state's citizens —in this case a child—as well as against his parent who pays taxes to the public school treasury. While the high court has opened the door a little on the concept of using state tax funds to support those valuable services parochial schools provide, it may also have gone out on a limb in doing so— those "just supposes" about advancing religion notwithstanding.

Reading 26

Women, Equality, and the Public High School

Bea Mayes

As a gatekeeper in the institutional web of our country, the high school is in a position to shape the expectations and choices of the students. Equality of individuals is one of the basic teachings of the high school. Does the public high school in its operation demonstrate equality between men and women? Recent changes in women's lives have been dramatic. In disregard of the consequences, the high school continues to demonstrate a sexist orientation in its organization and in the differential treatment accorded students. Recent federal legislation required school systems receiving federal monies to set up means of complying with federal regulations by October 21, 1975 and to complete a self-evaluation on sex discriminatory practices by July 21, 1976.

Fifteen million students attend high school in grades nine through twelve. Ninety-three percent of young people fourteen to seventeen years old go to publ and non-public schools. As many as 1.5 million young women and 1.5 million young

Source: Bea Mayes, "Women, Equality, and the Public High School." *Education* vol. 97, no. 4 (Summer 1977), pp. 330–335. Reprinted with permission.

men were graduated from American high schools during 1971–72. Nearly all 14 and 15 year olds, and 89% of 16 and 17 year olds are in school. High school attendance is expected, encouraged, and compelled. As a result the high school influences nearly all young people.

The Role of the High School in Society

A growing body of data describes differences in treatment given young women as opposed to young men. Differential treatment of young men and young women becomes more rigid and obvious as students approach the time when they will take up adult roles. The practice of differential treatment and expectations on the basis of sex is pervasive.

Sexism, as Amundsen (1971) points out, "is, as are all systems that maintain relationships of dominance and subordination, *institutionalized.*" It is "implanted and perpetrated by institutions centrally located in the political socialization process. . . . It has an *interest structure* that provides the underlying rationale and dynamic for the on-going process." Controls and discriminatory patterns are maintained through legal codes and, or, institutionalized behavior. They are so well entrenched that the people involved often are not conscious of operating in a sexist manner. However, as Amundsen notes, "In a democracy, sooner or later one has to conform with the basic principle of equality under the law."

The high school is a gatekeeper in the in-stitutional web of our country. It is therefore likely that the high school will implant and perpetrate the sexist dichotomy. Since the high school is an instrument of society and reflects its patterns, it follows that in twen-tieth century America the high school will be an instrument of sexist indoctrination and will channel young people into sex-prescribed roles.

Can it be true that in egalitarian American democracy the highest and most demanding school that all students attend inculcates sexist beliefs? Is it true that the education system instills in young women ideas of sub-ordination to men, beliefs in their own in-capacity, and a disposition toward passivity and non-participation? If so, such ideas are a direct contradiction to the expressed teachings of the high school. These teach-ings include a profound belief in equality among people and in their right to freedom, justice, and fair opportunity. Indeed, it may be said that high school curriculums center on the American value of equality. High school teachers set forth democratic heri-tage, describe the foundations of equality in American history, and reiterate Ameri-cans' beliefs in the rights of individuals. Not only do high school teachers teach about equality, but they also have the opportunity to demonstrate equality. So, if there is a conflict between the high school's espoused values of equality and its demonstrated treatment of men and women, then objec-tive data must reflect the incongruence.

Do the schools give the same treatment to young women students as they do to young men? Does the environment and structure of the school exemplify equality between men and women? Or do the data show that neither the hierarchical structure of the school nor the treatment accorded students demonstrates equality among women and men? Should it be shown that behavior pat-terns demonstrated in the high school dis-criminate against women, the consequences become increasingly vicious in light of re-cent changes in the conditions of life.

Consequences of Sexist Practices in Employment

Let us take a look at some data about women in our society. Not only do large numbers of women support or contribute to the support of their families, but the life ex-pectation of women has changed dramati-cally. Women are no longer primarily homemakers. Nearly 35 million women are part of the work force (U.S. Department of Labor, 1974 (a), 1974 (b), 1971). They con-stitute more than 42 percent of all full time workers. Nearly half of these women are working because of pressing economic need.

Even with a break in employment, the average woman has a work life expectancy of 25 years. The single woman averages 45 years in the work force. More than half of all women between 18 and 64 years of age are in the labor force. Half of these women who work full time earned less than $6,000 in 1973. The women's median income is 57.9% of the median earnings of fully employed men, $10,195. Women who work at full time jobs the year round on the average earn only $3 for every $5 earned by similarly employed men.

Almost 3 out of 5 women workers are married and living with their husband. Almost 2 out of 5 have children under 18 years of age. The 13 million working mothers have 26.2 million children among them. Six million of these children are under age 6.

Perhaps the most compelling statistics concern women who are raising families on their own and who are designated head of the family. Over 8 million children under 18 are members of families headed by women who are alone and who are the main support of their family (Weddman and Whitmore, 1973). Families headed by women workers (no husband present) had a median income of only $5,750 in 1972. In families headed by women who were not in the work force, including many who were on welfare, income was $3,495.

The corresponding family incomes for husband-and-wife families with children are $13,840 and $12,120, respectively. Nine million children, 14% of all children, are in families designated in 1972 as poor. Of the children in families where only the mother is present 54% are poor. Only 8% of the children in two-parent families are poor.

It seems clear that when women are widowed, divorced, or separated and must bear the burden of raising children alone, they must not only provide care for and be responsible for the youngsters, but they must do so on a comparatively meager income. As compared with children in a two-parent family, children in a family headed by a woman are six times more likely to be poor.

The data show that women do not, and have not, enjoyed the exclusive and protected position presumed to be theirs. At least half the women in this country have to work outside their homes for the larger portion of their lives. Amundsen notes in a comprehensive survey of the condition and status of women in America that the condition of being a woman has changed.

While a woman was once likely to spend a good part of her adult life employed in the breeding and rearing of children and their orderly induction into society, improved standards of living have led to a life expectancy of some 76 years for women in America. At age 30 most women have borne their last child. At age 35 all of their children are in school.

The implications of this change cannot be over estimated. When women are freed of the need to constantly watch and care for their children during the daytime hours, they have at least 35 active adult years to look forward to! Add to this change in freedom due to cultural changes the development and wide availability of oral contraceptives. These changes mean that for the first time in history women can choose when, how often, and if they want to become mothers. Cultural and technological advances have radically changed women's lives. For most women economic necessity dictates how they will use the newly found years that are theirs. The data show that most—more than two-thirds of American homemakers—join the job market later in life. What is more, these women almost always lack decent preparation for their new roles in the labor force.

Sexism in the Public Schools

As changes in economics, technology, and longevity are bringing more women into the job market, it is incumbent upon the schools to take cognizance. Women deserve decent preparation for the work they will undertake. They deserve the opportunity to make full use of their abilities. John Stuart Mills' pivotal questions are equally appropriate to the teachings of the high school: "What sort of human beings can be formed under such a regime? What development can either their thinking or active faculties attain under it?" When the high school prepares women for a protected future that does not exist and fails to prepare women for full partnership in the wage earning community, it is doing violence to the notion of equality of opportunity for all individuals. Furthermore, the continuance of sexist practices in public schools is illegal. The federal Title IX regulations of the 1972 Education Amendments were adopted by Congress July 21, 1975. These regulations prohibit sexist practices in public school admission requirements, employment practices, classroom composition, financial aid, extracurricular activities, and athletics. In many cases state regulations also prohibit sexist practices in other areas of education.

The practice of reserving for women those jobs and duties rated by the culture as low in status and pay fails to recognize the changes in the life conditions of women. It perpetuates a culture of poverty for certain groups of citizens, and violates the American belief in equality of individuals. If indeed the high school prepares women for a future that for more than two-thirds of them does not exist, then one must look at the mechanisms by which the high school imposes acceptance of such damaging practices.

One of these sexist mechanisms is the structure of the school itself. A second mechanism is the differential treatment accorded students within the school. Both these mechanisms concern institutional practices through which the school demonstrates its bias to students. Though in theory both offer the opportunity of demonstrating equal treatment of men and women, in practice there is discrimination.

Teaching is one profession into which women have made heavy inroads. Almost 7 out of 10 teachers are women. In elementary schools women compose 85% of the teaching staff. In high schools women constitute 46% of the teaching staff. (Women are only about half as likely to be high school teachers as they are to be elementary school teachers.) Yet women comprise only 20% of elementary principals and only 3% of high school principals. At top policy making levels women are even less evident. Of some 385 school superintendents in New Jersey only 3 are women. These three women supervise elementary school districts. No woman supervises a district that includes high school students (Walker, n.d. and Citizens' Advisory Council, 1972).

A survey of New Jersey school districts by Walker for New Jersey Women's Equity Action League (WEAL) showed that in 63 districts only 10% of the policy making administrators in 1973 were women. This was one year after federal legislation was enacted aimed at eliminating job discrimination against women. The survey showed that where there were women involved in school administration the women were at the bottom of the administrative ranks. Walker notes that 83% of the New Jersey students enrolled in programs granting an advanced degree in educational administration are male. Hence, the outlook for reversing the trend seems bleak.

Formally, salary differentials in teaching based on sex have been eliminated. Nonetheless, the high paying administrative positions go to men. In terms of salary, status and responsibility top level educational administration offers substantial rewards. It is absurd to think that most women, year after year, voluntarily turn their backs on this advancement. As in other job areas, the lot of women teachers is severely restricted in terms of social mobility. Not even 1% of the 14,379 school districts in the nation have women superintendents, only 7.5% have women deputy superintendents, and less than 3% have women assistant superintendents (Kampelman, 1973).

In the WEAL New Jersey survey women

"fared worst in regionalized high school districts and vocational schools where many had no women in any administrative policy making or supervisory role and few women teachers."

In summary, the point of these data is clear—the proportion of women in administration is far below expectation in a profession where women comprise 66% of school teaching staff. The number of women in policy making positions in public education dwindles to mere tokenism in a profession where women outnumber men by three to two. Neither the high school nor the school district demonstrates equality of women and men in hierarchical structure or in allocation of women and men to teaching positions throughout the grades. The message to students, both women and men, is one of marked difference between men and women in terms of status and power.

Furthermore, the data show that the high school does demonstrate inequality in its treatment of young men and women who are students. Sex differentiation persists in the student activities and the course work of the high school. Significantly, the girls' regular gym program in a typical high school demands little of girls, according to students. On the other hand, boys are continually urged to work hard. Gym is one of the few school classes that requires active physical participation, yet girls find that their involvement is minimal and demands are few. In addition, the non-academic activities of the high school continue to demonstrate sexist patterns. Most club activities seem to perpetuate dual-role realities for men and women.

Both the high school structure and the student program demonstrate a qualitative difference in the jobs and activities designated as women's as opposed to those designated as men's. Not only is the high school hierarchy overbalanced in terms of male participation, but the teaching staff of the high school is overbalanced in terms of men teachers when compared with other schools. The upper levels of school administration visibly demonstrate the lack of upward mobility of women. Clearly the demonstration by the high school of inequality among men and women is inappropriate to the times. It is especially inappropriate in an institution which centers its teachings upon American beliefs in equality among people.

Steps to Take for Improvement

For some teachers, especially girls' gym teachers, the direction is clear. Some girls certainly want a more demanding gym program. Aggressive competition in sports and overt prodding to physical exertion should be an accepted part of women's gym programs in the future. A strong, competent body, as we have been taught, is a foundation for future health and well being.

Teachers who are not gym instructors also have work to do. They can help students destroy the myths of sexist existence. Teachers and students can survey school practices, participate in consciousness raising activities, and be active in workshops in sexual stereotyping. Teachers can urge the school superintendent, the curriculum committee, or the teachers association or union to set up in-service courses for teachers and counselors. They can encourage both the district and the teachers association to set and follow through on goals for demonstrating equality in employment opportunity for women and men. Teachers can talk to principals, superintendents, and school boards about using resources such as the General Assistance Center at Teachers College, Columbia University; The Council on Interracial Books for Children, 1841 Broadway, New York City; and the New Jersey

State Board of Education program on Women's Equal Rights. Teachers can join and work with community groups whose purpose is to eliminate sexism.

As a final recourse, where nothing else works, teachers can take legal action. Any school system that is serious about eliminating inequality among students cannot adhere to sexist employment policies. When the school hierarchy demonstrates a sexist bias, it daily sets a sexist image and example before students. It tells them that sexism, rather than equality, is the order of things. Sensitive teachers should help bring about equality.

The federal Title IX regulations require all educational entities receiving financial assistance to have completed a self evaluation on sex discrimination practices by July 21, 1976. School systems were to have appointed a Title IX coordinator by October 21, 1975, and to have notified parents, adult students, and employees of the system's intent to comply with Title IX, and given them the name of the Title IX coordinator by October 21, 1975. Interested parents, students, and teachers can ask for this information from local school officials. In addition, parents, students, and teachers can ask the school administrator or Title IX coordinator some of the following questions:

- What percentage of the coordinator's time is devoted to Title IX?
- What percentage of girls and boys are in advanced math, science, economics, home economics, shop, language courses? How was the counseling process involved in the placement of students in classes?
- If interest inventories are given, do counselors use separate scoring methods and interpretation for girls and boys?
- Is financial assistance given to both sexes equally?
- Are work-study programs available on a non-discriminatory basis (who is training where)?
- What steps have been taken to sex-integrate physical education classes by July 21, 1976, for elementary students and July 21, 1978 for secondary students?
- Do girls and boys have comparable access to athletic facilities, equipment, publicity, and separate but equal locker rooms, toilet and shower facilities?
- Are students separated by sex in lines, academic games, helping assignments, e.g., library aides, audio visual aides?
- Do discipline and dress code requirements differ on the basis of sex?

The regional Offices for Civil Rights have been empowered to enforce Title IX. If some of the Title IX requirements have not been attended to, those interested can notify the appropriate regional office. A list of regional offices is available from the Public Information Office, Office for Civil Rights, HEW, Washington, D.C. 202001.

While eliminating sexism in employment is important to teachers, it is even more important to the school district since it affects not only employees but also the pattern of reality presented to students. Although there are other important facets of sexism in the high school, the realization of equality among women and men in (1) hiring and promotion practices, and (2) all phases of student participation will do a great deal to beneficially change the assumptions of all students.

It is up to teachers, parents, and students to refuse to allow the high school to reinforce dual-role sexist patterns which oppress women and limit them as human beings. It is up to the women and men who believe in equality to demonstrate their beliefs. It is up to all alert individuals to reexamine their assumptions and routines to be sure they are contributing to the realization of equality in the schools.

REFERENCES

Amundsen, Kirsten. *The Silenced Majority.* Englewood Cliffs, New Jersey, 1971.

Citizens' Advisory Council on the Status of Women. "Need for Studies of Sex Discrimination in Public Schools." Washington, D.C.: Citizens' Advisory Council on the Status of Women, 1972.

Kampelman, Maggie. "WEAL K–12 Education Kit." Washington, D.C.: Women's Equity Action League, Education Committee, 1973.

U.S. Department of Labor. "Fact Sheet on the Earnings Gap." Washington, D.C.: U.S. Department of Labor, Employment Standards Administration, Women's Bureau, December, 1971 (rev.).

————. "The Myth and the Reality." Washington, D.C.: Department of Labor, Employment Standards Administration, Women's Bureau, May, 1974 (a).

————. "Highlights of Women's Employment and Education." Washington, D.C.: U.S. Department of Labor, Employment Standards Administration, Women's Bureau, June, 1974 (b).

Walker, Lenore. "Women's Rights in Education: The Study of Sex Discrimination in the New Jersey Public Schools," *NJEA Instruction.* Trenton, New Jersey Education Association, n.d.

Weddman, Elizabeth, and Whitmore, Robert. "Children of Working Mothers." *Monthly Labor Review,* May, 1974, 50–58.

Guaranteeing 14th Amendment Rights to All Children

George H. Schauer

No state shall make or enforce any law which shall abridge the privileges or immunities of citizens of the United States. This statement from the 14th Amendment to the United States Constitution has been put to the test by concerned parents and citizens. The right abridged has been the privilege of attending public school by certain handicapped children. This article surveys the major landmarks which record the slow progress of American education in correcting these injustices. Generally the courts have been responsive in guaranteeing 14th Amendment rights to all children, regardless of background or handicap.

All persons born or naturalized in the United States, and subject to the jurisdiction thereof, are citizens of the United States and of the State wherein they reside. No State shall make or enforce any law which shall abridge the privileges or immunities of citizens of the United States; nor shall any State deprive any person of life, liberty, or

Source: George H. Schauer, "Guaranteeing 14th Amendment Rights to All Children." *Education* vol. 97, no. 3 (Spring 1977), pp. 233–235. Reprinted with permission.

property, without due process of law; nor deny to any person within its jurisdiction the equal protection of the laws (Amendment XIV, Section I, United States Constitution).

Tracing the action of school boards and the courts from 1873–1950 Empress Young Zedler (5) in 1953 gave clear evidence that the guaranteed removal of "troublesome" children so that others in the public schools would not be disturbed by their presence dominated our nation's thinking until the mid-twenties. Gradually during this early period the privilege of an education became a right to an education.

Special classes were formed for exceptional children in many areas during this period. A class for the blind was begun in Chicago as early as 1900. Unfortunately the right to education and the good intentions of educators concerned for such exceptional children resulted in very inappropriate groupings and settings in the guise of special education. It is not too difficult for individuals in education today to look back a few years and recall the special education class in the attic, or the basement, or the small, condemned cement block building behind the elementary school. Hopefully this is forever in the past.

The late 1940s brought to the courts the case of an Iowa deaf child who had been misplaced as retarded before a proper class for that disability had been formed. The 1950 decision in favor of the plaintiff showed at least on paper and in the legal textbooks that an important precedent had been established. Education is not only a right, but that education should be appropriate to the needs of the individual child.

It is a sad commentary on American education that this worthwhile and widely espoused goal has not as yet become universal. It has only been during the past five to seven years that litigation has caused educators to grudgingly accede to the rights of an American child to an appropriate public education. Very much to the point in this light is Edwin W. Martin's (4) conviction that such an education for the handicapped is not charity, it is a fundamental right as a citizen of this great nation.

Landmark cases are at present hard to find. Most cases eventually settle out of court and cannot be used as the basis for legal precedents. Most of the out of court settlements have at least in the local sphere resulted in the desired reforms. Many cases just seem to hang unresolved in the judicial halls, but fortunately a few cases can be cited which are paving the way for a cherished goal to be realized (1, 2).

In 1967 in the Hanson vs. Hobson case in Washington, D.C. the track system was abolished as being racially imbalanced. The low track was the black track, and many black schools had no advanced track. It must be stated that Washington, D.C. officials did nothing about the court order, nor did anyone else, until the 1969 Smuck vs. Hobson appeal reaffirmed the earlier decision. Today no one mentions the term "track system," but in most schools grouping in various forms continues to perpetuate the sorting system. Kirp (3) refers to schools as the super-sorters. The noted management expert, Peter F. Drucker, in his treatise on "The High Cost of Low Productivity in Education" acknowledges the school's ability to sort out the bright kids from the dumb kids at the earliest possible time.

One of the best sorting methods is to administer intelligence tests. This produces "scientific" evidence that one is "bright, or dumb." It was the use of IQ tests that prompted the Spangler vs. Pasadena Board of Education decision that racial imbalance in the special education program was at least partially caused by IQ test administration. The use of alleged culturally and language inappropriate tests and the Pasadena decision have proven to be important factors in the severe restrictions placed on the use of IQ tests in public schools by the legislature in California.

Other cases have been important in recent years even though they either have been settled out of court, became moot because of earlier settlements, or are still languishing in the courts. They at least have brought public pressure to bear. All have involved the infringement and denial of the equal educational opportunities guaranteed by the 14th Amendment to the United States Constitution for minority groups and/or handicapped children.

According to the research of Burello, DeYoung and Lang (1, 2) these cases include Diana vs. Board of Education (California), Covarrubius vs. San Diego Unified School District, Stewart vs. Phillips (Boston, Mass.), Guadalupe vs. Tempe Elementary School District (Arizona), Arnold vs. Talmapais Unified High School District (California), Larry P. vs. Riles (California), and LeBank vs. Spears (New Orleans, Louisiana). In a case decided by the courts in Utah (Wolf case) the plaintiffs, parents of a twelve year old mentally retarded child and the parents of an eighteen year old mentally retarded son, were guaranteed that the Utah constitution guaranteeing the right to an education for all Utah children included their children.

A recent case, Mills vs. Board of Education, Washington, D.C., resulted in the excuse that money was lacking and appropriate programs could therefore not be provided. In an appeal the court refused to accept this response and indicated that with the money they had an equitable distribution was to be made in such a fashion that no child is totally excluded from the public schools. Of interest also is that in addition to the six children excluded who were plaintiffs in the case, Washington, D.C., was instructed to list all excluded children for the court.

In this writer's estimation the most influential decree in the history of special education was the 1971 Pennsylvania Association for Retarded Children (PARC) settlement in an eastern Pennsylvania federal district court. This, too, was an out of court settlement, but at least nineteen states have begun making provisions based on that settlement. It simply stated that in Pennsylvania all children up to the age of twenty-one had the right to be in public school.

Organizations with acronyms such as COMPILE and COMPET, as well as the governor's right to education committee, all sprang into action and literally "beat the bushes" in an effort to find 50,000 excluded children in the Commonwealth. The use of circulars in state liquor store packages, circulars mailed with state welfare checks, circulars given to each school child in the public schools to take home, radio and newspaper announcements, a toll-free telephone number, and even three regional exhaustive census efforts to check their effectiveness was indeed a tremendous effort.

There were problems. It all had to be done in four summer months with no extra personnel (especially school psychologists). The two Masters appointed to oversee the program did yeoman work despite having other full-time employment and being able to devote only two or three days per month to the job. Threats from the courts persuaded the Department of Public Welfare to join the effort. Unfortunately the state's largest city, likely due to the sheer volume of legwork and paperwork, resisted participation.

In all about 13,000 excluded children were found, but no clearing house type of central processing was established. Consequently no one knows in what types of programs these children became enrolled. Many of the children because of the pressure of time were not properly evaluated, a lot of old records were just brought up to date.

However, despite the shortcomings, one aspect of the PARC decree makes it a monumental precedent setter, the due process provision.

Parents, and local school districts, each have the right to due process hearings prior to special class placement of a child. The great advantage is for parents, as school records may be examined, legal counsel obtained, and school personnel quizzed on their reasons for wanting such a placement. If the hearing officer's decision proves unacceptable a process of appeal, first to the State Superintendent of Education, and then to the courts, is provided. Either side may initiate due process (parents or local school district), either side may appeal as well. Also, parents, at state expense, may secure an independent professional judgment concerning their child. Even with all of these safeguards no clear method of arbitration was outlined for hearing officers and to date only the individual's personal decision-making skills have served as a guide. However, the system seems to work, and other states are using it as a model.

If nothing else the history of the struggle to guarantee 14th Amendment rights to exceptional children proves that the National

Association for Retarded Children since its founding in 1950 has time and time again demonstrated through parents, and really not educators, a tremendous knack at public-school relations coupled with a willingness to resort to the courts for a redress of grievances. That this has worked to the advantage of exceptional children should serve to challenge the complacent educator.

NOTES

1. Burello, L. C., DeYoung, H. G., and Lang, D. A. *Exclusion and rights to education and treatment.* Ann Arbor: University of Michigan, The Institute for the Study of Mental Retardation and Related Disabilities and The University Council on Educational Administration, 1973.

2. Burello, L. C., DeYoung, H. G., and Lang, D. A. *Special education and litigation: implications for professional and educational practice.* Ann Arbor: University of Michigan, The Institute for the Study of Mental Retardation and Related Disabilities and The University Council on Educational Administration, 1973.

3. Kirp, D. L. The great sorting machine. *Phi Delta Kappan,* 1974, 55, 521–525.

4. Martin, E. W. Individualism and behaviorism as future trends in educating handicapped children. *Exceptional Children,* 1972, 38, 517–526.

5. Zedler, E. Y. Public opinion and public education for the exceptional child—court decisions 1873–1950. *Exceptional Children,* 1953, 19, 187–198

Reading 28

The Serrano Case: Policy for Education or for Public Finance?

John Pincus

In the past decade there has been much research and discussion of two inequities in American school finance—one about equal educational opportunity as defined by student need, the other about differences in tax base per pupil among different school districts within a state.[1]

These arguments were soon translated into court cases, which tried to show that existing public school finance systems, spending some $60 billion a year on the 44 million students in their charge, are unconstitutional. The first argument, which claimed that equal educational opportunity was denied when differences in the educational needs of pupils were ignored, did not fare well in court. The landmark case, *McInnis* v. *Ogilvie,* was affirmed by the U.S. Supreme Court in 1969.[2] The Court rejected the claim that the Illinois state school finance system was unconstitutional because school funds were not distributed on the basis of children's educational needs and therefore denied them equal opportunity.

Source: John Pincus, "The Serrano Case: Policy for Education or for Public Finance?" *Phi Delta Kappan* vol. 59, no. 3 (November 1977), pp. 173–179. Reprinted with permission.

Despite this defeat, such cases raised important issues that the second type of argument attempted to resolve. It claimed that current school finance systems violate the equal protection clause of the Fourteenth Amendment. Schools generally raise most of their money through local taxes on property wealth. Therefore the quality of a schoolchild's education, as measured by dollars spent, depends on his school district's wealth, not on that of the state as a whole. At any given school tax rate, and for any given number of students, a property-rich district raises more money than one that is property-poor. It was argued that school finance systems should be fiscally neutral and should reflect only the wealth of the state as a whole, not that of individual districts.[3] This argument was therefore different from that of the *McInnis* case. In effect, it defined "equal opportunity" as the opportunity for each district to make its spending decisions on the basis of equal per-pupil revenue for equal property tax rates.

In *Serrano* v. *Priest* (1971), the California Supreme Court accepted the fiscal neutrality theory, saying that the California school finance system was unconstitutional on equal protection grounds in part because of invidious discrimination against the poor child, the quality of whose education, like that of the rich, was a function of the wealth of his parents and neighbors. The case was then tried on the facts, and a decision was rendered in favor of the plaintiff (1974) ordering statewide equalization of school district claims on wealth per student by 1980. The California Supreme Court affirmed the trial court judgment in December, 1976.

The trial included a lengthy and inconclusive airing of the relationship between school finance equalization and equal educational opportunity as measured by improvement in standardized test scores. The plaintiffs argued that they were entitled to more spending in their districts because only in that way could they have an opportunity to benefit from public education—better results could not be guaranteed by anyone.

It seems to have been assumed in the trials that rich children predominated in rich districts and poor children in poor districts. The standard examples were high-wealth, low-tax districts inhabited by the wealthy, like Palo Alto or Beverly Hills, and high-tax, low-wealth districts inhabited by poor people, like Lucia Mar or Compton. But these were all small towns. In the big cities the situation was otherwise. San Francisco and Oakland were property-rich but had many poor children. San Diego was not property-rich but was mostly middle class.

It has been estimated that the 1974 *Serrano* decision, if the then existing state-local school finance pool of $5.3 billion had been redistributed equally, would have led to no net increase in the funds going to poor children. Of course, the argument for equal claims on wealth per student is easy to defend on grounds of fairness. But the "fiscal neutrality" doctrine was originally seen in part as another approach to the *McInnis* issue, which had to do with disadvantaged

students. It has instead developed into something entirely distinct, although not necessarily less important: equality for poor *districts*.

The U.S. Supreme Court, in narrowly rejecting a similar case, *San Antonio Independent School District* v. *Rodriguez* (1973),[4] in effect made this point by stating that there was no evidence that the poorest people were concentrated in the poorest districts, and therefore poverty could not be adduced as grounds that the system operated to the peculiar disadvantage of some "suspect class" of people.

The California courts, since 1971 at least, have seen the matter differently. Even after the *Rodriguez* decision deprived state courts of Fourteenth Amendment grounds for disapproving the present California school finance system, they have continued to rely on the equal protection clause of the state constitution. In other states (Washington, Ohio, New York) similar cases are pending, and in many states (Florida, Kansas, New Mexico, Maine, Michigan) reform laws are now on the books.

The policy question that these legal debates reflect and also shape is: What are the effects of school finance equalization of the *Serrano* type?

The implications of a change to fiscal neutrality or other forms of school finance equalization can best be understood in light of California's present school finance system, which has evolved over many years. There were major changes in 1973 as a result of the passage of Senate Bill 90, which was itself partly a response to the 1971 *Serrano* decision.

California has 4.4 million public school students, and in 1975–76 about $6.6 billion was spent on them, 93% of it from state and local sources, the remainder from federal funds. About three-fifths of the state-local money is raised locally through local property taxes, the other two-fifths coming from state funds, as raised by general appropriation.

There is great variation among districts in spending per pupil. For example, in 1974–75 the lowest-spending elementary district in the state spent $620 per student; the wealthiest spent $5,174. For unified districts, the range was from $1,000 to more than $3,000.

But this variation is less striking than it appears. Districts that spend a great deal or very little are generally small. The great majority of unified districts spent between $1,150 and $1,450 per student in 1976–77, with comparable $300 spending ranges accounting for most elementary and high school districts.

This clustering of spending, despite the presence of extremes, is in large part explained by the operation of the school finance system as modified by S.B. 90. The system consists of:

- *A revenue limit,* in effect the amount of money the district spent per student in average daily attendance during 1972–73, plus an annual increment for inflation that varies inversely according to the district's level of spending. A district cannot maintain a property tax level that, after subtracting state aid, would produce revenues in excess of the revenue limit. Because rich districts have smaller inflation allowance than poor ones, the revenue limit system tends to equalize spending, although slowly.
- *Basic aid,* provided by the state and guaranteed by the constitution, in the amount of $120 per student. This tends to disequalize spending because it is really a subsidy to high-wealth districts.
- *District aid,* simply the proceeds of the local property tax; it is not aid in the usual sense of the word.
- *A foundation program,* a state guarantee of a minimum amount per student to each district. (In 1976–77 these levels were about $1,000 for grades K–8 and $1,200 for 9–12.) The foundation program defines a floor on school spending that rises annually through the operation of the inflation allowance.
- *Categorical aid,* provided by state or local government for special classes of students or special programs. Categorical aid is excluded from computation of the foundation program and the revenue limit.
- *Tax elections,* through which, by majority vote, local voters may approve school board proposals for school tax rates in excess of the revenue limit.
- *Property tax relief,* through state subsidy.

The net effect of this system, coupled with voter reluctance to approve higher property taxes, has been to raise the spending of low-wealth districts and curtail the growth of spending in high-wealth districts. Consequently, by 1981–82, under the present law, seven-eighths of all types of districts will be spending within a $200 range per pupil, providing voters continue to vote negatively in tax elections.

The S.B. 90 inflation allowance amounts to about 6% of the foundation program (about $60–$70 a year). Any spending above the foundation program is not subject to the inflation allowance, so that the $60–$70 allowance may represent only a 3% increase for high-spending districts. Meanwhile, local property assessments are rising by much more than 6% or 7% annually, but the school districts cannot use these additional revenue sources. Instead, S.B. 90 provides for property tax rate reductions when assessment growth outpaces revenue-limit growth.

In other words, S.B. 90 is both a property tax relief measure and a school finance equalization reform. In both respects it has been moderately successful. It has increased the homeowner's property tax exemption and restrained the growth of school property taxes. But it has also increased state costs for schooling, directly through the operation of the S.B. 90 foundation program and inflation allowance, and indirectly through reimbursing local government for loss of income occasioned by the homeowner's property tax exemption and through resulting increases in state categorical aid for disadvantaged youth, early childhood, handicapped youth, etc., which represent loopholes in S.B. 90 spending ceilings. Furthermore, S.B. 90 does little to reduce existing tax rate disparities among school districts.

Nonetheless, on the revenue and spending side, S.B. 90 makes substantial progress toward revenue equalization, an important aspect of *Serrano*. It is on the tax side that major difficulties are likely to arise under the 1976 reaffirmation of *Serrano*, which gives the state legislature less than four years to equalize spending opportunities among districts. On the revenue side, the decision does not allow the decade or more that S.B. 90 would require to achieve virtual equalization.

School finance reform was viewed as an educational reform by many of its original proponents. *Serrano* and other cases were advanced after the educational need doctrine failed to pass constitutional muster.

The *Serrano* argument aimed at giving each district equal opportunity for access to the property wealth of the state. If a district wanted an expensive education for its children, it could tax itself high and be guaranteed substantial revenue per student. If it taxed itself at the state average rate, its students would be educated at state average cost, and so on. The result would be greater equity among rich and poor districts.

This assumed that more spending was associated with better schooling and, in the eyes of many, that low-wealth districts were largely populated by poor people, or at least more so than high-wealth districts.

Serrano also implicitly assumed that an increase in total spending for education statewide was desirable. If equalization took the form of parcelling the present level of spending equally among all students, some high-spending districts would face a sharp drop in the level of educational spending. Presumably, this is politically unworkable. The more feasible policy is to increase the foundation level or offer a state-guaranteed tax yield, thereby raising revenues of lower-spending districts without significantly reducing the spending of rich districts. The result is to increase the share of state product going to public education above what it would otherwise have been.

These assumptions are questionable. In California, transferring money from rich districts to poor ones would simply change the incidence of financial gains and losses among the state's "pool" of poor students; the total numbers on each side would approximately offset each other.

The tax equity question is more complicated. At one level there is an unambiguous argument in favor of equalizing statewide, or, if it were possible, nationwide. But the incidence of such a new, equalized tax schedule may itself be no more progressive, or even less progressive, than the existing system, depending on who lives in poor districts and who lives in rich ones. *Serrano* would equalize school spending and tax burdens among political subdivisions, not among people; therefore judgments about fiscal costs and benefits are hard to compute. Of course, if spending increases were financed through a state income tax, the incidence would be progressive among taxpayers.

Despite these issues, the case for *Serrano* as an equalizing device for both spending and taxing remains strong, even though the case for it as a contributor to progressive educational taxation or to better schooling for the disadvantaged, or indeed for any class of students, is questionable.

In *Serrano,* the California Supreme Court's 1976 decision followed the lower court in seeking complete equalization of access to funds by 1980. This is likely to lead to major skirmishing between the legislature and the courts. Equalized opportunities can be achieved in various ways; but they are all unpalatable politically. There are political barriers to simply redistributing the existing pool of funds, although something close to that might be a sensible point of departure for negotiations between the executive and legislative branches. A second alternative would be to raise all districts to the spending level of rich districts (say $2,000 per student). This would cost, for example, about $3.5 billion a year and would require a doubling of school taxes statewide, or a 50% increase in income taxes, or a four- or five-cent increase in the sales tax.

A third alternative would be to redefine school district boundaries for tax purposes, either on a countywide basis or on a statewide basis through a guaranteed tax yield system or a statewide property tax. The county tax base system would be somewhat equalizing statewide, but probably not enough for the *Serrano* standard. A statewide system could easily meet *Serrano* but runs into a cost barrier, unless something is done to reduce the spending level of rich districts.

Therefore, it seems unlikely that the legislature will meet the *Serrano* criterion of equal access to spending by the 1980 scheduled date, although some acceleration of current progress under S.B. 90 is certainly politically feasible.

With respect to equalizing tax burdens among districts, the chances for legislative/judicial harmony by 1980 are even slighter. However, it is not easy to think of acceptable shifts on the scale of several billion dollars annually without resort to the tax base employed in collecting the federal income tax.

Furthermore, while S.B. 90 offered significant progress on the revenue side, it has done much less to reduce tax rate disparities. For example, in 1975–76 in Los Angeles County, El Segundo raised more money per pupil with a $2.13 tax rate than Claremont and Las Virgenes did with $5.85 tax rates.

In the 1976 decision, the California Supreme Court declared such tax differences to be intolerable, saying:

So long as the assessed valuation within a district's boundaries is a major detriment of how much it can spend for its schools, only a district with a large tax base will be truly able to decide how much it really cares about education.

The poor district cannot freely choose to tax itself into an excellence that its tax rolls cannot provide.

In a certain sense, S.B. 90 can be considered in large part as a general tax relief measure (much of the original funding of S.B. 90 went to property tax relief), sweetened by the special reduction for high-tax poor districts. Most people favor property tax reduction, and property-rich San Francisco, Pasadena, and Palo Alto are not likely to welcome property tax increases as a condition of maintaining their present levels of school spending, or even lower ones. Now that the court has called for equalized spending or equal tax revenues per unit tax rate, this is the implication, unless there is a shift in tax sources. Otherwise higher taxes will be called for, accompanied by lower property values in rich districts. The current price of land and buildings in Beverly Hills or Santa Monica incorporates the advantages of low tax rates. If *Serrano* makes their taxes rise relative to other cities, capital values of property will decline relatively.

But if the legislature accepts the reluctance of rich districts to pay higher property taxes, then some other change in taxation would be needed to meet *Serrano*. It seems unlikely that an acceptable combination of sales and income taxes could be relied on, unless the court requires only a modest degree of tax equalization.

Despite this, some further progress in equalizing tax rates is possible—for example, Governor Jerry Brown's recent suggestion of tying property tax reductions to the individual taxpayer's property tax burdens, measured as a fraction of his income; this is the so-called circuit-breaker, which for certain classes of taxpayers separates spending from tax rates. The scale that the governor proposed is inadequate in light of citizens' desires for the red meat of large-scale tax reduction; but this, of course, is the dilemma. A little free lunch is cheap to provide, but banquets run high.

It seems likely that the results of *Serrano* will not include any large short-run increases in rich districts' taxes or any reduction in their current spending levels. This probably points to a gradual reform, using some combination of general state tax sources for subsidy, while keeping the tax levels of rich districts stable as the rates of other districts are allowed to decline.

In short, revenue equalization is slow, but California has already started along that road. Tax equalization is slower, so the fulfillment of any equalizing order is remote. Nevertheless, *Serrano* should result in long-run progress toward equalizing spending and paying opportunities by school district, if not by class of student or taxpayer.

If the state supreme court finds such a rate of progress unacceptable, it could take the matter under its control as the New Jersey Supreme Court did in closing down the public schools until an acceptable method of financing is reached. From the viewpoint of the legislature, such an outcome would put the onus of higher taxes on the back of an "authoritarian" court.

In any event, a good deal of testing of the judicial-political winds will take place from 1977 to 1980. For example, in January of this year Governor Brown proposed an alternative that would eliminate basic aid to rich districts, reduce the tax rates of poor districts, and guarantee all districts that receive state aid an equal yield per dollar of tax rate. The result would be to eliminate much but not all of existing tax yield disparities, without much increase in state spending. This sensible remedy suffers from a possibly fatal defect: It is apparently inconsistent with the *Serrano* decision, because it does not fully equalize access; tax rates would still differ per dollar of tax yield. The result will be determined by negotiation with the legislature and more court tests, which will ultimately revolve around who pays and how much each party gains or loses. The most probable outcome at this writing (August, 1977) is legislation that provides more state aid than the governor proposed (including retention of the regressive basic aid system, apparently outlawed by last year's state supreme court decision), but includes his basic approach to equalization, to be followed by a new court test that may be decided in 1978.

Proponents of *Serrano* claim that the result will not be to guarantee anyone a better education but to give each district equal access to the resources that are needed in order to permit it to try to improve schooling.

But there is more to it than that. Unless most districts benefit, unless more money is spent, the legislature will be unable to speed up the pace of equalization.

But should the state, in the name of equity, provide public schools with more money than they would otherwise get? It seems likely that California voters would decline to approve more funds for equalization. They have recently been reluctant indeed to approve school tax elections for local purposes and have turned down statewide bond issues wholesale. What, then, would be a convincing rationale for raising the total level of school spending? Equalization per se, without more spending, has no appeal, except for state courts, eggheads, and the poor districts.

But if the public does not want to spend much of its money for equalization, would it be willing to spend more for better education? The argument would have to be that most children, not just the needy ones, benefit from more school spending, and by enough to merit the diversion of funds from private uses or other public uses.

The evidence on this score is quite unclear. First, statistical analysis of the relation between spending and educational outcomes runs into several barriers. The usual measures of educational outcome used in such analyses—standardized test score results and rates of high school graduation and college attendance—have their defects, because they provide limited information about what people learn in school.

Second, the statistical analysis tends to be dominated by acquired and inherited family effects—social class, wealth, and IQ of the student. Therefore, only about one-twentieth of the variation in achievement test outcomes is attributable to differences in school resources. But this figure may be misleading, because none of the statistical studies has included any measure of school or school district commitment to educational improvement.[5] Thus when, as in California after passage of S.B. 90, school districts have more money to spend, the educational results are variable. The analysis therefore tends to average together the results of districts that use the money for effective change and those that do not. In statistical terms, the problem is one of defining a variable that describes school and district management styles for implementing change.[6] Such a variable would allow us to separate the effect of effective districts from

those of ineffective ones. Under present conditions, a general increase in resources for education would result in better education for some places and the same or worse for others.

It is often claimed that the result would be merely to raise teacher salaries, particularly in an era of increasing teacher unionism. However, some evidence indicates that this is not what happens, at least in the short run.[7] Most of the money goes for hiring teachers and administrators and buying supplies. One-eighth to one-fourth of the funds remain for salary increases. In other words, large increases in funding lead directly to use of more resources in school districts, not simply to higher prices for the same resources.

This brings us back to the same problem: Should the public fund general increases in school resource use when it is likely that many of the additional resources will have no effects on measured outcomes?

In my opinion, the best application of *Serrano* would be one that imposed no extra costs on society but simply leveled spending at a specified tax rate, allowing districts to go above or below the combined ceiling/floor, if they so chose by local tax election, from a statewide property tax base. Governor Brown has proposed such a "guaranteed yield" system of tax revenues as part of his *Serrano* reform proposal.

Unfortunately, the pressures to sweeten the pot are likely to be overwhelming, and the social gains stemming from interdistrict equity are likely to be offset by the costs of higher school spending, with predictably doubtful results for educational outcomes. In the case of education, which is such an expensive public function anyway, it seems a pity to reinforce the current trend to increasing costs in public services by disbursing billions in the sole justification of an equity that could in principle be purchased at no net cost.

If California school districts do come closer to equalizing their spending per unit tax rate, what will be the result for the quality of schooling? As noted above, the evidence to date is that districts whose spending goes up hire more teachers, administrators, and aides, buy more equipment, improve the quality of maintenance, and increase salaries modestly, while the effects on student outcome, as usually measured, are uncertain and usually modest.

As has often been pointed out, the inconsistent results probably indicate that some districts make more effective use of resources than others do. Why is that so, and is there any way to hitch *Serrano* to encouraging greater effectiveness in resource use?

Most school districts, according to recent research at Rand, act to maintain the existing political and institutional equilibrium. School districts are hard to run smoothly, from a superintendent's viewpoint, because there are many competing interests to reconcile—those of school board members; teacher organizations; parents; various ethnic groups; lobbying groups that favor changes in curriculum, in discipline, and the like; principals and other administrators; students; nonprofessional staff. Therefore the objective of keeping the system running and suppressing "outside" interference from as many sources as possible becomes paramount.

There is nothing wrong, as such, with maintaining the status quo. But it does tend to conflict with the introduction of any substantial change into the system, because change is painful, creates resistance and strife, and requires a good deal of work in order to succeed. Nonetheless, the demand for change is also a fact of life. Therefore the district concerned primarily with maintenance introduces changes, but these changes are normally not of the kind that will actually alter the way the system operates (e.g., trips to the zoo, or Title I projects that reduce class size without changing curriculum). The more difficult kinds of projects, those that simultaneously reform curriculum and teacher relationships with other teachers, administrators, and students, are often adopted but rarely implemented in this type of district, because they would require a degree of support for change that simply is not there.

Therefore, for the district concerned with maintenance, increased spending from *Serrano* is not likely to be a particularly good use of public funds; moreover, if the district is property-poor, it is most likely to gain as a consequence of the associated tax benefits for its citizens.

Other districts operate differently, offering strong central support for change and encouraging principals and teachers to propose new approaches. Changes are not normally adopted in such districts unless there is an intention to implement them; evidence of this intent normally includes substantial teacher participation in both planning and implementation. Changes adopted are usually of a magnitude that makes it hard for the adopting schools to revert easily to old ways of doing things.[8]

Such districts therefore have the ability to use new funds systematically for educational improvement, at least within reasonable limits. To the extent that additional spending from *Serrano* goes to these districts, it is money better spent.

But even if *Serrano* funds could be tied to performance, which seems to be clearly not the case, the districts that now provide a good education would by and large benefit, while those that do not would suffer financially. This would be unacceptable politically, and it would appear to consign the weaker districts to perpetual mediocrity.

Therefore it would be unwise, in the name of educational betterment, to use *Ser-*

rano as a device for more educational spending, because most of the no-strings aid would not serve educational goals.

The alternative of tying increases in aid to the quality of district performance, using *Serrano* as a foundation plan, is more complicated. California's Early Childhood Education (ECE) program and the proposed legislation for high school reform (RISE) both include elements of this. ECE districts receive money for expanding the program to new schools only if the district's schools already in the program perform well. Each school in the program receives only about $140 per student but must present the state with a plan covering use of the school's entire resources. Progress is reviewed annually by the state.

It would be possible to condition increases in state aid on such measures of progress as parent and student satisfaction, higher test scores, more job placement, increase in college attendance, and other indices. There are three obvious disadvantages to any system based on educational performance: 1) inconsistency with *Serrano;* 2) reluctance of districts to accept this or any form of accountability (this reluctance is already evident in the ECE program); 3) penalties inflicted on effective schools in an ineffective district.

The method might be more consistent with *Serrano* if these payments were to be made *in addition to* foundation-level *Serrano* payments, as a form of categorical aid. The politics of the situation are hard to estimate. Would there be widespread support for a system of payments tied to performance in the manner of ECE or RISE? Finally, what about penalizing the effective school in the ineffective district?

If California were to decentralize a good deal of its educational decision making from the school district to the school and its parent community, then the system of re-

wards and penalties could be addressed to the school level, partly by-passing the district. Even then the problem persists for the individual teacher or student. Ultimately, as in the case of *Serrano,* any reward/penalty system that deals with groups of people is sure to permit inequities.

A further objection is that no system of outcome or activity measures can fairly define appropriate rewards and penalties, because the measures are inexact, and subject to manipulation.

Finally, it is argued that such accountability systems penalize schoolchildren rather than the poor performance of those who serve them. However, under *Serrano,* it is possible to assure each child a level of support close to the statewide average. Then the funds denied to his district would presumably not harm him, because his district has not demonstrated its ability to produce results.

This approach would have to be tied to a school-by-school plan and school-by-school results, in the manner of ECE or RISE. It would therefore require additional state supervision and would lead to greater conflict between the State Department of Education and the schools.

In sum, if increased funding is not tied to performance, a good deal of it will be wasted. If it is so tied, the weaker performers are likely to change the rules of the game. Meanwhile, the voters show no interest in providing more money for schools.

From all of this, I would predict that the lesson of *Serrano* will be the lesson of social policy in general: Government can allocate resources but it cannot specify results. Federal farm programs were designed to preserve the family farm—and actually encouraged its decline. *Serrano* and its predecessors were aimed at promoting better education for needy districts—and are likely to equalize spending with no systematic effects on educational outcomes. *Serrano* also presents the danger of increased school spending paid for by reduced private income, with less public spending on transportation, police, conservation, and the like.

The difficulty with all such policies is that policy makers understand rather little about how society and its institutions work. John Coons may well have been correct in suggesting that the real significance of *Serrano* lies in giving districts a better chance to try their hand at providing good education. Since that is likely to lead to substantially higher spending, and since there is no persuasive evidence about the results of such increases, we are left with a familiar policy dilemma. It is likely to be solved by compromise: spending less money than the courts in effect demand and more than the system would otherwise have tolerated, with unknown results for the quality of schooling and the public welfare.

If, as seems likely, *Serrano* ends up providing financial benefits to a large majority of school districts, then there will be little money left for targeted educational improvement. In that case reform would be the enemy of progress. The new California legislation may attempt to bridge that gap by offering a little of each.

The secret of educational improvement, if there is one, lies in two directions. One is more reverence and desire for teaching and learning by all of us and by all of our institutions. Since this is unlikely on a large scale, the second direction may be more practical: providing funds for schools, districts,

and programs that do help children to learn better, while allowing the others a decent stipend. This is the approach to school finance that I discussed above, and the obstacles are formidable. But no general school finance reform is likely to produce much more than pre-existing methods in the way of better-educated children. The *Serrano* solution that best reforms education is likely to be the solution that costs society least.

NOTES

1. Arthur Wise, *Rich Schools, Poor Schools* (Chicago: University of Chicago Press, 1969); John E. Coons, William H. Clune III, and Stephen D. Sugarman, *Private Wealth and Public Education* (Cambridge, Mass.: Harvard University Press, 1970); Harold Horowitz, "Unseparate but Unequal: The Emerging Fourteenth Amendment Issue in Public Education," *UCLA Law Review*, August, 1966, p. 1147.
2. *McInnis v. Shapiro*, 293 F. Supp. 327 (N.D. Ill.; 1968); *McInnis v. Ogilvie*, 394 U.S. 322 (1969).
3. Coons, Clune, and Sugarman, op. cit.
4. 36 L.Ed. 2d 16, 93 S.Ct. 1278 (1973).
5. See Harvey A. Averch et al., *How Effective Is Schooling?* (Englewood Cliffs, N.J.: Educational Technology Press, 1974); and John Heim and Lewis Perl, *The Educational Production Function: Indicators for Manpower Policy* (Ithaca, N.Y.: Institute of Public Employment, Cornell University, July, 1974).
6. See Paul Berman and Milbrey W. McLaughlin, *Federal Programs Supporting Educational Change, Vol. IV, The Findings in Review* (Santa Monica, Calif.: The Rand Corporation, April, 1975), R-1589/4-HEW.
7. Stephen M. Barro and Stephen J. Carroll, *Budget Allocation by School Districts: An Analysis of Spending for Teachers and Other Resources* (Santa Monica, Calif.: The Rand Corporation, December, 1975), R-1797-NIE.
8. Berman and McLaughlin, op. cit.

Yes, But What Are We Accountable For?

James L. Hayes, Everett McDonald, Albert Burstein, Dexter A. Magers, Gary Gappert, American Management Associations

Have you ever awakened uneasily in the dead of night, the left side of your face twitching, wondering deeply to yourself: How is educational accountability like a hurricane? Consider the answer:

Because a hurricane's winds travel in a huge circular pattern, someone in the center of a hurricane's path would first be hit by ferocious winds coming from one direction; then, as the eye of the hurricane passes over, the skies might become calm, blue and sunshiny; finally, as the other "half" of the hurricane circle hits, terrible winds would strike again, except this time they'd come from the opposite direction. Educational accountability is turning out to be an odd phenomenon, too—and one with at least three stages. We've lived through the first part: the storms, the panic, the hot air, the long-windedness, the rush of legislation, the roar of demands. And now public education seems to be enjoying the calmer, second stage: The accountability movement is relatively inactive, although it's still out there, moving, blowing—approaching. If the

momentum of this particular education movement is maintained, public schools will be hit by a third, stormy stage, although no one seems to know for sure where the winds are going to come from the next time around.

Educational accountability (to take a break from mangling metaphors and meteorology) seems to have arisen from an honest, albeit frustrated, attempt to improve education. Accountability was coughed up as a solution when the citizenry, reacting to anything from rising inflation to falling test scores, simply took the grip it has on public education—and squeezed. The result, over the last six or seven years, has been accountability legislation passed in three-fourths of the states and an entire accountability industry made up of those who are for it, those who are against it, those who are trying to explain it—and many, many of us who keep asking: "Huh?"

To take advantage of the current calm of accountability's eye and to attempt to answer that *Huh?* question, the American Management Associations* (in cooperation

Source: James L. Hayes, et al. "Yes, But What Are We Accountable For?" *American School Board Journal* vol. 163, no. 2 (February 1976), pp. 35–36, 38–39.

* The American Management Associations is a not-for-profit educational organization that annually con-

with the JOURNAL) recently sponsored a day-long discussion of educational accountability. James L. Hayes, president of the American Management Associations, conducted the meeting, which included these participants:

- Everett McDonald, a Warminster, Pa., superintendent who operates under state accountability laws;
- Albert Burstein, a New Jersey state assemblyman who has sponsored accountability legislation;
- Dexter A. Magers, a U.S. Office of Education senior program officer who works with states that are devising and implementing accountability legislation;
- Gary Gappert, an assistant commissioner for research and planning (Office of the New Jersey State Commissioner of Education) who has done extensive work in the field of accountability research.

What is educational accountability? One probably should approach that question the way lobsters approach lovemaking: back into it carefully. (A head-on answer to *What is accountability?* often gets involved in lofty generalizations: Accountability is an attempt to set goals for education and make someone accountable for reaching those goals. Or it gets involved in the descriptions of the 35 or so specific state accountability systems that currently are in operation.) One way to back into an understanding of accountability is to take a look at the forces that have affected its growth and direction. The meeting participants stressed three forces that have contributed to accountabil-

ity's current calm, and they sound like bywords for the Democratic party's nominating convention: confusion, politics, and money.

The confusion is basic, beginning with that question we mentioned previously: What is accountability? Now that people across the country are asking the question, a recess of sorts has been called to give experts, proponents and opponents a chance to answer. Everett McDonald, citing a recent study, says: "A man named Lesley Browder has examined 4,000 pieces of accountability literature and he says that 95 percent of the material contributes very little new information and that hard research data is even rarer. Browder claims that there are no commonly agreed upon definitions and that accountability actually needs refinement as a concept."

The confusion also has been spread by the widely varying ways in which accountability has been implemented in school districts and states across the country. Dexter A. Magers: "One extreme of the accountability spectrum is represented by the Colorado model in which the state simply monitors a process that goes on at the local district level. The state tells the local people to establish some goals and objectives, then measure where you are, and then report back to us. There are absolutely no statewide goals or standards of achievement as such. Now that has some difficulties, as you might obviously suspect—some local people simply don't set very high standards. The opposite kind of accountability model is typified by Florida, where the state establishes certain performance levels as being expected or normal. Then there is a requirement that progress be measured, usually by a statewide assessment or some kind of testing program.

"Both ends of the accountability spectrum are beginning to drift toward the middle. Florida is beginning to edge toward more

ducts training programs worldwide for more than 100,000 employees in private enterprise and public service organizations. A.M.A. representatives report that increasing numbers of educational organizations have requested the organization's assistance in meeting requirements of accountability legislation. Co-sponsorship of the accountability roundtable reported here is in partial response to such requests.

responsibility at the local level, while the program in Colorado is becoming a little more centralized."

Accountability *politics* are at a temporary stalemate. Whether they were trying to start or stop accountability, the "winners" of accountability battles across the country are holding onto their victories and waiting for their opponents' next move. And the temporarily vanquished seem to be pondering their defeat and gathering strength for another round of attacks.

That's certainly an oversimplification, but Albert Burstein gives credence to this stalemate interpretation when he describes opposition to New Jersey's accountability legislation: "There will be litigants who will test the language that we ultimately adopt in the way of legislation. And perhaps that's a good thing, because I believe the constant testing process ultimately results in a better-refined system."

Magers explains how the third force— money—has becalmed accountability: "A state in the West mandated that every student in its public schools be measured every year in every subject being studied. The state appropriated $90,000 to get the job done. Now this is like telling someone. 'Put a man on the moon and here's $1,500— now get cracking.' It was completely unrealistic. The tremendous cost of getting good information can be a great deterrent, so most of the accountability efforts at the moment are at a plateau of 'hold what we've got to refine; improve it.' Many of these efforts are cutting back to a much narrower scope and maybe this is good. It at least gives us a smaller piece that we can handle."

Could accountability be kaput as a major force in public education? Well, as Hubert Humphrey probably says these days when he walks down Pennsylvania Avenue: Anything's possible. But not likely. Accountability is surely going to "hit" again, both in terms of new legislation covering those districts that currently are accountability-free and in terms of stronger enforcement in states that already have passed accountability laws. School board members, according to several of the meeting participants, are potentially strong accountability proponents, *if those board members can be convinced that statewide accountability won't enfeeble local control.*

The more useful contemplation is not in writing an accountability eulogy but in trying to determine the characteristics of accountability's next round of activity. And Accountability Future is likely to be shaped by a set of tough twins called measurement and evaluation. Like the hurricane, it all goes around in a big circle: Accountability requires the setting of educational goals. Meeting those goals requires measurement of educational progress. Measurement almost surely requires an evaluation of educators (say teachers). Effective evaluation requires a means for rewarding good teachers and getting rid of incompetent ones. And evaluation and measurement (and therefore accountability) become nothing more than expensive exercises unless school board members and superintendents use them to make schools better.

Let's look at the goals-measurement-evaluation-improvement cycle one element at a time, starting with setting goals. Put bluntly: An accountability system isn't going to work if the control over the direction of local schools is taken away from the local citizenry. But once the accountability confusion (mentioned earlier in this article) is cleared up, it seems likely that a workable compromise can be struck: The state may require that goals be set in each district (and that all district goals include certain minimum standards), but the local citizens, through their school board, will be in final control of local educational goals.

The prognosis on measurement is dimmer, and you're familiar with the problems here: Education has no set, accepted, defined body of knowledge in the way that, say, medicine or physics do; if progress is to be measured against norms or averages, how does one account for the varying inherent abilities of individuals—but if progress is measured against an individual's own range of abilities, how is that range to be defined?; and how are all the disparate factors (children's abilities, teachers' skills, management savvy; proper funding) to be weighted when measuring educational progress?

Help in this area will have to come from education's research community, but that community is offering no solutions yet. Gary Gappert, in fact, cites a "crisis of measurement." Gappert asks: "How do you measure the output of public service, and do we really have the skills to measure the anticipated output of education, specifically? I feel that it's possible to measure some things, but it's a question of whether the things which we can measure are, in fact, the things that the public expects as the real outputs of education."

Gappert zeroes in on this second link—measurement—as one reason the accountability movement cannot own up when asked: Has accountability really changed anything so far? Answers Gappert: "We don't know, really. There is very little data to tell us one way or another. We've had accountability systems imposed by state legislatures and by state departments of education, but the results have not been measured."

Magers apparently is optimistic about the strengthening of the measurement link (but he reminds that the cost of good measurement is high). "I think we will find a rapidly changing technology of educational measurement," Magers says. "We're going to see a tremendous number of people working in this hot area of educational research and development. We're also going to see an increase in the militancy of teachers against these measurement efforts."

Hayes offers a succinct reason for teacher opposition: "Measurability is always a threat to security, even for the great performers." Measurement is a threat to teachers because it leads, as naturally as gin does to a hangover, to job evaluation. This progression along the accountability chain, from measurement to evaluation, may be natural but it is by no means inevitable. It can be blocked by these six letters: u-n-i-o-n-s; or more specifically, by these six: N-E-A-A-F-T (the National Education Association and the American Federation of Teachers).

McDonald explains how he has tried to convince his *administrative* staff that objective evaluation is not entirely evil: "We're reminding our administrators that they've been *subjectively* evaluated for years, but now they're going to get an *objective* evaluation. It took us two years to convince most of them they're better off with objective evaluations, but they don't all buy it because evaluation is a threat to them. The teachers know that evaluation might come to them later. They are organizing against it."

Magers tells of an accountability meeting held last summer during which half of the participants (teachers selected by N.E.A. and A.F.T.) "figured the whole meeting was a setup. They eventually had their own session and passed a resolution in which they indicated that student performance should in no way ever be used to judge a teacher. Just that flat and simple."

That pristine notion may get jostled a bit by proaccountability legislators. Explains Burstein: "It seems that reluctance to be judged is found in a greater degree in the educational sphere than in almost any other place. Perhaps that's because the tenure system and other protective devices have isolated education practitioners from the real world. All of us in other fields are being judged almost everyday on what we do. But in the educational sphere you have a job day after day no matter what, and as soon as someone begins to do anything that evaluates teacher performance, you get this negativism that we've been talking about."

Teacher negativism on evaluation arises from a stirring that is both pragmatic and basic: remaining employed. Although evaluation may emphasize rewarding good teachers and training ineffective teachers, any accountability system is a sham unless hopelessly incompetent teachers can be fired. Says Magers: "In this whole accountability concept from the grass roots up, there is no system of systematic improvement—including the removal of the teacher as a last resort. I don't think we should ever say that we can design a system that will improve the working parts, if one of the working parts is a person. And even that the person has got to stay, I think your system is fallacious. Although I think I would dodge the question as long as I could, we must indicate that the eventual outcome of accountability possibly will be the elimination of a few individuals who simply cannot perform."

School board members and superintendents are responsible for the final accountability link: using measurements and evaluations to improve education. In some districts, top school officials apparently are operating like some sort of mad chef who spends considerable money and effort in collecting and mixing expensive ingredients but then neither cooks nor serves the meal. Burstein: "School board members are dealing with matters of budget, which take an enormous amount of their time. They're dealing with a number of school buses that must be purchased for next year, or they're setting up an athletic program or arranging for some kind of contest. If board members are going to have the capability of filling the accountability job, they must get tuned-in to what's happening to the child in the classroom."

Burstein offers a specific example from New Jersey: "We've had an assessment program that has identified school districts with low reading scores. Now the school boards in those districts ought to be using those assessment results to find what is happening with their reading programs in the particular grades that are involved. Some are, but I don't think that most of the boards are doing that."

That bit of pessimism offers an appropriate setting for a topic few people want to connect with accountability: educational malpractice. Accountability Researcher Lesley Browder Jr. writes: " . . . the present state of education offers no definition for malpractice. Yet as the expectations, methods and procedures of educational practice become more highly stipulated (especially by state law), malpractice definitions (particularly those regarding forms of educational negligence) are likely to emerge."

In spite of the reasoning that accountability can make educational malpractice more manageable and in spite of the isolated educational malpractice suits that have been filed already, most observers (including those attending the A.M.A./JOURNAL meeting) downplay the potential impact of educational malpractice. But then, ten years ago many people would have scoffed at the idea that medical malpractice would someday vie for being the top controversy in medicine.

PART IV

Historical Foundations of Education

A study of educational foundations would not be complete without an examination of the history of American education. Teachers must know the history of our American educational system in order to appreciate the proud heritage of the teaching profession. A knowledge of the history of education also helps educators to better understand contemporary educational problems and, hopefully, to make wiser decisions regarding these problems. The readings in this section have been carefully selected so as to provide the reader with a view of the highlights of the history of American education.

One of the first major educational events in colonial America was the establishment of the Boston Public Latin School. This Latin grammar school was patterned after similar institutions that had existed in Europe for many years prior to their establishment in this country. The Boston Latin Grammar School was established in 1635, only five years after Boston had been settled. This school was a form of secondary school, and its function was to prepare boys for college.

In 1636, only one year after the establishment of the Boston Latin Grammar School, Harvard was founded. Although a number of colleges and universities had been established in Latin America prior to that time, Harvard was the first college to be established in the colonies. In fact, Harvard was the only colonial college for approximately sixty years, until William and Mary College was founded in 1693.

Important as they were, Harvard College and the Boston Latin Grammar School were but two small aspects of colonial education. Colonial education spanned 180 years (1607–1787), and, as one might expect, a good deal of activity took place during that long period of time. Robert Middlekauff, in his article, "Education in Colonial America," discusses the highlights of education during that 180-year colonial period. This article, of necessity, does not delve deeply into each aspect of colonial education, but rather attempts to capsulize the essence of its history.

For a period of time after winning her independence from England, the United States was so preoccupied with settling the pressing affairs of a newly formed nation that relatively little national energy was devoted to education. Beginning about 1820, however, there was a great deal of educational activity. About this time many states established statewide public school systems. Governors, legislators, and town councils started earnestly discussing the subject of education; many additional elementary schools were established; educational journals were published; more and improved textbooks were published; educational societies and institutes were organized; schools for the deaf and blind were established; Troy Seminary was established, providing the first higher education for women in this country; state school boards were organized; and special teacher-training schools called *normal schools* were established.

During this period of increasing educational activity there were a number of people who made substantial contributions to educational progress. Men such as Samuel Hall, Henry Barnard, Horace Mann, and Cyrus Peirce, among others, kept the issue of education before the public and led the fight for a universal free educational system. Space does not permit the inclusion of articles on all of these important educators, though each of their contributions was indeed great.

The second article in this section elaborates on some of these events, especially education's evolving role in the development of the American society. Wendell Pierce documents three primary forces that have historically shaped the development of American education.

An historical paradox is the topic of the next selection. This paradox deals with our nation's extremely high regard for education on the one hand, and a very low regard for teachers on the other. This interesting selection is authored by Myrtle Bonn.

"Master Dove's One-Room School," authored by Judith Selden, re-creates a 1775 one-room school in such a way as to help the reader learn much of the history associated with this uniquely American institution.

The last article, "The Historical Roots of the Parochial Schools in America," is co-authored by Peter and Alice Rossi. Many of the first schools in America were parochial schools. This was particularly true in the middle colonies, where people from a number of different religious backgrounds settled. The Rossis point out that while many religious groups have started parochial schools at various times in the past, only two have succeeded in establishing well-developed parochial school systems. These are the Roman Catholic Church and the Missouri Synod Lutheran Church.

Hopefully, when you have finished these selections you will realize that the roots of American education can be traced to Europe, but that the values, concepts, and organizational patterns of education in the United States today are unique in the world. You should also realize that, as our nation developed from the first thirteen states to the present fifty states, education changed from that for an elite few to education for the masses. In the current nuclear age, when the world is changing more in decades than it formerly did in centuries, educators should be familiar with, and appreciative of, the historical role that education has played in our ever-changing society. Despite some of the shortcomings of the current American educational system and despite the efforts of a few critics who advocate that we should return to European educational standards, history reveals that no other nation has accomplished what the United States has accomplished through mass education. It is important that we strive for educational improvements, but it is also important to remember that the

United States produces more goods and services, provides better opportunity for individual advancement, and enjoys a higher standard of living than most other nations in the world. A study of educational history helps us to realize that much of the credit for these achievements must be given to the educational system which has been developed in this country.

Education in Colonial America

Robert Middlekauff

When an American colonist discussed a "public school," he was not talking about the institution familiar to us since the nineteenth century; usually he simply meant a school open to anyone who wished to attend. The chances were that the school was privately owned and financed. The designation "public" was given to distinguish it from a school catering exclusively to a special group—usually a religious sect.

Indeed, the modern idea of "public education," implying a state-owned system of schools, supported by taxation, and administered by officials chosen by the community, which compels attendance of all children within a certain age group and which carefully separates itself from the educational efforts of private groups, did not exist in the colonial period. To be sure, the state sometimes participated in organizing and financing schools, but its role (outside of New England) was small. Indeed, several other agencies assumed the burdens of edu-

cation; chief among them were the family, apprenticeship, and private schools of various sorts.

Of these institutions early in the colonial period, the family carried the greatest burden. In the primitive conditions of settlement, other agencies did not exist. Parents had to give their children education—if any was to be given. Frequently, of course, children went untutored or picked up rudimentary vocational training while they were working.[1]

The family continued to be an important center of training even after colonial society developed. For colonial parents, like their English forefathers, frequently placed their children with other families for rearing and training. They had good reasons for doing so: some did not trust themselves to discipline their own children vigorously enough; others, wishing to see their children acquire certain skills, apprenticed them to masters capable of providing the appropriate knowledge.[2]

Throughout most of the colonial period, indentures, as the apprentice agreements were called, usually enjoined the master to see that his charge was taught the essentials

Source: Robert Middlekauff, "Education in Colonial America," *Current History* 41:5–8, 14 (July 1961). Copyright 1961. Used by permission of *Current History*, Inc.

of the Christian religion and to read and write. Apprenticeship, of course, was never simply an educational instrument. A master taking on a young boy or girl expected his charge to work as well as to learn. The indenture always provided that the apprentice would obey and serve his master for a specified time, usually seven years or until the apprentice reached twenty-one. The instruction a boy received was always in return for his service. Sometimes apprenticeship proved to be only an agency of work, as masters refused to teach their boys. In such cases, the apprentice's only protection was his parents—or the local courts.

Schools in the first years of settlement were scarce in all the colonies. Scattered settlement and scant resources discouraged attempts to maintain schools continuously. Thus in the first years education in schools was largely a temporary, even sporadic affair.

EDUCATION IN THE SOUTH

If education in the first years of settlement was much alike in all the colonies, it took on regional characteristics as colonial society matured. In the southern colonies—Virginia, the Carolinas, Maryland and later Georgia—where population always remained scattered on farms and plantations, geography prevented a neat structure of schools. Yet children were educated. A wealthy planter sent his sons to England to sit in one of the great grammar schools, or brought a tutor to the plantation, where he lived with the family. Smaller planters and farmers, especially in Virginia, sometimes combined their resources to build a "field school"—a building in a tobacco field, hence the name—and to hire a teacher to instruct the children living nearby. Boarding schools usually established by an ambitious college graduate or itinerant schoolmaster

appeared late in the colonial period and were usually found only in the larger villages like Williamsburg or Charles Town.[3]

Tutors, field schools, boarding schools were all maintained without any reference to public authorities. This was not true of most of the endowed schools of the southern colonies. Founded through the generosity of private donors, these schools were usually managed by county or parish officials—or a combination of both. Such officers found a place for the school's meeting, hired its master, and supervised its operation.

The most renowned of these institutions were the Symmes and Eaton schools. Both were founded around the middle of the seventeenth century from bequests of Virginians. Both were controlled by a board of trustees composed from county and parish officers. Symmes school secured incorporation in 1753; Eaton in 1759. During at least a part of its history each offered instruction in the classical languages as well as in reading, writing and arithmetic.[4]

Altogether nine such schools in Virginia survived at least a part of the colonial period. All in all, they were not of great importance for they took root in only seven parishes; eighty-three parishes had none.[5] In the colonial South only the grammar school at the College of William and Mary consistently received public funds.

THE MIDDLE COLONIES

The southern colonies were not unique; contributions from public treasuries in the middle colonies—New York, Pennsylvania, Delaware, New Jersey—rarely were given. Even Philadelphia and New York, large cities in the eighteenth century by English standards, did not direct municipal revenues into education.

An energetic and self-conscious denominationalism supplied Philadelphia with schools. First on the scene, the Society of Friends established elementary schools and a single grammar school shortly after Pennsylvania was settled. William Penn gave his encouragement by bestowing a charter on the grammar school in 1701. The Friends apparently needed no official endorsement, and throughout the colonial period they gave the schools vigorous support through private subscriptions and legacies.[6]

Other religious groups as eager as the Friends to preserve their identity and to perpetuate themselves maintained schools in Philadelphia. An Anglican parish school was begun in 1698, and the Society for the Propagation of the Gospel supported a charity school for poor children for most of the period before the Revolution. The Lutheran church opened a classical school around the middle of the eighteenth century, and the Baptists followed with the same type in 1755; the Moravians—never a rich group—began an elementary school in 1745.[7]

Besides these efforts—and probably equally important—were the numerous private school masters of Philadelphia. The average private master displayed a variety of skills to Philadelphians. If his newspaper advertisements accurately stated his qualifications, he could teach every thing from arithmetic to astronomy—including Latin and Greek, rhetoric, oratory, logic, navigation, surveying, bookkeeping, higher mathematics and natural science. His offerings were necessarily broad; he had to attract students since their tuition provided his sole means of support.[8]

New York, the other city of the middle colonies, could not match Philadelphia's denominational offerings. Still, its religious groups were important agencies of education. Under the Dutch in the first half of the seventeenth century, the Reformed Church maintained a school. After the English took

over the colony in 1664, the church, in an attempt to hold its children to the old ways and to the old language, opened several more. Though English culture eventually washed out the results, these attempts helped preserve Dutch homogeneity for years. As in Philadelphia the Society for the Propagation of the Gospel also proved active, sponsoring charity schools for children of the poor.[9]

New York could also boast numerous private schools in the eighteenth century with masters, judging from their claims in the newspapers, no less talented than those of Philadelphia. But on the whole, education was neglected in New York. Perhaps the most auspicious development of the pre-Revolutionary period was the opening of a grammar school by the newly-founded Kings College in 1762. The college and its school promised to renew interest in education beyond the elementary level.[10]

Small towns and villages in the middle colonies lagged badly in education. A few parish schools struggled along in several; private masters taught reading, writing and arithmetic and occasionally vocational subjects like surveying; apprenticeship supplied most of the skilled crafts. If a boy desired advanced training in the languages or higher mathematics, he had to travel to New York or Philadelphia. By the late colonial period apparently there were many boys who sought such instruction, for the city schools were filled with students from the country.

THE NEW ENGLAND AREA

This brief treatment of the southern and middle colonies suggests, perhaps, that a variety of agencies—each for its own purposes—promoted education. In New England a number of the same forces appeared: the Society for the Propagation of the Gospel sent out masters instructed to bring the dissenters back to the true faith; Baptists, Quakers and other religious groups strove to maintain schools purveying learning and their versions of Christianity; and in large towns and cities, private masters giving classical and vocational training flourished. Although this was in the familiar colonial pattern, New England, in education as in much else, departed from the familiar. The state made the difference by entering the field of education in Massachusetts, Connecticut, New Hampshire, and (before it merged with Massachusetts) in Plymouth.

New England was settled by Puritans who, unlike some of the radical sects they left behind in England, valued education. The Puritans came to the New World imbued with a sense of mission. They had left the Old World to complete the Protestant Reformation, to demonstrate that they held the true conception of church polity and religious doctrine. The success of their task depended in large measure, they were convinced, on an educated community. Hence they wished to erect a system of schools equal to the task.

They wasted no time in getting started. Six years after the Great Migration of the faithful began in 1630, the Massachusetts General Court set Harvard College on its distinguished road. Erecting and financing schools proved a difficult task (as did financing the college for that matter) and after a period in which private contributions were relied upon, the General Court of Massachusetts decided to compel towns to assume the burden.

Towns of at least 50 families, it decreed in 1647, must maintain a reading and writing master, and those of at least 100 families, a grammar master—as one who taught Latin and Greek was often called. Responsibility for enforcement of the law was placed with the county courts which were empowered to fine offending communities.[11]

With the exception of Rhode Island, the other New England colonies followed the Massachusetts example, though requirements and enforcement varied from one to another.

The statutes compelled local authorities to provide education; they did not force parents to send their children. Nor did the laws require communities to support their schools from taxes; finance was left entirely to the community's discretion.

Under the laws a pattern of control and finance appeared among New England villages. In its meeting—the most important institution of local government—the town handled the school in about the same way it did any public business. This was a fact of enormous importance, for, so located, the school could not avoid the impact of local politics and of public financial pressures.

Though the town meeting formulated school policy, it depended upon a committee (chosen in the meeting) or the selectmen (the most important officials chosen by the meeting) to carry it out. School committees and selectmen were usually the best men available—men who had education and political experience.

Committee functions varied little from town to town. Usually the committee hired the schoolmasters, found a place for the school to meet if a regular building was lacking, and handled the finances of the school. In most towns how the committee went about hiring a master was its own business, though it did have to satisfy the meeting. In Massachusetts a statute added another requirement: the local minister with one of his brethren, or any two neighboring ministers together, were supposed to approve the schoolmaster before he was hired. Though evidence is lacking, towns seem to have observed this statute. Only rarely did cases of noncompliance get into the county courts.[12]

SCHOOL EXPENSES

As local taxes on polls and property provided most of the money for ordinary expenses, so also they provided school expenses. Only in Connecticut could towns look to the provincial government for consistent financial help. Connecticut towns received an annual contribution out of provincial taxes, but few, if any, found this subsidy large enough to meet the expenses of their schools.

In every New England colony, there were towns which could rely on public lands for part of their school expenses. Donated by individuals, the colony, or set aside by the towns themselves, these lands could be rented or sold. Shrewdly invested, the income from such lands could often relieve the taxpayers of a large portion of school charges.

One other source of finance for schools existed—the parents of boys who attended. They could be assessed tuition for every child they sent to school and until the middle of the eighteenth century they occasionally were. In Watertown, Massachusetts, in 1700, for example, six pence a week was collected for each Latin scholar, four pence for a "writer," and three for a "reader." Few towns required tuition payments but many insisted that parents provide firewood in the winter. Parents also purchased paper, pens and schoolbooks for their children.

Town growth intensified financial problems and created new difficulties. As its once compact population increased and spread out, a village saw its single school become inadequate. Far from the original settlement, children could not attend the once centrally located school. Nothing, of course, prevented a town from providing a second more accessible school—nothing except money. To soften the clamor for education that arose from remote areas, many

towns decided to uproot their schools and send them out on the road. The school might "go round with the Sun" as it did in Duxbury, Massachusetts, for many years, meeting successively in the four quarters of the town for three months at a time.

Putting the school on the move had the obvious disadvantage of spreading learning very thin. A boy who had attended the school for nine or ten months out of a year when it was located in one place might only be able to attend the moving school the three or four months that it was near his house. If he was determined he might follow the school as it traveled from one spot to the next. But this was such a difficult and expensive process that probably few boys did it.

If many towns sent their schools into outlying sections, an equal number divided themselves into districts and established a school in each. Usually citizens in each district elected a committee charged with responsibility for hiring a master and providing a place for the school to meet. The authority of the district, and its committee, rarely included more important matters. Towns continued to hold taxing powers and understandably enough were reluctant to share them. Every town allocated annually a portion of its revenues to districts on the basis of their populations. Such divisions were often contested by jealous districts, but on the whole the system worked well.

The success of the system left Rhode Islanders unimpressed, and their legislature steadfastly refused to establish educational standards for its towns. The results for the colony's intellectual life were obvious: in the seventeenth century only one Rhode Island boy attended college. In the next century more traveled to Harvard and Yale but no college took shape in Rhode Island itself until just before the Revolution.[13]

Yet there were publicly supported schools

in Rhode Island, even a few which offered instruction in Latin and Greek. But most of these schools were in towns which had been transferred from Massachusetts to Rhode Island on the settlement of a boundary dispute in 1747. Thoroughly imbued with the educational tradition of Massachusetts, they probably never considered dropping their schools in removal from the Bay Colony's jurisdiction.

For the most part, Rhode Islanders relied upon private sources for the support of schools. Often this means failed them; and their schools, compared to those of the neighboring colonies, enjoyed a precarious existence.

Rhode Island's educational history obviously parallels much of that of the southern and middle colonies, where no public commitment to education existed and no private source of support was ever entirely reliable. In no colony did one group monopolize education. Rather, variety in support, in sponsors, in state participation, and in the forms institutions assumed characterized colonial education. Inevitably educational development followed an uneven course.

It did because it was an expression of a colonial society, which was altering at an uneven pace. Education itself, of course,

was a force in this process of change. As it helped shape colonial society, so also was it shaped. What emerged by the end of the colonial period was a peculiar blend of public and private, classical and vocational, religious and secular. Modern "public education" had not yet been conceived.

NOTES

1. Bernard Bailyn, *Education in the Forming of American Society* (Chapel Hill, 1960), pp. 15–16.

2. E. S. Morgan, *The Puritan Family* (Boston, 1956), pp. 37–38; and *Virginians At Home* (Williamsburg, 1952), p. 23.

3. Morgan, *Virginians At Home*, pp. 8–32.

4. G. F. Wells, *Parish Education in Colonial Virginia* (New York, 1923), pp. 32–39.

5. Ibid., p. 48.

6. Carl Bridenbaugh, *Cities in the Wilderness* (New York, 1955), pp. 123–24, 283; and *Cities in Revolt* (New York, 1955), p. 174.

7. Ibid., p. 284; *Cities in Revolt*, p. 174.

8. Bridenbaugh, *Cities in the Wilderness*, pp. 447–48.

9. Ibid., pp. 123–26, 287.

10. Ibid., p. 287; *Cities in Revolt*, p. 174.

11. S. E. Morison, *The Intellectual Life of Colonial New England* (New York, 1956), pp. 65–78.

12. This paragraph is based on an examination of manuscript court and town records.

13. Morison, *Intellectual Life*, p. 70.

Reading 31
Education's Evolving Role

Wendell Pierce

Since Colonial days, three evolving forces in American life have been influenced, shaped, and in some instances determined by that process of transmitting knowledge, skills, and values known as education.

The first of these has been political, expressed primarily in the creation and preservation of new forms of governance.

The second has been economic, reflected in the Nation's steady growth and its transformation from a primarily agrarian to a predominantly industrial-technological economy.

The third force has been social, initially the blending of disparate elements into a more unified whole and more recently a striving to provide equal opportunities for all.

Woven throughout these three forces, an integral part of each, has been an idealistic and inspirational human quality epitomized by a passion for change, improvement, reform, and renewal.

The indispensable condition, the *sine qua non* of the American experience, has been

Source: Wendell Pierce, "Education's Evolving Role." *American Education* (May 1975), pp. 16–29.

the first of these forces—the political. Although important economic factors also were involved, it was basically certain deep philosophical and pragmatic differences between England and the American Colonies over the form and function of government that led to the upheaval of the American Revolution and the subsequent creation of an entirely new and unusually dynamic political structure. Similarly, from the beginning of American history, government has been the central force in developing an educational system, and education and politics have been inextricably linked. In the Middle and Southern Colonies, the establishment of education came about when the governing bodies gave permission to various religious groups to establish schools or granted educational charters to businessmen or landowners. In the New England Colonies, the governing bodies used the authority they had received from the crown and parliament themselves to establish, support, and administer schools and colleges. Thus colonists setting out to found a new town in Massachusetts were required to reserve one building lot for the support of education.

It is interesting to note that the legislature

of the Massachusetts Bay Colony chartered the first college in Colonial America in 1636 (Harvard), that three years later the first public school supported by direct taxation was established, and that three years after that the first locally elected school board was formed. Thus, more than 100 years before the American Revolution, were created the basic models for the governance of American education. Two principles had emerged: educational institutions derive their authority to operate from government sanction, and local schools should have some degree of local control. The broad application of those principles, however, was to come about only with the gradual evolution of the Nation itself.

While the Declaration of Independence in 1776 provided a stirring intellectual rationale for what was yet to be, it was the Constitutional Convention 11 years later that produced the cornerstone upon which a nation could be built. When the Founding Fathers met in Philadelphia during that hot summer of 1787 to design a new form of government, schools and colleges were but two of many educational institutions. The family, the farm, the shop, and the churches were of equal if not greater importance.

Few conceived that the aim of formal education should be to give all children an opportunity to develop to their full potential. Common schools for youngsters of differing religions and backgrounds were rare, and the children of the poor usually received no schooling at all. When the Constitution went into effect in 1789, American education served for the most part to maintain the kind of class distinctions characteristic of Europe at that time. Formal educational endeavors were not considered of sufficient national bearing to warrant inclusion among the basic laws establishing the new Federal republic. Instead, education was one of the responsibilities reserved, under the Bill of Rights, to the individual for-

mer Colonies that collectively had become the United States of America. Events were in fact to render education the single most important prerogative of the Colonial legislatures that evolved into the governing bodies of the quasi-independent States of the new Federal union.

Very soon after ratification of the Constitution it became apparent that the new form of government required a new view of education. A government of the people, deriving its powers from the consent of the governed, required an educated populace. President George Washington recognized this proposition in his Farewell Address. "It is essential that public opinion should be enlightened," he said on that occasion, and he went on to urge the people to promote "institutions for the general diffusion of knowledge." Similarly, Thomas Jefferson, the author of the Declaration of Independence, said that "any nation that expects to be ignorant and free . . . expects what never was and never will be"; and James Madison, a prime mover in the development of the Constitution and the Bill of Rights, declared that "knowledge will forever govern ignorance; and a people who mean to be their own governors must arm themselves with the power which knowledge gives."

In any case, under the newly developed Federal system of "shared power," responsibility for providing the means by which the people could arm themselves for popular government was retained by the several States. The States thereby found themselves held accountable for the success or failure of popular government itself, both within their own borders and thoughout the young republic. Their deliberate but successful response to this challenge was to become the signal feature of American federalism.

By 1827—38 years after the founding of the new Republic—all of the original 13 States and all but two of the 11 that had since joined the union had made some provision for public or popular education, either through their State constitutions or by legislation. The Indiana constitution of 1816, for example, stated: "Knowledge and learning generally diffused through a community being essential to the preservation of a free government, . . . it shall be the duty of the general assembly . . . to provide by law for a system of education, ascending in regular gradation from township schools to a State university, wherein tuition shall be gratis, and equally open to all."

Thus was developed during the early and middle years of the 19th century the structure and substance of a completely new kind of school system, created and sustained by State governments. Given the latter circumstance, it was natural that the impetus, both philosophical and practical, should come not from professional educators but from persons active in the political arena. It was the politicians who took the lead in institutionalizing the educational component essential to the success of the new Constitution. The philosophical foundations had been provided earlier by such national statesmen as Thomas Jefferson, James Madison, and Benjamin Franklin. The practical process of implementation was led by State legislators, notably Henry Barnard of Connecticut and Horace Mann of Massachusetts.

Jefferson and Madison, although agreeing on the need for some kind of basic education for all, were from a classical tradition that considered Latin and Greek as the cornerstones of Western civilization. It was Franklin who provided the motivating principles for a more utilitarian approach. In his "Proposals Relating to the Education of Youth in Pennsylvania," he recommended three innovations: First, emphasis on English and modern languages; second, emphasis on mathematics and science; and third, emphasis on experimentation and practical application. ("While they are reading natural

history," Franklin wrote, "might not a little gardening, grafting, modulating, etc., be taught and practiced; and now and then excursions made to the neighboring plantations of the best farmers, their methods observed and reasoned upon for the information of youth?").

Whatever their differences of approach, however, Jefferson, Madison, and Franklin were agreed on the critical importance of an educated populace. And so, spurred by the principles enunciated by such revered leaders as these, the State legislatures set out to fulfill their education responsibilities. The Virginia Legislature, for example, finally enacted in 1796 a bill "for the More General Diffusion of Knowledge" that Jefferson had introduced in 1779, although amendments giving great power to local communities served to block effective implementation until the passage of new legislation in 1829. In 1812, the New York Legislature created the first statewide public school organization in the young Nation, providing a State Department of Public Instruction headed by a State Superintendent of Schools. In the 1830s and 40s, two New England legislators —Henry Barnard and Horace Mann—played prominent roles in a sweeping reform movement that was to spread, State-by-State, across the Nation. Out of that movement came a concept of education that was not only to serve the overall needs of the society but to respond to such special circumstances as the onset of massive waves of immigrants and a shift from an agrarian to an industrial economy.

In 1837, Mann gave up the presidency of the Massachusetts Senate to become the first secretary of a new State board of education. As a 26-year-old member of the Connecticut Assembly, Barnard introduced "An Act for the Better Supervision of Common Schools," and upon its passage in 1838 he followed Mann's example and became the State's first Commissioner of Education.

These two politicians-turned-educators personified the drive toward a uniquely American form of education—the character, financing, and control of which was to prove as revolutionary in its way as the Constitution it was created to preserve.

To support that Constitution by ensuring an educated electorate, the State legislatures were confronted by issues that remain familiar today: religion, finance, and governance. The adroit though usually slow and sometimes painful manner in which these issues were resolved during the first half of the 19th century largely determined education's role in the Republic's subsequent development.

Although silent as regards education the Federal Constitution did provide guidance on the religion issue. One of many experimental elements in that experimental document linked freedom of religion to the principle of separation of church and state. Neither the Federal nor state governments could interfere in religious affairs or provide public funds to support churches or church-related activities. Proponents of a universal system of public elementary schools took this thesis a step further by arguing that nonsectarianism would promote a greater sense of national unity, an important consideration in education for citizenship in a republic. While disputes over various forms of public aid to church-related education and over the role of religion in the school program and curriculum continue today, the original principle remains: Schools controlled by churches may not be supported by public funds. This proposition has not been taken as relieving the schools of all responsibility for imparting to their pupils some sense of ethics and morality. Rather, such instruction has increasingly become more generalized, oriented toward standards and aspirations of the society as a whole rather than to the tenets of a particular sect.

If schools were to be nonsectarian, how were they to be supported? Obviously, schools created by religious groups and financially dependent upon donations and the payment of tuition—as most were in Colonial America and during the early years of the Republic—were inherently exclusive and specifically unfair to the children of the poor. One step toward ameliorating this situation was the development of "free schools" where the children of what we now term low-income parents were supported by public funds and all others paid tuition. Advocates of equality argued that such an arrangement continued and in fact fostered class distinctions, and that these distinctions could be reduced only by financing the education of *all* children, regardless of parental means, through public funds raised through public taxation. Free public education limited to the children of poverty, they insisted, was simply an elitist extension of charity and in any event a divisive force in what was supposed to be a free and equitable society. If Jefferson and Franklin and Madison had been correct in holding education to be essential in maintaining the Republic, they reasoned, schooling should be free to all and supported through public taxation. Even those taxpayers who had no children in the schools would benefit from the existence of an educated electorate. Some of the warmest and in any case most decisive advocates of these principles were to be found among the elected officials of the States, and by one State legislature after another the concept of free public education was spelled out in the State constitutions.

As for how the necessary money was to be raised, the early public schools were variously supported by liquor and amusement taxes, land grants, special taxes on parents of students, lotteries, and—stemming from a Massachusetts law of 1647— what became the characteristic method of support, the property tax. The latter was particularly pushed by school districts established in some of the bigger cities under State legislation enacted even before the States themselves began to support education. Moreover, when the States did begin to share the cost, local property taxes continued to be the chief source of school funds, as indeed they are today, amidst much controversy. Among the major elements of this controversy are first, the feeling that local tax rates have been pushed just about to the limit, and second, that wide variances in the wealth of local jurisdictions seriously undermine the principle of equal education opportunity. The school finance issue is, in short, thorny and complex, and as with so many other basic questions in education, political decision-making would appear to be central to its resolution.

In any case, the pattern having been set that the schools would be nonsectarian and publicly supported, the question remained of how they were to be governed. Obviously, if public education were left entirely to the pleasures of local communities, its scope and quality would vary enormously, as in fact was the case in the early years. Thus there evolved the concept of local control under State mandate, with the States, through their constitutions and by legislation, establishing minimum standards and requirements for public schooling. State school superintendents and State boards of education, elected by the people or appointed by the governor, were held responsible for monitoring those standards and requirements. Meanwhile, the day-to-day operation and management of local schools was left to locally appointed teachers, locally selected superintendents, and locally elected school boards. Usually the latter were made independent of other local officials or agencies—kept immune, as agents of the State, from the routine of local politics.

This uniquely American method of shared power in local-State school governance made it possible for American education to be responsive both to specific local needs and, through the broad State mandate, to the greater needs of the larger society. To make sure those needs were met, the States ultimately enacted laws requiring all communities to establish and maintain public schools. And then, led by Massachusetts in 1852, they enacted compulsory school attendance laws. And so by the middle of the 19th century the States had by and large fulfilled the need to provide enough education for enough people to be reasonably certain that there existed a reasonably well-educated electorate—though to be sure, members of racial minorities, females, and the handicapped continued to receive short shrift.

Throughout, the primary motivating force and rationale for education had been education for citizenship. As Horace Mann wrote on his tenth annual report as secretary of the Massachusetts Board of Education: "Since the achievement of American independence, the universal and ever-repeated argument in favor of free schools has been that the general intelligence which they are capable of diffusing, and which can be imparted by no other human instrumentality, is indispensable to the continuance of a republican government."

Then in the middle of the 19th century, certain social and economic forces came to the fore to compel the educational system to expand its base and broaden its horizons, first in secondary schools and later in the colleges and universities. One of the most dramatic of these forces was an industrial revolution that shifted the American economy from an agricultural to an industrial base and displayed an almost insatiable appetite for the Nation's human, physical, and financial resources. Of the three, the human proved the most essential. A small, experimental democracy with a limited population composed primarily of farmers and traders had needed to provide the majority of its citizens with only enough education to enable them to read the Scriptures. Now the demand was for trained people ready to run the factories, build the railroads, staff the businesses, start up the new industries, and handle the financial affairs of an expanding and increasingly complex economy. Meanwhile the Nation itself was expanding, both in geographic size and in population. Schooling no longer was simply a democratic ideal but a practical necessity.

And so, during the latter half of the 19th century, public education increasingly included the availability of free, public high schools in addition to the "common" schools mandated earlier by State law. In the 1870s a number of court cases, particularly the *Kalamazoo* decision of the U.S. Supreme Court, established the principle that the use of tax funds for educational purposes need not be limited to the elementary level. Thus the concept of secondary and postsecondary education as a tuition-paying proposition necessarily reserved to only a few gave way to the goal of providing and even requiring as much education as possible for all. State after State adopted compulsory school attendance laws covering youngsters to at least age 14 or 16.

The enrollment statistics tell the story of what happened thereafter. In 1900, some 70 percent of all children aged six to 13 were in elementary schools, while about ten percent of those 14–17 years of age were attending secondary schools. By 1930, nearly 85 percent of elementary school-age children were enrolled, and the figure for high school-age youngsters had climbed to 50 percent. The current figures are almost 100 percent of all children aged 6–13 and more than 90 percent of those aged 14–17. Even more remarkable has been the growth of enrollment rates in postsecondary education. In 1900, less than five percent of all

youth aged 18–21 were attending colleges or universities. By 1930, this proportion had grown to 20 percent. Today it exceeds 50 percent.

This record contribution to the Nation's welfare is no better illustrated than by its economic impact, both on the individual and in the aggregate. Most easily measured is the financial benefit of education to the individual. As analyses by the U.S. Census Bureau show, the more education people have the higher their lifetime earnings are likely to be. For example, the lifetime worth of a 22-year-old male shows the following average variance according to different educational backgrounds: Less than eight years of schooling—$159,000; elementary school graduate—$192,000; one to three years of high school—$216,000; high school graduate—$264,000; one to three years of college—$301,000; college graduate—$388,000; five years or more of college—$443,000. Obviously, one of education's primary contributions has been to provide a greater number of individuals with greater personal income and employment security.

Nor is such private return the only justification for public support of education endeavors that now directly involve nearly 30 percent of the population and consume more than $100 billion annually—almost eight percent of the Gross National Product. As the individual benefits, so does the Nation as a whole. Higher personal incomes provide a direct benefit to local, State, and Federal governments in the form of larger tax returns. Communities in which the median income is high enjoy higher average per capita retail sales. And, harking back to that early American ideal, statistics indicate that the more education a person has, the greater that person's interest in political affairs. The percent of those casting ballots in Presidential elections, for example, increases in direct proportion to the level of education attained.

Beyond these matters, a number of economists in recent years have concluded that education is a far more vital factor in stimulating economic growth than previously had been recognized. Traditionally it had been held that while education produces and reproduces a body of skilled manpower, it had little to do with increased productivity as such. Physical capital and natural resources—these, it was maintained, are the keys to economic development. Economists today respond that such a position ignores the force of human capital—that education not only provides trained workers but carries with it the potential for creating and developing new goods, new technologies, new services. No other kind of capital, they say, combines all these features. Thus a number of economists now believe that the growth in real per capita income in the United States since 1930 has been due far more to advances in knowledge and education than to private capital investments. Moreover, their projections for the future indicate that this effect will be even more powerful in the future.

In any case, it is self-evident that nations with high education attainment levels tend to have higher per capita incomes, regardless of the level of their natural resources, than nations with high levels of natural resources and low education attainment levels. Switzerland and Denmark, with few natural resources, are cases in point. So are Colombia and Brazil, which have high levels of natural resources but low education attainment levels and low per capita incomes. The United States, with high levels of both natural resources and education attainment, has the highest per capita income in the world. The American labor force possesses more educational capital per person than that of any other country, and the result is to be seen in the Nation's extraordinary economic development.

But the Nation's schools and colleges have been expected to make further contributions—to provide more than education for citizenship and education for economic growth. From the beginning they have also been called up to fulfill a variety of social as well as political and economic functions. It was the schools, more than any other institution in American society, that provided the cohesion necessary for the creation of a sense of national unity. It was the schools that bore the prime responsibility for "Americanizing" the millions upon millions of immigrants that poured into the Nation from the middle of the 19th century through the second decade of the 20th. And it has been the schools and colleges of the country that have been in the forefront of more contemporary efforts to provide equal opportunities for those who once had been systematically excluded—women, blacks and other minorities, the mentally or physically handicapped.

Americans have deliberately used their schools and colleges as agents of social change. They have asked more of their education institutions than any people in history. In so dong they have exhibited what has been termed a "consistent, often intense, and sometimes touching faith in the efficacy of popular education." Paradoxically, education is considered so essential a part of the national experience that it frequently leads the list of scapegoats when the Nation suffers a reversal. When the Soviet Union was the first to orbit a man-made satellite, it was American education that was held to have failed. The more furious the debate over desegregation, the more visibly the schools have occupied the center of the storm. Criticism of education is something of a national sport.

Some of this criticism is justified, though it should be noted that there has always been a gap between expectation and performance. In any case, it is apparent that elaborate administrative bureaucracies, deemed essential to the management of mass education enterprises, frequently have proven to be barriers to social and economic mobility. More crucially, significant numbers of young people are not benefiting appropriately from their school experience, for reasons unrelated to native intelligence. According to the National Assessment of Educational Progress, the Achievement of young Americans who are poor or black, who live in the inner city or in rural communities or in the Southeast, lags behind national levels in a number of subjects.

And yet, as historian Henry Steele Commager has noted, "No other people ever demanded so much of education. . . . None other was ever served so well by its schools and educators."

There is a story that when an aging Benjamin Franklin was leaving one of the final sessions of the Constitutional Convention, a woman asked what kind of government the fledgling nation was to have. Franklin replied, "A republic, madam. If you can keep it." Thanks in no small part to the role of education, we've kept it.

Reading 32

An American Paradox

Myrtle Bonn

"Built like a scarecrow, a gangling, pin-headed, flat-topped oaf. But what would anyone expect? He was just a teacher." (That is Washington Irving's superstitious, simple, Ichabod Crane.)

"A ridiculous figure, his bald head covered with an ill-fitting wig . . . a man who had aspired to be a doctor but who had been forced by poverty to be nothing more than a schoolmaster." (That is Mark Twain's description of Old Dobbins.)

"Their teacher was a gaunt, red-faced spinster, with fierce, glaring eyes." (That is Thomas Wolfe in *Look Homeward, Angel*.)

These fictional teachers are part of a peculiarly American paradox—a paradox compounded of a high regard for education on one hand and the generally low regard that has usually been accorded teachers on the other. Time and the kind of people entering the profession have enormously elevated the status of teachers, of course, but historically they have drawn mixed reviews, as witness Willard S. Elsbree on the Colonial schoolmaster:

Source: Myrtle Bonn, "An American Paradox." *American Education* (November 1974), pp. 24–28.

He was a God-fearing clergyman, he was an unmitigated rogue; he was amply paid, he was accorded a bare pittance; he made teaching a life career, he used it merely as a steppingstone; he was a classical scholar, he was all but illiterate; he was licensed by bishop or Colonial governor, he was certified only by his own pretentions; he was a cultured gentleman, he was a crude-mannered yokel; he ranked with the cream of society, he was regarded as menial. In short, he was neither a type nor a personality, but a statistical distribution represented by a skewed curve.

Somewhere on that curve appeared Joannes Van Ecklen, who signed a contract in 1682 to "keep school" in the town of Flatbush, Long Island. Five hours a day, six days a week, from September to June, Joannes taught a class of about 16 children (some schoolmasters handled more than 100). He received the tuition fees plus a salary—with the use of a dwelling, barn, pasture, and meadow thrown in.

With no lesson plans to draw up, few papers to grade, no curriculum materials to select, no conferences to attend, Joannes would have run out of things to do, even after making quills, the most time-consuming adjunct to teaching. So it was understood he would take a second job—as minister's assistant, though had he lived elsewhere he might have been juryman, town crier, registrar of probate, or tradesman. (John Thelwell of Wilmington, Delaware, held so many extra jobs that someone recalled: "It would be easier to say what he did not do than to recount his numerous duties.")

As minister's assistant, Joannes was to "keep the church clean . . . serve as messenger for the consistory . . . give the funeral invitations, dig the graves, and toll the bell. . . ." He was of course paid extra for this moonlighting.

Considerably further up the social scale were the schoolmasters of New England's Latin grammar schools. Usually coming from wealthy or at least well-connected families, these pedagogues were charged with preparing the sons of other well-to-do parents for college, though many regarded this task as a barely bearable stop-gap until they could arrange more lucrative and prestigious careers.

Lowest on the teaching ladder in Colonial times was the "dame"—a housewife, often the spouse of the local minister, seeking extra income. She listened to the younger children recite their letters and the older ones read and spell from their primers while she sewed or knitted. It was the dame who polished manners, instructed the youngsters in how to bow and curtsy properly, and impressed on them the importance of avoiding such vulgarities as "stepping on vermin in the sight of others." The first dame to set up shop in Northfield, Massachusetts, reported that she cared for 20 youngsters during the summer months and found time to "make shirts for the Indians at eight pence each."

Procedures for hiring teachers were fairly uniform throughout New England. A select-

man or town father recruited candidates who then stood for approval by the minister and before a town meeting. Outlying areas settled for anyone answering an ad or located by hearsay. As for Joannes Van Ecklen, the people in Flatbush were doubtless more concerned with whether he held a license from the British governor of New York which guaranteed his religious conformity than with his academic achievements.

The schoolmaster's wages were usually low, since he was in most instances deemed an unproductive worker, a tolerated necessity, a cheap commodity. He represented the budget item that could most readily be squeezed for greater community economy. Whether such treatment was the cause or the effect, townspeople found that hiring a schoolmaster could be risky. One was accused of paying "more attention to the tavern than to the school"; another was fired for "obtaining articles from stores in the name of the rector and taking them to pawnshops." Contracts were usually written for a year and if the schoolmaster failed— whether for reasons of drinking, using profanity, piling up debts, behaving "unseemly" toward women, or simply for being unpopular with the community—he'd move on or make a change in his profession.

In a society where picking apples on the sabbath brought a fine, the schoolmaster's comportment was narrowly prescribed. Joannes Van Ecklen came a cropper when he and some other locals took issue with a group of wealthy landowners. He was promptly fired and replaced. He then added to his offense by setting up a competing school. This enterprise was halted by a cease and desist order, and Van Ecklen dropped out of sight for a while, though he seems later to have returned to teaching in Flatbush, presumably made more tractable by his experience.

Though political activity such as his was not to be tolerated, a much more common cause for dismissal in Colonial days and for a long time thereafter had to do with maintaining discipline. The schoolmaster with insufficient skill in keeping prank-prone boys in line could never feel secure. If he ousted troublemakers wholesale, his school gained a reputation for being too hard. If he permitted insubordination, he was a "poor manager." In any case, the whipping post, the ferule, and later the hickory stick became indispensable allies of some teachers. A North Carolina schoolmaster developed a set of rules starring the stick—three lashes for calling each other names, for example, two for blotting a copy book, three for failing to bow to visitors.

Some schoolmasters, especially those with advanced degrees, were accorded the title of Mister and assigned prominent pews in the church—important social indicators in Colonial times. While such teachers moved in aristocratic society, others arrived as indentured slaves bringing a lesser price than convicts.

Came the Revolution—and if the schoolmaster wasn't called to arms, he found himself in a nonessential career. In those schools that continued to operate, the teacher had trouble finding classroom materials. Hostilities had cut off what had in any case been a sparse supply of books, imported from England. Moreover, the content of the texts that remained had become instantly unsuitable, since they were of course British in character. Revised versions were ultimately issued, one of the most popular being, *A New England Primer* (which taught "millions to read and not one to sin"), but for some time spellers still contained honorary English titles and math books ignored decimal currency.

In the years between the Revolution and the Civil War, the idea of free, tax-supported schools took root and teachers seemed headed for a new lease on life. Education leaders rose to influence, literature

on the importance of education abounded, statutes appeared in State constitutions indicating a recognition of the obligation to provide education for all. What most impressed a New England schoolteacher during the early part of the 19th century, however, was his school's lack of an outhouse and the community's failure to provide a manageable building or even maintain a proper supply of firewood. He and his pupils nearly froze in the mornings and almost suffocated by the smoke later in the day. He figured out that his school had seen 37 teachers in 30 years.

Change nevertheless was in the wind, though not all were to welcome its arrival. There was the matter, for example, of teacher preparation. The notion that teachers, like bookkeepers, required special training was regarded by many oldtimers as an affront to their dignity and an unwarranted reflection upon their competence. But the country was growing in land and people, demand was increasing for a more sophisticated work force, and the need for teachers able to help build such a work force became acute. The result of these pressures was the establishment of numerous institutions specifically focused on teacher training—normal schools, as they were called. About a dozen came into being between 1834 and the Civil War, and for the remainder of the century they were established at a rate of two or three a year. Normal schools offered one year (and later, longer) courses that taxed neither the pocketbook nor the mind. Men were admitted, but it was young ladies who flocked to them.

The first normal school students came straight from elementary school; if they retained a smattering of what they had learned there they were acceptable. After a few years the standards were raised to require two years of high school. Not until after 1900 was high school graduation a prerequisite. Highbrow education was not the goal of these young ladies. Some may have had a desire to serve mankind through teaching, but many were seeking a profitable way to spend the time between school years and marriage.

With the institution of grade levels in the schools and the consequent separation of the younger from the older children, the argument no longer held that females made unsuitable teachers because they could not handle obstreperous older boys. It had to be conceded that they could at least cope with the younger children, the Boston Board of Education declaring, for example, that women were "infinitely more fit than males to be the guides and exemplars of young children"; that they possessed milder manners, purer morals, which makes "the society of children delightful and turns duty into pleasure."

Not everyone jumped on the distaff bandwagon. A Rhode Island superintendent insisted that no matter how well qualified, a female teacher could not be employed "for the same reason she cannot so well manage a vicious horse or other animal, as a man may do."

But the voices of dissension soon became muted, and before long, women were appearing in classrooms everywhere. In 1862, New Jersey reported: "It is somewhat remarkable that the number of female teachers has been gradually increasing from year to year, until it now exceeds the number of male teachers. . . ." Other States were soon to report similar experiences. The Civil War would ring the final knell to teaching as a predominantly male profession.

The average woman teacher, because of her youth, because she was not career minded, because she was ignorant of national affairs, did not involve herself with the State and local teachers' associations that were forming. She was seen as having no interest in educational reform and in any case insufficient knowledge and experience to contribute to it. Those who tried found themselves subjected to sometimes humiliating discriminatory practices. Women were, to be sure, welcomed by the new National Teachers Association, founded in 1857, which later became the National Education Association (NEA). But in those days if a female wanted to present a paper, regulations required that it be read for her by a male member.

Meanwhile as education leaders debated whether teaching could be reduced to a science and if physical culture and singing belonged in the "regular branches," the great body of teachers was more concerned with the practical problems involved in "boarding out" or the personal penalties their careers exacted of them.

The male teacher had long "boarded around" on the theory that close association with local families would give him a better understanding of the students and the community. Not that this was the teacher's idea. Living as a guest afforded little privacy, no guarantee of nourishing food or warm quarters, limited control over leisure time, and the frequent discomfort of long trudges to and from school. It was simply a cheap way to support the schools. A Pennsylvania county superintendent argued: "By this mode the burden of boarding the teacher is never felt; whereas if the teacher were boarded in one place, and money paid therefore, the cash flow of supporting our schools would be nearly double."

Historian Mason Stone tells of a Vermont schoolmaster who suffered a diet of tough gander. The bird was served at a Monday dinner and thereafter for each meal, including breakfast, for the rest of the week. The schoolmaster confided in his diary: "Dinner—cold gander again; didn't keep school this afternoon; weighed and found I had lost six pounds the last week; grew alarmed; had a talk with Mr. B. and concluded I had boarded out his share."

Because women were more trouble to board than men and fewer homes offered them hospitality, boarding around was gradually "phased out" during the second half of the 1800s. Nevertheless, the teacher continued to have little personal freedom and to be the object of close scrutiny—except, curiously enough, in the area of professional skills. Few laymen, or educators for that matter, were competent to judge teaching ability and fewer still bothered to try. The situation changed somewhat with the advent of county superintendents, but even then teachers could expect an inspection visit only about once a year. Moreover, county superintendents were elected to their positions, and some were merely inept political hacks who looked at outside paint with more diligence than they reviewed performance in the classroom. Many others, however, conscientiously did their best to cover their territories with horse and buggy and do whatever they could to make schooling more effective. The situation sometimes discouraged even the most ebullient of them. A Pennsylvania superintendent, for instance, found that "not a scholar in the school could tell me what country he lived in." Not that the situation was universally this dismal. There was at least one good teacher to match each poor one, and in many instances the teacher was held in the highest regard.

As many of the traveling superintendents observed, however, the situation was disturbingly spotty, and the feeling grew that if the schools were to have competent teachers, each community could no longer be left to set its own standards. With normal schools improving and communication facilities expanding, educators began to devise schemes to standardize—at least within

States—requirements for securing a teaching certificate. After the Civil War, authority to issue certificates began to move from local and county officials to the States. A teacher applying for a license was required to take a written examination prepared by State authorities. As long as local and county superintendents were responsible for grading the papers, however, they still controlled certification for all practical purposes.

Teachers needed only a tenth-grade education to be eligible for the tests—even in the 20th century. (Indiana in 1907 became the first State to require a high school diploma as a condition for all teaching certificates.) If they passed the written exam, they had a blanket certificate good for any subject at any grade level. Gradually, the idea of special certificates for special teaching assignments caught on, as did the notion that graduation from high school and, later, college would be a sounder basis for evaluation than a single test.

The typical teacher of 1911, according to the first study made of the characteristics of schoolteachers, was 24 years old, female, had entered teaching at 19, and had four years of training beyond the elementary school. Her parents were native born, her father was most likely a farmer or tradesman, and she had to earn her own way.

Fifteen years later, a similar survey showed little change. The teacher of the mid-Twenties came from a rural area or small town. She had never traveled more than a couple of hundred miles from her home, and had had little exposure to art or music. Light literature—popular magazines such as the *Saturday Evening Post* and *Ladies' Home Journal*—was her preference, and she scanned the newspaper daily. Attempts to elevate teacher preparation standards had meanwhile been launched, but then came the dislocations of World War I. In 1918, according to records of The National Education Association, half of the 600,000 teachers then in the classroom lacked special training and about one-sixth were without even a tenth-grade education. As late as 1926, 15 states still had no definite scholarship requirements for a certificate.

Teachers continued to be bound by petty restrictions that had little to do with their teaching. Before and immediately after the war, the management of their private lives extended even to being told to what charities they were obliged to contribute. Tenure was insecure, without provisions for sickness or old age. And to take a stand on a public issue was to commit professional suicide. Personal freedoms were similarly limited. Well into the 20th century, the common habit of tobacco chewing was adequate cause for denial of certificates to male teachers. A teacher who was for some reason invited to a party was not supposed to dance, and failure to attend church services regularly was taken as sure proof of moral decay. As late as the 1930s, one teacher complained: "I cannot be funny or act like a human being. I must possess all the dignity and peculiarities of an old maid."

Employment of teachers in their home towns was prohibited in Alabama, and a North Carolina county outlawed "quarreling among teachers." Between 1920 and 1930, school authorities in several communities refused to appoint teachers who bobbed their hair, painted their lips, or rouged their cheeks. Such restrictions often were embodied in State codes or written into contracts. A Virginia county school system rule still on the books in 1935 read, "Any conduct such as staying out late at night, etc., which may cause criticism of the teacher will not be tolerated by the school board."

As individuals, teachers were often praised, venerated, and even loved by the communities they served. As a class, they were stereotyped—congenital old maids of both sexes, too incompetent to compete in the world of work, too frustrated to take their place in normal society, somewhat odd in appearance and dress, lacking in social graces. "You can tell a teacher as far as you can see one," went one of the clichés. Or, "He who can, does; he who can't, teaches."

As with Americans generally, the arrival of the 20th century was accompanied by considerable gear-shifting with regard to teachers—in their status, in the way in which they were viewed, and in the way they viewed themselves. Both cause and effect were involved in a surge of activity chiefly conducted through local and State professional organizations at first, then rising to the national level—aimed at achieving better salaries, tenure, higher certification standards, a larger role in setting school policies, and greater personal freedom. In the beginning these moves brought few gains, but as a consequence of them the pattern was set. Teachers were determined to win a place in the sun.

Their efforts have not been universally welcomed or endorsed, particularly when their new-born militancy was translated into boycotts and strikes. Even then, however, the criticism has primarily been directed toward the organizations involved rather than teachers as such. Moreover, to the extent that their demands have been aimed at providing more competent instruction and more effective learning, teachers struck a responsive chord. Meanwhile teachers were becoming not simply more militant but better educated, more competent, more involved. And as it turned out, more highly respected.

Consider, for example, some results from a series of Gallup polls conducted for Phi Delta Kappa, the education fraternity. When asked if they would like their children to become teachers, three out of four parents said yes, they would, and when the sample was narrowed down to parents with children still in school, the ratio climbed to four out of five.

As for the teachers themselves, though they have changed considerably over the years, there is this constant: Like the Colonial schoolmaster, he or she is an individual, "neither a type nor a personality, but a statistical distribution represented by a skewed curve." Only today the curve is even less symmetrical. It includes blacks in cities and suburbs, people with Spanish surnames, Native Americans on and off reservations. As it includes people trained in traditional institutions who earned their credentials by taking traditional courses, so does it encompass people who have been certificated because they acquired and demonstrated specific competencies. It includes people who completed college in four years and went straight into teaching, and it includes people who have climbed a career ladder through multiple levels. It includes people who teach in a conventional manner in self-contained classrooms as well as individuals who work in "open" or "free" schools where youngsters are responsible for much of their own learning.

From a compilation of statistics about teachers by the National Education Association comes this odd assortment of facts: The median age of teachers is 35 years. A little over eight percent of all teachers are black. About 50 percent of all teachers come from blue-collar working class or farm backgrounds, but the percentage of teachers with fathers in one of the professions is increasing. There are more male teachers today than there were five or ten years ago, especially on the elementary school level. Seven teachers in ten are married. The percentage of men teachers with working wives has increased. Ninety-seven percent of all teachers hold at least a Bachelor's degree. The best prepared teachers tend to work in large school systems.

Finally, a statistic that serves as a kind of intangible monument to the teaching professionals who recognize the unending series of challenges they are called upon to meet and who have the will and the courage to meet them: Nine of every ten teachers plan to go on teaching.

Reading 33

Master Dove's One-Room School

Judith Selden

"There he is! The Master's coming!" Jeremiah Gladstone abruptly reversed his direction, abandoned the squirrel he had been chasing, and dashed toward the schoolhouse. Following 35 or so other boys of assorted ages, sizes, and backgrounds, he neatly vaulted the two-foot wooden fence, ran up the path, and pushed inside the door of the one-room, wooden building. The year was 1775 in the Massachusetts Colony, and Jeremiah Gladstone was nine years old.

Once inside, the boys wasted no time in finding their seats, for Master Dove was not noted for dealing kindly with tardy pupils. The Master arrived promptly at 7 a.m. in the spring and fall and 8 a.m. in the winter, and he expected to see his students in their seats when he arrived. Jeremiah was not interested in incurring the Master's wrath, so he wedged himself onto one of the backless benches in the first row, on the side of the room.

There were two rows of pine benches on three sides of the room, facing the huge pot-bellied stove in the center. Behind the

Source: Judith Selden, "Master Dove's One-Room School." *American Education* (June 1974), pp. 8–10.

benches, against each wall, there was a continuous, sloping shelf at waist level which the older students used—as a support to lean against while they were studying, and as a desk while they were writing. There was a narrower shelf under it on which they could store their books and supplies. Within the square of the outer benches, there was a line of lower benches for the smaller children. The space in the middle of the room served as a kind of stage for recitations.

The Master's desk was in the front of the room, next to the door. Jeremiah knew that inside that massive piece of oak were the tops, balls, marbles, and other forbidden items which Master Dove confiscated from his pupils with uncanny regularity. Just yesterday, Jeremiah himself had been the victim of the Master's quick hand, and had lost the prized penknife which his older brother Thomas had entrusted to him last summer. He had promised to guard it while Thomas was away at college in nearby Cambridge, and Jeremiah dreaded disappointing his brother.

While he brooded, the din in the classroom mounted to an earsplitting pitch. Then suddenly it stopped, and the room became silent. Jeremiah dragged himself out of his miserable reverie and waited expectantly for Master Dove to march through the door. As usual, he prayed that one of these days the Master would arrive having been transformed the previous night into a kind, twinkling man; maybe someone like his uncle Joseph, who always had a piece of maple sugar in his pocket and could make anyone laugh.

But, alas, today was not the day, for in strode Master Dove looking rigid and sour, brandishing the dreaded, ever-present ferule, with his three-cornered hat riding majestically atop his impeccable gray wig. Even his worn gray silk waistcoat with its rows of silver buttons rode rigidly on his lanky frame, as if reluctant to flow naturally for fear of being punished.

Jeremiah found it hard to believe that the schoolmaster had been born with such a sour disposition, and he was forever looking for some sad, mystical reason for Master Dove's transformation. The lad's father, who knew a lot about most things and didn't put much stock in sad mysticism, said that Master Dove was probably "of a sour bent" because he had to work very hard, not only teaching his pupils but also helping to maintain the school building, for which he was paid only £30 per year. Jeremiah thought that was a lot of money to pay such a crotchety person.

"Good morning, Master Dove," chanted the boys in unison, at no seeming cue other than the Master's arrival at his desk. He peered over the top of his square, tortoise-shell glasses, and gazed at his charges who shifted uncomfortably against one another.

Jeremiah knew by heart what the procedure for the day would be. It would start with the "first class" (the oldest boys) reading from the Scriptures. Then would come the thawing and watering of the ink, in preparation for writing, which consumed a major portion of the morning. Not a meticulous person by nature, Jeremiah didn't care much for the discipline involved in copying for page after page such phrases as "Contentment is a virtue" or "Procrastination is the thief of time"—two of Master Dove's favorites—until he had mastered the letters. He was consoled, nevertheless, by his fascination with the ink he used and the process of ink-making that his father had taught him when he started going to school. Together they had gathered the bark of swamp maple and boiled it in an iron kettle to give it a more perfect black color. When it thickened, they had added copperas, or green vitriol to it. Jeremiah loved to dip his quill pen into the ink and make huge swirls on his paper, but he knew that paper was scarce and must not be wasted.

After writing, it would be the turn of the second class to read from the Scriptures, and then the turn of Jeremiah's class. After that, the smallest children would be called out to read a sentence or two from their reader, the *Hornbook*, since they were not yet ready to read from the Scriptures. Jeremiah still had his *Hornbook*, which really wasn't a book at all. It was a thin board on which was pasted a printed leaf containing the alphabet and some short sentences. This was covered with a thin sheet of transparent horn to protect it from the invariably dirty fingers it would fall prey to.

Promptly at half past ten each morning, the boys were allowed to go outside for a short recess. On the way back inside, each child was permitted a drink of water from the pail near the door, but Jeremiah was always one of the last ones back inside so he generally got only a longing look at the water, and a menacing look from Master Dove.

The rest of the morning was spent working on spelling, and Jeremiah liked to make this part of the day into a game. While Master Dove read out words from the handsome *WATTS Compleat SPELLING-BOOK*, and then waited as the class spelled the words out loud, Jeremiah tried to see how often he could be the first to finish.

And then it was time for lunch. Jeremiah walked the half-mile home for lunch with his cousin George, who was 11 and in the first class, and George's brother Matthew, who was seven and, to Jeremiah's mind, a hateful pest. Jeremiah wished his own brothers were closer to him in age so they could walk home from school with him, but Thomas was 15 and studying at Harvard College, and Jabez was only three. Nearer his own age were his two sisters, ten-year-old Abigail, and Rebecca, who was eight and his favorite. Their days were spent at home with their mother, learning how to cook and sew, because as Jeremiah's father rightly said, "A gentleman has no interest in an educated woman." Jeremiah thought that this made sense because most girls were silly anyway, although he recently overheard his parents saying that some of the daughters of the townspeople were attending school for a couple of hours each day after the boys went home. Supposedly the schools were built for everyone, rich or poor, and to some people that even meant girls. Abigail and Rebecca, however, took dancing lessons instead because their parents thought that was more important.

After lunch, Jeremiah returned to school for the afternoon, which commenced with each class reading out loud in turn from *The New England Primer,* an 88-page, 3 1/2-inch by 4 1/2-inch leather-bound book which, except for some spelling lessons and an occasional illustration, didn't hold Jeremiah's interest. He knew it was important to learn the Westminster Catechism, but he had great difficulty memorizing the tedious questions and answers. He forced himself to concentrate on it because he knew he would have to recite a portion this Sunday in church, and he definitely didn't want to disgrace his family by not being prepared. Aside from the obvious embarrassment in church for any child who had not memorized his catechism, Master Dove's own brand of disapproval, manifested with the help of the ferule, was not something Jeremiah coveted.

When each class had completed its reading from the primer, there was more spelling, and finally some arithmetic. There was no textbook for this study, but Master Dove, like most schoolmasters, gave each boy pages of handwritten rules and problems from a manuscript sum-book which he had studied from when he was a boy. Jeremiah couldn't imagine that the Master had ever been a boy, much less one who had had as much trouble struggling with problems and sums as Jeremiah himself did.

The boys were usually weary by this time, because the day was long, and they knew it was almost five o'clock, the time that school was dismissed. The fire in the stove was waning, and Jeremiah was chilly and hungry. The dismally vacant walls and stained, gritty windows didn't do much to cheer him up, and he sorely wished there was something of interest in the classroom for him to look at. Across the room, two of the youngest boys were fidgeting and pushing each other, trying to see who would be forced off the bench and into the Master's wrath first. Jeremiah hoped that school would end before the Master caught them.

"And tomorrow, Jeremiah Gladstone will light the fire before school." Master Dove planted his hat firmly on his curls, and strode from the room. Jeremiah breathed a sigh of relief and suddenly, forgetting his fatigue, hunger, or the cold, ran from the schoolhouse to find that squirrel.

Reading 34

The Historical Roots of the Parochial Schools in America

Peter H. Rossi
Alice S. Rossi

The most widespread conception of American material well-being sees the great wealth of this country primarily as being poured into the hectic consumption of a glittering variety of chrome-trimmed conveniences and high-calorie foods. While there is some truth in this conception, as in any stereotype, the high national income manifests itself in a number of ways. The numbers of voluntarily supported religious and educational institutions, privately financed community services, and private public health organizations is impressive. America's better universities (and some of its least commendable) exist on private bounty, past and present, despite the fact that state governments provide inexpensive and generally good higher education in state universities.

Americans also maintain what is undoubtedly the largest privately financed elementary school system: the denominational

Source: Peter H. Rossi and Alice S. Rossi, "The Historical Roots of the Parochial Schools in America." Reprinted by permission of Daedalus, Journal of the American Academy of Arts and Sciences, Boston, Massachusetts, Spring 1961, "Ethnic Groups in American Life."

schools of the Roman Catholic Church. On a smaller scale, other denominations, notably the Evangelical Lutheran Church (the Missouri Synod), also maintain private elementary schools. At present some six and a half million pupils are enrolled in the denominational schools, constituting approximately 15 percent of the total elementary school population. Of these six and a half million, approximately 85 percent, or five and a half million, are enrolled in the parochial schools of the Roman Catholic Church.

Privately financed denominational elementary schools paralleling an excellent state-financed system can be found in other countries (for example, France), but the unique characteristic of the American denominational schools is their attempt to provide education on a mass basis. In France, Church schools primarily serve the upper classes. In contrast, our parochial schools recruit their pupils from all levels of society. These are not schools for the elite, primarily supported by high tuition rates, but a privately financed school system designed to serve the mass of Catholics, who, by virtue of their origins in Europe and the recency of arrival in this country, are spread throughout our class system, with heavy concentrations in the lower strata of American society. . . .

At the time of the adoption of the Federal Constitution, nine of the American states had established churches, with several denominations represented. Perhaps only the little state of Rhode Island had complete religious liberty as we conceive of it today. When supported as a state enterprise or as an arm of local government, the schools of the time were denominational in character, upholding in their instruction the doctrines of a particular church. Some of today's great secular universities were then primarily denominational seminaries: Harvard was a state-supported Congregational seminary. For some decades after the War of Independence, this condition persisted, for the First Amendment prohibited the federal government from establishing a national church but did not prevent individual states from giving special recognition to particular denominations.

The state churches of the eighteenth century did not last long into the nineteenth. Immigration as well as schisms in established denominations brought about a proliferation of sects, so that by 1840 the separation of church and state had taken place in every state within the Union. During the same period, interest was growing in public education. Public school systems were being established, and controversies arose over what were the religious teachings to be taught within them. In state after state the solution to the diversity of denominations was to make the new schools "nonsectarian."

As the public schools extended their coverage and became increasingly "nonsectarian," they came under fire from the more orthodox denominations, whose religious leaders felt that a secular education would weaken the faith of children. Several denominations began to consider the advisability of setting up parochial schools. In the 1840s, the Presbyterian Church urged its congregations to set up schools for children between the ages of five and twelve. The Presbyterian experiment was at best feeble, and by 1870 this denomination had given up its attempt. The various Lutheran denominations, which since their arrival in this country had maintained denominational schools, renewed their emphasis on the importance of church schools. In 1846 the Evangelical Lutheran Church (the Missouri Synod) was established. From its inception it emphasized denominational schooling, and today it operates the largest parochial school system among the Protestant denominations.

It was also during this period that the Roman Catholic Church began to grow to the stature of a major denomination. The heavy Irish immigration to the eastern seaboard cities, plus the arrival of many from the German Catholic states, swelled the ranks of the Church. To the Church leaders of the time, the "nonsectarian" public schools, in which the King James version of the Bible was used, were "Protestant" schools. Early in this period the bishops of the Church urged each parish to establish a denominational school; but it was not until the Third Plenary Council of the hierarchy, held in Baltimore in 1884, that the Church made it obligatory for each parish to set up its own school and for each Catholic to send his children to a parochial school. Catholic parochial schools—state-supported, if possible, privately financed, if necessary—were seen as the answer to the need felt for the religious education of Catholic youth.

Of the several nineteenth-century attempts to set up mass denominational school systems in the United States only the German Lutheran and the Roman Catholic efforts have successfully survived to this day. From the attempts of the other denominations only a few secondary schools have survived, but these are primarily serving an elite clientele.

It is crucial to an understanding of the contemporary functioning of parochial schools to consider the factors which have made for the success of the Roman Catholic and the German Lutheran denominational schools. Several salient features of the two successful parochial school systems are probably among the most important reasons for their success. To begin with, in both cases, more than denominational purity was at stake. In each case very self-conscious ethnic groups were identified with each denomination: the Irish and Germans in the case of the Roman Catholics, and the Germans alone in the case of the Lutheran Church. In each case the church was a major form of identification in the old country, and the strength of identification was augmented by their experience in the new land. Both the Irish and the Lutherans had had some experience in maintaining their church under unfavorable conditions: the Orthodox Lutherans against a reformed state church in Germany, and the Irish against the established church of England. The Irish in particular had developed the institutional devices for maintaining their church in a hostile environment and had also evolved customs favoring a heavy financial support of church activities. In addition, each group brought with it an experienced religious cadre, and when established in this country quickly set up organizations for the recruiting and training of future cadres.

In the case of the Lutheran schools, their ethnic character was quite obvious. These were German language schools in which religious subjects, at least, were taught in that language. German was the liturgical language of the Missouri Synod up to only a few decades ago, and even today the church leaders are largely from German ethnic stock. It should be noted that the success of the Lutheran schools was greatest in the rural areas and small towns of the Midwest, where many Germans had settled. Even as late as 1947 a majority of the Lutheran schools were one- or two-room rural schools. Although the amount of instruction conducted in German had decreased considerably since the anti-German hysteria of World War I, it seems likely that these schools have played an important part in keeping German as the most widely used foreign language in American households: in 1940, of the fourteen million Americans who spoke a foreign language as their "mother tongue," over three and a quarter million spoke German, more than twice as many as spoke the next most popular language, Italian.

While the rural isolation of the German Lutherans helped them maintain a viable denominational school system, the urban Irish Catholic schools derived a similar strength from their position at the bottom of the urban heap. The anti-Catholic movements of the nineteenth century helped maintain the strong attachment of the Irish to the Roman Catholic Church. The German Catholics benefited from very much the same geographical isolation as did the Lutherans.

Undoubtedly, these two denominations were aided in the struggle to maintain their parochial schools by their ideologies of non-compromise with their environments. Both the Roman Catholic Church and the Missouri Synod were militant and dogmatic bodies each of whose leaders insisted that their church alone was truly Christian.

The successful denominational schools, therefore, were those identified with particular ethnic groups and run by religious organizations which either already had, or quickly developed, the institutions for maintaining and recruiting a cadre of teaching personnel. In more recent times, the success of the French Canadian immigrants in establishing and maintaining an extensive foreign-language parochial school system provides another illustration of the importance of this pattern. As we shall see, these historical origins have left their mark on the Roman Catholic schools of today.

Although these are factors which apparently make for an initial success in establishing a successful denominational school system, they are not as well suited to the maintenance of such systems over long periods of time given the processes of assimilation which all ethnic groups in America sooner or later apparently undergo. As the period of its initial entry into this country recedes into the past, the attachment of each group to its national origins tends to be dissipated, and the continued success of

a denominational school system may perhaps be best assured by calling upon other types of motivation. The denominational schools, compared to the public schools, must provide as much or more aid to the aspirations of the emerging middle classes and at the same time lose some of their ethnic stamp. In this connection we note the heavier emphasis during the past two decades in both Roman Catholic and Missouri Synod schools on higher educational standards, and a corresponding decline of instruction in foreign languages. At present the Roman Catholic schools are more than holding their own, but the evidence seems to point to a considerable decline in the popularity of the German Lutheran schools.

PART V

Philosophical Bases of Education

The challenge of critical and logical thinking found in the study of philosophy, along with the association with the greatest minds of civilization, seems a sure way to produce the intelligent men and women necessary to insure the growth of democracy. It is suggested that a degree of philosophical involvement on the part of all teachers with regard to both classical and contemporary philosophical system of thought might provide the clues which teachers may best use in helping to develop the minds of their pupils. The growth of the comprehensive American system of education has obviously been aligned with the growth of the American democratic way of life. The American democracy depends upon an educated citizenry functioning within a framework of several simultaneously existing systems of thought. Teachers working within the framework of American democracy usually formulate a philosophy of education which they personally feel best enables them to work with their pupils. While the contemporary American teacher chooses the educational philosophy personally desired, most of the various views regarding education may be identified

as having been suggested within the classical philosophies of the historical past.

The relevance of philosophy to successful teaching practice is a loosely grounded notion in the minds of many of our youth who are preparing for teaching careers. In the first selection of part V, George Kneller suggests that philosophy is both natural and necessary, and, that educational philosophy depends on formal philosophy to the extent that problems of education are of a general philosophical character. The selection of Kneller's statement is intended to present a point of view toward the consideration of "The Relevance of Philosophy."

In order to sustain patterns of meaningful actions, teachers need to systematize their beliefs. They also need to be familiar with general terminology of philosophy if they are to order their beliefs under the various branch categories of philosophy. Proper utilization of terminology will enable teachers to communicate their personal philosophies and to understand the philosophical positions of others. Since much of the vocabulary of philosophy consists of words which have clear, straightforward meanings, lack of clarity arises when terms from our everyday forms of speech are loosely interpreted and/or used when solving problems of a philosophical nature. Linguistic analysis as part of the analytic movement in philosophy stresses clarity and analysis of terms as essential in the approach to educational problems. That part of the introductory terminology of philosophy considered here consists of the basic terms which have commonly accepted philosophical definitions. Familiarity with such terms will provide the reader with an overview of the positions described in the readings in this part.

J. Donald Butler specifies his purpose in the treatment of terminology entitled "The Vocabulary of Philosophy" as twofold: to define terms, and to show, by outline, some of the interrelationships between terms and the problems with which they are commonly associated. Four major categories of philosophy are given as metaphysics (theories of the nature of reality), epistemology (theories of the nature of knowledge), logic (science of exact thought), and axiology (general theory of values). Obviously no pretense can be made that study of a brief vocabulary outline substitutes for depth study of the original works of philosophers. However, since one of the purposes of this section of the book is to view the carry-over influence of the classical philosophical positions to the contemporary American scene, Butler's vocabulary outline serves this purpose well.

Philosophers have not been able to agree upon the number of formal philosophies which exist. Thus, attempts to group schools of philosophy by classification schemes may be viewed as questionable practices. Further confusion may arise when classifications are made under the headings of traditional views, contemporary views, and emergent views since most systems of thought have their origins with the ancient Greeks. As a matter of mere internal consistency, the educational views classified as traditional are drawn heavily from the classical philosophical schools of Idealism, Realism and Neo-Thomism. Experimentalism and Reconstructionism are considered as contemporary educational views. Existentialism is considered as an emergent approach to education.

In the past few decades, perennialist philosophy has been revived under the heading of Neo-Thomism. Growing numbers of intellectuals adhere to the thinking that the basic beliefs and knowledge of ancient cultures apply as well in our lives today. Historically, Thomism has been associated with the Roman Catholic church, but the revival of Perennialism in America is associated mainly with lay educators. Differences among the views of the lay and ecclesiastical Neo-Thomists, if judged by religious standards, would be considered vast. Yet, Roman Catholic educators have welcomed the revival of the Scholasticism of Thomas Aquinas and share many common educational views with lay perennialists.

The writing, teaching, and work of Robert M. Hutchins have brought the most public attention to the perennialist educational view. Hutchins makes a strong case for the need of a liberal education for every citizen before becoming a specialist. "The Basis of Education" outlines what he considers to be the best kind of education appropriate to free men.

One of the major conflicts in American education exists between the *Traditionalists,* whose primary interests are in the curriculum or in the so-called "subject-centered" activities in the school, and the contemporary *Progressivists,* who stress the importance of the experiences of life or "student-centered" activities as the emphasis in curriculum. The function of the progressive schools is to be an active leader in change. In this context, one can envision the antithetical positions of Traditionalism and Progressivism. John Dewey has been placed at the center of this conflict by many contemporary educators. A misconception with regard to Dewey is that many have fallaciously identified him as the father of Progressive education when, in fact, many of the notions of the Progressivists are independent of Dewey. It should also be noted that Dewey was a severe critic of several of the basic assumptions of the Progressive movement. To a large degree, the work of John Dewey has been subjected to attack by many identified with the Traditionalists' positions. Upon careful examination it seems that the meanings in certain of his works indicate that this American philosopher was dedicated to the reconciliation of the split between the Traditionalists and the Progressivists, since he felt that both views were important to education. Among the hundreds of books, essays, and other works Dewey produced in his long career, "My Pedagogic Creed," which he wrote in 1897, is uniquely significant. In its style and content, it may most clearly exemplify the reformist fervor of his Chicago period. Here is Dewey passionately, even flamboyantly, confident of his vision of the nature, purpose, and inevitable progress of education. At once a personal declaration and a revolutionary manifesto, it dispenses with supporting arguments or documentation. The resulting clarity, succinctness, and even eloquence have offered incomparable opportunities for interpretation, to both disciples and critics.

Theodore Brameld is a leading American philosopher of education. In the book excerpt, "The Culturological Context of Reconstructionism," he suggests that Reconstructionism views education as the instrument for reconstructing the social order. However, Reconstructionism is more frequently regarded as a part of Progressivism as indicated by the figure

taken from one of Brameld's earlier books and showing the position of Reconstructionism to the other educational views. A common central theme from the many books and articles written by Brameld is that we are in the midst of a world-wide crisis, with a new social order suggested as the only effective solution. The brief Brameld excerpt speaks to the culturological context of this educational view.

During the past several years, and particularly during the past decade, philosophers have increasingly taken issue with the so-called "nonsense philosophy" attempts by educationists. Out of the philosopher-educationist conflict, Existentialism has become increasingly popular as a newer philosophical approach to education. Existentialism rules out philosophy as a logical system of thought. An individual must discover meaning for his existence through experience rather than by the attempt to understand a set of predetermined propositions or truths.

The American system of education has, for the most part, been directed toward group processes and group norms. In such a context, Existentialism could not serve as a functional philosophy of education, since Existentialism is directed toward individual self-fulfillment. Educators have given considerable attention to problems and processes concerned with individual differences. However, much of their effort has been aimed at minimizing the individual difference variables by such tactics as forming homogeneous groupings for particular subject matter instruction. The rationale for these practices is that "group" instruction can proceed better since the individuals involved are better adjusted to the group. Existentialism advocates complete sensitivity to aspects of individual uniqueness. This does not necessarily imply that emphasis given to the development of the individual has no place in the public schools, because such activity would be contrary to the group orientation of the system. However, the existential classroom teacher would need to function from a conceptual base which rules out certain time-honored conventional notions.

Since Existential philosophers have not been greatly concerned with philosophical discussions of the issues of education, the selection by Gerald John Pine, "Existential Teaching and Learning," is a significant contribution. Pine provides a brief overview of common existential principles. Of greater significance are his comments about existential teaching and learning principles. The reading also provides a list of the existential conditions which facilitate learning.

A hoped for outcome among the "pure" philosophers associated with the Philosophical Analysis movement is the stimulation of the application of newer philosophical approaches to education. Philosophy is currently undergoing rapid growth, particularly with regard to its methods of analysis. Suggestions as to the application of newer philosophical methods call for discussion between philosophers and educators. In the absence of such discussion, the "pure" philosophers have contributed considerably to the literature purportedly to establish closer relations with philosophers of education. Close relations, however, do not exist universally, and an academic rift can be evidenced between philosophers and educators. For the most part, the central problem is whether a philosophy of education can be derived from a systematic position in general philosophy (definitional approach), or whether it can be derived from the application of analytical methods to educational problems.

Using the definitional approach, one might learn about philosophy by studying these positions and views and, from this study, derive a philosophy of education. Philosophical Analysis calls for "analyzing" a philosophy of education. William K. Frankena's article entitled "A Model for Analyzing a Philosophy of Education" is an example of analytical philosophy of education.

Humans are not born into the world with a predetermined value base. Prior to beginning school, children begin to develop values from the modeling and teaching of their parents. It is assumed that the school will provide every child the opportunity to acquire and further develop his or her beliefs. However, the young are often faced with inconsistent models, according to Jacob W. Getzels. In his article entitled "Schools and Values," Getzels outlines "some possible reasons for the trouble schools have in influencing values."

The concept of comprehensiveness as ascribed to the American public schools suggests that most school systems would utilize curriculum arrangements which would reflect aspects of each educational view. In practice, curriculums for most public schools do reflect the traditional educational views, the contemporary educational views, and the emergent educational views. Thus, the American public schools operate from a kind of eclectic educational philosophy. In such a milieu, various subgroups within the school communities may feel their specific needs are poorly met, particularly minority groups such as our black Americans, American Indians, and Chicanos. Other factors such as Supreme Court decisions, increased financial costs for educational programs, and parental demands also influence changes in practice and philosophy.

Reading 35

The Revelance of Philosophy

George F. Kneller

From time to time every teacher and student asks himself questions that are implicitly philosophical. The teacher wonders, "Why am I teaching? Why am I teaching history? What is teaching at its best?" And the student asks, "Why am I studying algebra? What am I going to school for anyway?" Taken far enough, these questions become philosophical. They become questions about the nature of man and the world, about knowledge, value, and the good life.

MODES OF PHILOSOPHY

Unfortunately, nothing illuminating can be said about philosophy with a single definition. Let us therefore think of philosophy as an activity in three modes or styles; the speculative, the prescriptive, and the analytic.

Speculative Philosophy

Speculative philosophy is a way of thinking systematically about everything that exists. Why do philosophers want to do this? Why are they not content, like scientists, to study particular aspects of reality? The answer is that the human mind wishes to see things as a whole. It wishes to understand how all the different things that have been discovered together form some sort of meaningful totality. We are all aware of this tendency in ourselves. When we read a book, look at a painting, or study an assignment, we are concerned not only with particular details but also with the order or pattern that gives these details their significance. Speculative philosophy, then, is a search for order and wholeness, applied not to particular items or experiences but to all knowledge and all experience. In brief, speculative philosophy is the attempt to find a coherence in the whole realm of thought and experience.

Prescriptive Philosophy

Prescriptive philosophy seeks to establish standards for assessing values, judging con-

Source: George F. Kneller, "The Relevance of Philosophy." *Foundations of Education*, 3rd edition. New York: John Wiley & Sons, Inc., pp. 199–202. Used by permission.

duct, and appraising art. It examines what we mean by good and bad, right and wrong, beautiful and ugly. It asks whether these qualities inhere in things themselves or whether they are projections of our own minds. To the experimental psychologist the varieties of human conduct are morally neither good nor bad; they are simply forms of behavior to be studied empirically. But to the educator and the prescriptive philosopher some forms of behavior are worthwhile and others are not. The prescriptive philosopher seeks to discover and to recommend principles for deciding what actions and qualities are most worthwhile and why they should be so.

Analytic Philosophy

Analytic philosophy focuses on words and meaning. The analytic philosopher examines such notions as "cause," "mind," "academic freedom," and "equality of opportunity" in order to assess the different meanings they carry in different contexts. He shows how inconsistencies may arise when meanings appropriate in certain contexts are imported into others. The analytic philosopher tends to be skeptical, cautious, and disinclined to build systems of thought.

Today the analytic approach dominates American and British philosophy. On the Continent the speculative tradition prevails. But whichever approach is uppermost at any time, most philosophers agree that all approaches contribute to the health of philosophy. Speculation unaccompanied by analysis soars too easily into a heaven of its own, irrelevant to the world as we know it; analysis without speculation descends to minutiae and becomes sterile. In any case few philosophers are solely speculative, solely prescriptive, or solely analytic. Speculation, prescription, and analysis are all

present to some degree in the work of all mature philosophers.

PHILOSOPHY AND SCIENCE

A great deal of information has been gathered by various sciences on subjects treated by philosophy, particularly human nature. But when we look at this information, we find that psychology gives us one picture of man, sociology another, biology another, and so on. What we have after all the sciences have been searched is not a composite picture of man but a series of different pictures. These pictures fail to satisfy because they explain different aspects of man rather than man as a whole. Can we unify our partial pictures of man into one that is single and complete? Yes, but not by using scientific methods alone. It is through philosophy that we unify the separate findings of science and interrelate the fundamental concepts these findings presuppose.

The philosopher considers questions that arise before and after the scientist has done his work. Traditional science presupposes, for example, that every event is caused by other events and in turn causes still other events. Hence, for science no event is uncaused. But how can we be sure of this? Do cause and effect exist in the world itself or are they read into the world by men? These questions cannot be answered scientifically because causality is not a finding but an assumption of science. Unless the scientist assumes that reality is causal in nature, he cannot begin to investigate it. Again, science deals with things as they appear to our senses and to our instruments. But are things in themselves really the same as they appear to us? The scientist cannot say, because things in themselves, as opposed to their appearances, are by definition beyond empirical verification.

Philosophy, then, is both natural and

necessary to man. We are forever seeking some comprehensive framework within which our separate findings may be given a total significance. Not only is philosophy a branch of knowledge along with art, science, and history, but also it actually embraces these disciplines in their theoretical reaches and seeks to establish connections between them. Once again, *philosophy attempts to establish a coherence throughout the whole domain of experience.*

PHILOSOPHY OF EDUCATION

Besides having its own concerns, philosophy considers the fundamental assumptions of other branches of knowledge. When philosophy turns its attention to science, we have philosophy of science; when it examines the basic concepts of the law, we have philosophy of law; and when it deals with education, we have philosophy of education or educational philosophy.

Just as formal philosophy attempts to understand reality as a whole by explaining it in the most general and systematic way, so educational philosophy seeks to comprehend education in its entirety, interpreting it by means of general concepts that will guide our choice of educational ends and policies. In the same way that general philosophy coordinates the findings of the different sciences, educational philosophy interprets these findings as they bear on education. Scientific theories do not carry direct educational implications; they cannot be applied to educational practice without first being examined philosophically.

Educational philosophy depends on general or formal philosophy to the extent that the problems of education are of a general philosophical character. We cannot criticize existing educational policies or suggest new ones without considering such general philosophic problems as (a) the nature of the good life, to which education should lead; (b) the nature of man himself, because it is man we are educating; (c) the nature of society, because education is a social process; and (d) the nature of ultimate reality, which all knowledge seeks to penetrate. Educational philosophy, then, involves among other things the application of formal philosophy to the field of education.*

Like general philosophy, educational philosophy is speculative, prescriptive, and analytic. It is speculative when it seeks to establish theories of the nature of man, society, and the world by which to order and interpret the conflicting data of educational research and the behavioral sciences. It is prescriptive when it specifies the ends that education ought to follow and the general means it should use to attain them. It is analytic when it clarifies speculative and prescriptive statements. The analyst, as we shall see, examines the rationality of our educational ideas, their consistency with other ideas, and the ways in which they are distorted by loose thinking. He tests the logic of our concepts and their adequacy to the facts they seek to explain. Above all, he attempts to clarify the many different meanings that have been attached to such heavily worked educational terms as "freedom," "adjustment," "growth," "experience," "needs," and "knowledge."

---

* Educational philosophy derives also from the experiences of education.

Reading 36

The Vocabulary of Philosophy

J. Donald Butler

The vocabulary of philosophy, while different from our everyday forms of speech, is not necessarily difficult. Some helpful explanation of meanings plus a bit of patient study will go a long way toward making the student feel at home among philosophers. In the following treatment of terminology the purpose is twofold: to define terms, and to show, by the outline arrangement, some of the interrelationships between terms and the problems with which they are commonly associated.

I. *Metaphysics.* Theories of the nature of reality.
   A. *Cosmology.* Theories of the nature of the cosmos and explanations of its origin and development.
      1. Some considerations in *cosmology* are
         a. *Causality.* The nature of cause and effect relations.

Source: J. Donald Butler, "Glossary: The Vocabulary of Philosophy." *Four Philosophies and Their Practice in Education and Religion,* 3rd edition. Copyright, 1951, 1957 by Harper & Row, Publishers, Inc. Copyright © 1968 by J. Donald Butler. Reprinted with permission.

         b. The nature of time.
         c. The nature of space.
      2. Two distinctive views in *cosmology* are
         a. *Evolutionism.* The universe evolved of itself.
         b. *Creationism.* The universe came to be as the result of the working of a Creative Cause or Personality.
   B. The nature of man as one important aspect of reality.
      1. The problem of the essential nature of the self. There are no particular terms but there are divergent answers which can be identified with general viewpoints.
         a. The self is a soul, a spiritual being. A principle of *idealism* and *spiritual realism.*
         b. The self is essentially the same as the body. A principle of *naturalism* and *physical realism.*
         c. The self is a social-vocal phenomenon. A principle held especially by *experimentalists.*
      2. The problem of the relation of body and mind.

a. *Interactionism*. Mind and body are two different kinds of reality, each of which can affect the other.

b. *Parallelism*. Mind and body are two different kinds of reality which do not and cannot affect each other. But in some unknown way, every mental event is paralleled by a corresponding physical event.

c. *Epiphenomenalism*. Mind is merely a function of the brain, an overtone accompanying bodily activity. It is an onlooker at events, never influencing them.

d. *Double Aspect Theory*. Mind and body are two aspects of a fundamental reality whose nature is unknown.

e. *Emergence Theory*. Mind is something new which has been produced by Nature in the evolutionary process, neither identical with body, parallel to it, nor wholly dependent upon it.

f. *Spiritualism*. (A definition common to most *idealists* and *spiritual realists*.) Mind is more fundamental than body. The relation of body and mind is better described as body depending upon mind, as compared to the common-sense description according to which mind depends upon body.

3. The problem of freedom.

a. *Determinism*. Man is not free. All of his actions are determined by forces greater than he is.

b. *Free Will*. Man has the power of choice and is capable of genuine initiative.

c. There is a third alternative proposed especially by the *experimentalists*, for which there is no name. Man is neither free nor determined; but he can and does delay some of his responses long enough to reconstruct a total response, not completely automatic but not free, which does give a new direction to subsequent activity.

C. Conceptions of and about God.

1. *Atheism*. There is no ultimate reality in or behind the cosmos which is Person or Spirit.

2. *Deism*. God exists quite apart from, and is disinterested in, the physical universe and human beings. But he created both and is the Author of all natural and moral laws.

3. *Pantheism*. All is God and God is all. The cosmos and God are identical.

4. The conception of God as emerging, for which there is no common name. God is evolving with the cosmos; He is the end toward which it is moving, instead of the beginning from which it came.

5. *Polytheism*. Spiritual reality is plural rather than a unity. There is more than one God.

6. *Theism*. Ultimate reality is a personal God who is more than the cosmos but within whom and through whom the cosmos exists.

D. *Teleology*. Considerations as to whether or not there is purpose in the universe.

1. Philosophies holding that the world is what it is because of chance, accident, or blind mechanism are *nonteleological*.

2. Philosophies holding that there

has been purpose in the universe from the beginning, and/or purpose can be discerned in history, are *teleological* philosophies.

3. It may be that a special case must be made of the *experimentalists* again on this particular question, as they do not find purpose inherent in the cosmos but by purposeful activity seek to impose purpose upon it.

E. Considerations relating to the constancy, or lack of it, in reality.

1. *Absolutism.* Fundamental reality is constant, unchanging, fixed, and dependable.

2. *Relativism.* Reality is a changing thing. So-called realities are always relative to something or other.

F. Problems of quantity. Consideration of the number of ultimate realities, apart from qualitative aspects.

1. *Monism.* Reality is unified. It is one. It is mind, or matter, or energy, or will—but only one of these.

2. *Dualism.* Reality is two. Usually these realities are antithetical, as spirit and matter, good and evil. Commonly, the antithesis is weighted, so that one of the two is considered more important and more enduring than the other.

3. *Pluralism.* Reality is many. Minds, things, materials, energies, laws, processes, etc., all may be considered equally real and to some degree independent of each other.

G. *Ontology.* The meaning of existence as such. To exist, to have being, means what?

1. Space-time or Nature is identical with existence. To exist means to occupy time and space, to be

matter or physical energy (e.g., *naturalism* and *physical realism*).

2. Spirit or God is identical with existence. To exist means to be Mind or Spirit, or to be dependent upon Mind or Spirit. (Especially true of *idealism.*)

3. Existence as a category which is not valid. This is held by those, especially the *pragmatists,* who insist that everything is flux or change and there is nothing which fits into the category of existence in any ultimate sense.

II. *Epistemology.* Theories of the nature of knowledge.

A. The possibility of knowledge.

1. *Agnosticism.* The position that conclusive knowledge of ultimate reality is an impossibility.

2. *Skepticism.* A questioning attitude toward the possibility of having any knowledge.

3. The affirmation of knowledge. The position that true knowledge of ultimate reality is possible.

4. The affirmation of functional knowledge. The position that knowledge is always fractional, never total, and functions in a present field or situation where it is needed, and that we can appropriate such fractional and functional knowledge (especially true of *experimentalists*).

B. The kinds of knowledge.

1. *A posteriori.* Knowledge which is based upon experience and observation.

2. Experimental knowledge. Not exactly the same as *a posteriori* knowledge because it is not regarded as something finally to be concluded from experience or observation, by induction. Rather, it is something to be put to work in

experience as a function which carries experience forward satisfactorily.

3. *A priori.* Knowledge which is self-evident. Principles which, when once understood, are recognized to be true and do not require proof through observation, experience, or experiment.

C. The instrument of knowledge.
1. *Empiricism.* The position that sensation, or sense-perceptual experience, is the medium through which knowledge is gained.
2. *Rationalism.* The position that reason is the chief source of knowledge.
3. *Intuitionism.* A position that knowledge is gained through immediate insight and awareness.
4. *Authoritarianism.* The position that much important knowledge is certified to us by an indisputable authority, such as the Bible, the Church, or the State.
5. *Revelation.* The position that God presently reveals Himself in the Bible and the Church.

III. *Logic.* The science of exact thought. The systematic treatment of the relation of ideas. A study of methods distinguishing valid thinking from thinking which is fallacious.
A. *Induction.* Reasoning from particulars to a general conclusion.
B. *Deduction.* Reasoning from a general principle to particulars included within the scope of that principle.
C. The *Syllogism.* A form in which to cast deductive reasoning. It is comprised of three propositions: The major premise, the minor premise, and the conclusion.
D. Experimental reasoning or problem-solving. A form of reasoning, largely *inductive* but using *deduction* as

well, which begins with a problem, observes all the data relating to the problem, formulates hypotheses, and tests them to reach a workable solution of the problem.
E. *Dialectic.* A method of reasoning in which the conflict or contrast of ideas is utilized as a means of detecting the truth. In Hegel's formulation of it there are three stages: *thesis, antithesis,* and *synthesis.*

IV. *Axiology.* The general theory of value. The nature of values, the different kinds of value, specific values worthy of possession.
A. The nature of value.
1. The interest theory. Values depend upon the interest of the person who enjoys them. Strictly speaking, they do not exist but are supported by the interest of the valuer. According to this theory, what is desired has value.
2. The existence theory. Values have an existence in their own right which is independent of the valuer and his interest. Values are not qualities or essences without foundation in existence: They are essence plus existence.
3. The experimentalist theory. That is of value which yields a greater sense of happiness in the present and at the same time opens the way to further goods in future experiences.
4. The part-whole theory. The key to realizing and enjoying value is the effective relating of parts to wholes.
B. Realms of value.
1. *Ethics.* The nature of good and evil. The problems of conduct and ultimate objectives.
a. The worth of living.

(1) *Optimism.* Existence is good. Life is worth living. Our outlook can be hopeful.

(2) *Pessimism. Existence is evil.* Life is not worth the struggle: we should escape it by some means.

(3) *Meliorism.* Conclusions as to the goodness or evil of existence cannot be made final. Human effort may improve the human situation. The final end cannot be assured, but we must face life, not escape it, applying all the effort and resources we can command.

b. The highest good or *summum bonum*. The end, aim, or objective of living which is above all other ends. In absolutist philosophies it is the ultimate end which by its nature cannot be a means to another end.

(1) *Hedonism.* The highest good is pleasure. Hedonist philosophies vary in their conceptions of pleasure, ranging from the intense pleasure of the moment to highly refined and enduring pleasure or contentment. *Utilitarianism* is a form of hedonism having society as its frame of reference. According to it, the greatest happiness of the greatest number is the prime objective.

(2) *Perfectionism.* The highest good is the perfection of the self, or self-realization. Perfectionism may also have its social frame of reference, envisioning an ideal social order as the ultimate objective of society.

c. The criteria of conduct. From one's conception of the highest good there follow logically certain practical principles for everyday living. Some examples are:

(1) Kant's maxim: act only on those principles which you are willing should become universal moral laws.

(2) Spencer's principle: action to be right must be conducive to self-preservation.

(3) Dewey's principle: discover the probable consequences of what you consider doing, by going through an imaginative rehearsal of the possibilities.

(4) The religious principle: obey the will of God; commit yourself completely to the fulfillment of God's purpose for yourself and the world.

d. The motivation of conduct. The kind and scope of the interests which guide conduct.

(1) *Egoism.* The interests of self should be served by an individual's actions.

(2) *Altruism.* The interests of others or of the social group should be served by an individual's actions. One realizes his own fullest selfhood in seeking the best interests of others.

2. *Aesthetics.* The nature of the values which are found in the feeling aspects of experience. The conscious search for the principles governing the creation and appreciation of beautiful things.

3. *Religious Values.* The kind, nature, and worth of values to be possessed in worship, religious experience, and religious service.
4. *Educational Values.* The kind, nature, and worth of values inherent in the educative process.
5. *Social Values.* The kind, nature, and worth of values only realized in community and in the individual's relation to society. Some more specific kinds of social values are the *political* and the *economic.*
6. *Utilitarian Values.* The kind, nature, and worth of values to be realized in harmonious adjustment to or efficient control of the forces of the physical environment.

Reading 37

The Basis of Education

Robert M. Hutchins

The obvious failures of the doctrines of adaptation, immediate needs, social reform, and of the doctrine that we need no doctrine at all may suggest to us that we require a better definition of education. Let us concede that every society must have some system that attempts to adapt the young to their social and political environment. If the society is bad, in the sense, for example, in which the Nazi state was bad, the system will aim at the same bad ends. To the extent that it makes men bad in order that they may be tractable subjects of a bad state, the system may help to achieve the social ideals of the society. It may be what the society wants; it may even be what the society needs, if it is to perpetuate its form and accomplish its aims. In pragmatic terms, in terms of success in the society, it may be a "good" system.

But it seems to me clearer to say that, though it may be a system of training, or instruction, or adaptation, or meeting im-

Source: Robert M. Hutchins, "The Basis of Education." The Conflict in Education. Copyright, 1953 by Harper & Row, Publishers, Inc. Reprinted with permission.

mediate needs, it is not a system of education. It seems clearer to say that the purpose of education is to improve men. Any system that tries to make them bad is not education, but something else. If, for example, democracy is the best form of society, a system that adapts the young to it will be an educational system. If despotism is a bad form of society, a system that adapts the young to it will not be an educational system, and the better it succeeds in adapting them the less educational it will be.

Every man has a function as a man. The function of a citizen or a subject may vary from society to society, and the system of training, or adaptation, or instruction, or meeting immediate needs may vary with it. But the function of a man as man is the same in every age and in every society, since it results from his nature as a man. The aim of an educational system is the same in every age and in every society where such a system can exist: it is to improve man as man.

If we are going to talk about improving men and societies, we have to believe that there is some difference between good and bad. This difference must not be, as the positivists think it is, merely conventional. We cannot tell this difference by an examination of the effectiveness of a given program as the pragmatists propose: the time required to estimate these effects is usually too long and the complexity of society is always too great for us to say that the consequences of a given program are altogether clear. We cannot discover the difference between good and bad by going to the laboratory, for men and societies are not laboratory animals. If we believe that there is no truth, there is no knowledge, and there are no values except those which are validated by laboratory experiment, we cannot talk about the improvement of men and societies, for we can have no standard of judging anything that takes place among men or in societies.

Society is to be improved, not by forcing a program of social reform down its throat, through the schools or otherwise, but by the improvement of the individuals who compose it. As Plato said, "Governments reflect human nature. States are not made out of stone or wood, but out of the characters of their citizens: these turn the scale and draw everything after them." The individual is the heart of society.

To talk about making men better we must have some idea of what men are, because if we have none, we can have no idea of what is good or bad for them. If men are brutes like other animals, then there is no reason why they should not be treated like brutes by anybody who can gain power over them. And there is no reason why they should not be trained as brutes are trained. A sound philosophy in general suggests that men are rational, moral, and spiritual beings and that the improvement of men means the fullest development of their rational, moral, and spiritual powers. All men have these powers, and all men should develop them to the fullest extent.

Man is by nature free, and he is by nature social. To use his freedom rightly he needs discipline. To live in society he needs the moral virtues. Good moral and intellectual habits are required for the fullest development of the nature of man.

To develop fully as a social, political animal man needs participation in his own government. A benevolent despotism will not do. You cannot expect the slave to show the virtues of the free man unless you first set him free. Only democracy, in which all men rule and are ruled in turn for the good life of the whole community, can be an absolutely good form of government.

The community rests on the social nature of men. It requires communication among its members. They do not have to agree with one another; but they must be able to understand one another. And their philosophy in general must supply them with a common purpose and a common concept of man and society adequate to hold the community together. Civilization is the deliberate pursuit of a common ideal. The good society is not just a society we happen to like or to be used to. It is a community of good men.

Education deals with the development of the intellectual powers of men. Their moral and spiritual powers are the sphere of the family and the church. All three agencies must work in harmony; for, though a man has three aspects, he is still one man. But the schools cannot take over the role of the family and the church without promoting the atrophy of those institutions and failing in the task that is proper to the schools.

We cannot talk about the intellectual powers of men, though we can talk about training them, or amusing them, or adapting them, and meeting their immediate needs, unless our philosophy in general tells us that there is knowledge and that there is a difference between true and false. We must believe, too, that there are no other means of obtaining knowledge than scientific experimentation. If knowledge can be sought only in the laboratory, many fields in which we thought we had knowledge will offer us nothing but opinion or superstition, and we shall be forced to conclude that we cannot know anything about the most important aspects of man and society. If we are to set about developing the intellectual powers of men through having them acquire knowledge of the most important subjects, we have to begin with the proposition that experimentation and empirical data will be of only limited use to us, contrary to the convictions of many American social scientists, and that philosophy, history, literature, and art give us knowledge, and significant knowledge, on the most significant issues.

If the object of education is the improvement of men, then any system of education that is without values is a contradiction in terms. A system that seeks bad values is bad. A system that denies the existence of values denies the possibility of education. Relativism, scientism, skepticism, and anti-intellectualism, the four horsemen of the philosophical apocalypse, have produced that chaos in education which will end in the disintegration of the West.

The prime object of education is to know what is good for man. It is to know the goods in their order. There is a hierarchy of values. The task of education is to help us understand it, establish it, and live by it. This Aristotle had in mind when he said: "It is not the possessions but the desires of men that must be equalized, and this is impossible unless they have a sufficient education according to the nature of things."

Such an education is far removed from the triviality of that produced by the doctrines of adaptation, of immediate needs, of social reform, or of the doctrine of no doctrine at all. Such an education will not adapt the young to a bad environment, but it will encourage them to make good. It will not overlook immediate needs, but it will place these needs in their proper relationship to more distant, less tangible, and more important goods. It will be the only effective means of reforming society.

This is the education appropriate to free men. It is liberal education. If all men are to be free, all men must have this education. It makes no difference how they are to earn their living or what their special interests or aptitudes may be. They can learn to make a living, and they can develop their special interests and aptitudes, after they have laid the foundation of free and responsible manhood through liberal education. It will not do to say that they are incapable of such education. This claim is made by those who are too indolent or unconvinced to make the effort to give such education to the masses.

Nor will it do to say that there is not enough time to give everybody a liberal education before he becomes a specialist. In America, at least, the waste and frivolity of the educational system are so great that it would be possible through getting rid of them to give every citizen a liberal education and make him a qualified specialist, too, in less time than is now consumed in turning out uneducated specialists.

A liberal education aims to develop the powers of understanding and judgment. It is impossible that too many people can be educated in this sense, because there cannot be too many people with understanding and judgment. We hear a great deal today about the dangers that will come upon us through the frustration of educated people who have got educated in the expectation that education will get them a better job, and who then fail to get it. But surely this depends on the representations that are made to the young about what education is. If we allow them to believe that education will get them better jobs and encourage them to get educated with this end in view, they are entitled to a sense of frustration if, when they have got the education, they do not get the jobs. But, if we say that they should be educated in order to be men, and that everybody, whether he is a ditch-digger or a bank president, should have this education because he is a man, then the ditch-digger may still feel frustrated, but not because of his education.

Nor is it possible for a person to have too much liberal education, because it is impossible to have too much understanding and judgment. But it is possible to undertake too much in the name of liberal education in youth. The object of liberal education in youth is not to teach the young all they will ever need to know. It is to give them the habits, ideas, and techniques that they need to continue to educate themselves. Thus the object of formal institutional liberal education in youth is to prepare the young to educate themselves throughout their lives.

I would remind you of the impossibility of learning to understand and judge many of the most important things in youth. The judgment and understanding of practical affairs can amount to little in the absence of experience with practical affairs. Subjects that cannot be understood without experience should not be taught to those who are without experience. Or, if these subjects are taught to those who are without experience, it should be clear that these subjects can be taught only by way of introduction and that their value to the student depends on his continuing to study them as he acquires experience. The tragedy in America is that economics, ethics, politics, history, and literature are studied in youth, and seldom studied again. Therefore the graduates of American universities seldom understand them.

This pedagogical principle, that subjects requiring experience can be learned only by the experienced, leads to the conclusion that the most important branch of education is the education of adults. We sometimes seem to think of education as something like the mumps, measles, whooping-cough, or chicken-pox. If a person has had education in childhood, he need not, in fact he cannot, have it again. But the pedagogical principle that the most important things can be learned only in mature life is supported by a sound philosophy in general. Men are rational animals. They achieve their terrestrial felicity by the use of reason. And this means that they have to use it for their entire lives. To say that they should learn only in childhood would mean that they were human only in childhood.

And it would mean that they were unfit to be citizens of a republic. A republic, a true *res publica*, can maintain justice, peace, freedom, and order only by the exercise of intelligence. When we speak of the consent of the governed, we mean, since men are not angels who seek the truth intuitively and do not have to learn it, that every act of assent on the part of the governed is a product of learning. A republic is really a common educational life in process. So Montesquieu said that, whereas the principle of a monarchy was honor, and the principle of a tyranny was fear, the principle of a republic was education.

Hence the ideal republic is the republic of learning. It is the utopia by which all actual political republics are measured. The goal toward which we started with the Athenians twenty-five centuries ago is an unlimited republic of learning and a worldwide political republic mutually supporting each other.

All men are capable of learning. Learning does not stop as long as a man lives, unless his learning power atrophies because he does not use it. Political freedom cannot endure unless it is accompanied by provision for the unlimited acquisition of knowledge. Truth is not long retained in human affairs without continual learning and relearning. Peace is unlikely unless there are continuous, unlimited opportunities for learning and unless men continuously avail themselves of them. The world of law and justice for which we yearn, the world-wide political republic, cannot be realized without the world-wide republic of learning. The civilization we seek will be achieved when all men are citizens of the world republic of law and justice and of the republic of learning all their lives long.*

* I owe this discussion to the suggestions of Scott Buchanan.

Reading 38

My Pedagogic Creed

John Dewey

ARTICLE I—WHAT EDUCATION IS

I believe that all education proceeds by the participation of the individual in the social consciousness of the race. The process begins unconsciously almost at birth, and is continually shaping the individual's powers, saturating his consciousness, forming his habits, training his ideas, and arousing his feelings and emotions. Through this unconscious education the individual gradually comes to share in the intellectual and moral resources which humanity has succeeded in getting together. He becomes an inheritor of the funded capital of civilization. The most formal and technical education in the world cannot safely depart from this general process. It can only organize it or differentiate it in some particular direction.

I believe that the only true education comes through the stimulation of the child's powers by the demands of the social situations in which he finds himself. Through these demands he is stimulated to act as a

Source: John Dewey, "My Pedagogic Creed." Number IX in a series under this title, in *The Second Journal* LIV, no. 3 January 16, 1897, pp. 77–80.

member of a unity, to emerge from his original narrowness of action and feeling, and to conceive of himself from the standpoint of the welfare of the group to which he belongs. Through the responses which others make to his own activities he comes to know what these mean in social terms. The value which they have is reflected back into them. For instance, through the response which is made to the child's instinctive babblings the child comes to know what those babblings mean; they are transformed into articulate language and thus the child is introduced into the consolidated wealth of ideas and emotions which are now summed up in language.

I believe that this educational process has two sides—one psychological and one sociological; and that neither can be subordinated to the other or neglected without evil results following. Of these two sides, the psychological is the basis. The child's own instincts and powers furnish the material and give the starting point for all education. Save as the efforts of the educator connect with some activity which the child is carrying on of his own initiative independent of the educator, education becomes reduced to a pressure from without. It may, indeed, give certain external results, but cannot truly be called educative. Without insight into the psychological structure and activities of the individual, the educative process will, therefore, be haphazard and arbitrary. If it chances to coincide with the child's activity it will get a leverage; if it does not, it will result in friction, or disintegration, or arrest of the child's nature.

I believe that knowledge of social conditions, of the present state of civilization, is necessary in order properly to interpret the child's powers. The child has his own instincts and tendencies, but we do not know what these mean until we can translate them into their social equivalents. We must be able to carry them back into a social past and see them as the inheritance of previous race activities. We must also be able to project them into the future to see what their outcome and end will be. In the illustration just used, it is the ability to see in the child's babblings the promise and potency of a future social intercourse and conversation which enables one to deal in the proper way with that instinct.

I believe that the psychological and social sides are organically related and that education cannot be regarded as a compromise between the two, or a superimposition of one upon the other. We are told that the psychological definition of education is barren and formal—that it gives us only the idea of a development of all the mental powers without giving us any idea of the use to which these powers are put. On the other hand, it is urged that the social definition of education, as getting adjusted to civilization, makes of it a forced and external process, and results in subordinating the freedom of the individual to a preconceived political status.

I believe that each of these objections is true when urged against one side isolated from the other. In order to know what a power really is we must know what its end, use, or function is; and this we cannot know save as we conceive of the individual as active in social relationships. But, on the other hand, the only possible adjustment which we can give to the child under existing conditions, is that which arises through putting him in complete possession of all his powers. With the advent of democracy and modern industrial conditions, it is impossible to foretell definitely just what civilization will be twenty years from now. Hence it is impossible to prepare the child for any precise set of conditions. To prepare him for the future life means to give him command of himself; it means so to train him that he will have the full and ready use of all his capacities; that his eye and ear and hand may be tools ready to command, that his judgment may be capable of grasping the conditions under which it has to work, and the executive forces be trained to act economically and efficiently. It is impossible to reach this sort of adjustment save as constant regard is had to the individual's own powers, tastes, and interests—say, that is, as education is continually converted into psychological terms.

In sum, I believe that the individual who is to be educated is a social individual and that society is an organic union of individuals. If we eliminate the social factor from the child we are left only with an abstraction; if we eliminate the individual factor from society, we are left only with an inert and lifeless mass. Education, therefore, must begin with a psychological insight into the child's capacities, interests, and habits. It must be controlled at every point by reference to these same considerations. These powers, interests, and habits must be continually interpreted—we must know what they mean. They must be translated into terms of their social equivalents—into terms of what they are capable of in the way of social service.

ARTICLE II—WHAT THE SCHOOL IS

I believe that the school is primarily a social institution. Education being a social process, the school is simply that form of community life in which all those agencies are concentrated that will be most effective in bringing the child to share in the inherited resources of the race, and to use his own powers for social ends.

I believe that education, therefore, is a process of living and not a preparation for future living.

I believe that the school must represent present life—life as real and vital to the child as that which he carries on in the home, in the neighborhood, or on the playground.

I believe that education which does not occur through forms of life, or that are worth living for their own sake, is always a poor substitute for the genuine reality and tends to cramp and to deaden.

I believe that the school, as an institution, should simplify existing social life; should reduce it, as it were, to an embryonic form. Existing life is so complex that the child cannot be brought into contact with it without either confusion or distraction; he is either overwhelmed by the multiplicity of activities which are going on, so that he loses his own power of orderly reaction, or he is so stimulated by these various activities that his powers are prematurely called into play and he becomes either unduly specialized or else disintegrated.

I believe that as such simplified social life, the school life should grow gradually out of the home life; that it should take up and continue the activities with which the child is already familiar in the home.

I believe that it should exhibit these activities to the child, and reproduce them in such ways that the child will gradually learn the meaning of them, and be capable of playing his own part in relation to them.

I believe that this is a psychological necessity, because it is the only way of securing continuity in the child's growth, the only way of giving a background of past experience to the new ideas given in school.

I believe that it is also a social necessity because the home is the form of social life in which the child has been nurtured and in connection with which he has had his moral training. It is the business of the school to deepen and extend his sense of the values bound up in his home life.

I believe that much of present education fails because it neglects this fundamental principle of the school as a form of community life. It conceives the school as a place where certain information is to be given, where certain lessons are to be learned, or where certain habits are to be formed. The value of these is conceived as lying largely in the remote future; the child must do these things for the sake of something else he is to do; they are mere preparation. As a result they do not become a part of the life experience of the child and so are not truly educative.

I believe that the moral education centers upon this conception of the school as a mode of social life, that the best and deepest moral training is precisely that which one gets through having to enter into proper relations with others in a unity of work and thought. The present educational systems, so far as they destroy or neglect this unity, render it difficult or impossible to get any genuine, regular moral training.

I believe that the child should be stimulated and controlled in his work through the life of the community.

I believe that under existing conditions far too much of the stimulus and control proceeds from the teacher, because of neglect of the idea of the school as a form of social life.

I believe that the teacher's place and work in the school is to be interpreted from this same basis. The teacher is not in the school to impose certain ideas or to form certain habits in the child, but is there as a member of the community to select the influences which shall affect the child and to assist him in properly responding to these influences.

I believe that the discipline of the school should proceed from the life of the school as a whole and not directly from the teacher.

I believe that the teacher's business is simply to determine on the basis of larger experience and riper wisdom, how the discipline of life shall come to the child.

I believe that all questions of the grading of the child and his promotion should be determined by reference to the same standard. Examinations are of use only so far as they test the child's fitness for social life and reveal the place in which he can be of the most service and where he can receive the most help.

ARTICLE III—THE SUBJECT-MATTER OF EDUCATION

I believe that the social life of the child is the basis of concentration, or correlation, in all his training or growth. The social life gives the unconscious unity and the background of all his efforts and of all his attainments.

I believe that the subject-matter of the school curriculum should mark a gradual differentiation out of the primitive unconscious unity of social life.

I believe that we violate the child's nature and render difficult the best ethical results, by introducing the child too abruptly to a number of special studies, of reading, writing, geography, etc., out of relation to this social life.

I believe, therefore, that the true center of correlation on the school subjects is not science, nor literature, nor history, nor geography, but the child's own social activities.

I believe that education cannot be unified in the study of science, or so called nature study, because apart from human activity, nature itself is not a unity; nature in itself is a number of diverse objects in space and time, and to attempt to make it the center of work by itself, is to introduce a principle of radiation rather than one of concentration.

I believe that literature is the reflex expression and interpretation of social experience; that hence it must follow upon and not precede such experience. It, therefore, cannot be made the basis, although it may be made the summary of unification.

I believe once more that history is of educative value in so far as it presents phases of social life and growth. It must be controlled by reference to social life. When taken simply as history it is thrown into the distant past and becomes dead and inert. Taken as the record of man's social life and progress it becomes full of meaning. I believe, however, that it cannot be so taken excepting as the child is also introduced directly into social life.

I believe accordingly that the primary basis of education is in the child's powers at work along the same general constructive lines as those which have brought civilization into being.

I believe that the only way to make the child conscious of his social heritage is to enable him to perform those fundamental types of activity which make civilization what it is.

I believe, therefore, in the so-called expressive or constructive activities as the center of correlation.

I believe that this gives the standard for the place of cooking, sewing, manual training, etc., in the school.

I believe that they are not special studies which are to be introduced over and above a lot of others in the way of relaxation or relief, or as additional accomplishments. I believe rather that they represent, as types, fundamental forms of social activity; and that it is possible and desirable that the child's introduction into the more formal subjects of the curriculum be through the medium of these activities.

I believe that the study of science is educational in so far as it brings out the materials and processes which make social life what it is.

I believe that one of the greatest difficulties in the present teaching of science is that the material is presented in purely objective form, or is treated as a new peculiar kind of experience which the child can add to that which he has already had. In reality, science is of value because it gives the ability to interpret and control the experience already had. It should be introduced, not as so much new subject-matter, but as showing the factors already involved in previous experience and as furnishing tools by which that experience can be more easily and effectively regulated.

I believe that at present we lose much of the value of literature and language studies because of our elimination of the social element. Language is almost always treated in the books of pedagogy simply as the expression of thought. It is true that language is a logical instrument, but it is fundamentally and primarily a social instrument. Language is the device for communication; it is the tool through which one individual comes to share the ideas and feelings of others. When treated simply as a way of getting individual information, or as a means of showing off what one has learned, it loses its social motive and end.

I believe that there is, therefore, no succession of studies in the ideal school curriculum. If education is life, all life has, from the outset, a scientific aspect, an aspect of art and culture, and an aspect of communication. It cannot, therefore, be true that the proper studies for one grade are mere reading and writing, and that at a later grade, reading, or literature, or science, may be introduced. The progress is not in the succession of studies but in the development of new attitudes towards, and new interests in, experience.

I believe finally, that education must be conceived as a continuing reconstruction of experience; that the process and the goal of education are one and the same thing.

I believe that to set up any end outside of education, as furnishing its goal and standard, is to deprive the educational process of much of its meaning and tends to make us rely upon false and external stimuli in dealing with the child.

ARTICLE IV—THE NATURE OF METHOD

I believe that the question of method is ultimately reducible to the question of the order of development of the child's powers and interests. The law for presenting and treating material is the law implicit with the child's own nature. Because this is so I believe the following statements are of supreme importance as determining the spirit in which education is carried on:

1. I believe that the active side precedes the passive in the development of the child's nature; that expression comes before conscious impression; that the muscular development precedes the sensory; that movements come before conscious sensations; I believe that consciousness is essentially motor or impulsive; that conscious states tend to project themselves in action.

I believe that the neglect of this principle is the cause of a large part of the waste of time and strength in school work. The child is thrown into a passive, receptive, or absorbing attitude. The conditions are such that he is not permitted to follow the law of his nature; the result is friction and waste.

I believe that ideas (intellectual and rational processes) also result from action and devolve for the sake of the better control of action. What we term reason is primarily the law of orderly or effective action. To attempt to develop the reasoning powers, the powers of judgment, without reference to the selection and arrangement of means in action, is the fundamental fallacy in our present methods of dealing with this matter. As a result we present the child with arbitrary symbols. Symbols are a necessity in mental development, but they have their place as tools for economizing effort; presented by themselves they are a mass of meaningless and arbitrary ideas imposed from without.

2. I believe that the image is the great instrument of instruction. What a child gets out of any subject presented to him is simply the images which he himself forms with regard to it.

I believe that if nine tenths of the energy at present directed towards making the child learn certain things, were spent in seeing to it that the child was forming proper images, the work of instruction would be indefinitely facilitated.

I believe that much of the time and attention now given to the preparation and presentation of lessons might be more wisely and profitably expended in training the child's power of imagery and in seeing to it that he was continually forming definite, vivid, and growing images of the various subjects with which he comes in contact in his experience.

3. I believe that interests are the signs and symptoms of growing power. I believe that they represent dawning capacities. Accordingly the constant and careful observation of interests is of the utmost importance for the educator.

I believe that these interests are to be observed as showing the state of development which the child has reached.

I believe that they prophesy the stage upon which he is about to enter.

I believe that only through the continual and sympathetic observation of childhood's interests can the adult enter into the child's life and see what it is ready for, and upon what material it could work most readily and fruitfully.

I believe that these interests are neither to be humored nor repressed. To repress interest is to substitute the adult for the child, and so to weaken intellectual curiosity and alertness, to suppress initiative, and to deaden interest. To humor the interests is to substitute the transient for the permanent. The interest is always the sign of some power below; the important thing is to discover this power. To humor the interest is to fail to penetrate below the surface and its sure result is to substitute caprice and whim for genuine interest.

4. I believe that the emotions are the reflex of actions.

I believe that to endeavor to stimulate or arouse the emotions apart from their corresponding activities, is to introduce an unhealthy and morbid state of mind.

I believe that if we can only secure right habits of action and thought, with reference to the good, the true, and the beautiful, the emotions will for the most part take care of themselves.

I believe that next to deadness and dullness, formalism and routine, our education is threatened with no greater evil than sentimentalism.

I believe that this sentimentalism is the necessary result of the attempt to divorce feeling from action.

ARTICLE V—THE SCHOOL AND SOCIAL PROGRESS

I believe that education is the fundamental method of social progress and reform.

I believe that all reforms which rest simply upon the enactment of law, or the threatening of certain penalties, or upon changes in mechanical or outward arrangements, are transitory and futile.

I believe that education is a regulation of the process of coming to share in the social consciousness; and that the adjustment of individual activity on the basis of this social consciousness is the only sure method of social reconstruction.

I believe that this conception has due regard for both the individualistic and socialistic ideals. It is duly individual because it recognizes the formation of a certain character as the only genuine basis of right living. It is socialistic because it recognizes that this right character is not to be formed by merely individual precept, example, or exhortation, but rather by the influence of a certain form of institutional or community life upon the individual, and that the social organism through the school, as its organ, may determine ethical results.

I believe that in the ideal school we have the reconciliation of the individualistic and the institutional ideals.

I believe that the community's duty to education is, therefore, its paramount moral duty. By law and punishment, by social agitation and discussion, society can regulate and form itself in a more or less haphazard and chance way. But through education society can formulate its own purposes, can organize its own means and resources, and thus shape itself with definiteness and economy in the direction in which it wishes to move.

I believe that when society once recognizes the possibilities in this direction, and the obligations which these possibilities impose, it is impossible to conceive of the resources of time, attention, and money which will be put at the disposal of the educator.

I believe that it is the business of every one interested in education to insist upon the school as a primary and most effective interest of social progress and reform in order that society may be awakened to realize what the school stands for, and aroused to the necessity of endowing the educator with sufficient equipment properly to perform his task.

I believe that education thus conceived marks the most perfect and intimate union of science and art conceivable in human experience.

I believe that the art of thus giving shape to human powers and adapting them to social service, is the supreme art; one calling into its service the best of artists; that no insight, sympathy, tact, executive power, is too great for such service.

I believe that with the growth of psychological service, giving added insight into individual structure and laws of growth; and with growth of social science, adding to our knowledge of the right organization of individuals, all scientific resources can be utilized for the purposes of education.

I believe that when science and art thus join hands the most commanding motive for human action will be reached; the most genuine springs of human conduct aroused and the best service that human nature is capable of guaranteed.

I believe, finally, that the teacher is engaged, not simply in the training of individuals, but in the formation of the proper social life.

I believe that every teacher should realize the dignity of his calling; that he is a social servant set apart for the maintenance of proper social order and the securing of the right social growth.

I believe that in this way the teacher always is the prophet of the true God and the usherer in the true kingdom of God.

Reading 39

The Culturological Context of Reconstructionism

Theodore Brameld

Although concern with far-reaching purposes and aggressive strategies is grounded in the long history of influential philosophic movements, no single school of thought can be called the chief source of that influence. There are many such sources. Like other philosophies, moreover, reconstructionism must be evaluated finally by the extent to which its motivations and intentions are rooted in the culture. These motivations and intentions are at once strongly negative and strongly positive: negative, because they are generated by acute dissatisfaction with several prime facets of our age; positive, because they give rise to constructive, organized, and future-oriented plans for a cuture, the outlines of which are already beginning to crystallize.

The central critique of modern culture contends that, magnificent as their services have been in the past, the major institutions and corresponding social, economic, and other practices that developed during pre-

Source: Theodore Brameld, *Patterns of Educational Philosophy: Divergence and Convergence in Culturological Perspective.* Copyright © 1971 by Holt, Rinehart and Winston, Inc. Reprinted by permission of Holt, Rinehart and Winston, Inc.

ceding centuries of the modern era are now incapable of confronting the terrifying, bewildering crisis of our age. Simultaneously, the transmissive, moderative, and restorative choices of belief represented in varying styles and degrees of expression by three alternative philosophies of education have likewise been found wanting. Meanwhile, the selected modern philosophic movements . . . (existentialism, analytic philosophy, neo-Freudianism, Zen Buddhism, and neo-Marxism) have responded to this crisis in multiple ways—some very deliberately and forthrightly, some obliquely or perhaps even unintentionally, but all contributing in various respects to the revolutionary compulsions that motivate the quest for an educational philosophy of cultural transformation. The need for a compass by which we can discover our lost bearings thus challenges the philosopher as he has been challenged only in previous periods of extreme crisis. He is under obligation, together with the physicist, economist, and all other scientists—bar none—to help build a rationally designed culture and to assume full responsibility for his discoveries.

Herein is the positive obligation of those

in our culture. Not only are they philosophers and scientists but also artists, teachers, and just everyday citizens who find themselves responding to the beliefs most significant for reconstructionists. A large body of knowledge-achievement is already available and waiting to be used. Belief in the practicability of a planned, democratic world civilization is bolstered by rich experience in recent years. The untouched resources available for providing economic abundance, better health, better education, richer esthetic enjoyment, and for satisfying still other ubiquitous wants (such as respect for all races) are vastly greater than those drawn upon thus far. To estimate these resources accurately, as well as to plan for their release and equitable use through organized democratic machinery, becomes our chief opportunity.

Reconstructionists, in brief, seek both to determine what obstacles lie in the way of achievement of our objectives and to determine how *the largest possible majority of people* can find strength and intelligence to

remove these obstacles. Above all, reconstructionists try to make certain that any design to be transformed, and any practices that may be implemented in building it, are rooted in defensible beliefs about reality, knowledge, and value. However gigantic this undertaking, they are convinced that Western civilization is at an end if man fails in them.

Accordingly, this philosophy of education, although like various others an interpretation of and response to contemporary problems, differs in significant ways. While these alternative philosophies, too, are stirred by the deep troubles besetting our age, they analyze them differently and their prognoses are usually less fundamental or less far-reaching. Instead of remaining satisfied with gradual moderation and transition, or with fairly constant perpetuation and transmission, or with intellectualized and/or theologized restoration, the reconstructionist throws in his lot unequivocally with those who believe (as some have always come to believe in critical times) that only thorough-

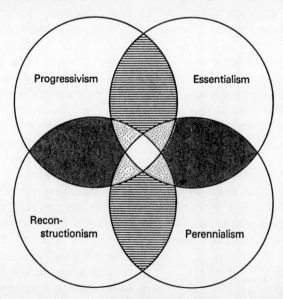

Figure 1. Brameld's view of reconstructionism as an educational philosophy. Adapted from Theodore Brameld, *Philosophies of Education in Cultural Perspective.* New York: The Dryden Press, Inc, p. 77.

going transformation of principles and institutions is any longer possible or suitable. The philosopher of culture, Cassirer, epitomizes this attitude when he asserts that the:

... great mission of the Utopia is to make room for the possible as opposed to a passive acquiescence in the present actual state of affairs. It is symbolic thought which overcomes the natural inertia of man and endows him with a new ability, the ability constantly to reshape his human universe.

To conclude, reconstructionism takes its position with the historic philosophies of vision. But its vision emerges out of the tangible, tested experiences of both the past and the present. It rests squarely upon the contributions of the physical and behavioral sciences, the pure and applied arts, and education. For this reason and without any rationalizing equivocations, its adherents would defend themselves as ultimately more practical than those who, in the name of common sense or caution, delimit their theories to the point of sterility and similar ineffectiveness.

Reading 40

Existential Teaching and Learning

Gerald John Pine

Today's students are deeply concerned with questions regarding the meaning of human existence. These questions are expressed in such terms as Who am I? Where am I going? What is the meaning of life? What is the meaning of *my* life? What is the purpose of learning? How relevant is education to life? The search for the answers to these queries is a significant element in the teacher-pupil relationship.

Common Existential Principles

A great deal of diversity may be found among such existential writers as Sartre, Heidegger, Kirkegaard, Marcel, Jaspers, and Buber. As a philosophical movement existentialism embraces a variety of viewpoints. However, running through these various existential viewpoints are several common denominators which can be identified and which have special relevance for those who hope to arrive at a more effective teaching

Source: Gerald John Pine, "Existential Teaching and Learning." *Education* vol. 95, no. 1 (Fall 1974), pp. 18–24. Reprinted with permission.

approach through the medium of existentialism.

1. The basic philosophical principle of existentialism is that *existence precedes essence.* Man chooses his essence; he exists first and then defines himself through the choices he makes plus the actions he takes. Thought without action is meaningless. Man is what he does.

2. At every moment man is free. He is free of external forces. He is free of himself—of what he has been. An individual's past life is history, it no longer exists *now* in the present. An individual is influenced by external agents or by his past life only when he chooses to be influenced by these forces.

3. Accompanying man's freedom is the awesome burden of responsibility. Each man is responsible for what he is. In choosing and acting for himself each man chooses and acts for all mankind. Man cannot avoid the weight of his freedom. He cannot give away his freedom and responsibility to the state, to his parents, to his teachers, to his

weaknesses, to his past, to environmental conditions.

4. Every truth and every action implies a human setting and a human subjectivity. There is a world of reality but it cannot be reality apart from the people who are the basic part of it. Reality lies in each man's experience and perception of the event rather than in the isolated event; e.g., two men may hear the same speech, the same words, the same voice. One man's reality may be that the speaker is a political demagogue, for the other man the reality is that the speaker is an awaited political saviour.

5. Man must rely upon himself and upon his fellow creatures to live out his lifespan in an adamant universe. Man's relationship to others must be that of self-realization for all and creature comfort (empathic love).

6. Man is not an object; he is a subject. Each man is unique and idiosyncratic. To view man scientifically is to view man as an object. Science fails to find the "I" in each man.

Existential Teaching/Learning Principles

Flowing from these common and vital existential principles a special facilitative human relationship between student and teacher can evolve. The existential teacher has translated existentialism into a teaching approach designed to increase freedom within the pupil, to assist the pupil in discovering meaning for his existence, and to improve his encounter with others.

The existential teacher sees teaching as more an attitude than a technique. It reflects the self of the teacher and represents a sharing of the teacher's self in a personal and human relationship with fellow human beings.

Teaching is viewed primarily as an encounter which implies a special kind of relationship requiring the teacher to be totally present to the student, to participate in the student's existence, to be fully with him. The teacher strives to know the student by entering the student's reality, and seeing as the student sees.

The student is not reduced to an object to be analyzed according to theoretical constructs. He is not diagnosed and evaluated by the teacher because diagnosis and evaluation are conducted in terms of externally established norms and standards.

The teacher who depends on cumulative records and test data to work with the student locks himself outside the student's internal world. Entrance into that world is gained by an emotional commitment in which the teacher gives of himself as a person.

Knowing the student as a person becomes more important than *knowing about* him. This demands teacher movement away from the traditional diagnostic approaches which mirror an external objective perspective to an internal, subjective one.

The existential teacher operates on the immediate view of human experience. Learning and behavior are a function of the immediate view of the student. There is no reliance on historical or external determinism.

The immediate view stresses the way the student sees his situation today, at this instant. The student behaves and learns at this time on the basis of his ways of seeing, choosing, and acting at this moment in time. What the teacher is and what he or she does in relationships with students is the key to developing facilitating and enabling relationships which help students move toward becoming more fully functioning self-actualized persons.

The existential teacher believes that each person has dignity—intrinsic value—because he exists and because he is a free being who defines his essence through the choices he makes and the actions he takes. Existential teaching offers a challenge to the teacher to implement fully belief in the dignity of man and deep respect for the individual. The value of the student is not determined by what he has done, what test scores he has achieved, what he has said, what clothes he wears, where he lives, how he speaks, what grades he has achieved, or how he relates to people. His value stems from his existence, his freedom to choose, and his capacity to become and to carve out his own life.

Emanating from this existential teaching attitude are existential principles and conditions which can be translated into an educational process that would enable students in a variety of situations, circumstances, and places to more fully realize their potentialities. These principles and conditions refer to learning as it occurs in schools, universities, adult education programs, continuing education programs in business and industry, and wherever else teaching and learning occur.

Existential Principles of Learning

Principle 1:   The learner is a free and responsible agent. Existentially speaking, he is a choosing agent; he is unable to avoid choosing his way through life. He is a free agent in the sense that he is absolutely free to establish goals for himself. There are no goals which he cannot choose. The beginning point in creating values and learning is the setting of goals. The learner is a responsible agent who is personally accountable for his free choices as they are revealed in the way he lives his life (Van Cleve Morris 1966).

Principle 2:   Learning is an experience which occurs inside the learner and is acti-

vated by the learner. The process of learning is primarily controlled by the learner and not by the teacher. Changes in perception and behavior are products of human meaning and perceiving rather than of any forces exerted upon the individual. Learning is not only a function of what a teacher does to or says to or provides for a learner. More significantly, learning has to do with something which happens in the unique world of the learner. It flourishes in a situation in which teaching is seen as a facilitating process that assists people to explore and discover the personal meaning of events for them.

No one directly teaches anyone anything of significance (Rogers 1969). If teaching is defined as a process of directly communicating an experience or a fragment of knowledge, then it is clear that little learning occurs as a result of this process and that the learning that does take place is usually inconsequential. People learn what they want to learn, they see what they want to see, and they hear what they want to hear. Learning cannot be imposed. When we impose ideas on people, we train them. When we create an atmosphere in which people are free to explore, to nourish, and to develop ideas in dialogue and through interaction with other people, we educate them. Very little learning takes place without personal involvement and meaning on the part of the learner. Unless what is being taught has personal meaning for the individual, it will be shut out from his field of perception. People forget most of the content "taught" to them and retain only the content that they use in their work, or the content that is relevant to them personally.

Principle 3:   Learning is the discovery of the personal meaning and relevance of ideas. People more readily internalize and implement concepts and ideas which are relevant to their needs and problems. Learning is a process which requires the exploration of ideas in relation to self and community so that people can determine what their needs are, what goals they would like to formulate, what issues they would like to discuss, and what content they would like to learn. What is relevant and meaningful is decided by the learner and must be discovered by the learner.

This means the curriculum as a set of experiences emerges from learners. Rather than fitting people to externally prescribed programs of experiences, we need to provide a growth-fostering climate in which people are free to construct their own curricula. No one person or agency can validly decide what must be learned by people as individuals or as members of groups. A curriculum consists of experiences freely chosen by free and responsible agents. The learners' choices of experiences define the curriculum.

Principle 4:   Learning is a consequence of experience. People become responsible when they have really assumed responsibility; they become independent when they have experienced independent behavior; they become able when they have experienced success; they begin to feel important when they are important to somebody; they feel liked when someone likes them. People do not change their behavior merely because someone tells them to do so or tells them how to change. For effective learning, giving information is not enough; for example, people become responsible and independent, not from having other people tell them that they should be responsible and independent, but from having experienced authentic responsibility and independence.

Principle 5:   Learning is emotional as well as intellectual. Learning is affected by the total state of the individual. People are feeling beings as well as thinking beings, and when their feelings and thoughts are in harmony, learning is maximized. To create the optimal conditions for learning to occur in a group, *people* must come before *purpose* (Gendlin 1968). Regardless of the purpose of a group, it cannot be effectively accomplished when other things get in the way. If the purpose of the group is to design and to carry out some task, it will not be optimally achieved if people in the group are fighting and working against each other. If the purpose of the group is to discuss current issues and problems in a given field with reason and honesty, then it will not be achieved if people are afraid to communicate openly. Barriers to communication exist in people, and before we can conduct "official business," we need to work with the people problems that may exist in a group. It might be said that in any group, regardless of the people problems which exist, enough group intellectual capacity remains intact for members of the group to acquire information and skills. However, to maximize the acquisition and internalization of ideas, it seems reasonable that the people problems would have to be dealt with first.

Principle 6:   Learning is a valuing experience. Learning implicitly or explicitly is an experience that expresses values. The data an individual chooses to internalize are functions of his values. The data an individual chooses to exchange and share are reflections of what he deeply cares about. The questions he seeks to answer, the skills he desires to acquire, the values he weighs and ponders over, the ideas he develops, ultimately emanate from the deeply rooted first concerns inherent in his nature—Who am I? What is my relationship to the world in which I live? These are human valuing questions which lie at the base of all learning. They are questions which belong to all men. Learning which deals explicitly and openly with these questions represents the highest and most relevant form of learning.

Principle 7:   Teaching is learning. Since learning is defined here as the process of changing behavior in positive directions, it follows that teaching is learning. The problem in this statement is with the word "teaching" which, in the traditional sense, refers to a didactic procedure built upon an *external stimulus-internal response* notion of motivation that results in a view of learners as organisms to be made into something. This view suggests that learners cannot be trusted to decide what is good and relevant for themselves—someone else (the curriculum maker) must decide; then some other people (teachers) must determine what forces should be exerted to keep learners moving through this "good experience." In such a situation, people are pupils or students (organisms to be made into something), but not necessarily learners.

An enhancing learning situation is characterized by a curriculum that is defined by the learner's choices of good and relevant experiences and by the presence of a teacher who is a learner. Learners are free and responsible persons who bring to any interaction and relationship an accumulation of experiences, ideas, feelings, attitudes, and perspectives. Learning occurs when free and responsible people are open to themselves, when they draw upon their personal collection of data and share their data in cooperative interaction. As a learner, the person designated "teacher" shares his data when they are needed by others, and he, in turn, draws upon the data that other persons contribute for his own growth and development. The direct dissemination of ideas, facts, and information in a structural relationship which permits little or no feedback from learners and which occurs for the purpose of altering behavior to accomplish an objective formulated by agents or agencies external to the learning group is *training.* Unfortunately, this is a definition which

all too accurately describes much of the behavior known as teaching.

Existential Conditions Which Facilitate Learning

Condition 1:   Learning is facilitated in an atmosphere which encourages people to be active. The learning process thrives when there is less teacher domination and talk and more faith that people can find alternatives and solutions which are satisfying to themselves. If the teacher listens to his students and allows them to use him and the classroom group as resources and sounding boards, the active exploration of ideas and the possible solutions to problems is facilitated. People are not passive and reactive receptacles into which we can pour the "right" values, the "right" answers, and the "right" ways of thinking. People are active and creative beings who need the opportunity to determine goals, issues to be discussed, and the means of evaluating themselves. They learn when they feel that they are a part of what is going on—when they are personally involved. Learning is not poured into people; learning emerges from people.

Condition 2:   Learning is facilitated in an atmosphere which promotes and facilitates the individual's discovery of the personal meaning of ideas. This means that the teacher, rather than directing or manipulating people, helps them to discover the personal meaning that ideas and events have for them. He creates a situation in which people are freely able to express their needs rather than to have their needs dictated to them. Learning becomes an activity in which the needs of the individual and of the group are considered in deciding what issues will be explored and what the subject matter will be.

No matter how permissive or unstructured a learning activity may be, there exist implicit goals in the activity itself—a teacher is never goalless. Learning occurs when the goals of the teacher accommodate, facilitate, and encourage the individual's discovery of personal goals and personal meaning in events. The art of helping people to learn requires the development of goals which provide sufficient elbowroom for people to explore and to internalize behavior that is satisfying and growth-producing to themselves.

Condition 3:   Learning is facilitated in an atmosphere which emphasizes the uniquely personal and subjective nature of learning. In such a situation, each individual has the feeling that his/her ideas, his/her feelings, his/her perspectives have value and significance. People need to develop an awareness that all that is to be learned is not outside or external to themselves. They develop such an awareness when they feel that their contributions and their value as people are genuinely appreciated.

Condition 4:   Learning is facilitated in an atmosphere which encourages openness of self rather than concealment of self. Problem solving and learning require that personal feelings, attitudes, ideas, questions, and concerns be brought to light and examined openly. To the degree that an idea, a thought, a feeling, or an attitude related to the topic at hand is held back and not openly expressed—to that degree are the processes of learning and discovery inhibited. People need to feel that they can try something, that they can fail if necessary without being humiliated, embarrassed, or diminished as persons. Openness of self occurs in an atmosphere free from psycho-

logical threat. People can invest themselves fully and openly in the collaborative and interactive process of learning when they know that no matter what they say or express, it will not result in psychological punishment or penalties.

Condition 5:   Learning is facilitated in an atmosphere in which difference is good and desirable. Situations which emphasize the "one right answer," the "magical solution," or the "one good way" to act or to think or to behave, narrow and limit exploration and inhibit discovery. If people are to look at themselves, at others, and at ideas openly and reasonably, then they must have the opportunity to express their opinions no matter how different they may be. This calls for an atmosphere in which different ideas can be *accepted* (but not necessarily agreed with). Differences in ideas must be accepted if differences in people are to be accepted, too.

Condition 6:   Learning is facilitated in an atmosphere which consistently recognizes people's right to make mistakes. Where mistakes are not permitted, the freedom and the willingness of people to make choices are severely limited. Growth and change are facilitated when error is accepted as a natural part of the learning process. The learning process requires the challenge of new and different experiences, the trying of the unknown, and therefore, it necessarily must involve the making of mistakes. In order that people may learn, they need opportunities to explore new situations and ideas without being penalized or punished for mistakes which are integral to the activity of learning. The teacher who feels and acts on the need always to be right creates a limiting and threatening condition of learning.

Condition 7: *Learning is facilitated in an atmosphere in which people are encouraged to trust in themselves as well as in external sources.* They become less dependent upon authority when they can open up the self and when they feel that *who they are* is a valuable resource for learning. It is important that people feel that they have something to bring to the learning situation rather than to feel that all learning means the acquisition of facts and knowledge from some external agent for use sometime in the future. People learn when they begin to see *themselves* as the wellsprings of ideas and alternatives to problems. Learning is facilitated when people begin to draw ideas from themselves and others rather than to rely on the teacher.

The most existential teacher is the teacher who creates the conditions by which he loses the teaching function. The person designated as "teacher," by creating an appropriate atmosphere and facilitating conditions, gradually moves from being a dispenser of information to becoming a resource person and learner, enabling persons in the group to emerge more strongly as vital human resources and active learners. The facilitating elements which the teacher tries to foster lead to free and open communication, confrontation, acceptance, respect, freedom from threat, the right to make mistakes, self-revelation, cooperation and personal involvement, shared evaluation, and responsibility. Successful "teach-ing succeeds by doing itself out of a job. It succeeds by becoming unnecessary, by producing an individual who no longer needs to be taught, who breaks loose and swings free of the teacher and becomes self-moving" (Van Cleve Morris, 1966: 153).

The teacher creates the climate for learning by becoming a facilitator who views *himself* as a learner and who authentically behaves as learner. He reveals himself as an inquiring, questing, and valuing person who conveys spontaneity, curiosity, warmth, and empathy; who listens and attends to others; who conveys acceptance and respect; who understands affective as well as cognitive meanings and intents; who confronts in a genuine and caring way. Such a person creates an atmosphere in which these qualities are internalized by members of the group. To the degree that the teacher becomes a facilitator and a vibrant learner—to that degree will learning become enhanced. He who teaches least teaches best.

REFERENCES

Gendlin, Eugene T., and Beebe, John. "Experiential Groups," in *Innovations to Group Psychotherapy.* Edited by George M. Gazda. Springfield, Illinois: Charles C. Thomas, 1968.

Morris, Van Cleve. *Existentialism in Education.* New York: Harper and Row, 1966.

Rogert, Carl R. *On Becoming a Person.* Boston: Houghton Mifflin Company, 1961.

Reading 41

A Model for Analyzing a Philosophy of Education

William K. Frankena

There are two sorts of things that go by the name of philosophy of education today, one traditional and one newish. The newish sort of thing is what is called "analytical philosophy of education." It consists in the analysis of educational concepts, arguments, slogans, and statements. For example, if one tries to define what is meant by teaching, to distinguish teaching from indoctrination, and to relate teaching to learning, or if one tries to determine what is meant by the slogan "Learn by doing!", then one is doing analytical philosophy of education. The analytical philosophy of education consists entirely of such inquiries. Since I am here seeking to show how to analyze a philosophy of education, this essay is itself an example of analytical philosophy of education. I say that this sort of thing is newish because, although educational philosophers have always included some of it in their works, it is only recently that some of them

Source: William K. Frankena, "A Model for Analyzing a Philosophy of Education." *The High School Journal* vol. 50, no. 1 (October 1966), pp. 8–13. Reprinted by permission of the University of North Carolina Press.

have come to think that their work should include nothing else.

The other kind of philosophy of education is what educational philosophers have done historically and what some of them still do. I shall call it "normative philosophy of education." It may be eclectic or non-eclectic; idealistic, realistic, or pragmatic; naturalistic or supernaturalistic; traditional or progressive. In all its forms, however, what distinguishes it from analytical philosophy of education is that it makes normative statements about what education, educators, and the schools should do or not do, about what the aims, content, methods, etc., of education should be or not be.

Now consider any such normative philosophy of education, for example, that of Aristotle, Rousseau, Dewey, Whitehead, Russell, Maritain, Brameld, or Phenix. Our problem is to find a scheme for analyzing it, that is, for understanding it and seeing how it is put together, for taking it apart and putting it together again. One cannot evaluate it in any systematic way until one has analyzed it to see just what it says and what its arguments are.

In general, a normative philosophy of education will include statements of three kinds. a) It must include normative statements about the aims, principles, methods, etc., of education, as Dewey does when he says that the schools should teach reflective thinking. b) It will probably include—and it should include—some bits of analysis, for example, definitions of education, teaching, and learning. c) Almost certainly it will contain some statements of empirical fact, hypotheses about their explanation, psychological theories, experimental findings, predictions, and the like, for example, Russell's statement that a child can be made to feel the importance of learning the dull parts of a subject without the use of compulsion. d) It may also contain statements of a fourth kind—epistemological, metaphysical, or theological ones such as Phenix's assertion that the meaning of a proposition is defined by the method of validating it or Maritain's doctrine that man is a sinful and wounded creature called to divine life. It is not always easy to tell which kind of a statement is being made in a given sentence, and many sentences in works on the philosophy of education are ambiguous and hard to classify.

To analyze a philosophy of education one must find out what statements of these different kinds it contains and how they are related to one another in the author's reasoning. This is relatively easy to do in the case of some authors, for example, Maritain, harder to do in the case of others, for example, Dewey or Whitehead. What follows is an attempt to provide a guide for doing so.*

Education is primarily a process in which educators and educated interact, and such

a process is called education if and only if it issues or is intended to issue in the formation, in the one being educated, of certain desired or desirable abilities, habits, dispositions, skills, character traits, beliefs, or bodies of knowledge (if it is intended to but does not, it is called *bad* education), for example, the habit of reflective thinking, conscientiousness, the ability to dance, or a knowledge of astronomy. For convenience, I shall refer to all such states as dispositions. Then education is the process of forming or trying to form such dispositions. Note that what I have just done is a rough analysis of the concept of education.

If this is so, then 1) the *main* task of a normative philosophy of education is to list and define a set of dispositions to be fostered by parents, teachers, and schools (and by the pupil himself). That is, it must say what dispositions are desirable and ought to be cultivated. In saying this it will, of course, be making normative statements, but the definitions of the dispositions listed will be bits of analysis. A complete normative theory of education will, however, do two more things. 2) It will give a line of thought to show that the dispositions listed by it are desirable or should be cultivated. Such a line of reasoning may take various forms, but they must all have the same general pattern. They must bring in some basic premises about the aims or values of life or about the principles to be followed in life—about what is desirable or obligatory. These, again, will be normative judgments, the most fundamental ones. Even Dewey brings in such premises, though he often writes as if he does not. In addition, they must show or at least give reasons for thinking that, if we are to live in the way that is desirable or in the way in which we ought to—if we are to live a good or a moral life—then we must acquire the dispositions listed. It is in this part of a philosophy of education that epistemological, ontological, or theological premises

---

* For similar attempts on my part, see "Toward a Philosophy of the Philosophy of Education," *Harvard Educational Review* 26 (1956); *Philosophy of Education* (Macmillan, 1965), pp. 1–10; *Three Historical Philosophies of Education* (Scott Foresman, 1965), pp. 6–12.

most often appear, but they are not logically required. What *is* logically required is, first, some normative premises stating basic goals or principles, for example, Aristotle's premise that the good life is a happy one consisting of intrinsically excellent activities like contemplation, and second, factual claims stating that certain dispositions are conducive to the achievement of those goals or to the following of those principles, for example, Aristotle's further claim that, if we are to achieve the good life as he sees it, we must cultivate such dispositions as moderation, practical wisdom, and a knowledge of mathematics, physics, and philosophy. If we think of basic normative premises as belonging to Box A, the other premises used here, whether they are religious, philosophical, or empirical, as belonging to Box B, and the conclusions as to the dispositions to be fostered as belonging to Box C, then we can represent this part of a philosophy of education as follows:

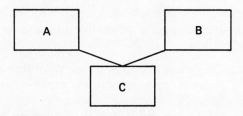

3) Finally, a complete normative theory of education will tell us what we should do in order to acquire or foster the dispositions recommended by it in Box C, that is, it will make further recommendations about means, methods, curriculum, administration, etc., hopefully accompanying them with its reasons for making them. This means that it will make normative statements of yet a third kind, and that it will support them by giving empirical evidence (discovered by observation and experiment or borrowed from psychology and other disciplines) to show that the methods and measures it advocates are necessary, helpful, or effective

in the formation of the dispositions in its Box C (and that other methods are not). The example cited from Russell earlier will do here; in it he argues that compulsion should not be used, since children can be gotten through even the dull parts of a subject without it. This example also shows that premises from Box A may come in even in this part of a philosophy of education, for Russell is assuming the normative principle that compulsion ought not to be used unless it is necessary. Actually, epistemological premises or other premises from Box B may also appear at this stage; for instance, Cardinal Newman uses his epistemological premise that theology is a body of genuine knowledge in an argument to show that theology should belong to the curriculum of a university. Neglecting such important points, however, we may represent this part of a philosophy of education as follows, taking Box C as giving the dispositions to be fostered, Box D as containing factual statements of the form "Method X is necessary, effective, or at least helpful in the formation of one or more of these dispositions (or the opposite)," and Box E as including recommendations of the form "Method X should (or should not) be used":

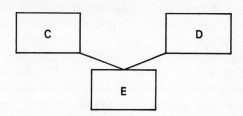

It should be added that bits of analysis may also show up in this part of a theory, for example, in a distinction between indoctrination and teaching or in a definition of compulsion.

It will now be clear that a full-fledged normative philosophy of education will have two parts, each probably including some bits of analysis; one part falling into the ABC pattern given above and the other into the CDE pattern. In its actual presentation, however, the two parts are often mingled and the patterns are often left unclear, for instance, in Whitehead's essays on education. Of the two parts, the first is the more properly philosophical, and the second is the more practical. Combining the two parts, we may represent a complete normative philosophy of education as follows:

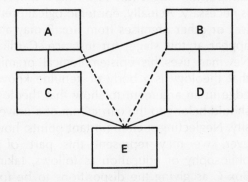

Here the dotted lines are intended to take care of the fact, noted earlier, that premises from Boxes A and B may be used in arriving at the recommendations made in Box E.

It will also be clear that there may be three kinds of normative philosophy of education: a) one that is complete in the way just indicated; b) one that does only what was described as the first part of the complete task, giving us only what falls into the ABC pattern, that is, one that provides us only with a list of dispositions to be fostered together with a rationale showing us that they should be fostered and why, leaving the task of implementation to educational scientists, administrators, and teachers; and c) one that simply begins with a list of dispositions to be cultivated and goes on to give us what falls into the CDE pattern or into what was referred to as the second part of the complete task, telling us what we should do to foster the dispositions listed most effectively and giving us the evidence and arguments to show why we should adopt those methods and procedures. A writer who does the third kind of thing might take his list of dispositions from some more philosophical work, or he might be eclectic, picking up the dispositions on his list from various sources, or he might simply take them to be the dispositions regarded as desirable by society, parents, the state, the church, school boards, or even the pupils themselves—remember how Bianca complains to her would-be educators in *The Taming of the Shrew*:

Why, gentlemen, you do me double wrong,
To strive for that which resteth in my choice:
I am no breeching scholar in the schools;
I'll not be tied to hours nor 'pointed times,
But learn my lessons as I please myself.

We can also now see just what one must do in order to understand any complete normative philosophy of education that is placed before one (an analytical philosophy of education is another matter). If one knows this, one will also be able to analyze any less complete normative philosophy of education.

1. One must first look to see what dispositions it says education should foster (Box C).
2. Next, one must try to determine the rationale given to show that education should foster those dispositions. To do this one must:
    a. See what its basic normative premises are—its basic values, principles, or ends (Box A).
    b. See what factual premises are brought in (implicitly or explicitly), empirical, theological, or philosophical (Box B).
    c. See how these go together to make a line of argument of the ABC pattern to show that the dispositions listed should be cultivated.

3. Then one should look for recommendations about ways and means of teaching, administering, etc. (Box E).

4. Fourthly, one must seek to discover the rationales for these recommendations. To do this one must:

    a. See what factual statements based on observation and experience are brought in (possibly borrowed from psychology, etc.) (Box D).

    b. See if any premises from Boxes A or B are used here.

    c. See how these go together to make a line of argument (or a battery of separate arguments) to show that the ways and means recommended should be used in the cultivation of the dispositions listed (Pattern CDE).

5. All along, of course, one should notice any definitions or bits of analysis that occur and see how they fit into the discussion.

Reading 42

Schools and Values

Jacob Getzels

I should like to consider very tentatively some possible reasons for the trouble schools have in influencing values.

All children acquire their fundamental "codes for future learning" or "learning sets" in the family during the period ascribed to primary socialization. One of the sets is the language code, the other the value code. The language code gives the child the categories for structuring and communicating his experiences. The value code tells him what in his experiences is important. In a sense, language becomes the medium through which the child perceives and expresses experience, and values determine what in his experience he will accept or reject.

Typically, the school requires an achievement ethic, with consequent high valuation on the future, deferred gratification, and symbolic commitment to success. It assumes that every child has had an opportunity to acquire beliefs, that anyone can get to the top if he tries hard enough, and that if he

tries he, too, can reach the top. The future, not the present, is what counts; one must use the present to prepare for the future. Time, therefore, is valuable and must not be wasted—"time is money"—and the school assumes that timed tests carry the same urgency for everyone. It is expected that the pupil will be able to defer gratification through symbolic commitment to success; he will study geometry now to become an engineer later. These are the values not only of the school; they are also the values of the families in which many of the children are reared. Such children acquire from their earliest years a value code compatible with the school values, just as they acquire a language code compatible with the school language. There is no reason for them to change, and the school provides no model for change.

In contrast to this, other children have experienced primarily a survival or subsistence ethic, with consequent high valuation on the present rather than the future, on immediate rather than deferred gratification, on concrete rather than symbolic commitment. Where these children live, hardly anyone ever gets to the top; often one cannot

Source: Jacob Getzels, "Schools and Values." *The Center Magazine* (May/June 1976), pp. 28–30. Reprinted with permission.

even move across the street. Time is not important or potentially valuable if there is not going to be anything to do with it anyway. And what does an appeal to symbolic success mean where the only success the child has seen can be measured realistically solely by subsistence and survival? In contrast to the other children, these children face severe discontinuities in values when they come to school—discontinuities which often have a profound effect on their behavior toward school and on the school's behavior toward them.

These children are often accused of failing in school because they are intellectually apathetic and physically aggressive. The issue may be turned around and the question raised whether they may not be intellectually apathetic and physically aggressive because they fail. For what can be more tormenting than to be confronted day after day with a situation in which the language and value codes seem different in inexplicable ways from those to which you are accustomed—and more, a situation in which you cannot succeed and from which you are not permitted to escape without threat of severe punishment?

This is a situation in which learning cannot take place, and surely not the learning of new values. The reaction to this type of frustration is hopelessness and rage. In school, the hopelessness is manifested in apathy, intellectual withdrawal from the source of frustration; and the rage is manifested in aggression and in physical attack upon the source of the frustration. The patterns of apathy and aggression maintained over the compulsory years often become stabilized into deep-seated maladjustment.

In view of these circumstances, the customary teacher-training and placement procedures are dysfunctional. Little differentiation has been made between prospective teachers for one locality and those for another. The distinctions in training and placement have all been made vertically, that is, between those who will teach in one age grade or another, but not horizontally, that is, between those who will teach the same grade but in different localities.

Yet even a cursory visit to Woodlawn and Winnetka reveals that the differences in teaching the same grade—say, the eighth—in Woodlawn and Winnetka are infinitely greater than teaching two different grades—say, the eighth and ninth—in the one locality or the other. Despite this, the teachers for the eighth and ninth grades are prepared in different teacher-training programs, but the teachers for localities as different as Woodlawn and Winnetka are prepared in the same teacher-training program. The consequence of the neglect to differentiate teacher training programs by locality of the school in addition to the age of the pupils is the failure of so many teachers to perform effectively in so many of our schools. They not only cannot cope with the children's values, they also cannot cope with their own commitments when confronted with the children's values.

We all know of cases in which generous, sensitive, and humane teachers have established schools in neighborhoods where, until then, the atmosphere had been one of terror, threats, and outright violence directed against the instructors. Within a year, these desperate youth have, under the influence of loving and understanding teachers, replaced suspicion with trust, hostility with affection, and cynicism and selfishness with openness and helping.

But even these achievements—remarkable as they are—seem to be accompanied by nagging, troublesome questions about values. The teachers in these schools ask themselves whether they have simply imposed their values, possibly at the cost of unfitting their students in their fight for survival; they wonder whether they have merely substituted their goals for those of the students and, to achieve those goals, constructed a curriculum which may be a subtle act of aggression against their students, a curriculum which does not seriously, sympathetically, and objectively weigh what is of merit in the culture of their students.

The present circumstance in the schools seems to be that the insensitive and thoughtless educators do not bother to ask the question, what values? while the sensitive and thoughtful ones, who do ask, are often uncertain—or at best apologetic—about the answer.

The human organism is not born into the world with a ready-made set of culturally adaptive behavior and values. Instead he must acquire a set of values. He must inevitably learn to put the question to himself, "May I yield to the impulse within me, or will I, by doing so, imperil the highest values of my society?" He must learn, on the one hand, to suppress or to modify certain of his drives. He must learn, on the other hand, to acquire certain culturally adaptive attitudes and values. One of the functions of the school has customarily been to help the child do just this.

But the word "learning" or "schooling" is something of a euphemism here, for it is not the same kind of learning as, say, memorizing the multiplication tables, or the capitals of the states, or the pledge of allegiance. The child's learning, or, perhaps better here, his interiorizing of social values is a much more intimate and complex process. Learning, imitation, conscious emulation play a part, to be sure. But a fundamental mechanism by which we interiorize values in schools as elsewhere is identification. As the child struggles to integrate and to maintain a stable self-image from among his fragmentary perceptions of who he is and where he belongs, he is led to view himself as at one with another person. The parents are the child's earliest objects of identifica-

tion. Later he may add older siblings, favorite neighbors, community heroes, certain members of his peer group, and of course school personnel. In making these identifications, the child not only assumes the outward manners and expressive movements of his "significant figures" but also attempts to incorporate their values and attitudes.

It is in this context that the school situation can acquire an eminence second perhaps only to the home—an eminence that it does not have now. To be sure, many aspects of the child's personality and values are already formed by the time he enters school. But the way in which these aspects are developed and modified may depend on the character of his educational institution. The teachers become, or at least can become, significant figures for the child. But where values are concerned, it is not so much what people say the child should do that matters as the kinds of models the significant figures provide that is important. It is not sufficient to teach values, it is also necessary to offer appropriate models for identification.

When we find ourselves in a period of rapidly changing values, such as we are now undergoing, the various significant others in the school and community provide uncertain and inconsistent, if not contradictory, models for the child. The problem of course is not the variety of values, which is not only inevitable but desirable. The problem rather is that the values are latent and unexamined; the ambiguities and differences are often invisible and underground, as it were.

In such a situation, identification, if it occurs at all, provokes conflict and anxiety. For to identify with one model means, knowingly or, what is worse, unknowingly, to reject another model. To accept the parent's values may mean to reject the teacher's values, to accept the teacher's values may mean to reject the religious leader's values, to accept the religious leader's values may mean to reject the political leader's values, to accept the political leader's values may mean to reject everyone else's values. And none of this is to say anything about the ever-threatening discrepancy between the operative secular values and the conceived sacred values.

As a result the child faces, consciously or subconsciously, an extraordinarily difficult problem in adaptation. The solution may be to seek safety in either inflexible incorporation of one model or to renounce all models. In the one case we have over-identification, and consequent restriction and rigidity of purpose; in the other we have under-identification, and consequent confusion and derangement of purpose. Both represent a serious inadequacy in personal development as a consequence of inadequacies in prevailing models and values. And while we are loudly urging our children to acquire appropriate values in school, the children may more properly—albeit mutely —be asking the school the prior question: *"What* values?"

PART VI

Structuring School Programs for Youth

As the American educational system enters the 1980s, it faces increased social and educational demands of the society. While some of these demands have been manifested by the federal government's concern for social problems, other demands have come from a general dissatisfaction of society with the product of the schools. The national mood is one of accountability, yet the concerns for individuality, knowledge acquisition, and "due process" hold high priority for all youth attending school. There is no doubt that this implies better trained teachers at both the preservice and inservice levels.

Although an examination and study of school programs have not generally been considered as an area of educational foundations, the preservice teacher needs to be cognizant of current efforts to improve programs. Too often, school programs tend to be offered within a traditional framework of current and past practice. The major failure of innovative practices during the 1960s and 1970s was that they did not cater to economic and social changes taking place in society. School enrollments have dropped and with that drop has come less

economic support. Yet, there is the demand for increased individual programs for all kinds of learners, from special education to gifted. School programs of the 1980s must search for new ways to meet these demands.

This part of the text is not intended to direct or teach prospective teachers how to structure programs for youth. That task is best accomplished through a formal curriculum course or a direct curriculum development experience. It is the intention of the authors, however, to identify those school program issues that will impinge upon program development during the 1980s.

The "back-to-the-basics" movement has been embedded in the accountability movement of the 1970s. Although this movement has been allied with a national swing to conservatism in the United States, it can also be traced to the social change of the family. Ben Brodinsky presents a case for the school being expected to provide what the home has failed to do. In actuality, the major thrust of this movement has been directed at increased attention to the three R's. Supported by employers who cite lack of performance on the part of their employees, colleges who have had to establish remedial programs for their students, Princeton reports of poor SAT performances, and cost figures which show basic three R programs as more economical, this movement has seriously dampened the creativity and humanistic efforts of the 1960s and 1970s. The most serious charge against this movement has been the threat of producing a new generation of minimal competencies and minimal mediocrity.

Despite the clamor for change in the schools, attention to programs for individualizing instruction remains consistent. Joel Davis presents a model for individualizing instruction based upon behavioral objectives. The model is built around three major components which he identifies as analysis, synthesis, and operation. Since this model is behaviorally organized, it calls for the use of criterion-referenced tests where the pupil does not compete against a group, but works toward some pre-established competency. Considerable emphasis is given to the roles of diagnosis and prescription.

Work-study programs received increased attention during the 1970s and will most certainly continue into the next decade. Although earlier intended for the lower and some middle class students, Peter Scharf and Thomas Wilson present a fresher definition of work experience for the 1980s. This definition embraces a career education concept and suggests experiences in the work-business world for all students. Asserting that this more encompassing definition is consistent with John Dewey's philosophy, all learners are to experience a bond with formal school learning and the real world. It is intended that learners placed in this type of learning environment will develop new moral perspectives about the world of work and the career options available.

Technology continues to challenge the face-to-face human encounter in the instructional process. Wm. Clark Trow discusses the impact of computer-assisted instruction (CAI) in education and recounts the major criticisms that have been directed at the medium. Rather than give open support to the criticisms of CAI, Trow asserts that the most important aspect of school programs is planning. Technology is merely a means for delivering good programming and should not become the program itself. Where it can be used to maximize the achievement of objectives, it should be considered as an educational tool.

One of the increasing pressures for school programs during the 1980s will be early education for young children. Supported with funds and legislation from the federal level, early childhood education has grown by leaps and bounds. Unfortunately, there has not emerged as quickly those numbers of competent teachers needed to staff these programs. Lilian G. Katz, a prominent early childhood educator, presents four propositions which she cites as necessary prerequisites for all early childhood educators. These propositions center on teaching teachers as we wish them to teach, knowing how the young learner understands what is to be learned, the rate at which teachers respond to young learners, and the congruence of the social setting of teacher training with early childhood programs. Katz strongly supports the modeling impact of early childhood educators. If the early childhood educator behaves as a learner with young learners, young learners will become better disposed to lifelong learning.

Public Law 94–142 has mandated mainstreaming for mildly handicapped learners. In addition to the impact of this law on special education teacher training programs, the law has compelled all teacher training programs to be vitally concerned with the handicapped learner. In a timely article, Colleen S. Blankenship and M. Stephen Lilly discuss how preparatory programs for regular educators need to be adjusted for the teaching of children with mild learning and behavior problems. In addition to the new task for preservice teacher training programs, the Bureau of Education for the Handicapped financially supports inservice training programs in order to help implement P.L. 94–142. Blankenship and Lilly caution that crisis training for this social need should not be undertaken without carefully planning and executing programs systematically.

This section is concluded with a presentation by William J. Gephart on curriculum evaluation. Since accountability will remain a theme for the 1980s, Gephart discusses the various roles that government, community groups, parents, and educators play in the curriculum evaluation process. The major thrust of his presentation centers on what information should be gathered, by whom, and who should have access to it.

In summary, this section of the text has been offered as a means of alerting the prospective teacher to some of the major issues involved in structuring programs for youth. Whatever the program of a particular school district, that program still must be offered within the context of an open society. As a social institution of the state, the public school continues to be subject to the dictates of the society it serves. Yet, in spite of this type of societal coexistence, the school functions as a distinct entity and it must establish and put into operation a program which it perceives as being consistent with its role in American society.

Reading 43

Back to the Basics: The Movement and Its Meaning

Ben Brodinsky

There is a movement in American education which irritates some educators, baffles others, and raises high the hackles of still others. Its stirrings put many a school administrator and scholar on the defensive. It is usually led by parents, ministers, businessmen, and politicians. National in scope, it is weak in some parts of the country, strong in others. In some communities the movement makes itself evident through polite editorials or strongly worded resolutions by PTAs; but sometimes it shows teeth and muscle—and the results are bitter controversy, curtailed school funds, defeated bond issues, and, in at least one place (Kanawha County, West Virginia), violence and bloodshed.

In some instances the movement focuses on a single objective—drill in the three Rs; in others, on a wide range of aims—including patriotism and Puritan morality. "It certainly lacks conceptualization," one curriculum expert told me as we were discussing the movement's underpinnings, "and it seems to thrive without organized and iden-

Source: Ben Brodinsky, "Back to the Basics: The Movement and Its Meaning." *Phi Delta Kappan* vol. 58, no. 7 (March 1977), pp. 522–527. Reprinted with permission.

tifiable leadership." When that leadership is assigned to the Council for Basic Education, its officials squirm. "There are those who infer that CBE is interested only in reading, writing, and arithmetic," says George Weber, a CBE spokesman, "but basic education, to us, is by no means limited to the three Rs. We want to promote instruction in the basic intellectual disciplines for all students." The CBE is a great friend of the arts, and this fact alone may disqualify it for leadership among those whose adamant cry is "Back to basics!"

What *do* back-to-basics advocates want? Since they have no spokesman, platform, or declaration of principles, we must fall back on a composite. Here is what, at various times and in different places, back-to-basics advocates have demanded:

1. Emphasis on reading, writing, and arithmetic in the elementary grades. Most of the school day is to be devoted to these skills. Phonics is the method advocated for reading instruction.

2. In the secondary grades, most of the day is to be devoted to English, science, math, and history, taught from

"clean" textbooks, free of notions that violate traditional family and national values.

3. At all levels, the teacher is to take a dominant role, with "no nonsense about pupil-directed activities."

4. Methodology is to include drill, recitation, daily homework, and frequent testing.

5. Report cards are to carry traditional marks (A, B, C, etc.) or numerical values (100, 80, 75, etc.), issued at frequent intervals.

6. Discipline is to be strict, with corporal punishment an accepted method of control. Dress codes should regulate student apparel and hair styles.

7. Promotion from grades and graduation from high school are to be permitted only after mastery of skills and knowledge has been demonstrated through tests. Social promotion and graduation on the basis of time spent in courses are out.

8. Eliminate the frills. The *National Review,* a conservative journal, put it this way: "Clay modeling, weaving, doll construction, flute practice, volleyball, sex education, laments about racism and other weighty matters should take place on private time."

9. Eliminate electives and increase the number of required courses.

10. Ban innovations (a plague on them!). New math, new science, linguistics, instruction by electronic gadgets, emphasis on concepts instead of facts— all must go.

11. Eliminate the school's "social services" —they take time from the basic curriculum. "Social services" may include sex education, driver education, guidance, drug education, and physical education.

12. Put patriotism back in the schools. And love for one's country. And for God.

Such a list, read as a totality, would cheer only the most rabid protagonists of back to basics. It chills even the most conservative of educators. It brings out the defensive mechanisms in most professionals.

"Where is back? What is basic?" said one educator during an interview on the subject. He echoed two questions which usually come up in the back-to-basics controversy. From my notes, made during interviews with educators, here is a composite of the views of those who either reject the movement, join it grudgingly, or accept only a few of its tenets:

"Back to basics? Look, we're moving *forward* to basics. We're broadening our basics to teach children to think, analyze problems, make wise decisions, develop confidence in themselves. As for the three Rs, why return when we've never left them? . . ."

"We're not going to repeal the twentieth century and we can't hold back the twenty-first. We're not going to give up everything we've learned about children, teaching, and learning during the last 50 years. . . ."

"Nothing new, nothing new here. There had been cries for basics long before Socrates started teaching what he thought was basic. In this country, demands for fundamentals crop up every decade. . . ."

"I'm suspicious of easy answers and snappy slogans. Back to basics is a simplistic solution for complex educational problems. If we carry it out as a national policy, it will throw us back 100 years. . . ."

"What was basic yesterday is not basic today and won't be 10 or 15 years from now. What is basic to one group of people is not necessarily basic to another. One person's frills are another person's basics. . . ."

"We do need to get back to the basics, but it is essential that we first identify the basics we want to get back to. . . ." (These words, attributed to W. Ross Winterowd, professor of English, University of Southern

California, have gained a kind of fame in the nationwide controversy.)

Finally, after such litany, there frequently came the troubled question, "What could spawn such demands in this year of 1976 after a hundred years of progress in education?

A search for causes leads the investigator to such factors as nostalgia in the 1970s; the public's whetted appetite for accountability; the nation's periodic swing to conservatism; the high divorce rate and the disintegration of the family, leading to demands that the schools provide the discipline which the home no longer can; the excesses of permissiveness; and a bundle of causes in which Dr. Spock, TV, and creeping socialism are crammed into the same bag.

More realistically, the whys and wherefores of the back-to-basics movement can be found in these developments:

1. Parents, often at the behest of educators, have taken a larger part in school affairs. As they delve deeply into the task, they don't like, or don't understand, what they see. They try to reshape policies and programs in accordance with their views.
2. Blacks and Hispanics claim, rightly or wrongly, that their children are ignored or shortchanged with respect to instruction in basic skills. The ghetto has been a hotbed for the basics.
3. Over the years, teachers have been urged to focus on creativity, on humanistic objectives, on development of independent thinkers. It has not always been clear to the classroom practitioner whether these were to be in addition to, or instead of, mastery of the skills. Confusion of educational goals has opened the way for the single-minded advocates of the three Rs.
4. Employers have long complained that high school graduates do not make pro-

ductive workers because allegedly they cannot read instructions on the job and lack ability in arithmetic. To the slogan, "Johnny can't read, write, or figure," *Forbes*, a journal for industrialists, added, "And Johnny can't work, either."

5. Colleges have also long complained that the typical high school graduate is unprepared for college. Consequently, colleges have had to lower their standards of admission and to resort to remedial courses in English, math, and science. College officials join in the clamor that the schools should do a better job of teaching fundamentals.
6. As proof of their complaints, employers and colleges cite the 12-year drop in national test scores, which allegedly show a decline in student achievement. When the Gallup poll asked a sampling of parents in 1975 what, in their opinion, was the reason for the dropping scores, 22% of the respondents said, "Courses are too easy; there is not enough emphasis on basics."
7. Partisans of the basics often revolt against a) the growth of *super*-professionalism in education and b) the proliferation of the school's services and activities. The charge is that, first, educationists have made the schools a theater for experimentation—more in their self-interest than in the interest of the children. Neither the new report card, new math, nor the new textbooks have improved the educational product, they tell us. "Educators keep on making changes for the sake of change," said a Pasadena critic during a recent battle over basics. The second charge is that the public schools have grown into huge bureaucratic machines, with overstuffed curricula and oversized staffs. The schools have taken on services and programs which belong to the home, the church, and social agencies—from

serving breakfasts to giving the Pill to schoolgirls. And the schools seek to hide their shoddy performance under a mantle of "professionalism" and by using cover-up lingo which makes no sense to the layman.

8. Finally, there is the financial crunch. It is cheaper to finance a bare-bones, stripped-down school program than the runaway programs of the past decade. Such fundamentalist reasoning scores with taxpayers beset by inflation and rising school budgets.

Since back to basics covers a range of convictions and dogmas, some educators embrace some of them, even if they reject most of them. It is not uncommon to find schoolmen and -women enthusiastic for the cause. When Robert L. Brunelle took the post as New Hampshire's state commissioner of education in August, 1976, he did so with a ringing call for a return to basics: "If you can't read, you can't learn anything." Scattered throughout the country are other educators who go along with fundamentalist concepts.

But to the probable surprise of basics hard-liners, educators counter simplistic demands for the three Rs with a new educational trinity: 1) minimal competency, 2) proficiency testing, 3) a performance-based curriculum.

Around these technical terms cluster aims and concepts toward which educators at state and local levels are working at a slow but increasing tempo. These include, in addition to emphasis on the three Rs, the development of life (or survival) skills—that is, competencies needed for personal growth and for successful existence as citizen, consumer, jobholder, taxpayer, and member of a family.

To achieve this double layer of skills, educators are looking to a curriculum based not on textbook facts but on standards of performance. To check whether the performance-based curriculum works, educators are turning to tests of proficiency. No student is to go from grade to grade or to graduate from high school unless he or she can prove, by test results, the mastery of a minimal body of skills and information. This is the direction in which American education is starting to move—but as one educator put it, "It's a slow rush." Many school districts, perhaps a majority, are making no move in this direction. They are waiting for a national pattern to develop or for state laws to push them into action.

Although more than four-fifths of the nation's school boards believe their schools should put greater emphasis on reading, writing, and arithmetic, according to a National School Boards Association survey, few boards have adopted policies to set into motion formal back-to-basics programs. NSBA officials who keep track of policy development in the nation's school districts have found less than half a dozen policy statements reflecting the fundamentalist party line. Why?

"Consider what it would mean to policy development to go all the way back to the basics as some partisans demand," said a school board member. "It would mean restructuring the board's policy statements on philosophy, goals, instructional program, discipline, homework, study halls, retention, promotion, graduation, report cards, counseling, extracurricular activities—to mention but a few topics. No board is about to do that."

What, then, *are* school districts doing?

Without bothering to rethink districtwide goals or philosophy, some school boards are permitting *some* of their schools to get on the basics track.

Seventeen schools in Philadelphia (including a middle and a junior high) have gone basic—meaning that the principals demand neatness and decorum and that teachers stress reading and mathematics and require regular homework. Parents, largely black or Spanish-speaking, wholeheartedly support these moves.

The Philadelphia schools are among about half a hundred in the country which have adopted back-to-basics practices. Others include the highly publicized Myers School, in Charlotte, North Carolina; the Hoover Structured School, Palo Alto; and the John Marshall Fundamental School, Pasadena.

The Council for Basic Education, as a service to the cause, keeps a monthly tally of such schools and is pleased to add new ones to the list. The CBE reports that under consideration for fall, 1977, is the establishment of fundamental or traditional schools in Madison, Wisconsin; Mesa, Phoenix, and Scottsdale, Arizona; Montclair, New Jersey; Montgomery County, Maryland; and San Diego.

As a parallel service to the cause, the Education Commission of the States keeps tally of schools moving toward minimal competency testing. Among another half a hundred schools adopting this practice, it lists Craig, Alaska; Gary, Indiana; Cedar Rapids, Iowa; and Providence, Rhode Island.

Looking up and down the line of actions taken by the nation's schools, we find a range of efforts from cosmetic to regenerating.

Some school districts are applying the Madison Avenue solution, advertising widely that, "Yes, we have been, are, and will be teaching the basics," then putting the spotlight on any project or activity dealing with skills. District 66 in Omaha, Nebraska, spent nearly two years on just such an effort as one way of "talking back to the back-to-basics tiger."

Thus any existing Right-To-Read project (a Title I activity), remedial classes in language arts and math, or the reintroduction of phonics, partly, wholly, voluntarily, or on a compulsory basis, are cited by school administrators as a return to basics.

A community moderately satisfied with its traditional program and not under the spur of state law to do anything about basics can get ahead of the school critics by a modest initiative. In May, 1976, Superintendent James Kennedy of Manchester, Connecticut (population 50,000), decided on a pilot program to test the 650 tenth-graders in the system for proficiency in language arts and mathematics. Passing the test has not been made a graduation requirement, but, if the school board should make it so, students would be given opportunities during their remaining high school years to master the skills the tests require. Even so modest an effort has aroused the interest of many New England school officials to whom proficiency testing is still novel.

A shift of emphasis in regular activities often serves as a response to demands for basics. In Hartford, for example, Superintendent Edythe J. Gaines is restructuring the annual budget so that basics get top priority and a little bit more money than the year before. The budget Gaines presented to her board for 1976–77 was "priority oriented," she said, "toward 1) basic thinking skills in reading and other language arts, including applications . . . and 2) basic thinking skills in mathematics, including applications. . . ." The word "applications" is important, reflecting a determination to test students at regular intervals to see if they have mastered the skills.

When a school system gets a new superintendent—particularly if young, activist, and black—a dramatic shift toward the basics often takes place, not because of pressure groups but because the new educational leader wants it that way. This is what happened in Oakland when Ruth Love, who made Right-To-Read famous, arrived in the Bay city in November, 1975. Love set up "an educational scoreboard" with specific goals and moved toward a tight schedule of completion. The top items (of a dozen or more) on Oakland's scoreboard are given by Superintendent Love as follows:

"Children who complete the third grade will be able to perform basic skills."

"A program of intervention will be provided for children who are or who fall one year behind grade-level expectations in basic skills."

"Graduates will possess the academic resources for higher education, advanced training, or a marketable skill."

Intervention strategies in Oakland may mean simply giving individual attention to students who need extra help, or requiring students to work in math labs, or assigning them to separate classes where they spend a full school day on reading and math. To assure that graduates "possess the academic resources" for post-high school work, Oakland requires students to pass proficiency tests in reading, writing, and computation.

In Salem, Oregon, under state mandate but with much local initiative, Superintendent William M. Kendrick and his staff have made the high school diploma the omega of the basic skills program.

"The traditional high school diploma has been based on two legs," says Kendrick, "attendance (seat time) and course requirements (exposure). . . . Now we've added a third leg—demonstrated performance."

Graduation from Salem secondary schools depends upon completing all of 35 "competency performance indicators" (CPIs). Grouped under "personal development," "social responsibility," and "career development," the CPIs, or skills a student must demonstrate before getting his diploma, include:

Read a 200-word article and answer questions. . . . Read and state three conditions of an apartment rental agreement. . . . Cite advantages and disadvantages of various credit plans. . . . Balance a checkbook. . . . From a list of 30 foods, select and describe a balanced menu for breakfast, lunch, and dinner. . . . Given a simulated paycheck stub, identify from five to seven payroll deductions. . . . Demonstrate knowledge of voting procedures. . . . Identify helpful and harmful effects of garden and household chemicals. . . . Prepare a job application. . . .

Salem's entire curriculum is being revised to focus on the 35 performance objectives. The elementary schools are expected to lay the groundwork for later success in the competencies. "This will bring our schools together with one objective—that of assuring each student a program which will allow him to acquire skills for survival in today's complex society," says Kendrick.

Florida is back-to-basics country—land of the much-touted Accountability Act of 1976. Not all Florida county school systems have been galvanized into action by the act. Polk County, for example, reported late in 1976, "We have started looking into our curriculum to see what changes need to be made to conform to the act." One change likely to be introduced in many Florida school systems is more classroom time for language and math. In Hillsborough County (Tampa) "a minimal time frame" for primary grades calls for more than 13 hours a week of teacher and pupil activity in reading and writing and five hours in math; similar time allotments are called for in the intermediate grades. Such schedules go a long way to satisfy those who claimed that the three Rs are being neglected in Florida.

Duval County (Jacksonville) public schools are pleasing back-to-basics advocates by using a test measuring whether the person has mastered the basic reading skills "necessary for survival in everyday life." Students are asked to demonstrate whether they can follow a recipe, understand a rental agreement, understand an appliance warranty, evaluate a charge account agreement, pick out bargains in a grocery ad, determine long-distance telephone rates, and acquire essential facts from an insurance policy. A number of Florida state legislators are impressed with the Duval test (similar to many others now in use in the country); they want to make passing such tests part of graduation requirements for every public school student in the state.

When a school system bears down heavily on minimal competency, it need not narrow its curriculum. This is illustrated by the Denver public schools, which offer courses and services some might call "frills": the arts; health, psychological, and social services; film making; sex education; and bachelor survival for boys. Yet community pressure for basics have been relatively weak in Denver in recent years. This may be due to a simple action by former Superintendent Kenneth Oberholtzer: Some 15 years ago he persuaded his board of education to require that each high school graduate successfully pass tests in language, arithmetic, reading, and spelling. At that time the move was practically unheralded. For nearly a decade Denver stood almost alone as the major school system with such a requirement. Today the Oberholtzer move is hailed as an act of educational statesmanship and a "touchstone in the movement to assure proficiency in high school graduates."

State agencies have traditionally been weak in leading educational reform, leaving that role to the cities and wealthy suburbs.

This time it's different. State legislatures, state boards of education, and state education departments have leaped forward in the basics/minimal competency movement. The Education Commission of the States in Denver has tried hard to keep up with events. "It's a fast-moving scene," said Chris Pipho of the ECS. "Daily bulletins are needed to keep up with the action."

Some "bulletins" during 1976 reported the death of proposed legislation for mini-

mal competency or performance-based programs in Arizona, Connecticut, Louisiana, Pennsylvania, and Tennessee—although planning for these purposes continued in their state departments of education.

One bulletin, flashed to the educational community after a quickie survey by the National Center for Educational Statistics in August, 1976, reported that 22 states had no plans or activities for statewide standards to be used in developing performance-based curricula or for controlling promotion and graduation from public schools. In the 29 states that were planning (and this could mean anything from discussing a preliminary statement to drafting legislation) or doing something concrete, the chief concerns were: providing multiple opportunities to pass a required test of competence for progression through the grades and introducing new proficiency tests for high school entrance and high school graduation.

These are, of course, also the goals of the scores of bills introduced into state legislatures during the past two to three years. In a first phase, much of the legislation dealt with proficiency tests for high school entrance and graduation. Under pressure of school critics, bills in state capitols became broader in scope, as illustrated by Florida's catch-all Educational Accountability Act of 1976 and New Jersey's "Thorough and Efficient" Public School Education Act of 1975.

Although the Florida act is ostensibly concerned with accountability, the back-to-basics advocates are mostly interested in the provisions that mandate the testing of basic skills in grades 3, 5, 8, and 11. Students who do not meet minimum standards, by performance, must be given extra help or placed in remedial programs. The state will provide technical assistance (a term not clearly defined) to school districts where pupil deficiencies are identified.

By July 1, 1977, Florida school districts will move pupils forward, grade by grade, on the basis of performance rather than on social promotion. By 1978–79, Florida districts will have to establish performance levels for high school graduation, in addition to the normal course requirements. Students unable to meet such standards must get "remediation" from their schools. Boards of education are authorized to award differentiated diplomas to correspond to the varying achievement levels of graduates.

The state of New Jersey mandates "thorough and efficient education"—a phrase whose vagueness still puzzles school boards. The law calls for each school system to develop a curriculum which contains "all elements of basic skills necessary to function in a democracy" and sets up checkpoints in the school program to make certain that students receive the kind of instruction they require.

Under a State Board of Education schedule, New Jersey's State Department of Education administered tests in October, 1976, to grades 4, 7, and 10. The results went back to school districts in January. Students found in the low 20% bracket were given immediate attention. The statewide plan, for any student scoring below the 65% mastery level, goes into effect next September. Before this date, school districts must file in Trenton their basic skills improvement plans. What these are to cover and how they are to be put to work will worry New Jersey educators throughout the long summer of 1977. But as far as New Jersey State Education Commissioner Fred G. Burke is concerned, "Ours is the most comprehensive basic skills effort in the nation, because it will assure a learning program for every student with basic skills needs."

Equally sanguine about *their* plans are state officials in other parts of the country.

In Oregon, where taxpayers have condemned "worthless" high school diplomas for nearly a decade, school systems are now deep in programs raising and tightening high school graduation requirements. As first mandated by Oregon's State Department of Education in 1972, graduation depends upon a student's ability to master competencies in three areas—personal development, social responsibility, and career development (in addition, of course, to the usual credits for courses and attendance). Districts were given authority to develop their own performance indicators.

A 1976 revision of the state plan now allows districts to develop indicators for either the three previously mandated areas or to develop replacements for them. How the student is to demonstrate his competence to function as a learner, a citizen, consumer, and family member is up to the local board. Georgia officials said late in 1976 that they may adopt the Oregon plan.

California, where interest in basics is endemic, passed legislation in 1976 requiring student testing at least once during the seventh through ninth grades and twice between grades 10 and 11. For those failing to demonstrate minimal proficiency, the law provides teacher/parent conferences and remedial classes. No student will receive a high school diploma after June, 1980, unless he passes the required proficiency tests.

New legislation in the state of Washington requires school districts to develop learning objectives in behavioral terms. State funds may be withheld from the local districts for noncompliance. Meanwhile, a standardized test was given in 1976 to all fourth-grade students in reading, math, and language arts. Results are now used by schools to compare children's achievement levels with those of other pupils in the district, the state, and the nation. Plans for remedial action remain to be developed.

Virginia's Standards of Quality Act of 1976 requires the State Board of Education to set up minimum statewide educational objectives and a statewide test in reading, language arts, and math—all this not later than September, 1978. The high school diploma is also a point of concern in this state, because Greensville County, Virginia, is the home of Superintendent Sam Owen, who has become a hero among back-to-basics advocates because he "got tired of handing out rubber diplomas." Greensville County graduation requirements, although no different from those being adopted in other districts, have been publicized as models.

And so state actions continued throughout 1976 and into 1977. The plans that came into being were remarkably alike in purpose and in content. It was test and teach, teach and test—to assure competence in basic skills and the mastery of a minimal body of information thought necessary for graduation.

Among many state plans, only the time schedule was different. Missouri mandated its students to take tests starting July 1, 1977; Alabama, Massachusetts, and Vermont were working toward a fall, 1977, deadline for the start of testing; New York State decided to require three new tests for graduation, effective in June, 1980. Educators predicted that by 1984 (Orwell, can you hear?) nearly all the states will have incorporated minimal competency testing into promotion and graduation requirements. And then, what then?

What *will* be the outcome of the back-to-basics movement? "There is potential for some good and much harm," said one educator. Among possible beneficial effects is, first, the chance that during the next decade the public schools will produce a cadre of better readers and youths better skilled in computation—and possibly even in writing. Second is the possibility of restoring the authority of the teacher in the classroom, where it has been eroded by policies of pupil planning and pupil direction of school activities. Next: "The barnacles of multitudinous goals and activities may be stripped from school systems where they have fouled the curriculum," said a Maine superintendent, "and that would be to the good." Finally, even the most conservative of laymen may begin to value individualized instruction, since many of the remedial plans call for teaching on a one-to-one basis.

These possible advantages will be more than outweighed, according to concerned educators, by the growth of state power at the expense of the local school board. Many educators cite interference in local school affairs and eventual total control by the state as strong possibilities. "We're moving toward state superboards of schools," one superintendent said.

Testing, testing, testing will spread to an extent hitherto undreamed of. School districts are feverishly looking for proficiency tests and are adopting them as soon as they can find them. The test-making industry is making plans to expand. "What worries me most," said a curriculum director, "is that we shall actually be asking teachers to teach to the test—a practice already condoned."

But the overriding worry of many educators to whom I spoke was the possibility that the public schools "are moving toward producing a generation of minimal mediocrity." By stressing mechanical skills of communication and computation, by denigrating the arts and creativity, by dehumanizing the learning process and placing it under rote and autocracy, American education, it is charged, will lose the great generating power which has kept the nation free, inventive, and productive.

Reading 44

Design and Implementation of an Individualized Instruction Program

Joel J. Davis

This article describes a procedure for determining an optimal individualized instructional program. The model (see Figure 1) incorporates certain critical features lacking in many contemporary schemes: it proceeds in a systematic manner; it addresses the interaction of cognitive processes and instructional task demands; it provides for continuous evaluation and modification; and it deals with measurable behaviors.

The model is divided into three components (adapted from Tuckman and Edwards, 1973). The first component, analysis, contains the following three activities: (1) the determination of post-instructional behaviors; (2) the translation of these behaviors into behavioral objectives; and (3) a specification of a sequence for the presentation of the objectives. Following analysis is synthesis, which involves: (1) determination of learner competencies and processes; (2) description of materials; and (3) establishing the instructional setting. The outcomes of each of these steps are integrated into an

Source: Joel J. Davis, "Design and Implementation of an Individualized Instruction Program." *Educational Technology* vol. XVII, no. 2 (December 1977), pp. 36–41.

instructional program. This program, along with evaluation and modification, comprises the final component of the model, operation.

The remainder of this article details each of these activities.

I. ANALYSIS

1. Specification of Post-Instructional Behaviors

The educational process consists of providing a series of environments which permit a student to acquire new behaviors or modify existing behaviors. Within this context learning is defined as the exhibition of new behaviors which are demonstrated at a satisfactory level of competence and regularity under appropriate circumstances. When learning is viewed in this manner it becomes apparent that the initial step in the implementation of any instructional program must be a determination of the terminal behaviors a student will display if instruction has been successful.

Terminal behaviors can be approached on

two levels. The first, more abstract level, includes the long-term goals of education. Attainment of these behaviors is often the product of many years of schooling. Examples of behaviors at this level are of the form:

1. The student displays the fundamental skills of reading and writing.
2. The student displays a knowledge of civics.
3. The student displays an understanding of astronomical concepts.

Global behaviors are too broad to be successfully translated into short-term instructional programs. As a result, these behaviors must be rewritten as a series of specific behaviors which indicate the terminal performance capabilities of students completing a single instructional unit. For example, the first global behavior could be divided into specific behaviors such as:

1. The student can name and recognize letters of the alphabet.
2. The student can write a simple letter or paragraph.
3. The student can understand and answer inferential questions.

It is on this level that description of terminal behaviors should be written. The increase in specificity over global behaviors allows a more finite determination of appropriate instructional activities.

Once the terminal behaviors have been determined, it becomes necessary to ascertain the cognitive level at which these behaviors occur. This is necessary if the instructional sequence is to contain all the appropriate prerequisite skills. The most applicable description of the levels of cognitive functioning can be found in the *Taxonomy of Educational Objectives* (Bloom, 1956).

In sum, the first step of the model requires the determination of post-instruc-

tional behaviors and the cognitive level at which those behaviors occur. The more clearly defined the terminal behaviors, the more effectively the instructional materials can be selected and sequenced.

2. Translation of Terminal Behaviors into Behavioral Objectives

A behavioral objective is a statement which specifies a testable condition. An objective, if it is to be useful, must describe a behavior in a manner such that all who read the description can agree whether or not a student's actions satisfy pre-defined criteria. The type of statement required, therefore, must contain the following components: a statement of performance; a statement of the conditions under which the performance is to occur; and a statement against which the performance is to be evaluated (Mager, 1962).

The model requires that the behaviors specified as the outcomes of a successful instructional program be analyzed as to their component skills, with each skill being rewritten as a behavioral objective. The translation of terminal behaviors into behavioral objectives allows one to readily determine the behaviors relevant to the instructional task. Additionally, this procedure clarifies the type of learning to be undertaken and the required conditions of learning and subsequent evaluation.

3. Sequencing of Behavioral Objectives

Structural analysis (Tuckman, 1968) is a technique for specifying the sequential relationships among a set of behavioral objectives. This approach makes possible the specification of a sequence of instructional objectives, that, when arranged in a pre-specified logical order, maximizes move-

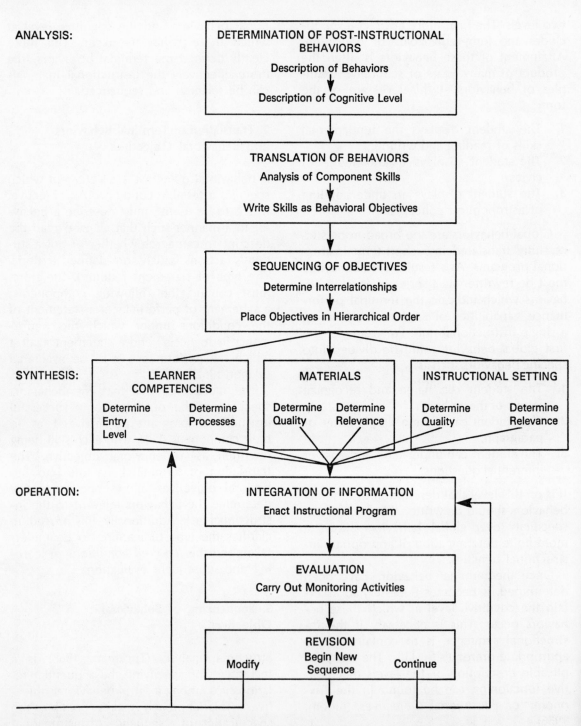

Figure 1. A model for an optimal individualized instructional program

ment from entry into the sequence to the attainment of the terminal behavior.

Structural analysis is based upon two major premises. First, that learning is a sequential process where the attainment of complex behaviors is dependent upon the acquisition of the prerequisite lower order skills. Second, that the establishment of an appropriate sequence is one of the essential conditions underlying learning (Bloom et al., 1971; Gagne, 1970).

The importance of determining the sequence of instructional elements lies in the fact that it enables one to avoid omitting essential steps in the presentation of knowledge. Since each subordinate skill has been identified as such because it is hypothesized to contribute to the learning of a related higher-order skill, it follows that higher-order behaviors will be more readily acquired if the subordinate skills have been learned *and* are available for recall. The sequence, therefore, identifies the ordered relationships of a set of skills where substantial amounts of positive transfer are expected from lower-order skills to connected ones of a higher position.

This phase of the model requires a determination of the interrelationships of the previously defined objectives. A procedure for determining the interrelationships of objectives is shown in Figure 2.

II. SYNTHESIS

1. Learner Competencies

The majority of students in any classroom have the potential to acquire the terminal behaviors desired as end-products of instruction. It is therefore the responsibility of the instructional planner to determine a procedure by which any student will be able to acquire these behaviors.

The primary cause of failure for many students is placement at a level in the instructional sequence for which they have not mastered the prerequisite skills. Effective instructional programs are predicated upon providing instruction specific to the needs of each student. If this is done, a majority of students may be expected to achieve mastery of the subject.

This phase of the model requires that a determination be made of each student's competencies, in order that each may be placed at the appropriate level in the instructional sequence. Tests must be administered before the onset of instruction in order to acquire information on the skills which a student already possesses.

The type of tests required by this system are criterion-referenced tests. "A criterion-referenced test is one that is deliberately constructed to yield measurements that are directly interpretable in terms of specified performance standards" (Glaser and Nitko, 1971, p. 653). In order to satisfy this definition, criterion-referenced tests must have the following characteristics (Nitko, 1974):

1. The classes of behaviors that define different achievement levels are specified as clearly as possible before the test is constructed.

2. Each behavior class is defined by a set of test tasks in which the behaviors can be displayed in terms of all their important nuances.

3. Given that the classes of behavior have been specified and that the test situations have been defined, a representative sampling plan is designed and used to select the test tasks that will appear on any form of the test.

4. The obtained score must be capable of expressing objectively and meaningfully the individuals' performance characteristics in the class of behavior tested.

Criterion-referenced tests are therefore constructed to supply information about a stu-

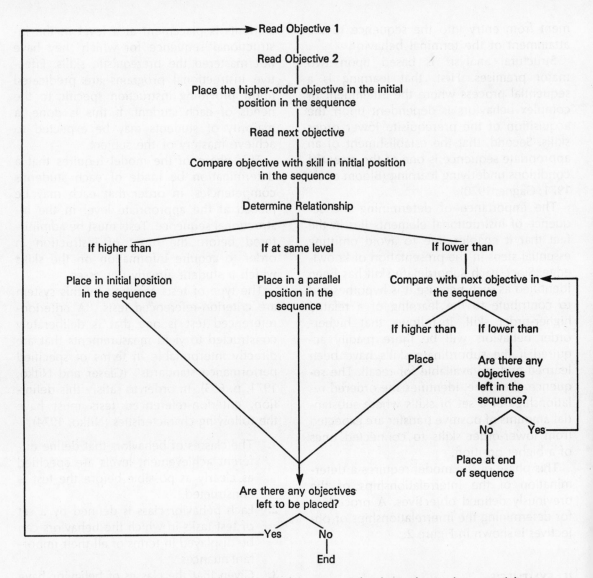

Figure 2. A program for determining the sequential relationships of a set of behavioral objectives

dent's performance relative to a specified domain of tasks.

Once the test items have been generated, it becomes necessary to develop a test procedure that will rapidly locate a pupil's performance level at the appropriate position in the instructional sequence. A procedure designed to accomplish this task has been presented by Ferguson (1970).

Ferguson's program attempts to place a student at an objective level such that if he were tested on all the objectives below that location he would demonstrate mastery, and if he were tested on all the objectives above that location he would demonstrate a lack of mastery. It was found that the most effective procedure was to begin testing objectives in the middle of the instructional hierarchy, and then, depending upon the student's responses, test either higher or lower objectives.

The placement of a student at the proper objective in an instructional sequence is necessary if instruction is to be appropriate to the student's competencies. However, if instruction is to be maximally useful and relevant, it is also necessary to determine the underlying processes responsible for incorrect responses on the criterion-referenced tests. Analyses must be performed to ascertain the causes of errors.

An error analysis entails a review of all incorrect items on a test in order to discover patterns of errors. The procedure involves making a determination of the processes used by the student to move from the stimulus (the test question) to the response (the answer to the test question). Error analysis allows instruction to be individualized to the needs of different students operating at the same objective level. See Ashlock (1976) and Harris and Sipay (1975) for discussions of the procedures of error analysis.

2. Materials

Instructional materials are most effective in guiding learning if they are of high quality and the characteristics of the materials are related to the needs of the learner. As a result, it is necessary for the instructional planner to perform an analysis of the strengths and weaknesses of all materials employed. This section describes a framework for performing this analysis.

Tyler and Klein (1974) have presented a series of criteria by which to determine the quality of any instructional material. The most important criteria are:

1. Objectives should be specified operationally.

2. Objectives should be consistent with each other.
3. Learning activities should be directly related to the behavior and content of the specified objectives.
4. Learning activities must be arranged so that the behavior of the student is developed.
5. The technical manual must describe in detail the types of behaviors which the teacher is to utilize.
6. Documentation must be provided to substantiate claims of effectiveness.

Once a set of materials has been selected, it is necessary to determine the point in the instructional sequence at which they are most relevant, applicable and appropriate. The instructional material used must provide activities maximally related to the objective and desired terminal behavior.

3. Instructional Setting or Mode

Individual students may need very different types of instruction in order to attain a set of desired terminal behaviors. That is, the same content and objectives can be learned by different students as the results of very different types of instruction. There is evidence, for example, that some students learn quite well through independent study while others may need highly structured instructional situations (Congreve, 1965). Further, it appears reasonable to expect that some students will need more concrete illustrations and explanations than will others; some will need more examples to get an idea than others; some will need more manipulatives than others; some will need more approval and reinforcement than others; and some may need to have several repetitions of an explanation while others may be able to grasp it on the first presentation (Bloom et al., 1971).

This phase of the model requires a determination of the instructional needs of each student. This is in agreement with Carroll (1963), who defines the quality of instruction in terms of the degree to which the presentation and explanation of the elements of the task to be learned approach the optimum for any given learner. The diagnosis of a student's instructional needs is a complex process, a discussion of which is beyond this article. The reader is directed to Bloom et al. (1971), Glaser and Nitko (1971), and Harris and Sipay (1975) for detailed discussions in this area.

III. OPERATION

1. Instruction

The implementation of an effective instructional program entails interrelating the decisions reached in the synthesis phase of the model. The information on learner competencies and processes, materials and instructional options must be correlated in order to provide an instructional condition appropriate to each specific learner. When correlated correctly, each student will receive an instructional program designed to meet his or her specific needs and characteristics.

2. Monitoring and Evaluation

The model requires that student performance be monitored and assessed at established decision points. Achievement measures similar to those used for initial placement must be obtained. This collected information indicates whether a learning criterion has been achieved; and, if not, in what respect the performance is deficient. If appropriately done, teaching, instruction and testing should all merge into one another.

Testing information is used by the student and teacher to make decisions about future instructional needs. The evaluation can determine one of three courses of action, depending upon the student's performance. First, it can indicate that the objective has been mastered and that the student is ready

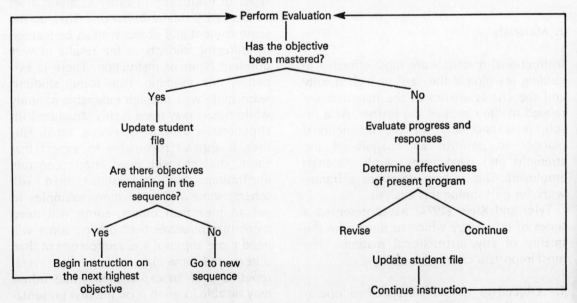

Figure 3. Monitoring and evaluation in the instructional program

to proceed to the next level. Second, it can indicate that learning is proceeding but is incomplete and that additional time and instructional reinforcement are needed. Finally, it may indicate that no learning has taken place, and that a reanalysis of student placement, materials and instructional mode is needed. This decision-making procedure is illustrated in Figure 3.

SUMMARY

The model presented is an attempt to set forth a set of general requirements governing the creation of an effective instructional program. However, the success of any program is limited by certain constraints. These include: the extent to which the proposed learning hierarchies are psychologically real; the extent to which individual differences in ability and learning characteristics are accurately diagnosed; and the extent to which alternative instructional techniques and educational experiences are developed which are adaptive to the individual characteristics of each learner. The success of any program is directly related to the extent to which these criteria are satisfied.

REFERENCES

Ashlock, J. *Error Patterns in Computation (Second Edition)*. Columbus, Ohio: Merrill, 1976.

Baker, P. and R. Schutz. *Instructional Product Development*. New York: Van Nostrand, 1971.

Bloom, B. (Ed.) *Taxonomy of Educational Objectives: The Classification of Educational Goals. Handbook 1: Cognitive Domain*. New York: David McKay, 1956.

Bloom, B. et al. *Handbook on Formative and Summative Evaluation of Student Learning*. New York: McGraw-Hill, 1971.

Carroll, J. A Model of School Learning. *Teachers College Record*, 1963, *64*, 723–733.

Congreve, W. Independent Learning. *North Central Association Quarterly*, 1965, *40*, 222–228.

Davis, F. and J. Diamond. The Preparation of Criterion-Referenced Tests. In C. Harris, M. Alkin and W. J. Popham (Eds.), *Problems in Criterion-Referenced Measurement*. Los Angeles: Center for the Study of Evaluation, 1974.

Ferguson, R. A Model for Computer-Assisted Criterion-Referenced Measurement. *Education*, 1970, *81*, 25–31.

Gagne, R. *The Conditions of Learning*. New York: Holt, Rinehart and Winston, 1970.

Glaser, R. and A. Nitko. Measurement in Learning and Instruction: In R. L. Thorndike (Ed.), *Educational Measurement (Second Edition)*. Washington, D.C.: American Council on Education, 1971.

Harris, A. and F. Sipay, *How to Increase Reading Ability (Sixth Edition)*. New York: David McKay, 1975.

Mager, R. *Preparing Instructional Objectives*. Palo Alto: Fearon, 1962.

Nitko, A. Problems in the Development of Criterion-Referenced Tests: The IPI Pittsburgh Experience: In C. Harris, M. Alkin and W. J. Popham (Eds.), *Problems in Criterion-Referenced Measurement*. Los Angeles: Center for the Study of Evaluation, 1974.

Tuckman, B. *Structural Analysis as an Aid to Curriculum Development*. New Brunswick, New Jersey: Rutgers University, 1968.

Tuckman, B. and K. Edwards. A Systems Model for Instructional Design and Management: In *Introduction to the Systems Approach*. Englewood Cliffs, New Jersey: Educational Technology Publications, 1973.

Tyler, L. and M. Klein. Evaluation Within the Context of Curriculum Development and Instructional Materials: In G. Borich (Ed.), *Evaluating Educational Programs and Products*. Englewood Cliffs, New Jersey: Educational Technology Publications, 1974.

Reading 45

Work Experience: A Redefinition

Peter Scharf and Thomas Wilson

Work Experience/Study Programs have been historically associated with the ritual of "training" lower class students in public high schools to perform the more menial tasks of an industrial society. The assumptions underlying such programs included such notions as:

- lower class students were destined for labor-oriented careers and would not profit from academic instruction;
- middle class (typically academically able) students had no time available from their academic studies to explore work experiences;
- instruction related to work study students had to be presented in a rote fashion. Work study students could not profit from intellectual stimulation and that instruction should be geared to the: a) "practical" techniques of work, and b) the inculcation of the accepted work ideology (Protestant ethic).

This paper offers that such notions are misleading in two respects. First, they are clearly inconsistent with a democratic creed. Certain students end up being "sorted" into a social caste of under-educated "laborers." Second, "rote" learning techniques fail to provide the kinds of experiences likely to facilitate necessary developmental growth. We offer instead that work experience programs:

- should rework the class ideology and be redefined in terms of experiences that might be applicable to students other than the traditional marginal students (academic and economic) who have until now constituted the major target population of work experience programs;
- should be reconceptualized in terms of psychological assumptions underlying work experience instruction and instead of operant habitual training, an interactional-cognitive developmental model be utilized to provide for students' cognitive/moral growth through meaningful work experiences.

Our approach, then, is to examine these two reconceptualized notions in some detail and then offer a concrete, functioning program designed to implement the two redefinitions.

Source: Peter Scharf and Thomas Wilson, "Work Experience: A Redefinition." *Theory Into Practice,* vol. 15, no. 3 (June 1976), pp. 205–213.

Reworking the Class Ideology of Work Experience Programs

Perhaps the most critical flaw of traditional work experience programs is that they have existed mainly for economically deprived youth rather than for all students. The problems with this assumption are manifestly obvious for they lead to channeling "economically" deprived youth into lower status, lower security, lower paid vocations and already economically advantaged youth into prestigious professional careers. This is damaging in several respects. Capable working class youth tend to overlook careers which might require college training. As well, middle class youth of average ability ignore skilled-labor careers which might be more economically viable than are current marginal professional careers (e.g., a career as a tool die maker vs. a career as a high school teacher). In addition to stratifying the interests of youth prematurely and often inappropriately, the overall social consequence of such programs is to create a fixed under-educated working class with anachronistic skills and a white-collar, social advantaged elite with overpopulation and insecurity.

The implication of this broad critique implies that *all* students should be given access to experiences in the work-business world. Coleman (1974) argues that such experiences are more meaningful to students than are traditional programs and, as well, prepare students for available work roles (which purely academic programs clearly do not). While it is true that many jobs require specific intellectual and/or technological skills that only advanced academic training (probably college level) can provide, early emersion in the work world gives students a chance to identify which skills are needed for particular work roles. Then the student can realistically define a personal strategy for acquiring needed skills. This type of ex-perience makes as much sense for white-collar (computer operator), semi-professional (teacher), or professional (lawyer) roles as it does for blue-collar jobs (auto-mechanic).

This strategy implies that all students might become more aware of the vocational options available in American society through interaction with a broad range of work settings. For example, a student who now would be blithely channeled into "going to college" would, in the new context, become aware of alternative valid, meaningful non-college vocations. Similarly, a student heading towards a trade-oriented career would become aware of college as a viable option through interaction with more academically-oriented students as well as with college educated professionals. This approach to work experience, we believe, is ultimately more consistent with the democratic creed than is the class-defined work experience program. Students are offered a range of options to choose from with a reasonable reality context for each choice. With suitable counseling on the requirements for each career option, the student is given a reasonable opportunity to match his values, needs, and abilities with a tentative career choice.

Beyond the skill level, such work experiences for *all* youth would have monumental effect in terms of social growth. In presenting a case for an alternative of school and work, Coleman (1974:158) states it well:

The proposal here, however, is for school work alternation for college preparatory programs as well as vocational programs. The aim of such programs should not be primarily to "learn a skill," but to gain experience in responsible interdependent activity—and the importance of such experience is not limited to youth with manual labor destinations.

This ideology is not totally new in American educational thought. Dewey's *Schools for Tomorrow* (1906) documented cases of well defined and executed educational experiments which linked in a meaningful way the work of the school and the world of work such as the Gary School experiment. Founded in the new town of Gary, the school was transformed into a micro-work environment. Custodial, food, and maintenance functions were shared by the students, but in such a way that students had to resolve policy issues as well as perform the concrete work involved. Nutrition, resource allocation, systematic accounting and futuristic planning were all the tasks of student managers. Many "academic" lessons were derived from conflicts from the task of physically and economically maintaining the school.

A more modern example is Richmond's *The Micro-Society School* (1974). Richmond advocates a micro-economy school which parallels the economic world at large. Students create banks, tutoring services, protection services, restaurants, employ others and even stage revolutions. In both the Micro-Economy School and the Gary interventions, there is the idea that exposure to work be neither demeaning or simply manual application. Such examples of successfully uniting work experience with sound academic content (as well as opening experience in the work world to all students) provide models with which to help us design contemporary programs. Coleman (1974) suggests similarly that youth are overschooled and underexperienced. Rather than channeling students into dead-end vocational careers, properly reflective work experiences can provide students with both practical expertise as well as a reality context for classroom intellectual experiences. Even in conventional terms, contact with real life institutions give traditional subjects greater meaning. For example, a youth who has worked in a factory might find a book like Sinclair's *The Jungle* a powerful educa-

tional experience. In contrast, for a youth who has no contact with institutions outside the school, peer group and family, the same book might not have value. So too, jobs involving arithmetical operations might stimulate an interest in math as might a job involving interpersonal contact (sales, counseling, etc.), stimulate an interest in psychology or sociology. The overall thrust of all these innovations is providing experience in the work world which makes sense only if it is common for all students, and not merely a means for segregating the youth community into a pre-working class and pre-professional elite.

Reconceptualizing the Psychological Assumptions Underlying Work Instruction

Most traditional approaches to work study assume a behaviorist orientation towards student learning: Specifically, students are taught to perform specific job skills and develop work-oriented attitudes.

In terms of job requirements, students are taught skills tied to specific technologies. The skills are taught usually in a rote manner (e.g., "press green button to lift drive shaft, then lower blue lever. . . ."). Often advanced behavioral techniques, e.g. computer guided instruction, or programmed learning are used, but still within this general behavioristic pattern of learning.

Work values are taught in a similar fashion. Teachers repeat cliches about "cleanliness in the job interview," "the importance of being on time" or "the value of diligence." Often, successful lower-class models (either black or poor) who "made it" are eulogized. In some programs there have been efforts through token economics or similar strategies to reward particular work behaviors and attitudes. Students who show particular Protestant ethic virtues (punctuality, diligence or cleanliness) are rewarded through use of tokens or other rewards. Such a learning strategy raises three critical issues.

1. There are some powerful indications that the skills approach even where effective is not functional due to a rapidly changing technology. Often students trained to operate with particular technologies find that the technology has shifted even before they graduate from the skills program. The high unemployment rate among "successful" job corps graduates is an indication of this problem. Training students in concrete skills may not make much sense for a time of rapid technological change.
2. The training of attitudes is apparently ineffective. Few of the studies reviewed indicate any long term success with any of the models attempted. Such efforts as those of Hartshorne and May (1930) found that the attitudes reinforced two years before were not retained and even where they were retained over a short period of time, they did not correlate with any known measure of behavior. Rokeach (1973) reports essentially the same: attitude change cannot theoretically be expected to lead to behavioral change. Particular value contents are short lived and cannot be trained through rote, associationist training (Kohlberg, 1969).
3. Finally, there is a serious ethical issue raised in the training of work attitudes. The attitudes chosen characteristically represent those of the teachers and school administrators rather than those of the students. To students, they often appear as impositions from without, reminding us of the efforts to teach "proper tooth brush use" to immigrant children at the turn of the century. Most generally, the work attitude approach involves efforts to impose one cultural "bag of virtues" on a particular group of children. Since these values are arbitrary and not chosen by the students, it represents a highly questionable educational act by the school.

Both the training in skills and proper definitions of moral responsibility can be viewed from a quite different psychological perspective. This is from the cognitive developmental orientation—that tradition beginning with John Dewey (1916) and George Herbert Mead (1934) and including Piaget (1960), and Kohlberg (1969). Where the behaviorist position is that specific skills and attitudes should be taught by reward, modeling and punishment, the cognitive-developmental school offers that only by students interacting with a broad range of technical and moral problems can they develop the necessary capacities to solve a variety of complex tasks in more adequate, comprehensive ways. Thus, skills should not be taught as isolated capacities by rote. Rather the focus should be on allowing the student to develop the necessary mental structures to solve a range of practical problems. Similarly, it is futile to teach specific positive work attitudes such as hard work or punctuality. Rather, the school should focus on the student's capacity to solve adequately a range of moral problems and dilemmas.

The developmental approach has been well documented in terms of formal research. Piaget (1966) has documented an invariant sequence of logical stages which have been found to describe a universal order of learning mental operations. Children move through the stages sequentially and each higher stage represents a more adequate mode of thinking about physical and social problems.

The Stages:

1. (Birth–2 years) *Sensori Motor:* Learning here is based primarily on immediate experience through the five senses. The child has perceptions and movements as his only tools for learning. Lacking language, the child has neither the ability to represent nor symbolize thinking, and thus no way to categorize experiences. One of the first sensori-motor abilities to develop is that of visual pursuit—the ability to perceive and hold a visual object with the eyes. Later, the capacity of object permanence—the ability to understand that an object can still exist even though it cannot be seen—develops. Lacking vision during this period prevents the growth of mental structures.

2. (2–7 years) *Pre-Operational or Intuitive Mode:* During this period, the child is no longer bound to the immediate sensory environment, and it builds upon abilities such as object permanence from the sensor-motor stage. The ability to store mental images, symbols (words and language as a structure for words) increases dramatically. The mode of learning is a freely-experimenting intuitive approach—one that is generally unconcerned with reality. Communication occurs in collective monologues in which children talk to themselves more than to each other. Use of language during this period, then, is both ego-centric and spontaneous. Though use of language is the major learning focus at this age, many other environmental discoveries are made—each using the free-wheeling, intuitive approach.

3. (7–11 years) *Concrete Operations:* This period sees the dramatic shift in learning strategy from intuition to concrete thought. Reality-bound thinking takes over, and the child must test out problems in order to understand them. The difference between dreams and facts can be clearly distinguished, but that between a hypothesis and a fact cannot. The child becomes overly logical and concrete so that once his or her mind is made up, new facts will not change it. Facts and order become absolutes.

4. (11–16 years) *Formal Operations:* At this stage, the child enters adolescence and the potential for developing full formal patterns of thinking emerges. The adolescent is capable of attaining logical-rational or abstract strategies. Symbolic meanings, metaphors and similies can be understood. Implications and generalizations can be made.

In terms of the problems of work study programs, the focus has to be on the transition between concrete and formal operations. Junior high school and high school students will be divided between concrete operational and formal operational youth. The ways that skills are learned according to this model directly conflicts with the associationist model described earlier. Where the associationist-conditioning model focused on the acquisition of particular skills, this model offers that the overall capacity of the student to think through practical problems is critical. For example, a concrete operational student, when faced with a problem at work—for example fixing a radio—will focus on the simple rules for fixing the machine, e.g.,

1. Disconnect wire.
2. Look for blown-out tube.
3. Find new tube.
4. Reinsert in #3 socket.

A formal operative student will begin to discover the dynamics and logical principles governing the functioning of the radio. Why do tubes blow out? What are better ways to build a radio? Also, when there is doubt about the causes of malfunction, the formally operational student is able to reason through which of a number of possible causes is the real cause for the malfunction.

This formally operational capacity clearly has an advantage over the concrete operational approach. When technologies shift, the formally operative student is able to adapt to them. The student can move from being a radio repairer to possibly an engineer or designer as he or she is able to conceive of the radio as an abstract electronic system and think of ways to redesign it to give it new capacities. The concrete operational worker is more or less stuck in the role of a rote technician.

Key to Piaget's approach is the notion of *assimilation* and *accommodation*. Piaget defines assimilation as the taking in of impressions into one's own available cognitive structures. Accommodation is defined as the testing of such structures against the world. In terms of creating a meaningful and effective work experience for students, it is assumed that there be a balance between assimilation and accommodation. Work cannot be simply a totally theoretical (assimilatory) experience—(e.g., reading about work environments), nor can it be pure accommodation (simply working without any external input). Rather, work experience should involve both opportunities for the student to explore practically the world of work, as well as a means to stimulate the intellect of the adolescent.

Another compatible way of thinking about the same problem is to use Dewey's Reflection-Experience paradigm. Dewey argued that educational experience could be thought of as a continuum, the optimum effectiveness being at the midpoint between purely experiential and purely reflective educational experiences (Dewey, 1916). The diagram below represents Dewey's Model:

Pure Experience		Pure Reflection
(Working at McDonald's)	Optimum Effectiveness	(Reading about work)

Experiences that are purely reflection are meaningless, as are experiences which are purely experiential. The goal is to give students valid, existentially powerful work experiences and at the same time provide opportunity 1) in which they can actively reflect about those experiences, and 2) in such a way that does not violate the power and immediacy of those experiences. Such reflective and experiential educational moments should stimulate the student towards more mature thinking about both technical and social worlds.

The experience reflection model is also most appropriate for moral education. Kohlberg (1969) describes a realm of social development and attempts to define the conditions which might stimulate development in the aspect of moral thought. The theory (guided by eighteen years of observations by Kohlberg and his colleagues) argues that moral thinking develops sequentially through six stages of moral thinking. In a variety of cultural contexts, individuals have been found to move through the stages in the same order though the speed of development and final stage achieved varies.

These studies likewise indicate certain conditions associated with rapid and complete moral development. One condition is that individuals are provided opportunities for resolving moral conflict. A second postulate offers that moral change is associated with active role-taking and participation in the maintenance functions of "secondary institutions." Finally it has been found that moral change occurs where individuals accept an institution's moral climate as being legitimate and just as understood at the person's stage of moral maturity.

The implication of Kohlberg's theory is that simply teaching students "good work attitudes" is totally inadequate. As we indicated earlier, while it is possible to condition attitudes for a short period of time, we cannot expect that these attitudes will endure, nor will they correlate with behavior. Additionally, particular attitudes are culture-bound and will appear imposed by students and will be rejected. The alternative we pose is a reflective work study experience setting wherein the students face real-life moral and social conflicts and attempt to resolve them in a group context with a general goal of developing a more mature moral and social consciousness on the part of the student. Instead of seeing work study as a means for facilitating "good work habits," it becomes a means of presenting new opportunities for interaction and conflict to stimulate moral development.

A Concrete Program to Create a New Work Experience Program at Newport Harbor High School, Newport Beach, California

Given our argument that an effective work study program requires a new sociological and psychological base, we are in the process of creating a work study program which would:

1. Involve a new population of work study students, not drawn from class distinctions but from (1) those identified as alienated, and (2) those who volunteer.
2. Try to match students with role-models and environments suited to their needs.
3. Create a model of related instruction geared to stimulating students thinking in a reflective manner about first, their own characteristic way of "learning," and second, their experiences at work, the nature of work in American Society, and their futures in the work world in the society.

As indicated earlier, the typical work experience class is comprised of the bottom of the academic barrel. The model here assumes that work experience should be a valuable component of *all* efforts at general education in the high school. The experience of real life involvement, we believe,

has particular importance for students whom the school has not reached with traditional programs and/or who demonstrate symptoms of alienation. This grouping is distinguishable from students who are socially and economically destined for lower class careers: Such groups of alienated youth might be bright underachievers, those bored with academic experiences, or genuine low achievers in traditional realms.

While we have developed a model of alienation and means to measure it, its presentation here is beyond the scope of this introductory paper. It suffices to say that our rather comprehensive model attempts to combine the work of Maslow (1968), Rokeach (1973), Rotter (1968), Keniston (1965), Schwartz and Stryker (1970), and Stokols (1975).

Though there should be a primary focus on students we define as alienated and who are not maximally benefitting from traditional programs, clearly the work experience program should be open to all students and a broader range of students should be encouraged. Our arguments for this mix of students is that it will foster a more democratic open class structure and that the mix of lifestyles and talents will enrich all students involved.

Perhaps even more essential to the program is the identification of types of work settings which might provide an appropriate context for a meaningful work experience. The primary goal is to get students in roles where they interact with older possible work role models, involve them in interesting, challenging work tasks and which, in some way, yield insight and information about a possible future career. For example, such settings as McDonald's where the "counter kids" are all of high school age is less preferable than, say, a setting where through informal apprenticeships the student is able to role-test and interact with significant older individuals in an intensive manner. The "old" non-regimented craft-shop with masters working with apprentices is a prototype of such a psychologically advantageous setting.

In addition, the nature of the work involved is critical to the meaningfulness of the work experience. Settings where students are provided a variety of operations—say repairing machinery or even sales—are preferable to an assembly line or mechanical (impersonal) counter job. Work which is intellectually stimulating is preferable to routine work.

Finally, settings where students interact with professionals or master-craftsmen are preferable to things which stratify older and younger workers. These relationships might be called "natural projective apprenticeships" and are obviously desirable. For example, the student interested in education might be an apprentice to a day care teacher. Likewise, the student interested in engineering or architecture might apprentice himself or herself to an architect. The student interested in being a mechanic may find a suitable role model in the garage. The dynamics of such relationships are not simply informational but involve what Erikson (1950) calls the process of "adolescent future projection and identity formation." The adolescent tries to project himself or herself in a future orientation and decides on a career to create the self he or she wants to be. This contact with an older person is critical in forming a vocational identity choice. The adolescent in such a relationship is fundamentally asking himself, "Do I want to be like this older person?" The answer to this question may provide a significant event in the adolescent's choosing of a future career.

In addition to providing rich work experiences for all students, we will strive to match students according to the students' vocational interests, personal style and level of moral expectation. The basic model to be proposed involves measuring the work setting in terms of moral atmosphere, alienation environment, and organizational climate and then matching the student in such a way that the setting provides upward moral/social conflicts for the student.

The related instruction consists of groups of about fifteen students who meet weekly for four hours with a faculty member to (a) reflect upon their own learning styles, and (b) reflect upon their work experiences.

Reflection Upon Learning Styles

This occurs through the utilization of REAL (Relevant Experiences in Active Learning) "mini-pacs" developed by the Northwest Regional Laboratory, Portland, Oregon. The packages come in pairs and focus upon a basic issue experienced by all learners such as, "Why Learn Anything?" or Letting Someone Teach You." One version of each pair has a format and illustrations appropriate to youth and the other is appropriate to adults.

Below is a description of the materials which may be found in each Minipac.

Directions. The direction papers contain the methods for using the materials and specify which materials are to be used with which method.

Key Ideas Booklet. This booklet gives a brief discussion of the Minipac topic in terms of a set of important psychosocial ideas. For example, the Key Ideas Booklet for the "Being Helped" package contains a brief explanation of what being helped means and eight key ideas discussed in the Key Ideas Booklet.

Audio Cassette. The tape contains examples of the key ideas as they appear in human experiences. These human experiences are illustrated by interviews, confrontations, and music. There may be different cassettes for students and for adults.

Search Booklets. There are two search booklets in each Set I Minipac. One introduces the learners to completing needs assessments, problem identification, dilemma clarification, and values clarification through recalling specific information that is relevant to the learners' past experiences. The other booklet includes directions for performing various activities that call for behavioral outcomes rather than just knowledge. Set II Minipacs have one Search Booklet that combines these foci. The learners may be involved in some writing, drawing, manipulating, and simulation situations as they respond to the search directions.

Self-Assessment Booklet. This booklet (called "Where Are You Now?") invites learners to evaluate their behaviors in working with the ideas of each Minipac. The evaluation includes open-ended questions, fill-in statements, checklists, and a card sort. Each is designed to provide self-checks regarding cognitive-affective learnings, attitude changes, and the degree of increased self-awareness relative to the key ideas.

Use of the package is completely self-directed and is accomplished either individually or in a leaderless small group. A package explains the dynamics of the issue it focuses on and suggests ways that the user can have experiences to learn. The materials don't tell the user what a person should do in any way. They are, rather, intended to enable the user to recognize the human dynamics of issues so as to better determine ways to cope with them in his or her own style and according to his own desires. Such recognition is intended to make the issue of responsibility for the factor of choice in behavior an explicit one. The idea and design of these self-directed minipack-

ages derives directly from a theoretical model of social-psychological self-evolution based upon the work of Erikson, Piaget, Kohlberg, and Maslow (June 1972).

Reflection Upon Work Experience

This involves the creation of a discussion climate in which students feel free to bring up problem issues which occur in the work setting. Such problems are then dealt with within the group and resolution is sought after collective effort.

The issues which might result are obviously many. One example might be labeled an ethical conflict which might occur. In one pilot session, a student working in a mental hospital offered the group the following:

"I was working with the little mentally disturbed girl, Frances. The nurse was ignoring her so I went to talk to her. The nurse bawled me out because she said that the girl was being punished, and everyone was supposed to ignore her. I went and talked to her, even though I might get fired for it. . . ."

The goal of the leader is to get the group to help the student deal with the moral conflict posed (doing what one considers right for the patient vs. conforming to the norms for the institution). The leader in this discussion raised several issues to the group:

Why did the nurse want the students to ignore the girl? Were these reasons justified?

What would happen to the girl patient if the student got fired? Who would relate to her then?

When is it right to violate the rules of the institution? What are the responsibilities for a person who violates such rules?

The goals are not to preach a particular answer, but to get the students to reflect on the issues posed. The leaders will be trained in using the models reflection/experience and moral education (Kohlberg 1969), and will try and encourage better reasoned responses, rather than the "right response." The goal is to encourage students to better think about their responsibilities in a work setting, rather than to rebel or conform to the system. The group, after a resolution of such a conflict, will attempt to assist the student involved to better deal with his or her work role.

Another type of issue might involve the context of work. Students working in fast food chains (e.g., McDonald's) might reflect upon the effect of such institutions upon the nation's nutrition and local ecology. Leaders might suggest surveys of customer opinions or other such observations.

Another type of issue involves students choosing a vocation. Students might project as to what kinds of work they would find meaningful in the future. Through role-plays and projective exercises the leaders could involve the students in defining potential career options while encouraging them to plan realistically for such careers.

Other issues which might arise are:

personal conflicts at work; the nature of the organization of work; power in the work world; effects of capitalism on work; ways to make work more interesting, etc.

Such issues would be dealt with in an open, non-indoctrinative manner where students and leaders would reflect in an intellectually stimulating and supportive manner about the issue being discussed. There would be a focus upon resolving the conflict on the intellectual level as well as contracting with the students solutions to be applied in the work setting. Thus, if a student brought to the group a dilemma dealing with a disagreement with a supervisor over a particular matter and the group concluded that the student was in the wrong, he or she might be reasonably expected to

apologize to the boss as compliance with the contract made with the group. The related instruction then serves as a moral basis for relating to the job as well as an intellectual forum to air problems occurring in the work world.

CONCLUSIONS

This paper has attempted to formulate a new conceptual outline for Work Experience programs. It offers a new sociological principle for selecting work experience students as well as suggests a new psychological strategy with which to formulate supplementary educational training. The program suggested by this paper is now being implemented at Newport Harbor High School, Newport-Mesa Unified School District, Newport Beach, California. We are conducting a careful evaluation of the program to determine the project's impact upon reduction of student alienation and increased maturity of moral thinking. We hope the results of this research are in the anticipated directions and that it is possible to create work experience programs which will have moral and intellectual impact upon a broad range of students.*

* Research for this article was funded by Title III of the Elementary and Secondary Education Act in cooperation with the University of California and the Newport-Mesa Unified School District.

REFERENCES

Coleman, J. *Youth: Transition to Adulthood.* Chicago: University of Chicago Press, 1974.

Dewey, J. *Democracy and Education.* New York: Free Press, 1916.

Dewey, J. *Schools of Tomorrow.* Boston: D. C. Health, 1906.

Erikson, E. *Childhood and Society.* New York: Norton, 1950.

Hartshorne, H. and May, M. A. *Studies in the*

Nature of Character. Columbia University, Teachers College. Vol. I: *Studies in Deceit.* Vol. 2: *Studies in Service and Self-Control,* Vol. 3: *Studies in Organization of Character.* New York: Macmillan, 1928–30.

Jung, C. *Improving Teaching Competencies Program: Basic Program Plans.* Portland: Northwest Regional Education Laboratory, 1972.

Kenston, K. *The Uncommitted: Alienated Youth in American Society.* New York: Harcourt, Brace, Jovanovich Inc., 1965.

Kohlberg, L. "Stage and Sequence: The Cognitive-Developmental Approach to Socialization" in *Handbook of Socialization Theory and Research.* Edited by D. Goslin. Chicago: Rand McNally, 1969.

Maslow, A. *Toward a Psychology of Being.* New York: Van Nostrand Reinhold Company, 1968.

Mead, G. *Mind, Self, and Society.* Chicago: University of Chicago Press, 1934.

Piaget, J. "The General Problem of the Psychobiological Development of the Child," in *Discussions on Child Development.* Vol. 4. Edited by J. M. Tanner and B. Inhelder. New York: International Universities Press, 1960.

Piaget, J. "Cognitive Development in Children." *Piaget Rediscovered: A Report on Cognitive Studies in Curriculum Development.* Edited by R. Ripple and V. Rockcastle. Ithaca: Cornell University School of Education, 1966.

Richmond, G. *Micro-Society School.* New York: Harper and Row, 1973.

Rokeach, M. *The Nature of Human Values.* New York: Free Press, 1973.

Rotter, J. "General Expectancies for Internal versus External Control of Development." *Psychological Monographs,* LXXX, No. 1 (1966), pp. 1–28.

Schwartz, M. and Stryker, S. *Deviance, Selves, and Others,* 1970 (Monograph). Cited in A. McCord. "Happiness as Educational Equality," *Society,* XII, No. 1 (November/December 1974), pp. 65–71.

Stokols, D. "Toward a Psychological Theory of Alienation." *Psychological Review,* LXXXII, No. 1 (January 1975), pp. 26–44.

Reading 46

Educational Technology and the Computer

Wm. Clark Trow

When the printing press appeared, and later the electric light, the telephone and the automobile, there was no question about what we should do with them. But opinions differ on how to use the computer, particularly what its role should be in education. The magazine *Phi Delta Kappan* recently published an article by William C. Norris [1] suggesting that technology should take over the job as the chief cook and bottle washer of the whole educational menage. According to a footnote, Norris is "chairman of the board and the chief executive officer of one of America's largest producers of computers and related electronic hardware," which may or may not have influenced his thinking.

However, the *Kappan* editor, recognizing the importance of the subject, asked a score or so of well informed educators [2] to comment on the Norris essay. Although favoring the use of technological hardware, these critics pointed to the weaknesses they saw in the plan Norris recommended. This and, of course, his own comments were all that

any one of the contributors saw of the symposium, so it seemed desirable for someone to write a summary of the contributions of both the original author and the critics. At any rate, this is what is attempted in the present article.

First, we can note some of the weaknesses of present educational procedures that led Norris to recommend reform.

Second, we can consider Norris' main proposals for a developing technology—the computer-assisted instruction (CAI) which he recommends.

Third, we should report some of the criticisms of these proposals.

Fourth, we should provide suggestions as to what seems to be needed to get educational reforms under way. As one of the contributors put it, "We desperately need new . . . guidelines that come to grips with the realities of educational reform."

I. Criticisms of Present Educational Procedures

Mr. Norris does not spend much time on the flaws and failures of present educational

Source: Wm. Clark Trow, "Educational Technology and the Computer." *Educational Technology* vol. XVII, no. 12 (December 1977), pp. 18–21.

practices, probably because they are well enough known to all who are professionally engaged in educational work. In general, they are the high costs which make secondary and higher education prohibitive for many qualified young people (and have already bankrupted some schools), the incompetence of many teachers and other school personnel, the inability of the graduates of our schools to solve the national problems of our day—energy, health, unemployment, etc.—and the duplication of effort and fragmentary attempts at educational reform.

II. Norris' Proposals for a Developing Technology

Even this brief summary suggests the direction taken by the Norris proposals. To use his language, there should be less emphasis on *labor-intensive* and more on *capital-intensive* productive technologies. These "intensive" terms seem to mean overworking the personnel vs. overworking the hardware, respectively.

The plan calls for a system involving a national and an international network of learning centers, computer-controlled. There is inadequate space for a complete description here. Suffice it to say that after an excursion into inputs and outputs, the exposition runs into a eulogy of a computer system (PLATO), e.g., "infinite patience, the epitome of personalization, nearly limitless versatility, and delivery of uniformly high quality . . ." But it is much more than that. And other advantages of CAI are listed, including conversation, discussion, employment of AV communications, with a virtually inexhaustible memory, working 24 hours a day, seven days a week.

There is no need to enlarge on these advantages; rather, we should note the suggestions that Norris gives for procedure. These will be alluded to later in connection with my comments and suggestions. But, first, let us note the objections of the critics to employing this *Wunderkind*.

III. Criticisms of Computer-System Control of Education

There are two chief criticisms of the Norris plan. One is the cost. Since this is a criticism everyone has of present-day education, apparently "more research is needed" in this sector. For the present, however, the fragmented approach is no doubt more expensive, for the advantages gained, than most schools can afford. Quite possibly the quantity production of large computer-controlled systems such as Norris advocates would be less expensive.

The second major criticism, which is woven into the fabric of the comments of the critics, is that of teacher resistance. Back of every innovation lies the threat of displacement, and if not that, the general objection to being removed from the decision-making role.

Besides these major objections there are several others, a brief resume of which follows: The listings do not do justice to the several contributions, but it is believed that they represent fairly accurately the total pattern of opinion.

- CAI has been tried; it is not a cure-all. Experimental projects nearly always wither on the vine as soon as the special funds are withdrawn.
- There are many things a computer can't do as well as the regular school and *vice versa*. Therefore, each should do what it can do best.
- Education is more than presenting ideas to a group of students, their grasping of these ideas, and internalizing them. It is an active process on the part of the student from which he or she brings educational procedures into the competition of the

marketplace, and gains satisfaction from his or her learning efforts.

- A voucher system magnifies this competition and so has some attraction; but it is not popular, especially in economic times like the present.
- No reason is given as to why the idea is a good one educationally—no educational rationale. True, it adapts to varying learning rates, but not to varying learning styles.
- The most effective first step in developing a technology of teaching should be an analysis of the behavior of the student, not an exploration of the possible uses of hardware. Computers can teach complex materials through supplying immediate results and progressive steps, but so can much simpler materials.
- Norris does not mention the availability of low-cost, technologically advanced educational materials in the home.
- Many still question whether the best way to get "higher quality education at lower cost is for private companies to provide the technologies, management, marketing, and leadership."
- The search for profits may not be the best objective, though quite legitimate in the industrial community.
- Education is more than visual and auditory communications to which a learner is asked to respond.
- The computer is properly used only as an adjunct to education.
- One critic wants to know what the "cost trade-offs" are between conventional classrooms and CAI programs, whether the possibilities for extreme individualization are really advantageous, and if the voucher system is used, whether it will increase the social isolation of the schools.
- Computer rhetoric is no longer helpful. What is needed is a sufficient number of high quality courses at low cost. Industry can barely afford the high costs of technology for training in vocational skills—a problem which Norris overlooks.
- Norris's "system" cannot claim to be an educational system. It is a scheme for bringing education into private corporate enterprise. Norris seems to remain oblivious of the dehumanizing concomitants of "technological" solutions of social problems. He would make education less "labor-intensive," i.e., more profitable to the industrialized private sector, but without eliminating teaching jobs—which would be the neatest trick of the month.
- A new linkage of schools and industry as presented by CAI can hardly be expected to deliver by itself all the objectives of quality education. But it should be more clearly realized that CAI is not the equivalent of educational technology.

IV Alternative Suggestions

If these views are *typical* of what is to be expected from American educators, it rather looks as if the Norris-type technology is not slated to usher in a new era in education. Where, then, can we look for the needed changes?

Many suggestions for reform have appeared in the educational literature that have served to please or disappoint a small professional audience. But they are soon forgotten. There are some rather clear reasons for the neglect, aside from cost and teacher resistance, and the other criticisms that have been listed in the *Kappan* article. One is that many of us are so interested in our own ideas that we do not show adequate concern for the ideas of our colleagues. Or we talk to each other in our meetings and in our journals, but fail to spread the gospel, as we see it, to the people whose influence and votes are necessary for the sale of our product. Or we can't get together on any basic principles or procedures.

The only persons, so far as I know, who almost single-handedly initiated basic educational reforms that became widely adopted were Pestalozzi, Herbart, Froebel, and Dewey. Besides expounding their views, they all operated practice schools of one sort or another in which to try them out. But, of course, the many who have operated such schools have promoted no lasting reforms. If consensus is not to be had, perhaps sufficient agreement is possible, with allowances for variations of emphasis here and there.

And if there are no giants these days, we have the advantage of the contributions of the days when there were. These should keep us from what seems to be the major error of the Norris approach and to which some of the critics delicately alluded, *viz.*, getting the cart before the horse. The question which should concern us is *not* "In what new ways can technology be used?" It is rather, "What methods and apparatus are needed to get the results we want?" What results *do* we want, and how can they best be obtained? In my opinion, three preliminary conditions are essential:

- First, we need a detailed list of goals or objectives.
- Second, we need a list of school subjects and activities through which, in part, the objectives are to be obtained.
- Third, we need scales with which to measure degrees of excellence in each.

1. The goals or *objectives* are the things we are hoping to teach. They involve skills (vocational, athletic, asthetic, socio-political and ethical), verbal usage, rational thought and problem-solving. We hope these will be learned as a consequence of instruction and school experiences. They are applicable in school and out.

2. It is hardly necessary to list the school *subjects* here. They are for the most part quite familiar, and Norris has provided a useful partial list. On it, industrial and vocational training are already quite at home, and continuing education and developing countries are new arrivals.

3. And the *scales* of excellence refer to measures of proficiency. Criterion-referenced measures are objective in that they employ standard units like feet and inches, minutes and pounds. Norm-referenced measures (usually A-B-C, etc.) are based on the distribution of scores in the group. Thus, an individual would score high in an inferior group and lower in a superior group.

The criterion-referenced marks are, of course, practically essential for the desired flexible individualization of instruction. They encourage students to move at their own rate (though not necessarily alone), whatever their age, or whether they are average, handicapped or superior. And they tend to keep pupils from being placed in permanent groups (grades) where they do not "fit in."

Ideally, then, all education becomes special education to the extent that it is adapted to what are known to be the individual learner's interests, abilities, aptitudes and needs. If what is to be taught can be handled ably and economically by computer, all well and good. If the computer performance does not furnish the derived satisfaction with learning and with the goals sought, these goals should be provided for in other ways. The inspirations of Haim Ginott,[3] whose untimely death was a great loss to education, could advantageously be studied and enlarged to include school situations.

The idea, then, is not to try to figure out

how much "education" CAI can deliver, but to provide the education desired, using the best means that can be devised.

NOTES

1. W. C. Norris, Via Technology to a New Era in Education. *The Phi Delta Kappan,* February 1977, *58,* 451–453.

2. Education Reaction to "Via Technology." *Ibid.,* 454–459.

3. H. Ginott. *Between Parent and Child.* New York: The Macmillan Co., 1965; and *Between Parent and Teenager.* New York: The Macmillan Co., 1969.

Reading 47

Challenges to Early Childhood Educators

Lilian G. Katz

For early childhood educators there is no shortage of challenges: We face constant demands requiring an increasing range of skills, understandings, responsibilites, and commitments. I want to address some challenges facing us in our roles as teachers, whether we are teachers of children or of adults. These challenges will be discussed in terms of principles, i.e., propositions which, although not always true, seem sufficiently general to be useful for organizing information, making plans, evaluating and experimenting with diverse aspects of teaching. Although the principles are enumerated as a sequence of four, they are interrelated in meaning, and intersecting in their referents.

I. THE PRINCIPLE OF CONGRUITY

The first principle is the way we teach teachers should be congruent in many basic

Source: Lilian G. Katz, "Challenges to Early Childhood Educators." Reprinted by permission from *Young Children* vol. 32, no. 4 (May 1977), pp. 4–10. Copyright © 1977, National Association for the Education of Young Children, 1834 Connecticut Avenue, N.W., Washington, D.C. 20009.

aspects—but not all—with the way we want them to teach children. At first glance this principle seems to be a restatement of the truism, "Practice what you preach!" But the principle of congruity is offered not just to safeguard ourselves against hypocrisy. The principle's usefulness seems to derive from two presuppositions. The first is that we probably constitute a model for many of our learners, and the principle of congruity may remind us to maximize the opportunities to teach by example. The second and more critical presupposition is that there are some elements of teaching which are applicable to all teaching, whether of young children or adults in teacher education. These elements are enumerated below and together with the principle of congruity they constitute a set of *generic* principles of teaching.

A note of caution concerning this first principle: The use of the term "congruity" is intended to suggest a kind of consistency, harmony, or concordance between the way we teach teachers and the way we want them to teach. In no way is it intended to imply isomorphism or identicality between teaching teachers and teaching children.

The principles are addressed only to those elements of the role of learner, and hence teacher, which may reasonably be thought to apply to all teacher-learner encounters regardless of age or experience.

II. THE PRINCIPLE OF KNOWING THE LEARNER'S UNDERSTANDING OF WHAT IS TO BE LEARNED

Let us take it as a useful idea that we cannot teach anything important to someone we do not know. Obviously this is not always true. We have all been taught by a lecturer addressing a large group, or by writers whom we have never met. It is likely however that successful teaching of large groups is related to how well the lecturer or writer "knows" the audience. I have intentionally used the qualifier "important" here to refer to our constructions of those aspects of reality that are relatively central to our lives and our work. This includes such constructions as our explanations of the behavior of others, our identification of cause-and-effect relationships in events which matter to us, our conceptions of those things about which we have relatively intense feelings, concerns, anxieties, and hopes.

This second generic principle of teaching is meaningful if we assume that a major function of a teacher is to help the learner to improve, refine, develop, or in some way modify his or her understanding (construction of reality) of the concept, task, idea, or skill to be learned. In order to fulfill this function the teacher must *uncover* what the learner's understanding of the task or concept to be learned actually is. It is in this sense that the teacher must know the learner.

Most teachers fret over how much "material" must be "covered." Certainly, adequate coverage of many content areas pre-

sents persistent problems, but adequate uncovering of the learner's construction of relevant reality may help us make better informed decisions about what "material" it is most appropriate to "cover" at a given time (Duckworth 1972). It seems reasonable to assume that every learner does have some understanding of the task, problem, or concept to be learned, but the understanding may be insufficient, incorrect, or inappropriate in some way.

Differentiation of Understanding

Of all the ways in which understandings may vary, let us examine one variable in particular: the extent to which the learner's understanding of the situation, task, or concept is *differentiated* or complex. Take, for example, my relatively undifferentiated understanding of the game of tennis. I know that at least two people play with rackets and balls on a court with lines, and that they hit the ball across the net to each other. By contrast, my son's understanding of tennis is highly and finely differentiated. His understanding includes concepts of games and sets, singles and doubles, rallies and volleys, loves and deuces, types of shots, as well as some intricate minutiae of appropriate dress.

Another example of variations in differentiation or complexity of understanding can be seen when we consider that a five-year-old has an understanding of where she comes from, i.e., reproduction. But when she is ten years old, her understanding will be even further finely differentiated. That understanding will include facts, concepts, and theory at a range of levels of abstraction and concreteness, with subsumed interdependent facts, concepts, and theory, as well as a variety of images, memories, ideas, and associated feelings. One can say, then, that as a five-year-old, she had an understanding of the phenomenon, but it was not as finely differentiated as it could ultimately become.

I am presupposing that a teacher is one who has a relatively finely differentiated or complex understanding of what is to be learned, and accepts the responsibility for helping to increase the extent to which the learner's understanding matches or at least includes the teacher's understanding. If our understandings of most relevant events/phenomena are not more fully differentiated, more useful, more appropriate, more accurate and plausible than those of our learners, then we lack the professional authority to be their teachers. This is not to say that learners are to be discouraged from developing understandings which are either better or different from the teacher's.

The second principle is thus the principle of knowing the learner's understandings of what is to be learned. This is a *generic* problem for all teachers of all learners. If I want to teach a student, for example, techniques of conversing with children, one essential approach would be to uncover that student's construction or understanding of the *teacher-child conversation situation*. It does not necessarily follow that when I uncover that construction I can teach the student a more useful construction. Success will be a function of the repertoire of teaching skills I bring to the situation. It may not be necessary to probe each individual student's construction of the situation or task. From knowledge and insight gained from experience I may be able to make inferences about students' constructions. Nevertheless, it seems reasonable to hypothesize that the probability of successful teaching of important learnings increases with increased knowledge of the learner, in particular, knowledge of the individual learner's construction of the relevant reality.

The Informality Hypothesis

A related hypothesis is that the greater the informality in the learning situation, the greater access the teacher has to relevant knowledge of the learner's understanding. This knowledge increases the probability that the teacher will respond appropriately (if appropriate responses are in the teacher's repertoire). Informality in classrooms has been a popular topic in early childhood education. Its popularity, however, seems to be related more to ideological positions than to the pedagogical principle of knowing the learner.

There probably is an optimum amount of informality for each classroom unit and perhaps for each individual. This optimum informality hypothesis is derived from two concerns. First, there may be a degree of informality beyond which the students perceive the classroom proceedings and their own progress to be stalled. A second concern is that teachers, especially of adults, may become too close to their students and thus risk losing their capacities for the *reasoned* judgment required for evaluation of students' progress.

Another implication of the second principle is that it may be helpful to teach students tactics and strategies by which to inform teachers where they are, how they are constructing the problem to be solved, what confuses them, and how they understand whatever is to be learned. For example, we can teach children to say to us, "I'm lost," "Hold it," "Go over that again," "I don't understand," "I'm confused," etc. On one occasion I recommended to a first grade teacher that she teach her pupils to signal her in this way. She expressed agreement with the soundness of the procedure, then, after a pause, said quite spontaneously, "But they'll interrupt the lesson." She chuckled as she realized the meaning of her protest. This teacher's comment informed me that covering the "lesson" had a high priority in her understanding of teaching.

The second principle also implies that we must be careful about teaching our learners to agree with us excessively, or to give us too quickly what we appear to want. We do this sometimes when we confuse conversations with what are really interrogations. Take, for example, an advisor who said to the teacher, "Why are those books on a table in the middle of the room instead of in that corner?" This was an interrogation because it was a question in which the right answer was given away. Ultimately the advisor wants the advisee to take the appropriate action, but she could probably achieve this by giving an order. If the advisor wants the advisee to solve problems on her own beyond the immediate situation, however, she should address the modification of the advisee's understanding.

I saw another example of interrogation when a group of college students was asked, "What are the three d's of education?" The respondents were quickly informed that one purpose of the question was to uncover what was in the questioner's mind. Surely there is a place for interrogation. Perhaps we want to know whether a young child knows his address and phone number. In such a case we can put it to the child honestly that we want to find out whether he knows it, and then interrogate.

While interrogation is useful for some types of assessment, it may undermine some important aspects of teaching. For example, let us look at the possible consequences of the advisor's interrogation about the books on the table. First of all, chances are that her question or interrogation reduced the likelihood of subsequent open communication. It is unlikely that in a subsequent encounter the advisee would share with the advisor her confusions and doubts about organizing the room. Indeed, such a question—depending perhaps on the tone of voice and facial expression—is likely to set in motion an adversary relationship between advisor and advisee, since the interrogation implies the passing of judgment or a "putting down" of the advisee. I do not intend to take issue with the adequacy of the advisor's advice. My major point here is that the advisor's task is to help the advisee understand the situation in closer proximity to the advisor's understanding. The probability that the advisor could help the advisee improve or refine her advisee's understanding of room arrangements, for instance, would increase if the advisor first uncovered how the advisee understood the situation. Then, with the knowledge thus obtained, the advisor could share some insights, concepts, or facts which best "match," in Hunt's (1961) sense of the term, the advisor's own understanding. In other words, interrogations inform learners that *we* know the right or best answers, solutions, and ideas. We hope that this is so! But it is through conversations in which we *probe* others' thoughts and ideas, in which we solicit their views, opinions, and wishes that we become informed of *another's* understandings of the relevant phenomena. The latter is the crucial step in teaching.

III. THE PRINCIPLE OF TIMING

The implications and hypotheses drawn from the second principle lead to a third one regarding timing. Two aspects of timing are important. One is the pace or rate at which teachers respond to learners in teaching-learning encounters. Another is the rate at which teachers' competence develops.

Pacing

I have in mind those frequent encounters in which, for example, a learner reveals an incorrect, inappropriate, or oversimplified understanding of a concept or situation. The teacher recognizes the incorrectness of the concept and may offer a correction. The question of concern here is whether there is a *right* or *better* time to offer this correction. When teaching student teachers we often have such timing decisions to make: We want to balance the rate at which we offer suggestions (which imply things could be going better) with the rate at which we offer encouragement and support (which implies that things are going well). Learning, change, and the development of understandings unfold and occur in time. Certainly all of us make errors in teaching by responding too fast or too slowly. However, it seems a reasonable hypothesis that greater latency, which allows more of the learner's behavior to unfold, increases the quantity of information upon which the teacher can formulate an appropriate response. Perhaps this hypothesis is merely an elaboration of the virtue of patience. According to my present understanding of teaching, patience resides in the relationship between latency and knowledge of the learner. Hypothetically there are likely to be optimal latencies for every teaching-learning encounter.

Developmental Stages

A second aspect of the third principle is that no one enters a social position as a veteran, and that it is useful to think of teachers as having developmental stages with associated concerns and developmental tasks (see Fuller and Bown 1974; Katz 1972). In addition to concerns and tasks, it seems reasonable to hypothesize that understandings of teaching develop as experience accrues. Teachers' understandings of teaching are less finely and fully differentiated earlier in their careers than they become later on. The differentiation could be expected to increase in such things as the number of levels

of analysis and conceptions of the teaching situation.

Presumably the teacher of teachers has a finely differentiated understanding of teaching. By proposing the principle of timing I intend to encourage the teacher educator to take a developmental view of the learners (as the learners should of children). The point is to focus on the kind of insight-sharing and information-giving which contribute to the steady but long process of refining understandings. We should understand our responsibility more often to be one of helping the learner to *develop* rather than just to *change*. Change is easy and can be achieved quickly. Perhaps an extreme example helps to illuminate the difference: Just point a gun at a teacher and you can make behavior change! But leave the room and after 30 minutes, what endures? The focus on development implies attention to questions of timing over the longer course of modifying, refining, and differentiating understandings of phenomena which are important to the learner.

IV. THE PRINCIPLE OF SOCIOINTELLECTUAL AMBIENCE

Every educational program has a characteristic ambience or atmosphere which is perceived by most of the teachers and learners participating in it (see Katz 1974). "Ambience" may be defined as "the feeling tone which expresses something about the feelings generated by the total set of relations between staff and recruits" (Wheeler 1966, p. 82). The sociointellectual ambience of teacher education settings should be congruent with the ambience we want students to create in early childhood programs. One of the most important challenges facing early childhood educators today is to strengthen the intellectual vitality of the sociointellectual ambience of both teacher education and early childhood education settings. In teacher education settings intellectual vitality may be achieved when staff members exhibit their concern, curiosity, and involvement in the disciplines relevant to education, and may be supported and strengthened when staff members engage students in activities in or through which they try to advance the conceptual and knowledge base of the field.

From my observations of early childhood programs in several countries, I have the impression that we are not providing activities and experiences of the kind into which children can sink their "intellectual teeth." In some programs, children dabble in a wide variety of activities which seem pleasant enough. In other programs, children engage in many routine academic tasks which also lack intellectual vitality. A major goal of early childhood education is to help children make sense of their experiences and environments. In other words, we are responsible for helping young children to develop, refine, improve, or deepen their understandings of the salient aspects of their day-to-day lives. The intellectual vitality of our programs can be strengthened when we encourage and help children to reconstruct these aspects. This can be achieved by actually building, making, and reproducing some aspects; by dramatizing others; and by encouraging the observing, recalling, recording, or discussing of their perceptions and understandings of their experiences.

For this goal to be more fully realized, children in early childhood education programs will have to have stronger attachments to the teaching adults and the relationships between adults and children must be characterized by greater intensity than they typically are now (Katz, in press). Strength of attachment has to do with adults' usefulness as models as well as sources of demands, support, and encouragement. Intensity has to do with the role of concentration in teaching and learning. In my own teaching experience I find that the process of uncovering students' understandings of relevant phenomena requires my full concentration on the unfolding events in the teaching situations.

Since we cannot "cover" everything we want learners to know, we must try to teach in such a way as to increase the likelihood that learners will go on learning. In other words, teaching should strengthen the learner's disposition to be a learner. Those of us who teach teachers are responsible for helping students become lifelong students of their own teaching. Some students learn by explanations; some learn from examples and illustrations; some learn from the model we provide; and some learn from all three of these aspects of our teaching. If we practice the first principle and teach in ways which are congruent with the ways we hope students will approach young children, we may measure up to some of our most urgent challenges.

REFERENCES

Duckworth, E. "The Having of Wonderful Ideas." *Harvard Educational Review* 42, no. 2 (May 1972): 217–231.

Fuller, F. F., and Bown, O. H. "Becoming a Teacher." In *Teacher Education: The Seventy-Fourth Yearbook of the National Society for the Study of Education, Part II,* edited by K. Ryan. Chicago: University of Chicago Press, 1975.

Hunt, J. M. *Intelligence and Experience.* New York: Ronald Press, 1961.

Katz, L. G. "Developmental Stages of Preschool Teachers." *Elementary School Journal* 73, no. 1 (1972): 45–50.

Katz, L. G. "Issues and Problems in Teacher Education." In *Teacher Education,* edited by B. Spodek, pp. 55–56. Washington, D.C.: National Assocation for the Education of Young Children, 1974.

Katz, L. G. "Teachers in Preschools: Problems and Prospects." *International Journal of Early Childhood*, in press.

Wheeler, S. "The Structure of Formally Organized Socialization Settings." In *Socialization after Childhood*, edited by O. G. Brim and S. Wheeler, pp. 51–107. New York: John Wiley & Sons, 1966.

Reading 48

Essentials of Special Education for Regular Educators

Colleen S. Blankenship and M. Stephen Lilly

The mainstreaming movement has resulted in the need to re-evaluate and restructure special education teacher education programs. The former practice of training special education graduates to assume the role of teachers in self-contained special classrooms for the "mildly handicapped" is outmoded. The practice of integrating "mildly handicapped" students into regular education programs, and the emphasis upon noncategorical teacher training, demands a very different sort of teacher preparation program.

In the last ten years, an increasing number of special educators have spoken of a cooperative relationship between special and regular education, with regular educators assuming a greater responsibility for the education of students with learning and behavior problems, assisted by special educators who can function in a supportive and consultive role (Lilly, 1975; McKenzie, Egner, Perelman, Schneider, & Garvin, 1970;

Source: Colleen S. Blankenship and M. Stephen Lilly, "Essentials of Special Education for Regular Educators." *Teacher Education and Special Education* vol. 1, no. 1 (Fall 1977), pp. 28–35. Reprinted with permission.

Reynolds, 1975). The need to prepare both regular and special educators to assume these new roles is of paramount importance if mainstreaming is to result in quality educational experiences for children.

The focus of this article will be on the preparation of regular educators to teach children with mild learning and behavior problems. The issues to be addressed include: the present level of training offered regular educators, the need to provide regular educators with pre- and inservice training in special education, and considerations in planning preservice programs. A preservice program for undergraduate education majors will be presented, and delivery systems for providing inservice training to regular educators will be discussed. Finally, conclusions will be drawn concerning pre- and inservice training for regular educators.

Present Level of Training

One of the first concerns expressed by many special educators relative to mainstreaming is, "Are regular classroom teachers equal to the task of educating the mildly handicapped?" (Brooks & Bransford, 1971, p. 259). The consensus has been that few regular educators have received training which would equip them to teach children with mild learning and behavior problems (Brooks & Bransford, Gearheart & Weishahn, 1976). It can be expected that, at most, regular educators may have listened to one introductory lecture on exceptional children.

The certification requirements for teachers and other educational personnel are only now beginning to include coursework in special education. At this time, only five states require regular classroom teachers to take even one course in special education. While this is a step in the right direction, there is a danger that this practice may delude us into thinking that one course will somehow be sufficient. The question is not one of the number of courses which should be required, but rather one of content of the courses to be offered. Of the states passing new certification requirements, only the legislation from Missouri specifies that the course should include information on teaching techniques. None of the remaining four states requiring a course in special education has set any restrictions on the type of course to be taken. In those states, a teacher could satisfy the certification requirement by enrolling in a single survey course on exceptional children. While we might expect teachers enrolling in such a course to increase their knowledge of handicapping conditions, it is unrealistic to expect that a survey course would contain the more practical and skill-oriented information which would be of assistance to teachers in regular classrooms.

It is safe to assume that the present level of training afforded regular educators is not equal to the demands which will be placed upon them in instructing children with mild learning and behavior problems. It is incumbent upon special education teacher education institutions to work cooperatively with general educators to assure that all regular teachers will receive sufficient training in teaching children with mild learning and behavior problems.

Need for Preservice and Inservice Training

In the past ten years an increasing number of "mildly handicapped" students have been returned or allowed to remain in the mainstream of education. The continued emphasis which will be placed upon special education in the regular classroom is evident in the passage of PL 94–142, which requires placement of children in the least restrictive environment. For the majority of children with mild learning and behavior problems, the least restrictive environment will be a regular classroom.

The need to provide preservice and inservice education to regular classroom teachers has a wide base of support. The training of regular educators has been identified as an area of concern by the Bureau of Education for the Handicapped. BEH funding, which was nonexistent in 1974–1975, has increased to over 3 million dollars for preservice education of regular educators. Similarly, funding for inservice training over the last three years has increased from 1½ million to over 4 million dollars (Comptroller General, 1976).

Numerous special educators have voiced support for training regular educators, as have state, local, and university special education administrators (Comptroller General, 1976). As Gearheart & Weishahn (1976) aptly pointed out, "The question is no longer one of 'should all teachers learn how to deal with handicapped children?' but rather, 'what should they learn?'" (p. vi).

Planning Preservice Programs

There are a few difficulties which must be overcome if we are to provide regular educators with preservice training in special education. First among them is the characteristic separation which exists among departments within colleges of education. In recent years, some special educators have come to realize that they share common interests with their colleagues in curriculum and instruction, particularly in the areas of remedial reading and arithmetic.

Several benefits could be derived from a closer association between regular and special education teacher educators at the college level, among them the opportunity to engage in cooperative research. One area which needs to be explored concerns the applicability of applied behavior analysis techniques in regular classroom settings. As Lovitt (1975) pointed out, logistics research concerning the application of measurement techniques to children in regular classrooms has been a neglected area of study. The results of research in this area could be of assistance in selecting and modifying the measurement skills to be included in preservice courses for regular educators.

It will take more than common interests, however, to get departments to work together. The impetus for change would most likely arise within departments of special education. What is needed is an organizational structure which encourages discussion and development of cooperative teacher education programs.

A second difficulty which may hamper the development of preservice programs concerns the manner in which training in special education can be incorporated into on-going teacher preparation programs. There are at least two solutions to this problem. The first would be to make the completion of a course(s) in special education a college requirement for regular educators. This approach has a number of pitfalls. First, it suggests little control over the training to be offered. Unless the course(s) are specified, students would be free to choose

from among special education courses, some of which may be knowledge-based rather than skill-oriented. Second, if regular educators enroll in methods courses designed to prepare resource teachers, the course may not focus on the skills which are directly relevant to the regular classroom situation. Third, the requirement of a single course denies departments of special education the opportunity to systematically develop model training programs for regular educators.

A second option would be to offer a minor, or an area of concentration, in special education to regular educators; a minor which does not result in special education certification. This approach has much to recommend it. First, it implies a cooperative effort between different departments within a college of education. Second, it does not entail adding additional coursework to the regular education teacher preparation program. Third, it allows a greater degree of direction on the part of special educators over the training to be provided. Fourth, it encourages the development of courses which are specifically designed for regular educators and tailored to the demands of the regular classroom.

If training in special education is offered on an elective basis, then it stands to reason that some regular educators will receive appropriate training while others will not. There seems to be a trade off between the need to train all regular educators and offering comprehensive programs to a limited number of persons. In the initial stages of developing training experiences for regular educators, we would be wise to err on the side of quality training for a few, rather than mediocre training for the masses.

The second option for providing preservice training to regular educators was seen as the most attractive possibility by the Department of Special Education at the University of Illinois. Planning was begun in 1975 by the Department of Special Education in cooperation with the Department of Elementary and Early Childhood Education to develop an undergraduate program to provide future classroom teachers with the necessary skills to deal with children with mild learning and behavior problems in the regular classroom. The decision to offer preservice training to regular educators, the decreased demand for teachers in self-contained classrooms for the "mildly handicapped," and the increased demand for resource teachers, led to a restructuring of programs offered by the Department of Special Education.

At the time planning was initiated to develop the undergraduate area of concentration in special education, a decision was made to discontinue admittance to the undergraduate EMH program. At the present time, two on-going programs dealing with the education of children with mild learning and behavior problems are offered through the Department of Special Education. One is the Resource/Consulting Teacher program, a master's level program preparing experienced teachers to assume special education resource teaching positions; and the other is the Specialized Instruction (SI) program for undergraduate elementary and early childhood education majors. The SI program is described in the following section.

Specialized Instruction Program

The intent of the SI program at the University of Illinois is to provide regular educators with the necessary skills to deal with children with mild learning and behavior problems in the regular classroom. Program development was based on the following assumptions: graduates are expected to seek regular teaching positions in grades K–9 and it is anticipated that supportive help from a special educator, analogous to a Resource/Consulting Teacher, will be available.

Several parameters served to define the nature of the program. First, the emphasis was to be on a functional approach to behavior problems. Second, a list of hypothesized job skills were to form the basis for establishing performance objectives to be attained by students in the SI program. Third, practicum experience was to be provided to allow for the application of learned skills in a regular classroom setting.

Due to the desire to provide an intensive and well supervised practicum experience, enrollment was limited to approximately 20 undergraduate education majors. The students were selected on the following basis: sophomore standing, cumulative GPA of 3.5 (5 point scale), elementary or early childhood education major, and expressed interest in the SI program. Although enthusiasm was not included among the selection criteria, it has proved to be an unexpected bonus.

Students in the SI program begin their coursework in special education during Spring Semester of their sophomore year. The first course deals with trends and issues in special education. During the students' junior year, they enroll in one special education course per semester; the first focusing on assessment and remediation of social behaviors and the second dealing with assessment and remediation of academic behaviors. The practicum experience, which occurs during the senior year, is arranged so that half of the students enroll during the Fall Semester and the other half during the Spring Semester.

The SI program was conceptualized around the role that a regular classroom teacher would assume in educating children with mild learning and behavior problems. Essentially, the role requires the teacher to act as a team member, a student and program advocate, an instructional planner and implementer, and a behavioral manager. Mastery of a set of skills is implied in each of the aforementioned functions ascribed to a classroom teacher. Each of these functions will now be addressed, accompanied by a description of the major skills to be mastered.

Team member. The intent of the SI program is to prepare regular educators to assume a major responsibility in educating children with mild learning and behavior problems. It is not anticipated that they will be able to function as program planners and implementers without the supportive help of special educators, nor is it intended that they should. Rather, it is expected that regular educators will function as team members in planning and implementing educational programs for exceptional children.

The emphasis on involving regular educators in program planning is evident in the federal regulations for PL 94–142, which require the presence of a child's regular or special teacher, or both, at the placement and planning conference. It stands to reason that due to the number of students with learning and behavior problems who will be placed in regular classrooms, a significant number of regular educators will be involved in jointly planning and carrying out individualized education programs. Therefore, regular classroom teachers need to acquire those skills which will allow them to function as members of an educational team.

Some of the skills which are stressed in the SI program include: 1) identifying needed supportive services and making appropriate referrals, 2) participating in placement and planning conferences, 3) working cooperatively with other team members, and 4) communicating progress to a child's parents and to other team members. Students in the SI program are given the opportunity to act as team members via role playing exercises which are incorporated into their coursework. During the practicum ex-

perience, SI students meet with the parents of at least one child with whom they have been working, to discuss the child's progress.

Student and program advocate. A regular classroom teacher is in a rather unique position to advocate placement in the least restrictive environment. His/her very presence at a placement or planning conference for a child can signify a willingness to integrate the student into the mainstream of education. Who is in a better position to know the demands which will be placed upon a handicapped child than the teacher of the regular class in which the child will be placed? Based on the child's present level of performance and the demands of the setting, the regular educator is in a good position to request the provision of an appropriate level of special education services to allow the child to function in the regular classroom.

In order to serve as an advocate, SI students must have a knowledge of the literature pertaining to least restrictive placement, legislation, litigation, and the services of professional organizations. SI students are given the opportunity to demonstrate their advocacy skills via simulation exercises which are part of their coursework.

Instructional planner and implementer. As an instructional planner, a teacher must be able to accurately assess a student's present levels of educational performance. In all cases, a teacher will find it necessary to go beyond the results of standardized tests in order to precisely identify a student's strengths and weaknesses. Knowledge of and the ability to use criterion-referenced tests and curriculum-based assessment devices should be of great assistance to teachers in planning instructional programs. One of the major goals of assessment should be to identify skills in need of remediation and to describe them in measurable terms. Based on a child's performance during assessment, the teacher will need to sequence the skills which, when mastered, will result in the amelioration of identified academic deficits. Attention must also be given to the selection of instructional materials. A teacher must be prepared to adapt materials when possible and to create instructional materials when none exist.

Once a teacher has identified a starting place for instruction, it is necessary to select an instructional technique which can then be systematically applied. A thorough knowledge of a variety of instructional techniques and their uses will be needed if teachers are to select appropriate interventions. In order to precisely identify academic deficits and to determine the effectiveness of corrective techniques, a teacher must be familiar with measurement techniques and become proficient in their use.

The specific skills which students in the SI program are expected to master include the ability to: 1) conduct criterion-referenced and curriculum-based assessments, 2) describe instructional problems in behavioral terms, 3) construct and use task analyses, 4) write instructional objectives, 5) sequence instructional objectives, 6) generate and select teaching techniques, 7) observe and chart academic data, 8) make data-based decisions, and 9) adapt/create instructional materials. Students demonstrate their knowledge of these skills by completing a number of projects in their courses, and by planning and implementing instructional programs for children during the practicum experience.

Behavioral manager. A teacher can be expected to encounter a number of behavior problems with which he/she will have to deal in order to provide a proper learning environment. Being able to reduce the occurrence of socially inappropriate behaviors

and to increase the occurrence of appropriate ones are critical skills for a teacher to possess.

An aspect of significant concern is improving the behavior of "mildly handicapped" children to the extent that they are able to successfully interact with their nonhandicapped peers. A teacher is seen as being in a pivotal position as the facilitator of interaction to increase the social acceptance of "mildly handicapped" students by their classmates.

It is a wise teacher who can make use of natural reinforcers in the classroom, arrange group contingencies, and use self-management techniques to improve the behavior of students. The teacher who can effectively employ behavioral management techniques will be in a good position to structure the learning experiences of students and assure success in the regular classroom for students experiencing problems.

In order to increase the ability of SI students to deal with social behavior problems, they are expected to be able to: 1) use a variety of observation techniques, 2) identify problem behaviors in measurable terms, 3) record and chart social behaviors, 4) select appropriate intervention techniques, 5) make use of behavioral management techniques, and 6) make data-based decisions. Coursework offers the opportunity for SI students to complete a number of projects requiring the application of behavioral techniques to classroom behavior problems. During the practicum experience, the students design and implement strategies for improving a child's study and social behaviors.

It should be stressed that the SI program confers no new teaching certificate. It does provide, however, an opportunity for regular educators to take a substantial block of coursework in special education and to gain experience in teaching children with mild learning and behavior problems in the regular classroom setting. It is anticipated that due to the nature of the program, graduates will have a distinct hiring advantage as they seek positions as regular classroom teachers. In order to help assure that this occurs, each graduate of the SI program will have a special set of materials in his/her placement credentials describing the SI program and assessing the student's performance in the program.

Inservice Training

Recently, Ed Martin, Deputy Commissioner of Bureau of Handicapped, U. S. O. E., commented that "efforts to provide training and experience for regular classroom teachers are not keeping pace with the efforts to mainstream" (1976, p. 6). While this is not excusable, it is certainly understandable considering the number of regular educators (approximately 1.8 million) who require inservice training in special education.

If inservice training of regular educators is to be effective, it must overcome at least two obstacles. The first deals with teachers' attitudes and the second concerns the mystique which has surrounded special education. It is not so difficult to understand the reticence felt by some regular educators, such as those questioned by Hall & Findley (1971), concerning their willingness to teach low achieving pupils. Nor is it difficult to understand why some regular educators feel they cannot teach "mildly handicapped" youngsters without the aid of special equipment (Shotel, Iano, & McGettigan, 1972). These teachers have simply accepted the mystique which surrounds special education and which has been fostered by maintaining self-contained classrooms, thereby implying that regular classroom teachers were not capable of teaching children with mild learning and behavior problems.

Several special educators have placed a great deal of stress on changing teachers' attitudes (Brooks & Bransford, 1971; Shotel et al., 1972) and some researchers have been successful in bringing about desirable attitude changes (Brooks & Bransford, Glass & Meckler, 1972). An undue emphasis upon changing attitudes to the neglect of providing teachers with the skills necessary to teach problem students should not be encouraged. Changing attitudes is a tricky business; sometimes attitude shifts are accompanied by concomitant changes in behavior and sometimes not. A more direct approach is to focus on improving the skills of classroom teachers. It seems unlikely that a teacher could maintain a "poor attitude" toward a child if he/she possessed the skills to individualize instruction and to demonstrate that the child was making progress as the result of his/her teaching efforts.

The skills approach to inservice training has the support of a number of school district administrators, who when asked for suggestions concerning inservice training responded that it should be 'practical and specific," include "both observing special educators and working with the handicapped," and provide "follow-up" to assist participants in their regular classes (Comptroller General, 1976, p. 11).

If everyone agrees that inservice training of regular educators is necessary, the question then becomes, "How is inservice to be provided?" There are at least three options: 1) onsite training conducted by special education personnel who are employees of the school district, 2) onsite instruction provided by specialists under contract as consultants to the school district, and 3) stipends for short-term study at colleges or universities. When school district administrators were asked to indicate their preference of the above mentioned options, they rated onsite training by contracted specialists as the most desirable and stipends for short-term campus study as the least desirable alternative (Comptroller General, 1976). The preferences of school district administrators seem to suggest a rather cautious view concerning the capabilities of school district special education personnel to conduct inservice training. This may be due to the fact that insufficient numbers of special educators have been trained to serve in a role analogous to that of a Resource/Consulting teacher. If sufficient numbers of special educators were trained in that capacity, it would seem logical that they would be in the best position to provide the kind of "practical" information and "follow-up" which school district administrators indicated they desired for inservice training. In recognition of this reality, trainees in the master's level Resource/Consulting Teacher program at the University of Illinois are taught to plan and implement inservice workshops as a part of their preparation for that role in the public schools.

CONCLUSION

Based on the discussion thus far, the following recommendations concerning pre- and inservice training of regular educators seem warranted:

1. A single survey course in special education is not sufficient to prepare regular educators to assume the responsibility of educating children with mild learning and behavior problems. What is needed is a program which stresses skills and includes practicum experience in a regular classroom setting. While the clear implication of this statement is that training of regular educators will be a task of greater duration than many special educators would like, the alternative is likely to be mass training, almost sure to result in sparsity and mediocrity of application.

2. Training of regular educators should focus on increasing direct teaching skills, on the assumption that successful experiences in teaching children will result in positive attitudes toward the children being taught. If programs are initiated which focus on change of attitudes of regular educators, assessment of concomitant changes in teacher behavior should be an integral part of such endeavors.

3. Departments of special education, elementary education, secondary education, vocational-technical education, etc. should engage in cooperative planning to develop quality preservice programs in special education for regular education students.

4. College and University Departments of Special Education should consider reallocation of scarce financial and human resources from undegraduate preparation of special educators for self-contained teaching situations to training of regular educators to deal constructively with learning and behavior problems in the regular classroom. This is not to say that continued preparation of special educators is not needed, as is implied in the Comptroller General's report (1976) on the federal role in special teacher preparation. Rather, it is suggested that the majority of special education teacher training should be done at the master's level, and an increasing amount of our capability for undergraduate education should be focused on regular educators.

5. Inservice training should be skill-oriented and be conducted onsite, preferably by special educators who work in the schools as Resource/Consulting teachers and who can provide follow-up assistance to regular educators.

As mentioned earlier, the question is no longer whether regular educators should be trained to deal with learning and behavior problems in the classroom, but rather, how such training should be provided. It is the opinion of these authors that the monumental task of providing such training to regular educators must be approached with patience, and with constant attention to quality as well as quantity of effort. We must remain constantly aware of ill-advised and often ineffective efforts to prepare large numbers of special educators during the 1950s and 1960s, and insist that new undertakings be systematically planned and executed. Undoubtedly, the need for training of regular educators will outstrip our capability to deliver such training in the foreseeable future, for the change process in education is political in nature and does not follow a logical, developmental pattern. Even if change in education tends to be chaotic, however, we must be systematic in our response to it. The current demand for special education training for regular educators offers a unique opportunity for improving the educational experience of countless children, and our response to the challenge must be nothing short of the best we have to offer.

REFERENCES

Brooks, B. L. & Bransford, L. A. Modification of teachers' attitudes toward exceptional children. *Exceptional Children*, 1971, 38, 259–260.

Comptroller General. Training educators for the handicapped: A need to redirect federal programs. Report to the Congress by the Comptroller General of the United States, General Accounting Office, 1976.

Gearheart, B., & Weishahn, M. W. The handicapped child in the regular classroom. Saint Louis: C. V. Mosby, 1976.

Hall, M. M., & Findley, W. G. Ability grouping: Helpful or harmful? *Phi Delta Kappan*, 1971, 52, 556–557.

Lilly, M. S. Special education—A cooperative effort. *Theory into Practice*, 1975, 14, 82–89.

Lovitt, T. C. Applied behavior analysis and learning disabilities—Part I: Characteristics of ABA, general recommendations, and methodological limitations. *Journal of Learning Disabilities*, 1975, 8, (7), 432–443.

Martin, E. Integration of the handicapped child into regular schools, *Minnesota Education*, 1976, 2, 5–7.

McKenzie, H., Egner, A., Knight, M., Perelman, P., Schneider, B., & Garvin, J. Training consulting teachers to assist elementary teachers in the management and education of handicapped children. *Exceptional Children*, 1970, 37, 13, 143.

Reynolds, M. C. Current practices and programs in training the mainstream educator. In R. Johnson, R. Weatherman & A. Rehmann (Eds.), Handicapped youth and the mainstream educator (Vol. 4). Minneapolis: University of Minnesota, 1975.

Shotel, Julano R., & McGettigan, J. Teacher attitudes associated with the integration of handicapped children. *Exceptional Children*, 1972, 38, 677–683.

Reading 49

Who Will Engage in Curriculum Evaluation?

William J. Gephart

The title question for this article is a multi-edged sword. Considered one way, it seems to ask for a prediction of the lineup. Who or what agencies will be in on the action at some point in the future? Considered another way, it asks who has the right to evaluate curricula. Should the federal government be messing around in curriculum evaluation? Should the courts? By what right do they enter this arena?

Considered still another way, the question seems to ask who has the obligation, the responsibility, to engage in curriculum evaluation? Who has *got* to do it? Finally, from still another vantage point, the question seems to be a plea. Will *anybody* engage in curriculum evaluation? Please?

Some people will fuss that the "Feds" don't have the right to evaluate the curriculum. After all, the Constitution gave control of education to the states! So, why should

Source: William J. Gephart, "Who Will Engage in Curriculum Evaluation?" *Educational Leadership,* vol. 35, no. 4 (January 1978), pp. 255–258. Reprinted with permission of the Association for Supervision and Curriculum Development and William J. Gephart. Copyright © 1978 by the Association for Supervision and Curriculum Development.

the government get into curriculum evaluation? Others will fuss about the involvement of parents or community groups, after all, they aren't *trained* in education! And the courts, what do they know about education?

All of these concerns are moot. The fact is, all of these groups, and more, *will* evaluate the curriculum. There is no way we can stop them. Judging, contrasting, comparing, and assessing are continual behaviors of humans. No, we don't have to worry about which group will evaluate the curriculum, or which group has the right or the responsibility. They all do, and they all will! Trying to stop them would be like trying to keep the reader of this material from making judgments about how good or bad it is.

Our concern ought to shift to *how* these different groups evaluate the curriculum. That's where the problem is! Will these evaluations be systematic or subjective? Will the inevitable evaluations be public or private? And, will the evaluations be structured so that they are not rendered useless by the levels problem?

Curriculum evaluation is both simple and complex. It is a problem-solving process. As such, it is uniquely effective when we intend to make a choice, and when we don't have information that tells us the relative worth of the different options.

Curriculum evaluation focuses on four general classes of choice making. The first class is choosing between goals. Educators and their publics can conceive of far more goals than can be attended to by the curriculum. Our resources are limited, and so is our time. We need to choose which goals our curriculum is to be oriented toward.

The second class of choice making comes when a specific educational goal has been selected and there appear to be several programs or ways of accomplishing it. Now a choice has to be made as to which program plan seems best. The third class of choice-making occurs once a plan is selected and implementation is underway. Now the choice making focuses on the modifications that may be needed to keep the program moving toward accomplishing the chosen goal.

The final choice-making class comes when a program has been carried out. Are the results good enough that we should build the new program into the continuing operation? Or, are the results such that another test run with some modifications is warranted? Or, are the results so bad that the program or goal ought to be dropped?

The activities that make up the curriculum evaluation process include: (a) the specification of the alternatives that are going to be considered in the choice making; (b) the determination of the variables the decision makers will use in making their choice; (c) the collection and analysis of data; and (d) reporting the relative worth of the alternatives to the decision makers.

As asserted earlier, our problem is not who will evaluate the curriculum, but rather, how will they evaluate. Systematically or subjectively? Publicly or privately? Most evaluations are subjective and private. For example, as a reader, you have perhaps considered several options as you have read to this point in this article: continue reading; put the article aside until some other time; put it aside and forget it. As you have been reading, you may or may not have been conscious of considering those options. And, you probably did not *consciously* consider the array of variables (for example, clarity of the message, quality of the logic in the message, the importance of the concepts) that could be used in deciding to read on, set it aside, or throw it away.

But, you have made a decision. You are still reading. You have been evaluating at least some of the options, and you have made a choice. That evaluation is a subjective and a private evaluation. You did not do it by design. You did not articulate the alternatives. You did not specify the variables to be used in determining the relative worth of all of the options. And, you probably would have a hard time describing when and how you chose to continue reading.

Subjective, private evaluations are not all bad, particularly when an individual is making choices for himself or herself. But, when the decisions to be made involve many people and when the options considered are complex, systematic and public evaluations are preferred.

Three Types of Information

Systematic evaluations start with the delineation of the decision situation. This requires the determination of three types of information.

1. Who will make the decision? Is it an individual? If so, who? Is it a group? If so, are they functioning as a group or sequentially? At what decision levels are they going to make the choice? (More on this levels problem later.)

2. What are the alternatives? What set of options *will* be considered by the decision maker(s)? What are the characteristics of each of the alternatives?
3. What variables *will* the choice maker(s) use in determining the relative value or worth of the alternatives? (For example: cost, political acceptability, ease of implementation, extent to which learning is increased, aesthetic character, and so on.)

Once this information is in hand, the systematic evaluator constructs a matrix for each decision-making level involved. The rows of that matrix are labeled by the alternatives being considered; the columns by the variables to be used to differentiate their worth. Each cell in those matrices indicates a type of data that needs to be generated and interpreted in the evaluation study.

Notice the imperative in points 2 and 3 mentioned earlier. In designing an evaluation, it may be possible to identify more alternatives than the decision makers can or will consider. A systematic evaluation is one in which the evaluator first checks to see if the selection of alternatives and variables is a closed or open matter. If it is open, the evaluator identifies those other options (program alternatives and criterion variables) and calls them to the attention of the decision maker(s) for *possible* inclusion in the study. In this action, the evaluator assists the decision maker(s) to a conscious consideration of the options in a decision situation.

In an evaluation that does not delineate the options *before* collecting and interpreting data, it is possible to close out options on incomplete data. Two problems develop in such evaluations. Sometimes we examine the alternative programs sequentially and decide that one of them is not possible for one reason or another. As we move on to the remaining alternatives, we may forget about the alternative we have closed out. In so doing, we do not consider that alternative on all of the criteria. If that alternative rated poorer than the others on that first criterion but in fact was better on all the other criteria, a poor evaluation report would be submitted.

The second difficulty encountered when alternatives and criterion variables are not articulated in advance is also one of applying differential criteria. In this case, we consider program alternative A using a known set of criterion variables. The same occurs for program alternative B. Another program, option C, is uncovered, and we set out to evaluate it. As we apply the set of variables, we learn about another criterion that someone wants us to use. We apply it to program option C, but not to the other options. Again, the relative worth of all the programs can be distorted. Evaluation, done systematically, should produce data about the relative worth of *all* the program alternatives on *all* the criteria to be used in the decision.

The public-private dichotomy presented earlier is basically a concern for reliability in evaluation. Public evaluations are done in a manner in which the procedures to be followed are made known. Private evaluations can sometimes be reconstructed after the fact. However, we are all well aware of major differences between reconstructed logic and logic in use. Think back for a moment to a recent evaluation you made; perhaps the judgment of how good that meal was in a restaurant. There are a number of qualitative labels you could have used ranging from excellent ("Among the best meals I've had." through average to terrible ("I wish I'd refused to pay for it." or, at least, "I'll never eat there again."). Or you could have used some other qualitative labels, for example, "The best (or worst) Italian meal," "The best (or worst) service I've received," and so on. Were you conscious about considering all of those options? Did you think about the criteria you used to determine which of these worth labels was the best one for that situation? Probably not; you were performing a private evaluation (even though you may have made the results of it public by communicating your appreciation or lack of it to the waiter or management). Another person in that same situation would conduct his or her private evaluation. The two of you might come to different conclusions about the quality of the meal. Or you might come to the same conclusion but for different reasons.

We make a great number of private evaluations. That is how it should be. But, when we are faced with decisions that involve many people, decisions among complex alternatives, decisions in which there is a degree of accountability involved, we need to do public evaluations.

The many people and agencies who will evaluate the curriculum should understand one more point about public evaluations. The public aspect of an evaluation is determined by the degree to which the evaluative procedures are specified in advance and replicable by other competent evaluators. It does not necessarily mean that the results of the evaluation are broadcast from the front page of the newspaper.

At two earlier points in this article the phrase, "the levels problem," was used. This is another facet of the evaluation process that must be understood by those who would evaluate curriculum. Failure to understand it and deal with it in an evaluation effort can render the work useless.

An illustration of the levels problem can be seen in an example used by Mary Jean Bowman at a 1969 meeting of the National Symposium for Professors of Educational Research (NSPER). She made the point that the first thing that must be attended to in a cost-benefit analysis is the nature of the specific decision(s) being served. She asked the NSPER participants to consider the decision milieu in which offering or participating in *additional* higher education activities is involved. One decision in that milieu is made by the individual about participating or not. Another decision is made by the institution about offering additional higher education opportunities or not. Still another decision in that milieu is made by society, are those opportunities needed or not.

Bowman called the group's attention to the fact that the alternatives in each of these three decisions are different, associated but different. Further, the data needed to determine the relative worth of the options differs from one decision level to another. For example, consider costs. The costs to participants include tuition, fees, and foregone earnings. None of those are costs at the institution level of decision making. At this decision level costs include facilities, faculty salaries, and maintenance. Tuition is a benefit at the institution level of decision making. This illustration points out that a move from one level of decision making to another creates subtle changes in the alternatives being considered and subtle changes in the criterion variables.

We can see a levels problem in the evaluation of teaching. If we are evaluating *my* teaching to help *me* become a better teacher, we are at one level of decision making. If we are evaluating my teaching to help administrators make decisions about placement, pay, or termination, we are at another level of decision making. The data needed for these two levels are different. The same holds for curriculum. A teacher's evaluation of curriculum to help a child learn is one level of decision making. An administrator's evaluation of the curriculum of a school (undertaken to help children learn) is another level. The state or federal evaluation is still another. So is the parental, the teacher's union, and so on. Each of these decision making levels will be concerned with a somewhat different set of alternatives. Because of that, their data needs will differ.

Educators, politicians, and the lay public continually overlook the decision levels problem in evaluation. They act as if the same data bits can (and should) be used at all levels. Failure to recognize this and to design evaluations appropriate to the decision level can have a very harmful effect as the many groups and agencies carry out their inevitable evaluations of the curriculum.

In summary, the question, who will engage in curriculum evaluation, is misleading. It suggests that some should and others should not. The fact is all of us, and all of our groups and agencies, will evaluate—we are humans and that is the nature of the beast. Our concern should be modified! We should be concerned about *how* they will engage in curriculum evaluation. And in that concern we should work toward making their evaluations more systematic (in contrast to subjective), more public (in contrast to private), and more sensitive to differences in data needs at the differing levels of decision making inherent in the differing groups.

PART VII

American Education and the Future

Historically, American education has been oriented to the past and present, transmitting culture and responding to societal needs. As societal needs became apparent, schools reacted in responsive fashions. The addition of vocational training to the curriculums of secondary schools is illustrative of the schools responding to the societal need for trained manpower. More recently, federal programs such as Headstart have attempted to provide enriched preschool programs for children of poverty. School integration, stimulated by *Brown v. Board of Education of Topeka 1954,* is illustrative of schools being viewed as one type of potential solution to a societal problem.

Society changes, and as it does, to a certain extent, so do the roles and curriculums of schools. Many of the societal problems of the present, if not resolved, will continue to plague generations of the future. Current trends, such as the rapid depletion of natural resources and the pollution of air and water, could lead to world disasters.

In recent years, deliberate and concerted efforts have been made to study and relate the past and present to potential futures. This emerging discipline has been referred to as futuristics, futures research, policies research, and futures studies. In general, the discipline deals with forecasting potential futures, and hopefully determining desirable futures. Questions addressed by futurists include: What will the future be like if there is no change in the present trends? What can the future be like? What should the future be like? Can a desirable future be created?

The first article in this section, "Population and Education: How Demographic Trends Will Shape the U.S.," by Joseph Coates, describes and analyzes trends such as the birthrate and its effect on school enrollments, increasing numbers of women in the work force, likely demands for altered curriculums and new school-centered services, and changing family lifestyles and their potential impacts on school curricula and services. The effects of the immigration of non-English speaking students, and local population mobility on schools are also discussed. John Goodlad's "The Future of Learning Into the Twenty-First Century" speculates about schools and learning in the year 2000. Goodlad states " . . . much of the subject matter of today's learning is unrealistically narrow and antiseptic." He further states, "All that we can predict with certainty is that the central issue of the 21st century, as it is of this one, will be the struggle to assert truly human values and to achieve their ascendancy in a mass, technological society. It will be a struggle to place man in a healthy relationship with his natural environment; to place him in command of, rather than subservient to, the wondrous technology he is creating; and to give him the breadth and depth of understanding which can result in the formation of a world culture, embracing and nurturing within its transcending characteristics the diverse cultures of today's world." What will learning, teaching, and the role of schools be like in the year 2000? Provocative questions such as this are discussed by Goodlad.

Two major issues that education faced in the 1960s and 1970s were a fiscal crisis, and achieving equal opportunity. Pierce, in "Emerging Policy Issues in Public Education," forecasts that because of the decline in school enrollments and a decline in the pressures to increase teacher salaries, claims on the public purse for education will be relatively reduced. Pierce also forecasts that efforts to shift support of local schools away from local property tax are likely to moderate. He states, "The 1960s and early 1970s witnessed a variety of proposals to transform schools into instruments of social reform." He forecasts that the emphasis in the 1980s will be in making schools responsive to community preferences. In his opinion, "References to responsiveness, efficiency, and liberty have already begun to replace equality as the dominant values in many educational policy debates."

The late 1970s can be characterized as the "back-to-basics" years. A major issue of the 1980s may center around the improvement of performance of students in public schools. Pierce speculates that lively topics of debate will include: the organization of the schools, what is to be taught in the schools, how it is to be taught, and who governs public education.

The last two articles in this section deal with two rather specific educational topics related to the future: education as a lifelong process, and nonsexist education for all children. Few people disagree that education is a lifelong process; yet it has only been in recent years that the formal education system has begun to adapt to the concept. Both early childhood education and post-secondary education have witnessed significant growth in the past few years. Shane and Weaver, in "Education as a Lifelong Process," believe that "lifelong learning in a world recreating itself will take the form of a seamless learning continuum extending virtually from birth until incapacitating old age takes over." Is lifelong education desirable? How can our existing system be modified to accommodate lifelong learning? What research and what existing trends support the concept of lifelong learning? Shane and Weaver address themselves to such questions.

McCune and Matthews in "Building Positive Futures: Toward a Nonsexist Education for All Children," describe, define, and explain the case for eliminating sex role stereotyping. The roles of both men and women in society have changed, yet existing stereotypes continue to be perpetuated. Questions addressed by McCune and Matthews include: Where did this sex role problem come from—is it part of women's liberation? When we change a child's sex roles, aren't we threatening his or her sexual identity and orientation? Aren't we questioning traditional values, which are a parent's prerogative to maintain? What are implications for schools and for educational change? The article concludes with goals and actions directed toward effective nonsexist education for the development of a future society in which every child and adult is freer to achieve her or his full potential.

Population and Education: How Demographic Trends Will Shape the U.S.

Joseph F. Coates

Birthrates in the United States have declined significantly over the past 18 years, with 28% fewer children being born now than were born in 1959. This "baby bust," which has followed the post-war baby boom, has already reduced the number of children enrolled in elementary school by about 10%, and a drop of another 7 or 8% by the mid-1980s is certain. As the children born during the baby bust become older, their numbers will affect high school enrollments. During the 1980s, enrollments may drop as much as 25%. These statistics represent a basic, nationwide trend, but other demographic factors—those which most concern planners on the regional, state and local levels—make school planning much more complex and uncertain than simple aggregate fertility rates suggest.

Other trends that will affect education:

- Women are increasingly entering the work force and staying longer. This will

Source: Joseph F. Coates, "Population and Education: How Demographic Trends Will Shape the U.S." The Futurist (February 1978), pp. 35–42. Published by the World Future Society, P.O. Box 30369 (Bethesda), Washington, D.C. 20014.

create more demands to change curriculum and add new school-centered services.
- Continued immigration will place special burdens on school systems in major cities, where immigrants tend to settle.
- Local mobility—the ease with which populations move within this country—will create increasing uncertainty among education planners.

The principal impact of these demographic trends occurs at the state and local levels. Since this is where most education planning is done, improved demographic study must begin at these levels. To see just what problems arise from these trends, it is useful to examine them in detail.

The Changing Family

The traditional image of the family—mother, father, and children, around which public policy has been framed—is increasingly at odds with reality. The growth of the single-parent family is one of the major demographic trends affecting schools. Approximately 45% of children born in 1976 will have lived with a single parent for some time before reaching 18 years of age. Between 1970 and 1976, the number of children living with a divorced mother increased by two-thirds, and the number living with a single mother increased by about 40%. The number of female-headed families with children has increased by over 250% since 1950. These families comprise 41% of all poverty-level families; the limited income of these families creates new demands and stresses on all public services, including schools.

Another factor relating to marriage and the family which can influence the school is the tendency of women to defer marriage. In 1970, 12% fewer 20-year-old women had been married than in 1960. The decline in the number of married 24-year-olds was only 7%. This suggests that women are not turning away from marriage in any great number; they are merely delaying it. During that period of deferral, women tend to enter the work force or to continue their education in order to prepare for work.

The entry of women into the work force is perhaps the demographic trend that most profoundly influences curriculum, services, the child's environment and the whole family structure. The shifting roles that women assume as they enter the work force create a demand for curriculum changes to prepare women for their entry. And working mothers need services to take care of their children.

The effects on schools of women in the work force will be great. First, there will be a decline in volunteerism. At a time when the school system is experiencing greater demand for volunteers to meet the pressures for more services, fewer women will be available. An example of this has been experienced by the League of Women Voters. Much of the envelope-licking and stuffing that once was done with free labor now must be done on a fee-for-service basis because so many of the League's members have moved into the work force. Similar effects will soon be felt by schools.

Demographers associate increasing female participation in the work force with a decline in the number of children a family will bear. And education encourages participation in the work force. In the future there will be a cycle in which education promotes work, work promotes a decline in fertility, and declining fertility increases the problems of elementary and secondary schools. The increasing number of dual-income families, especially among middle-class managerial and professional households, provides more discretionary money, money which may lead such families to send their children to private schools or to relocate their residences outside of central cities. The exodus of middle-class families may bring about a big-city public school system whose sole purpose is to educate the underclass.

Female participation in the work force may lead to changes in the purposes and structures of public schools. Schools will face an increased demand to overcome stylized gender roles associated with occupational choices. Career counselling may change to meet new work-sex roles. The new role models for girls will probably increase the number of students desiring vocationally-oriented curricula and counselling. Deferred marriage and earlier entry into the work force may create a demand for curricula that focus upon independent living, and training in financial management and personal affairs. Those who live in the lowest economic strata and are burdened by small children or single parenthood need education that focuses on improving one's economic status through continuation course certification and specially-tailored high-school programs.

The increased demand for day care and

Working Women—and Men

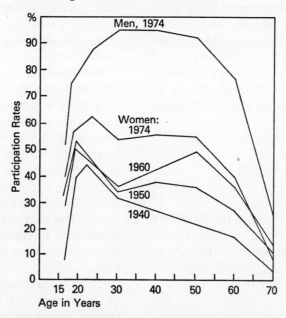

Labor force participation rates for men in 1974—and for women in 1974, 1960, 1950, and 1940. More women are entering the work force, and fewer are dropping out during the childbearing years. This trend is increasing demand for child care.
Chart: Juanita Kreps, ed., *Women and the American Economy*, 1976.

nursery care for preschool and young school children of working mothers may be met by the school systems. For children roughly aged 7 to 13, the school day is not quite long enough to accommodate the needs of single-parent working households. There are efforts in some communities to extend the length of afternoon care, not by extending the school day, but by extending the use of school buildings. Some 15% of children in this age group can be usefully served by extending the use of facilities from 3 p.m. to 6 p.m.

The family is becoming less of a dominant factor in the socialization of the child. A child now entering the first grade may have been exposed to nursery school or day care. He may have been involved with Head Start

or related programs, or have had extensive exposure to television. The size of his family is different from what it was for children born 10 years ago. Organized religious groups, grandparents and other members of the family, and adult neighbors seem to be playing a declining role in the socialization of children.

The reduced amount of time available for parenting in families where females work may create a demand for new school services that deal with functions traditionally learned at home. Schools may need to teach the skills of eating, drinking, dressing, social behavior, deportment, manners, self-control, and other functions to compensate for reduced parental care. In view of the underuse of schools and of surplus teacher capacity, the possibility of extending school functions into these areas may seem quite attractive to teachers' unions. However, a word of caution is necessary: Data from social psychological literature indicate that children put together with large numbers of other children for extended periods of time may suffer a reduced mental development.

Immigration and Non-English Speaking Students

Immigration accounts for one-fourth of net population growth in the United States. Since immigrants tend to settle in metropolitan areas, continuing immigration will create a chronic source of stress for big-city school systems.

There is an interesting relationship between high school dropout rates and the language spoken at home. Where English is the language spoken, or where English is spoken along with some other non-English language, the dropout rate is between 8 and 10%. But where a language other than English is the only language spoken at home, the dropout rate rises to 38%.

Among the specific population of those of Spanish origin, the situation is even worse. The principal non-English language spoken in the United States by people four years old and over is Spanish, spoken by almost 10 million people. Among school-age children, about five million speak Spanish as their primary language. Where English is spoken among families of Spanish descent, the dropout rate of their children is 14 to 15%. Where only Spanish is spoken, the dropout rate is 45%.

Among students who do not measure up to standard performance, non-English speaking students represent the biggest problem. Only 10% of English-speaking students are two or more grades below their peers. In grades one through four, approximately 17% of the non-English speaking students are two grades below mode; at the high school level, some 35% are two or more grades below mode.

The implication of these statistics is significant when they are coupled with the long-term movement of American society toward that of an information society. Approximately 55% of the work force is now in the information business. This situation raises questions about the value of bilingual education, and whether it denies students the chance for an economically useful education. The data suggest that, as now taught, students of foreign origin may be precluded from getting their first foot up on the economic ladder.

If the higher cost of bilingual education of students whose primary language is not English precludes other priorities, the level of education of English-speaking students may be reduced, further accelerating the decline of the urban school systems. Whether or not bilingual education continues, the steady stream of foreign-born students will renew the kinds of cross-cultural stresses associated with students who are hard to acculturate. This often results in delinquency and poor school performance, particularly for urban school systems. And proposed changes in the status of new illegal immigrants might encourage them to make greater use of the school system for their children. This will especially affect big-city schools and the smaller communities in the Southwest and in California.

Local Mobility and Internal Migration

Internal mobility and migration are perhaps the demographic factors that most perturb education planners at the state and local level. Between 16 and 18% of the U.S. population moves annually. The data reveal some evidence that people seem to be attracted to the city for work and other opportunities; but as they enter the childbearing years, people have a tendency to move out of central cities.

The overall effect of internal migration is a trend of movement out of the city and into suburban and rural areas. From 1970 to 1974, cities experienced a net exodus of 1.8 million people. The eight largest cities saw a net out-migration of 1.2%. Population growth in rural areas during this same period was 5.6%, contrasting with a growth of 4% for the nation as a whole. Educational management in these nonmetropolitan and small-community growth centers may run into special problems, because such growth was unexpected. The tax base may be inadequate to meet the demands caused by the influx of people, and the social values of the new migrants may be substantially at odds with those of the local people. The redistribution of population will create an acute problem for education planning in boom towns. In order to come to grips with the energy crisis, we will open up coal resources in Wyoming, the Dakotas, Colorado and other areas in the West, and Kentucky and southern Illinois in the east. One can reasonably anticipate surges in population for which the local communities in these areas will be totally unprepared.

There is a long-term trend toward the equalization of regional incomes. Once the nation's economic backwater, the sun belt areas of the South, the Southwest and southern regions east of the Rockies are all currently undergoing economic growth. In the early 1930s, regional income varied from 50% below average to 50% above the national average. In 1974 this range had narrowed to about 15% to 20%. Equalization may reduce regional differences in cost and quality of education, undercutting regional

disparities of funds available per child on a statewide basis.

Migration in and out of metropolitan areas is having the effect of concentrating minority students within the big cities and non-minority students outside of those big cities. This phenomenon, along with concern about the quality of schools, and about the curricula, are increasing white and middle-class dissatisfaction. There are only a small number of options open to middle-class parents who do not wish to have their children experience the effects of the decline in metropolitan school systems. One alternative is to withdraw the pupil to a private or parochial school. The data suggest that families that have the financial option of sending their children to private schools tend to exercise it. Even families with incomes in the $10,000–$15,000 range often send children to private schools.

For families without the income to send their children to private schools, the alternative may be a change of residence. Other options include early graduation and entry into college—a process that may stimulate programs of graduation based on credentials—and tracking, or grouping students by ability. In any case the net effect of all these alternatives open to a white or middle-class population—those dissatisfied with school systems in urban areas–is resegregation.

Teenage Childbearing

The only group in the United States now undergoing significant expansion in birthrates is that of females under age 15. Of the 3,144,198 live births in the United States in 1975, 12,642 were born to girls under 15 years of age. This situation has several implications for the educational system. Young motherhood interferes with the ability of the mother to continue her education. Children who are born to young mothers are far more likely to suffer a variety of congenital defects. These children born to adolescent mothers are themselves more likely to bear children at an early age, thus further burdening the school system.

Junior high school curricula, services and goals have never come to grips with the onset of puberty. Especially critical is the increasing rate of early sexual activity among boys and girls of junior high school and high school age, creating both immediate and long-term social and educational problems and needs associated with adolescent childbearing.

Decline in Enrollment

The national decline in enrollments does not imply universal distress—nor is it a universal phenomenon. A decline is occurring predominantly in the Midwest, Mid-Atlantic, and Pacific states, while the South and Southwest are experiencing a boom. To complicate matters further, both enrollment declines and increases often occur in the same state, with different small districts experiencing both shrinking and growing student populations. Especially hard hit by the general trend will be the big cities, already in great fiscal distress.

Thirty-seven states have experienced enrollment declines since 1970. Sixteen of these states have lost at least 4% of their students. Simultaneous with the declining enrollments has been an increase in minority enrollment in big cities. In the period between 1968 and 1974, the average student minority enrollment was 67.1%. School enrollment in the 27 largest cities peaked in 1970, and is now back at the level it was in 1962. The exodus seems to have occurred primarily among middle-class and white students. Looking at a sample of those 27 cities, one finds that the percent of minority school enrollment in almost every case is substantially above the percent minority population in the city.

For example, Atlanta has a 52% minority population; minority students there comprised 85% of the school system in 1974. Denver's population is 11% minority; in the schools, 47%. St. Louis is 41% minority; the school system is 70% minority. And the same is true of impoverished families. The percent of students from poor families in the big cities is far in excess of the percent of families in poverty: 33.4% versus 11.6%.

Response to Decline in Enrollment

In the face of declining enrollment, there are three general strategies available to school administrators: One alternative is to shrink by reducing staff and the so-called "frills" such as sports, music, and art. The second alternative is to expand services to current educational clientele. Places to expand include after-school care, courses in personal development, expansion of curriculum, and smaller classes with more individualized attention.

A third solution for school systems facing declining enrollment is to expand services to include new clientele. Preschool day-care may be part of this solution. Another is the entry of school functions into health services (such as immunization). and community center functions. But the most important new client for secondary school systems may be the adult. Adults have the need for credentials, courses teaching career skills, hobbies and recreation, and training of economic value, such as car and home repair. And one can anticipate that the coming increase in costs of energy will create a demand for courses teaching home conservation.

The Need for Improved
Demographic Studies

Familiarity with local circumstances can play a major part in determining whether or not a given forecast is useful to policy planners. In general, however, there is not enough expertise at the state and local levels to meet this need. The Census Bureau's state-level population projections are about 10 years old. The upcoming Census of 1980 will give substantial opportunity to improve the means of collecting data on a local level. The need

for demographic research relevant to plans concerning adult education, day care, nursery care, and after-school services is increasing along with the increased demand for such services. Such demographic data is essential for the wise policy-making needed to build effective educational systems for the future.

Reading 51

The Future of Learning Into the Twenty-First Century

John I. Goodlad

The Right to Learn

In a nation that speaks of inalienable rights, the right to learn must be paramount. Yet that right, in its full meaning, has been denied to many in this nation. It has been denied because of color, religion, poverty, infirmity, and residence. And it has been denied because of our often mindless adherence to many unproductive teaching concepts and practices.

The right to learn is the goal we seek for the 21st century. We want for our children a range of learning opportunities as broad as the unknown range of their talents. We want a learning environment that nurtures those talents. We want our children to know themselves and, secure in that knowledge, to open themselves to others. We want them to have freedom, and the order, justice, and peace that the preservation of freedom demands. . . .

Source: John I. Goodlad, "The Future of Learning Into the Twenty-First Century." From John E. Roueche and Barton R. Herrscher, *Toward Instructional Accountability: A Practical Guide to Educational Change.* New York: Cambridge Book Company, 1973, pp. 2–13.

What and How to Learn. Schools and teachers have been with us for so long that they have often been equated with education and, worse, with learning. Yet the infant learns to walk and to talk, to trust and to distrust; he learns fear and love and hate—all without benefit of school. By the age of five, the child has sat before a television set for at least the number of hours he will spend in the first three grades of school. Yet we still equate learning with school.

Although we believed, until recently, that school was the most powerful part of the learning environment, we know now that it is not.

But school is still the formal instrument created for the explicit task of educating our young, and in many ways it is the most important educator. Its answers to the questions of what and how to learn have both reflected national strengths and weaknesses and contributed to their formation.

The world has become increasingly complicated by technological advances and challenged by inequities in the human condition, all unfolding against the backdrop of an unknowable future.

As preparation for coping with these uncertainties, much of the subject matter of today's learning is unrealistically narrow and antiseptic. Those who have selected and prescribed it have done so through the biases of their Western culture, looking more to the past than to the future. For example, by denying to the young the richness of African, Asiatic, or Latin American heritages, to say nothing of the exciting variations of our own black and brown and yellow and red cultures, we have too often ignored and implicitly denigrated other cultures at an inestimable cost to all our children.

The full extent of the denial of the right to learn is even greater, however, for we tend to paint only pretty pictures of life, out of deference, supposedly, to the tenderness of children. In so doing, we magnify our hypocrisy for all to see. Even the youngest of our offspring soon become aware that we wage war while talking peace, that children go hungry in the richest land on the face of the earth, that even leaders cheat and lie. They come to understand that what we say and what we do are very different things. They see with the uncluttered vision of children the gap between rhetoric and reality.

What is to be learned is refined by our filtering system until, too often, it has little power to grip the learner and thus defrauds or cheats him. From the truly exciting possibilities of a culture—or conscience—embracing mankind, we slide to the homogenized "adventures" of Dick and Jane and a field trip to the supermarket.

With regard to the "how" of learning, we have only begun to question the outworn notion that certain subjects or concepts are to be learned by all individuals at successive stages of growth at stipulated times in sterile places. Reading is for the first grade, long division for the fourth, and fractions for the fifth and sixth. All of this takes place between the hours of nine and three in a big

box divided into cells. Preschool prepares for adjustment to the first box, and six or seven years in that box prepares for adjustment to a next larger box.

In this lockstep, as in so many other ways, we teach that each phase of life is instrumental to the next rather than of ultimate value in itself. We see the man we want the child to become rather than the child seeking to become himself. In the words of Hannah Arendt, "Man sees wood in every tree."

Toward Better Schools. This is the winter of our educational discontent. Until recently, we believed that we had only to provide some new subject matter here, inject a heavier dose of phonics there, or tighten the discipline a little, to improve both the system and society. Better schools (defined in largely quantitative terms) would mean more jobs, a brisker economy, safer cities, and more aware, dedicated citizens. Or so we thought. Dwindling confidence in these relationships reflects both declining public confidence in the schools and the tenacity with which we cling to the "learning equals school" equation. Painfully, we are coming to realize that grades predict grades, that success in school begets success in more school but is no guarantee of good workers, committed citizens, happy mothers and fathers, or compassionate human beings.

The schools have been poked and probed, judged and weighed—and found wanting. Whereas for many years they fulfilled brilliantly the primary purpose for which they were founded—the creation of one nation out of millions of immigrants—recent decades brought them new kinds of clientele whose needs could not be met with the formulas and procedures that had been used previously.

For a brief span of years, we believed that serious problems existed only in the schools of our great cities. Increasingly we have come to understand that suburban and, to an even greater degree, rural schools do not assure the diet or provide the vitality our children deserve. Even the middle-class school around the corner reveals ragged edges surrounding a soft center. The failures of our schools are apparent in dropout rates, in barely minimal learning on the part of many who do remain in school, and in growing alienation among the young of all colors and classes.

At the root of the problem is an implicit denial of diversity. The schools have become great sorting machines, labeling and certifying those who presumably will be winners and losers as adults. The winners are disproportionately white and affluent. The losers, too often, are poor and brown or black or red.

But many of the winners are losers, too. For they are shaped, directed, and judged according to a narrow conception of what is right and proper. This process begins very early; the environment of expectations, rewards, and punishments is established before mother and child leave the hospital. And in the home, infants are encouraged in their efforts to walk and talk, but their responses to sound, color, and smell are ignored or stifled. This process of channeling energy and talent is refined and perfected in the schools through a network of expectations, rules, grades, required subjects, and rewards for what is wanted and the subtle extinction of the great range of talents and achievements which are not wanted.

Do we paint an unduly dark picture? Perhaps, for sunny islands of contrasting practice are known to all of us. But study and reflection reveal that the contrasting examples are, indeed, islands in an otherwise gray sea. Those few must be tended and nurtured because of both their precious rarity and their potentiality for guiding change.

Massive Task of Change. A massive task of change lies ahead. We cannot take joy from these islands of success while we kill at home and abroad. We cannot point pridefully at those who have "made it" while half of us believe that life has passed us by. We cannot rejoice with our sons and daughters when their brothers and sisters do not graduate with them. We cannot congratulate ourselves on our talents when half of our talents have withered or died.

The inflated rhetoric we have used in describing our accomplishments far exceeds their nature and extent. Among many of our people there is a sense of outrage induced by the discrepancy between what is and what could be. Thankfully, however, not all our energies are used up in anger. We have more than a little hope that a new era can be both described and created. At the core of this hope is a fresh awareness of children: of their intrinsic rather than instrumental value, of their ability to learn, and of the kind of learning they could and should have as we look to the 21st century.

Other generations believed that they had the luxury of preparing their children to live in a society similar to their own. The primary—although seldom attained—aim of education was thus to transmit the existing culture to the young. Ours is the first generation to have achieved the Socratic wisdom of knowing that we do not know the world of the year 2000, in which our children will live. Although it is only 30 years in the future, we cannot truly envisage it and the range of demands it will impose on 21st-century man.

Requirements for the 21st Century. To speak, as we have in the past, of giving our young the "tools" with which to survive, to speak of techniques and "subjects" as the essential components of education, is to speak of trivialities. And, it is to send our children unequipped into the unknowable.

All that we can predict with certainty is that the central issue of the 21st century, as it is of this one, will be the struggle to assert truly human values and to achieve their ascendancy in a mass, technological society. It will be the struggle to place man in a healthy relationship with his natural environment; to place him in command of, rather than subservient to, the wondrous technology he is creating; and to give him the breadth and depth of understanding which can result in the formation of a world culture, embracing and nurturing within its transcending characteristics the diverse cultures of today's world.

We ask first, then, not what kind of education we want to provide but what kind of human being we want to emerge. What would we have 21st-century man be?

We would have him be a man with a strong sense of himself and his own humanness, with awareness of his thoughts and feelings, with the capacity to feel and express love and joy and to recognize tragedy and feel grief. We would have him be a man who, with a strong and realistic sense of his own worth, is able to relate openly with others, to cooperate effectively with them toward common ends, and to view mankind as one while respecting diversity and difference. We would want him to be a being who, even while very young, somehow senses that he has it within himself to become more than he now is, that he has the capacity for lifelong spiritual and intellectual growth. We would want him to cherish that vision of the man he is capable of becoming and to cherish the development of the same potentiality in others.

The education of this kind of human being is necessarily an enabling process rather than an instructional process. It requires opening the whole of the world to the learner and giving him easy access to that world. This implies enormous respect for the child's capacity to learn, and with the

granting of respect goes, by implication, the granting of freedom.

Learning in the Year 2000

When we look to education in the century to come, we see learning not as a means to some end but as an end in itself. Education will not be an imitation of life but life examined and enjoyed. A prescribed age for beginning to learn—or for ceasing to learn—will be meaningless. So will age as a criterion for determining what needs to be learned. And so will the standard school day and the standard academic year.

Diffused Learning Environment.   Compulsory education—or compulsory attendance, as it might better be called—will be a thing of the past. School as we now know it will have been replaced by a diffused learning environment involving homes, parks, public buildings, museums, business offices, guidance centers. Many such resources that are now unendorsed, unofficial, unrecognized, unstructured, or unsupervised—and unused—will be endorsed and made fully available for learning. There will be successors to our present schools, places designed for people to gather for purposes of learning things together.

The mere availability of a broad range of options will signify what we believe will be an important, and essential, change in our national value system. The word *success* will have been redefined, and a far wider range of choices—of study, of taste, of career, of "life style"—will be legitimized and seen as praiseworthy. Little boys will not be made to feel that they must grow up to be aggressive, or even affluent, men. Little girls will not need to feel that domesticity is the necessary end-all and be-all of existence. A career in science will not have higher status than a career in the creative arts. We will, in short, give substance to our longstanding but never fulfilled commitment to honor and develop the entire range of human talent.

Effects of Technology. Modern technology will help us realize our goals. The profound significance of the computer, when properly used in learning, is that it introduces an entirely new source of energy into the educational process. It is energy which is not affected by the night before, by viruses, or by unmanageable children. Subjects missed this year can be picked up next year. Single subjects can be pursued intensively for periods of time governed only by the whim of the learner. The 50-year-old need not humble himself by going back to school with 12-year-olds to get what he wants. He may go directly to the energy system, which is not aware of age, color, place of birth, or time of day.

It is possible that advanced technology will return the family to the center of the stage as the basic learning unit. Each home could become a school, in effect, via an electronic console connected to a central computer system in a learning hub, a videotape and microfilm library regulated by a computer, and a national educational television network. Whether at home or elsewhere, each student, of whatever age, will have at the touch of a button access to a comprehensive "learning package," including printed lessons, experiments to be performed, recorded information, videotaped lectures, and films.

Role of Schools. The moment so much teaching energy is made available throughout the 24-hour span of the day to all individuals at any place, school need no longer be what we have known it to be. It may then be used for latent and other functions we have not until now fully recognized. It will be the place where human beings come

together, not for the formalities of learning subject matter, but for the higher literacy that goes far beyond reading, writing, and arithmetic.

And so the schools of the 21st century, by whatever name they are known, will continue to play a major role in advancing insight and knowledge. But these "school learnings" will center more closely on developing man's ability to know himself and to relate to others. We expect that students will come together to speak and to listen, but in a greater variety of ways than they now do in schools. Heavier stress will be laid on learning different forms of rationality and logic and on ways to deal with crisis and conflict. The individual will be helped to develop a greater consciousness of his thoughts and feelings, so that he may feel and experience life and at the same time stand outside his immediate experience, so to speak. For 21st-century man would be a sentient being with both the freedom that comes from understanding and the accompanying control of impulse. The schools of the 21st century will have as part of their "curriculum" helping the young to understand their own antecedents, as they do today, but in infinitely more direct and vital ways.

Function of Teachers. In such an educational world, everyone will be from time to time both teacher and learner, but there will still be great need for teachers who, for the first time, will be free to engage in truly human tasks. No longer will they need to function as ineffective machines imparting "facts" by rote, since real machines will have taken over that function.

Some will spend many hours preparing a single lesson, to be viewed by thousands or even millions of individuals of every age. Others will evaluate such instructional programs. Some will staff counseling centers. Others will be engaging with groups of all ages in dialog designed to enhance human communication and understanding. The freedom and sense of potency we want for our children will be experienced, at long last, by their teachers. The entire enterprise will be directed toward increasing the freedom and the power of each individual to shape himself, to live at ease in his community, and in doing both to experience self-fulfillment.

From Today into Tomorrow: Recomendations

We have sketched a kind of learning Utopia. Achieving it will not be easy. In fact, without massive, thoughtful, social reconstruction, we will not get there at all. To stand aside—unconcerned, uncommitted, and unresolved—may very well be to assure no 21st century, least of all our Utopia.

We must actively aim toward a future in which the promise of American public education is truly fulfilled; when quality education, broadly conceived, is accessible to every American of every age and in every walk of life. We believe that the following three recommendations summarize what must be done if we are to move toward our Utopia.

Reordering National Priorities.   We recommend that national priorities be reordered, with spending of money, materials, and energy for war and defense subordinated to wars against racism, poverty, and pollution, and action on behalf of education.

Department of Education.   We recommend that a Department of Education, with full Cabinet status, be established and backed by a National Institute of Education in addition to the present United States Office of Education. The Department of Education shall contribute significantly to the reordering of national priorities, establish national educational policies, and promote constructive change in educational practice, all directed toward the full development of individual potential and the welfare of our society.

The immediate charge to this Department is

1. provision of resources for salvaging the growing number of school districts now on the verge of financial collapse
2. comprehensive implementation of what we now know to be quality education
3. increased educational experimentation through a wide variety of educational institutions, with public accountability

We make our recommendations in light of our conviction that school is a concept, not a place, that schooling and education are not synonymous.

Continuing Dialog Culminating in our 200th Birthday.   We recommend that a continuing dialog on our findings and conclusions be commenced now, to be held in towns and cities throughout the land, and culminating in the celebration of our 200th birthday, as a nation with learning as the theme.

Moral and Financial Commitment.   The first step toward implementing these three recommendations is moral commitment. Like all moral commitments, it must be backed by resources and action. There is much talk about the need to reorder national priorities. We add our voices to the millions seeking life-giving rather than death-dealing, conservation rather than the wanton pillaging of our resources, and the freeing and nurturing of the human spirit rather than the proliferation and worship of material objects. We sound a special call for full and genuine commitment to the right to learn.

The signal announcing this commitment

will be the long-awaited injection of large-scale government funds into learning: for encouraging experimentation in the schools we have, for the creation of schools specifically charged with experimentation, and for transcending the schools by bringing new learnings into them and by taking boys and girls to the whole range of resources outside of them. For a time, at least, we must infuse these funds as though we were at war—because, of course, we are at war: with ignorance, prejudice, injustice, intolerance, and all those forces crippling and restricting young and old alike.

Reform in the Schools.   The first phase of reconstruction pertains to the schools we have. Supposedly, the decade of the sixties was one of school reform: in the curriculum, in the organization of school and classroom, and in instruction. But recent studies reveal that the appearance of change far outruns the actuality of change. Put simply, the list of unfinished business is formidable.

In spite of emphasis on the need for identifying goals, few schools have a clear sense of direction. In spite of the obvious futility of "teaching" the world's knowledge, schools still emphasize the learning of facts rather than how to learn. In spite of our golden era of instructional materials and children's literature, the textbook is still the prime medium of instruction. In spite of growing knowledge about individual differences in learning, what children are to learn is still laid out by grades, years, months, and even days. In spite of increased insight into how learning occurs, teaching is still largely telling and questioning. In a diverse, complex society, our schools demonstrate almost monolithic conformity and enormous resistance to change. Close scrutiny reveals a deep-seated inability to come to grips with the problems those in the schools say they have.

The top agenda item, then, in seeking to

enhance learning in the seventies is unshackling the schools. The process must begin by decentralizing authority and responsibility for instructional decision making to individual schools. Simply dividing large school districts into smaller districts is not the answer. Schools, like individuals, are different in size, problems, clientele, types of communities served, and the like. They must create programs appropriate to their local circumstances, encouraged and supported in the diversity such a process necessarily entails.

Experimental Schools.   Many schools are not ready to take quick advantage of sudden freedoms. Too long fettered by the larger system, their staffs will be timid and uncertain. *We recommend, therefore, that substantial government funds be allocated for the deliberate development of schools, accountable to the public, whose sole reason for being is experimental.* Designed for purposes of providing alternatives, such schools could provide options in the community and thus would attract more supportive parent groups. In time, such schools would provide models for replication in networks of cooperating schools seeking to learn from each other.

Such schools need not arise solely within "the system." We are at a time in history when the need to break out of established patterns is critical. We need alternatives wherever we can find them. Some of the "free" schools springing up around the country offer diversity and should be encouraged to the point where their practices truly reflect their underlying philosophies.

We urge that support be given to schools endeavoring to abolish grade levels, develop new evaluation procedures, use the full range of community resources for learning, automate certain kinds of learning, explore instructional techniques for developing self-awareness and creative thinking, reschedule the school year, and more. Most of all, we urge that substantial financial support be given to schools seeking to redesign the entire learning environment, from the curriculum through the structure of the school to completely new instructional procedures.

Early Childhood Learning. Especially needed are well-developed models of early learning. We know now that the first five years of life largely determine the characteristics of the young adult. And yet we fail these years shamefully through neglect, through narrow, thoughtless shaping, or through erratic shifts from too little concern to too much concern. . . . We believe that it is impossible to provide the kind of learning environment we envisage in the absence of coherent, well-planned, and integrated health services to children from birth on. We believe also that early childhood centers are appropriate places for mothers-to-be to receive prenatal medical care and education and we urge their widespread establishment. There is ample evidence that commercial interests exploit the undiscriminating drive of many Americans to see to it that their children are well prepared for school. There also is abundant evidence that millions of parents fail to provide their children with the guidance, support, and social and intellectual skills they need for productive independence.

Two successive governments have promised and failed to deliver on a vast effort for expansion and improvement in the education of young children. A National Laboratory in Early Childhood Education suffered a crippled birth under one administration and is now starving to death under another. *We need research on the developmental processes of the young; educational programs based on what we now know; thousands of adequately prepared teachers to staff nursery and play schools; and exem-*

plary models of programs stressing cognitive, aesthetic, motor, and affective development.

Teacher Education. High on our list of "old business" is the overhaul of teacher education from top to bottom. The continuing debate over the value of "methods" courses, whether to have more or fewer of them, and how to regulate teacher education by legislative fiat only reveals the poverty of our approaches to the problem. Shuffling courses about is not the answer. Required are change strategies which take account of the fact that preservice teacher education, in-service teacher education, and the schools themselves are dependent, interrelated, and interacting components of one social system, albeit a malfunctioning one.

It becomes apparent, therefore, that financial resources must be directed toward those strategies that link schools seeking to change with teacher-education institutions seeking to shake out of established patterns. In brief, the teacher for tomorrow's learning must be prepared in school settings endeavoring to create a new kind of tomorrow. Most of today's teachers are prepared for yesterday's schools.

The tasks for the seventies may not have the heady appeal of the slogans for the sixties but they have a meaty substance about them, an "action" appeal for students, teachers, parents, private foundations, and all levels of government. Those who prefer doing to talking should find challenge enough in simultaneously redesigning the schools we have, creating alternative models, and arranging for teachers to find their role in these new settings for learning.

Electronic Education. But we need not wait for the 1980s to get a good start on other components of our visions for the year 2000. In fact, some roots are already taking hold. School, however reformed, is but one of the child's resources for learning. He spends more time and perhaps learns more, for better or for worse, in the electronic embrace of another—television. Television, in turn, is but one of several powerful teachers of electronic genre. The computer has even greater potential because of its ability to coordinate an array of devices: filmed or videotaped cartridges, records, graphic symbols, paper printouts, and responsive surfaces—devices for sight, sound, touch, and even smell.

We must stop talking about the possibilities of electronic educational aids and engage in experimentation on a much broader scale. To date, educational television has teetered on the brink of disaster, its limp fare failing to compete with commercial products, especially advertising. "Sesame Street" demonstrates vigorously that this need not be. It also demonstrates that successful use of television for desirable learning by children requires substantial financial backing for air time, for production, for evaluation, and especially for research into what constitutes appropriate subject matter. Ten years from now, the initial use of this instrument to teach children numbers and the alphabet will appear primitive indeed.

One of the major tasks involved in bringing electronics productively into children's learning involves a kind of research; namely, determining appropriate roles for human and machine teachers. The cant of audio-visual education insists that equipment be only an extension of human teachers. For computers, for example, to be mere extra arms of human teachers is to cripple both. We must recognize the fact that electronic devices constitute a new kind of instructional energy that is indefatigable, relatively immune to changes in the weather, and contemptuous of time of day or day of week. The human teacher, on the other

hand, is sharply limited in energy pattern, highly susceptible to chills, immobile in times of flood and snow, and sensitive to time of day. Clearly, the tasks for human and machine teachers should be both different and complementary.

When we come to recognize fully the characteristics and possibilities of electronic energy, most of the "givens" of schooling collapse. Learning need not take place in a box, from nine to three each day, five days a week, 180 days per year. There need not be a school beginning at age five, a graded school, or a "balance" of subjects throughout the day. Nothing need be "missed" because of absence; it can be picked up tomorrow by asking the machine to retrieve whatever is wanted. Something resembling a school—and this something might take many forms—is needed for those important human activities of interaction, exploration, finding one's self through others and others though one's self.

A needed form of experimentation, beginning now and continuing unabated into the 21st century, is that of creating options to schooling and legitimizing them. Soon, it will be common practice to show a variety of cassette tapes through a home television set. CATV promises a new set of options. And just behind both of these developments lies the home computer television terminal plugged into several video outlets, capable of playing its own records and cassettes, and providing printouts of the learning and cultural options currently available in the community. Taking advantage of these alternatives must be accepted and encouraged.

One way for us to grow accustomed to this nonschool freedom is to use much more vigorously the learning resources lying outside of school. Children should be excused from school for blocks of time in order to gain access to a nonschool teacher, to serve as apprentice to an artisan, or to practice a hobby in depth. The biggest block to the kind of learning future we are endeavoring to describe is not its availability. It is our individual difficulty in seeking to shake ourselves loose from the viselike grip of our present stereotyped thinking. Let us begin simply, with the young man who wrote: "All the world is a school, and you don't need permission slips to get out into the halls, and everybody should exchange classrooms, and—Hey! What about the lawns?"

Call to Action.   We had better begin now because we will need all of our imagination and our wisdom to cope with some of the critical moral questions soon to be thrust upon us. We now know that drugs are being used deliberately, under medical supervision, to intervene in the learning processes of children. Electronic means are being used to assist in the treatment of childhood disorders. The field of biochemistry is breaking new ground in seeking to understand and improve learning processes. Independent of these activities, drug use ranging from mild exploration to dangerous abuse is now a fact of life. Who is to be judged deviant and needful of chemical or electronic treatment? What restraints are to be placed upon the use of drugs for educational, self-serving, or destructive purposes? And who is to make what decisions for whom?

The question of who is to make what decisions for whom probably is the most pressing educational question both today and tomorrow. It is at the core of current discussions of accountability, voucher systems, and the like, in schooling. It is at the core of any minority-group demand for self-determination and equality. Ultimately, it brings us into the matter of who owns the child and who is to determine his freedom. To come back to where we began, the right to learn means the freedom of each individual to learn what he needs in his own way and at his own rate, in his own place and time.

This interpretation of the right to learn will not be easily understood. Nor are we likely to come easily to full acceptance and support of the flexibility and experimentation required to design the future of learning. We urge our leaders at all levels to work toward public understanding and support. We urge that celebration of this nation's 200th birthday in 1976 be taken as the culmination of a nationwide dialog about and assessment of our entire learning enterprise, a dialog that might well find its initial focus in the discussions and recommendations of the 1970 White House Conference on Children and Youth. Such a theme would herald the placement of human concerns at the top of our national priorities and would focus the eyes of our citizens on this accomplishment. The 20 million people expected to attend the year-long celebration could be given the opportunity to participate in a reasonable facsimile of the learning we have described for tomorrow.

We can think of no more appropriate celebration of the birth of a free nation than a demonstrable commitment to make real the most fundamental freedom: the right to learn.

Reading 52

Emerging Policy Issues in Public Education

Laurence C. Pierce

Anyone attempting to predict future issues underlying educational policy cannot help but approach the task with humility. For one thing, we often misunderstand an issue when it is first emerging. We judge it to be a different problem than it later turns out to be. For example, the much-discussed taxpayers' revolt of the late 1960s, on subsequent analysis, was no revolt at all. Instead it was a predictable and designed response of a democratic fiscal system to increases in the supply of education beyond that preferred by many communities. Similarly, the strong demands for equal educational opportunity in the early 1970s now appear to have sprung from a desire that education be more responsive to students' individual educational requirements rather than from a desire for all children to be treated equally.

For another thing, we have generally failed to predict major upheavals even a year or two in advance. It was only a few years ago that education was still heralded as a major growth industry. Only a few fore-

saw the leveling off and eventual decline in school enrollments. Almost no one predicted the strong demands by women for equal treatment in education, or foresaw the decline in student performance on national achievement tests.

It is with some hesitancy, therefore, that I reflect on future educational policy issues.

The most helpful way to begin an analysis of emerging policy issues in public education is to identify current issues which are likely to fade as time goes on. This will make it easier to see the problems likely to remain.

Education's Fiscal Crisis

For a variety of reasons, the fiscal crisis of public schools will probably recede soon as an important educational policy issue. The pressures for increased educational spending should taper off as enrollments decline —first in primary and secondary education, and by the middle 1980s in higher education. The teaching force, which consumes a large percentage of educational dollars, has already stabilized. Fewer teachers are being

Source: Laurence C. Pierce, "Emerging Policy Issues in Public Education." *Phi Delta Kappan* vol. 58, no. 2 (October 1976), pp. 173–176. Reprinted with permission.

hired. Enrollments in teacher preparation programs have fallen. The need for new school facilities will also decline, thus reducing claims on the public purse.

Much of the rapid growth in educational costs in the 1960s and early 1970s resulted from increases in teacher salaries. According to the Advisory Commission on Intergovernmental Relations, public education salaries increased by 167% between 1955 and 1973 compared to 129% in the private sector, and in 1973 were 8% above comparable private industry salaries.[1] Since teachers' salaries have caught up with other salaries, at least relatively, teacher salaries will increase more slowly in the future.

Not only will school enrollments and pressure to increase teacher salaries decline, efforts to shift support of local schools away from local property taxes are also likely to moderate. Property taxes may be onerous for many, but so are other taxes. The failure to find an acceptable substitute for property taxes has weakened the argument for their elimination.

The bad reputation of property taxes grew when unexpectedly high numbers of school budgets and bonds (which increase property taxes) were rejected by local voters. The shift in voter willingness to pay higher property taxes was interpreted by many educators as dissatisfaction with this form of taxation, rather than with the level of educational and other local services. Yet a recent study of school tax referenda showed that higher rates of voter rejection are associated with large school budget increases than in the past.[2] Another analysis found that voter rejection resulted from an increasing tendency of school boards to set proposed supplies of education at levels exceeding demand.[3] In other words, voter rejection of school budgets may not be a revolt against property taxes so much as a revolt against rapid increases in the costs of educational and other public services. These findings are supported by voter rejection of measures in a number of states to limit or replace local property tax support of schools.[4]

Attacks on property tax support of schools will diminish for other reasons as well. Conventional views of the regressiveness of property taxes have been weakened by evidence that property taxes fall most heavily on the owners of all kinds of capital.[5] Furthermore, many states now have property tax relief programs which reduce the burden on elderly and low-income property owners and renters. Property values are also rising rapidly in most areas, so that tax rates have leveled off or are declining.

Another reason why pressures for increased educational spending will subside is the growing belief that many of the most intractable problems of public schools cannot be solved with increased educational expenditures. As more high- and middle-income families leave the central cities, the costs of teaching minimum educational competencies to the students left behind will undoubtedly increase. The government should and will continue to provide compensatory education grants for its neediest citizens. But higher school expenditures will not eliminate the educational failures resulting from such factors as poor nutrition, family instability, or lack of job opportunities for urban youth. Nor will higher expenditures by themselves insure the coherent and supportive educational environment that children require for learning. Problems of truancy, violence, vandalism, and despair often prevalent in urban schools require a number of noneducational solutions as well as a basic restructuring of the school systems.

The Pursuit of Equal Opportunity

In the next five years the pursuit of equal educational opportunity will strike out in a new direction. The change will result, in part, from the countercyclical content of much public policy. Equality and liberty survive in dynamic tension as underlying values in American public policy. Mass public education was proposed by political leaders dissatisfied with the social inequalities in American society. Public schools were to be the vehicle by which young people could escape the social disadvantages of birth. Throughout its history, however, education policy has fluctuated between programs to increase equality and those to encourage initiative and individualism. The 1960s and early 1970s witnessed a variety of proposals to transform schools into instruments of social reform. The reaction of the 1980s will be a greater emphasis on making schools responsive to community preferences. References to responsiveness, efficiency, and liberty have already begun to replace equality as the dominant values in many educational policy debates.

Current reexamination of the goal of equal educational opportunity is more than a cyclical reaction, however. Programs and policies to promote equal educational opportunity have not accomplished their implicit purpose of enhancing social equality.[6] What little equalization has occurred has too often come at the price of increased uniformity and mediocrity in education.

The task of providing equal educational opportunity is complicated by widespread ambivalence about its meaning. Intellectually, we may define equal educational opportunity as a condition in which all students can develop their full potential without regard to social or economic backgrounds. Emotionally and politically, however, the goal of equal educational opportunity has meant bringing the educational achievement of minorities and economically disadvantaged students up to white, middle-class standards. No one really favors equally low standards; we all want equally high standards. The problem, of course, is that

public schools alone cannot produce this result. Factors outside their control (family, nutrition, housing, etc.) play too important a part in the educational achievement of children. Faced with an impossible goal, policy makers have devised surrogates for equality which are measurable but really have little to do with what equal educational opportunity means. Racial balance, equal access to resources, and equal spending are poor substitutes for the educational improvement of minorities and the poor.

Furthermore, although many people may say they favor equality of treatment, they in fact do not. They want schools to be responsive to the particular educational needs of their children. Equal dollars per student, equal class sizes, equal course offerings all discourage schools from matching their services to the particular mixture of their students' needs. It is quite possible, for instance, that while one group of students may benefit from a particular mix of classroom teachers, counselors, vice principals, and office clerks, another group of students might benefit from fewer counselors and administrators and more teachers, teacher aides, and tutors.

Decisions about the correct mix of services and personnel for any aggregate of students are difficult to prescribe under the umbrella of equal educational opportunity. The result will likely be suited to the majority and will probably not acknowledge that minority groups have systematically different educational needs. Without individually tailored mixtures of staff and services, it is difficult to accomplish anything more than superficial dollar equality among schools and students.

This superficial dollar equality is illustrated in a post-*Hobson* v. *Hansen* anecdote. A senior French teacher was moved from one Washington, D.C., high school to another because her high salary was contributing to an expenditure imbalance. By shifting her to a school with lower per-pupil expenditures, school administrators attempted to comply with Judge Skelly Wright's decision calling for dollar equality. However, the educational effect of the transfer was to deprive one group of students of a French teacher in mid-semester. Moreover, no students at the school to which the teacher was transferred elected to take advanced French, so she was assigned to clerical tasks and hall monitoring.

Equality will continue to be a strongly held value which significantly influences public policy. However, our inability to achieve equality through public schooling, and its inherent inconsistency with the equally strongly held values of efficiency and liberty, will require a new examination of the meaning of equal educational opportunity. The major problem we face in public education is to develop educational mechanisms that are responsive to the educational needs of our diverse population, and by so doing to encourage educational excellence. I believe the essence of equal educational opportunity is in improving the quality of education available to minorities and the poor. Too often today, excellent education is available only to those who can move to the suburbs or can afford private education.

Emerging Issues

The overarching educational policy issue during the next decade will be how to improve the performance of students who attend public schools. The outstanding flaw in our elementary and secondary schools is that an unacceptably large proportion of young people, most noticeably in the cities, emerge from the system without the minimum skills necessary for either higher schooling or for entry into a career. The fault may well lie in the lack of articulation between the levels of public schooling or

in the way we place young people in jobs. The fact remains that our schools are turning out young men and women unable to cope with the postsecondary world of work or education.

Real progress probably requires some change in non-school institutions as well as changes in schooling. Programs to improve the nutrition, health, housing, and family situations of Americans may be essential to improve significantly the performance of children in schools. Currently there is little evidence to support this speculation. Until such evidence is available, educators and policy makers will look for ways of reforming the schooling process to enhance the life chances of students who now pass through our schools only to fail outside.

Already policy makers are demanding accountability and taking a more direct role in the operation of schools. For example, the courts have ordered schools to provide educational services for handicapped students. A number of legislatures have enacted legislation establishing minimum competency standards in an attempt to insure that every child develops basic educational skills. Underlying the increasing political intrusions into educational decision making is the view that current educational problems are the result of incompetent school administrators and teachers. (Ironically, educators often encourage this view by saying that schooling is a matter of people working with people; that if you have good people, then the education system will be good.) Although the need for greater political control by representatives of the public may be justified, the assumption that educators are incompetent is not. There is little evidence to support the view that educators are less competent or more foolish now than in the past, or that, as a group, they are less concerned about the welfare of their clients than professionals providing other public services.

Another view is that public education's difficulties arise from the institutional arrangements through which schooling is provided—difficulties which can only be solved by reforming the institutions themselves. My guess is that the content of public education policy will increasingly be concerned with the organization and operation of schools. Financing and policy outcomes of schooling will still be discussed, of course. However, the issues which generate the liveliest debates will be about the organization of schools, what is taught in schools, how it is taught, who governs public education, etc. A review of several of these issues will illustrate my point.

Size as an Issue

The recent history of public education has been one of increasing centralization. Schools have become larger; districts have become fewer and larger; and the states' share of educational costs has increased, as have the number of federal programs and regulations. There are many reasons for this trend. Centralized educational management usually results from the need to control an increasing number of educational programs offered by public schools. District administrations have grown to coordinate new programs, to administer regulations of state and federal agencies, and to insure uniform standards throughout their districts. State educational agencies have grown in order to implement educational programs enacted by state legislatures and to coordinate federal programs within their boundaries.

Attempts to gain greater control through centralization, however, have left many districts out of control. Administrators in many large urban systems simply do not know what is happening in their schools. Budget information is often missing and inaccurate. Personnel records do not accurately reveal what services are being provided by teachers. Increasing numbers of specialists and consultants roam about with little supervision. Even students are becoming elusive, spending more time in school hallways or in the streets than in classrooms. Despite the best efforts of administrators and teachers, urban children seem increasingly immune to learning.

Part of the problem is size. Urban school districts and schools are too big. Education is still a highly personal endeavor. It requires great commitment from teachers and students in order to succeed. Teachers need to know students and their families. They also need to work closely with the school principals and administrators who provide the guidelines and resources for classroom instruction. Much of this intimacy is lost in large school systems. Teacher commitment and morale are low because teachers are being blamed for the failures of an educational program over which they have little or no control. They don't know the children in the classes because the children change schools so frequently; they don't know the students' families, who are equally transient; and they don't have much influence over education programs in an impersonal school bureaucracy. A first step in the reform of public education, therefore, is to determine the appropriate size of educational units. This is likely to become an important policy issue.

Control and Accountability

A major battle is developing over who should control public schools. The sides for the battle, however, have only begun to be chosen. A struggle will continue between legislators and education professionals. I have already mentioned legislators' interest in the educational process. In over 40 states legislators have enacted some kind of ac countability legislation. The trend is likely to continue. In the future, legislators will require demonstrable results to justify additional funding.

Legislators are also likely to find themselves battling with educators over the question of citizen control. The demand for greater citizen control has been brewing for many years. The urgency of those demands has been heightened by the rapid unionization of public school teachers. Important educational policy decisions are now being negotiated outside the traditional forums for school decision making. Parents and citizen groups, finding themselves frozen out of the negotiations process, are turning to the legislature for redress. Third-party bargaining, negotiations "in the sunshine," and community schools are only some of the proposals being considered to increase citizen involvement in educational decisions.

Battle lines at the district level are less clearly drawn. Under most collective bargaining statutes, union representatives negotiate with representatives of the school board on matters of compensation and working conditions. Organizationally, superintendents and their staffs are part of management and sit across the table from teacher representatives. Most administrators were formerly teachers, however, and their salaries are often tied to the negotiated settlement. They find themselves in the middle, in other words, between the school board's interest in protecting its constituents and the union representatives' interest in protecting teachers.

Usually forgotten in the struggle for control of education are individual teachers. Teachers are criticized for the failures of students, yet the battle between management and teacher representatives will further weaken their influence in the classroom. Union leaders so far have been insensitive to this problem. I would not be surprised to see many teachers siding with parents and citizen groups in their demands for more influence at the school site, as a step to restoring teachers' influence in the classroom.

A POLICY PROPOSAL: SCHOOL-SITE MANAGEMENT

If policy makers turn their attention to institutional reform as a way of improving the performance of public schools, what are some of the possible changes? One alternative would be to improve the technical abilities of educational managers. Management by objectives and planning-programming-budgeting systems are designed largely for this purpose. Another alternative would be to transfer educational choices to the family by providing education vouchers which could be used wherever parents decided. Both of these proposals have been widely discussed. Neither has proved to be politically feasable, however.

An intermediate reform is to delegate many program, budgeting, and personnel responsibilities to individual school sites. Both school-site management (or administrative decentralization) and education vouchers rest on the assumption that public schooling will be improved if consumers are given greater responsibility for deciding what educational services are provided. Education vouchers rely on the principles of competition and free choice. Parents who are dissatisfied with the performance of one school will transfer their children to another school which they believe better serves their children's needs.

As an alternative to greater choice, school-site management would offer consumers a greater voice in school affairs.[7] Consumers would be given greater responsibility in education by increasing their participation in educational decisions. When students' performance declines, school-site management would encourage parents to change the school's program rather than simply withdraw their children.

The essence of school-site management is a shift of decision-making responsibility from the school district to the school site. Under current state laws, school districts are legally responsible for providing educational services. They are empowered to raise money and are the recipients of state school support funds. School-site management would leave these legal relationships intact. In order to provide families with greater control over school affairs, however, important aspects of educational decision making would be delegated to the schools.

The reasons for doing this should be clear. The most important contact between school personnel and families takes place not at the district level but at the school site. Parents and students are more interested in their particular school than in the district, and consequently they are more likely to become involved at the school site. Furthermore, by dividing up districts into school units, the opportunities for parent participation are increased, while the scope of educational problems considered and the number of people involved at any one meeting are reduced. This makes it easier to respond to parent preferences, since only the preferences of parents with children in one school have to be considered; having to compete against fewer people increases the chance of any one parent to influence school policy. Finally, school-site management gives those education professionals most familiar with a student's problems—the principal and teachers—greater responsibility for the education of children. The educational needs of children within a school and between schools are not always the same. The principal and teachers in a school are in the best position to respond to those differences.

A fully implemented school-site manage-ment system would include parent advisory councils, promotion of school principals to positions as the most influential educational managers in a district, school-site budgeting, school-site negotiations on matters of educational program, school-by-school performance reporting, and open enrollment.

Implementing school-site management would not be easy. Comprehensive change brings out both the intense opposition of those who would lose by the change and incredulity among those who would be helped. Both PPBS and voucher proposals have fallen prey to these two forces. Professional educators whose lives would have been most affected by PPBS and vouchers have usually opposed both reforms. Despite valiant efforts by reform proponents to mobilize public support, the public has remained uninterested.

The political feasibility of school-site management is an important question. Opposition would come from several places. Many superintendents and central office personnel would oppose decentralization, because it will diminish their role and influence. Frequently, proponents of administrative decentralization seek to rally support for their proposals by emphasizing the incompetence of school administrators. This focus misses the major reason for decentralization and solidifies administrative opposition.

The purpose of school-site management is to encourage greater program flexibility, which is impossible with centralized school administration. Furthermore, school-site management would not eliminate the need for a central administration. Rather, it would free the central administration to spend more time on those things it does best, such as carrying on financial transactions with external agencies and insuring that district activities are being performed properly. Many financial, monitorial, auditing, and testing functions would remain the responsibility of the central administration. Most program planning and personnel planning, however, would be delegated to the school site.

Another likely source of opposition would come from union leaders. In many districts unions are in the process of establishing their relationships both with teachers and district management and are likely to oppose any reform that complicates their organizational task. They would particularly oppose the delegation of most personnel functions to individual schools, however, because it would mean dealing individually with many principals, rather than with the school board or its representative.

Union opposition might prove fatal to school-site management if most teachers were also opposed to the idea. The question of teachers' attitudes is complicated; attitudes are likely to vary considerably among districts. A key element of school-site management is strengthening the role of the teacher in the classroom. If teachers are given greater control in the classroom and more influence over school policy, they are likely to support the reform, or at least some parts of it. Teacher support is essential for the plan to work; it is also the key to diluting union opposition.

Some elements of school-site management have been enacted into law in Florida. The concept is also being discussed in some urban districts, such as San Francisco.[8] School-site management is a decision-making arrangement that enables school districts to make many hard economic decisions in ways that are responsive to the consumers of public education. It counteracts the trend toward increasing centralization in public education and is therefore consistent with demands for greater citizen participation in public decision making.

Finally, school-site management provides a mechanism for making professional educators more accountable for their performance. Accountability would shift from the district level to the school site. If a school failed to meet the expectations of its constituents, parents could ask that the principal be replaced, or they could try to change the school's curriculum and methods of instruction, or they could send their children to a different school. School-site management, in summary, would provide citizens with a stronger voice and a greater choice in public education than they now possess. Both are probably necessary to restore confidence in public schools, as well as to improve their educational performance.

NOTES

1. Neal R. Peirce, "Federal-State Report: Public Worker Pay Emerging as Growing Issue," *National Journal,* August 23, 1975, p. 1199.

2. Arthur J. Alexander and Gail V. Bass, *Schools, Taxes, and Voter Behavior: An Analysis of School District Property Tax Elections* (Washington, D.C.: Rand Cooperation, 1974).

3. Michael Boss, "Revolution or Choice? The Political Economy of School Finance Referenda," unpublished paper, Department of Political Science, Indiana University, Bloomington.

4. Donna E. Shalala, Mary F. Williams, and Andrew Fishel, *The Property Tax and the Voter* (New York: Institute of Philosophy and Politics of Education, Teachers College, Columbia University, 1973).

5. Henry Aaron, *A New View of Property Tax Incidence* (Washington, D.C.: Brookings Institution, 1974); and Willard Gaffney, "The Property Tax Is a Progressive Tax," *Proceedings of the National Tax Association,* 1971, pp. 408–26.

6. Christopher Jencks et al., *Inequality* (New York: Basic Books, 1973).

7. For a discussion of these two alternative strategies, see Albert Hirschman, *Exit, Voice, and Loyalty* (Cambridge, Mass.: Harvard University Press, 1970).

8. See Superintendent Robert F. Alioto, "An Education Redesign for the San Francisco Unified School District," San Francisco, January 6, 1976.

Reading 53

Education as a Lifelong Process

Harold G. Shane and Roy Weaver

Throughout history there have been notable persons who during their life exemplified the process of lifelong learning. With the approaching Bicentennial Year of 1976, a glance backward to 18th century colonial America affords a view of such a person. More than any other contributor to intellectual and political growth during the early development of the nation, Thomas Jefferson epitomized the concept that learning is a lifelong process.

During his lifetime, Jefferson was acknowledged as a statesman, architect, scholar, scientist, and author. As a statesman, he served with distinction as an official of the House of Burgesses, Governor of Virginia, Secretary of State, Vice-President, and President of the United States—the first to be inaugurated in Washington. While President, he applied his architectural knowledge to his role in the government both by creating the office of surveyor of public buildings and by providing leadership in planning the future development of

Source: Harold G. Shane and Roy Weaver, "Education as a Lifelong Process." *Vital Issues* vol. 24, no. 10 (June 1975), pp. 1–4. Reprinted with permission.

the Capital. Completion of the first buildings on the University of Virginia campus further highlighted his architectural skills and efforts.

Jefferson's familiarity with French, Italian, Spanish, Greek, and Latin, as well as his writings in philosophy, government, and science, provided access to the intellectual community of his day and brought him merited recognition as a scholar. The *Manual of Parliamentary Practice* which he wrote served as a framework for parliamentary procedure in the U.S. Senate. His writings in philosophy prompted his election as president of the American Philosophical Association, a post he held for eight consecutive years. More than any other contribution his work on the *Declaration of Independence* guaranteed his recognition as an able and versatile writer.

As a scientist he is remembered as an American pioneer in the realms of paleontology, ethnology, geography, and botany. On the basis of his scientific endeavors and his widespread recognition as one of the most prominent thinkers in America he was elected *associé étranger* of the Institute of France at the beginning of the 19th Century.

This was an honor that was shared by no other American in Jefferson's lifetime.

Thomas Jefferson stands as an exemplar of the process of lifelong learning. Unending pursuit of individual intellectual growth he viewed as a universal goal for humankind. He emphasized the latter position when he wrote in 1816 to du Pont de Nemours: "Enlighten the people generally and tyranny and oppression of both mind and body will vanish like evil spirits at the dawn of day."

Developments Likely to Influence Lifelong Education

Both the present world and the world of the 21st Century differ substantially from Thomas Jefferson's world. Nonetheless the "general enlightenment of the people" remains an integral part of America's educational commitment. In an age when the rapidity of change threatens to obscure reality and to inhibit decisive action, the lifelong study of persistent problems and opportunities for self-realization within and without U.S. society becomes vital. Such featured "real world" crises as exponential population growth, depletion of natural resources, the inroads of pollutants on the biosphere, the quest for more meaningful forms of governance, and a search for a revitalized moral framework in troubled times, represent a partial list of the social awareness and action component of the lifelong curriculum.

The need to create the future by exploring alternative futures and by designing controlling mechanisms to shape tomorrow becomes even more essential as we begin to recognize the enormous power of the forces now shaping institutions and life styles in our changing culture. The development of skills—including "process" skills—for implementing alternative future designs based on wise projection of interrelated events and for coping with the unexpected run parallel to the preceding two components of a future-oriented curriculum. A curriculum that anticipates the next century should be founded on: (1) novel approaches to the challenges of dealing with reality *now*, and for coping with the probable and possible tasks that will confront us tomorrow and (2) the necessary basic educational experiences for functioning effectively as a planetary culture. The writers believe lifelong learning in a world recreating itself will take the form of a seamless learning continuum extending virtually from birth until incapacitating old age takes over. Let us examine more closely this seamless concept of education.

Such a pattern of continuous education recognizes: (1) the diversity and uniqueness of persons—their diverse self-concepts and learning styles, their varying interests and backgrounds and (2) the organismic, holistic nature of learning as a timeless, evolving, continuous process. A lifelong continuum suggests itself when points one and two are accepted. Education becomes a day-and-night-year-round opportunity, open and accessible to persons of any age. The structure encourages a smorgasbord of offering, both formal and informal, devoid of arbitrary and uniform standards of performance. A sequential examination of the seamless curriculum should clarify the idea of a lifelong learning continuum. Let us begin with experiences for younger learners.

Early Childhood Education

An increasing body of research identifies the period of prenatal development as one of critical importance to the early physiological and intellectual growth of the newborn or very young child. As a result, the biochemical make-up of the mother during gestation may have a profound influence on human potential. From the time of birth until the age of two the environment provides certain initial patterns which influence subsequent learning. Such influences as the diet of the child, the extent to which he is permitted to interact verbally and socially with others, opportunities to play in stimulating surroundings, the amount of love given by parents, and the like, establish a learning style that the child carries with him for decades to come.

Because of the critical nature of the early months and years to the child's ongoing development it is imperative that a nurturing physical and educational environment be provided at an early age—especially for children from homes where such an atmosphere cannot be assured. On or near the child's second birthday, non-school preschool experiences, we suggest, should provide the young learner's first direct contacts with the educational community.

Direct contact with the school program, in the lifelong continuum, would begin near a child's third birthday. In a minischool situation a child would join a small group of from six to eight other children his age in a "developmental" program emphasizing socializing and cognitively enriching experiences. It should be stressed, however, that this program deliberately avoids a traditional "academic" experience. Rather, it is intended to develop a carefully planned and guided program of personalized growth.

Around the age of four in the seamless curriculum, a child would be transposed, that is, moved without conspicuous promotion, to the *pre-primary component* of the continuum. Such a change would resemble the entrance of a mid-year transfer pupil to a school after having moved to a new district. This *pre-primary component* departs dramatically from the typical contemporary kindergarten in that it provides planned "readiness" experiences aimed at building

and improving on preceding growth. In other words, the component stresses education as opposed to supervised care, entertainment, or premature exposure to, say, formal reading instruction.

Ideally, the nature of the pre-primary continuum inherently encourages the optimum development of each child prior to entry into the primary years. Realistically, fast-learning and maturing children might be transposed from the pre-primary component into the primary school in less than a year, and as early as at age five, whereas less mature, disadvantaged children or children with learning disabilities might participate in "readiness" experiences until as late as age eight or nine.

Although the primary years, as an integral part of the early childhood segment of the lifelong learning continuum, generally would involve children from six to nine years of age, grouping would not be based on chronological age. To the contrary, groups would be comprised of cross-age participants in a variety of inquiry, exploratory, expressive activities. Each learner would be helped and encouraged to "create himself."

The Middle School Years

Movement from the primary years to the middle school years would be characterized by "uninterrupted flow." When in the judgment of the teaching staff a child is deemed ready to function in a predominantly 9–12 age bracket, he would be moved to this new group environment. As in the primary segment of the continuum, a child might remain for less than a year or for as many as several years depending on individual needs, physical growth rate, and social development. In each case the child would move at his own pace and without reference to group norms. As a result, the elementary age might range from 5–15 year olds—excluding the 2–5 year olds in the early childhood segment of the continuum.

Transcending Secondary School Conventions: The Paracurriculum

At heart of a reorganized structure for the secondary school phase of the continuum is the importance of programs tailored to individual needs and to personalized goals. Patently, a number of alterations would be required in present high school practices to facilitate uninterrupted, open entry-and-exit opportunities. Effective utilization of educational technologies, individually guided instruction, cross-disciplinary approaches to knowledge, flexible scheduling designs, and differentiated staffing patterns promise to ease the transition to a seamless learning continuum at the early and mid-adolescent levels.

The concept of the *paracurriculum* is a vital aspect of the continuum we are describing because of its departure from most contemporary thinking and some legislation governing compulsory education. The term "paracurriculum" is designed to emphasize the significance of out-of-school experiences—formal and informal—which assist the learner in maximizing the potential coping and controlling powers he needs in a given environment. The formal paracurriculum—the world of non-school experiences which tomorrow's school would plan and incorporate— parallels the curriculum as its name suggests. It also supports and supplements conventional instruction in conventional schools. The non-school experiences such as work experiences, travel, and social service, usually (but not always) would be supported by pay or financial assistance to the student, and would temporarily, and sometimes permanently, replace in-school programs.

As a rule, between the ages of 13–15, an adolescent for whom a non-school experience would be deemed appropriate, could engage in one of several out-of-school activities. The primary responsibility of the educational institutions to which the student was associated would be to provide a psychological support system; that is, to develop a close working relationship with the student to assure ongoing in-depth counseling, to maintain communication with the student's parents, to assist in identifying cooperative businesses and social service agencies within the community, and to arrange meaningful travel experiences. Specific activities might include work in libraries, hospitals, welfare agencies, and preschools, or "with-pay" employment when proper safeguards are insured to avoid exploitation of child labor.

A strategic advantage of the paracurriculum over the conventional curriculum resides in the fact that after approximately a decade of guided experiences the student does not drop out of the educational continuum but moves at a 90 degree angle into planned paracurricular learnings. By offering a seemingly endless list of in-school and out-of-school experiences uniquely designed for each learner, the paracurriculum could come close to eliminating "left-outs," "drop-outs," and "push-outs."

While the flexibility of the open entry, exit, and re-entry of the paracurriculum would be especially functional in the secondary and immediate post-secondary range, it is not at all contingent on age or level. Opportunities for contributions to community service, temporary apprenticeships, and travel would be available to children at an early age as well as adults later in life. The paracurriculum concept also affords a person in his fifties or sixties the chance to move into the curricular realm from the paracurricular field in which he has been working so as to retrain for a post-retirement vocation, to learn a meaningful avocation for leisure time, or to seek education simply for self-satisfaction or pleasure.

Post-Secondary Education

This segment of the lifelong learning continuum is an extension of the paracurriculum. It includes both non-collegiate post-secondary learning opportunities and those contained in a university setting. A person enrolling in either the collegiate or non-collegiate setting may have completed the equivalent of four years of secondary education or may have been a part of work-related non-school experiences. In either instance, he would be admissable and afforded easy entrance to the resources of schooling if he chooses to finish educational activities aimed at providing either personal satisfaction or the improvement of his vocational marketability.

In the paracurriculum, then, education continues as a seamless continuum in which both paracurricular and curricular offerings are intertwined and linked administratively by infinite entry-exit-re-entry opportunities. The conventional university degree program would continue to provide certification or similar credentials to insure that qualified persons enter a given professional or service field. At the same time, post-secondary education as envisioned by the writers would encourage persons of an increased age span to participate on a continuing or continual basis in what traditionally has been termed adult education.

Necessary changes in the current structure of education to bring the lifelong learning concept to fruition include: (1) recognition for and further development of programs for "mature learners"—i.e., the opportunity for anyone to enroll in any educational program on a non-credit basis, with the preroga-

tive of taking for-credit examinations if they desire certification in a field at the post-secondary level; (2) an expansion of the function of the arts and science components from their traditional role in the liberal arts college to encompass offerings in a "communiversity" setting designed to meet the needs and interests of learners of all ages and all backgrounds; (3) development of a psychological support base and a flexible attitude toward groupings with widely-ranging multi-age learners; and (4) formulation of policies to assure the ease of continued exit and re-entry by learners without stigma or penalty.

Deployment of Staff

Without a substantial reorganization of school staffing patterns the seamless curriculum cannot become completely successful. The personalization and individualization of learning calls for teaching partnerships as well as increasing professional specialization. The concept of differentiated staffing promises an effective management system; one that can be created to meet the diversity of experience, multi-age groupings, and variability of needs and interests characteristic of learners in a lifelong seamless continuum.

Unlike conventional staffing procedures based on a ten month academic year, more members of a staff would be maintained since a continuum would provide year-round unending educational opportunities.

With the increased number of resource persons on the staff and because of the more varied professional skills made available to learners in the teaching partnership, certain members of the staff might serve as consultants to other community learning centers, and may work temporarily in more than one educational setting.

School Plant Planning and Use

Just as the lifelong learning continuum demands rethinking in terms of staff deployment, so too does the present-day perspective on school plant design and function. To begin with, the paracurriculum concept, coupled with the conventional curriculum, acknowledges that in-community settings as well as in-school settings must be considered as coordinate educational resources. In other words, the concept of "school plant" as envisioned here extends beyond the walls of schools, thus becoming a facility which encompasses businesses, industrial complexes, social service agencies and comparable institutions. Similarly, the function of available facilities must be reordered to include such services complementary to the learning process as: (1) guidance centers, (2) computer facilities, (3) research and development centers, (4) instructional system and media technology centers, (5) biochemical and psycho-social centers, (6) learner resource and communication centers, and (7) program planning and performance assessment centers.

Securing a Support Base for Lifelong Learning

From a brief description of a seamless lifelong learning continuum it becomes apparent that there exists no need for alternatives to schools, but rather a need to foster *more alternatives within a reorganized and revitalized educational community.* A number of the concepts discussed have been anticipated by such labels as "socially useful work," "continuing education," "work-study programs," "open education," "personalized instruction," "courses by newspaper," "educational options," and so on. A cooperative planning effort on the part of local, state, and federal agencies along with individual citizen action could move the lifelong learning concept to the forefront of educational development.

Granted that not every individual would be expected to become a notable historical figure such as Thomas Jefferson, each person nevertheless deserves the opportunity to explore and to develop the boundless limits of his human potential—a right requiring immediate reaffirmation in a world which sorely needs a well-educated species capable, throughout life, of defusing and then eliminating a threatening roster of humankind's problems.

Reading 54

Building Positive Futures: Toward a Nonsexist Education for All Children

Shirley D. McCune and Martha Matthews

"Sex-role stereotyping," "sexism" and "sex discrimination"—we have all heard these terms increasingly in recent years. They refer to critical educational problems we are moving to alleviate in our classrooms. But many of us still find ourselves uncertain as to what these terms mean and unsure of what they imply for our professional and personal lives.

Even as we may work to insure that our young children, male and female, are active in both the block and doll corners or that our middle-schoolers engage in both wood-shop and cooking experiences, we hesitate in the face of troubling questions: "Where did this sex-role problem come from—is it part of women's liberation?" "When we change a child's sex roles, aren't we threatening his or her sexual identity and orientation?" "Aren't we questioning traditional

Source: Shirley D. McCune and Martha Matthews, "Building Positive Futures: Toward a Nonsexist Education for All Children." *Childhood Education* vol. 52, no. 9 (February 1976), pp. 179–186. Reprinted by permission of Shirley McCune and Martha Matthews and the Association for Childhood Education International, 3615 Wisconsin Ave., N.W., Washington, D.C. Copyright © 1976 by the Association.

values, which are a parent's prerogative to maintain?" "What are the implications for schools and for educational change?"

How we respond to such concerns will be shaped by some of our most basic perceptions, values and experiences. In this article and those that follow, we seek to examine these questions and to provide suggestions that may assist in meaningful response.

SOURCES OF CONCERN ABOUT SEX ROLES

In the past decade criticism has been mounting with regard to the quality and relevance of the experiences our schools have provided children in preparing them for their adult roles. Two primary forces have stimulated this criticism. First, we have come to recognize and to reevaluate limitations placed on individuals by virtue of their race, ethnic group or social class. Second, as the rate of change in our society constantly accelerates, we are taking a new look at the relationship between this societal change and our educational institutions. Often we find ourselves caught between pressures for maintaining the past and for anticipating the future.

Both of these forces are reflected in the current concern with sex roles in education. In defining sources and manifestations of inequality, we have come to recognize sex as one basis for "sorting" children and for providing differential opportunities. As we become aware of changes in the roles of women and men, we see that such sorting on the basis of sex limits the optimal growth of *all* children.

Since the turn of the century, industrial and technological development has produced major transformations in the nature of work and paid employment. Statistical data document the following significant changes in the life patterns of women since 1900:[1]

- Women from every age group, marital and parental status are entering the labor force in increasing numbers; 90 percent of females now in high school will work at some point in their lives.
- Women are having fewer children; the proportion of a woman's adult life devoted to childbearing and childrearing is therefore decreasing.
- More women are becoming heads of families; growing numbers are assuming full responsibility for care and support of children.
- The percentage of women living alone or with persons unrelated to them is steadily growing; women between the ages of fourteen and thirty-four or over sixty-five comprise significant proportions of this group.

As the roles and lives of women have changed, so have those of men. With women's increased entry into the labor force, many men have assumed new responsibilities in maintaining home and family. Males and females are obviously having to relate differently to one another, both at work and in the home.

None of us is unaffected by these changes; they shape not only our lives but also the future lives of our children.

DEFINING THE ISSUES

Let us look now at some data on relationships between traditional sex-role differentiation and actual sex differences.

Eleanor Maccoby and Carol Jacklin recently completed a comprehensive analysis of over two thousand books and articles relating to possible psychological differences between males and females.[2] From their review, they concluded that a number of traditional beliefs about nonreproductive sex differences are myths, some are supported by research evidence, and others remain inadequately tested. Some of these conclusions are summarized below:

Myths

1. *That girls are more "social" than boys.* (Fact: Both are equally interested in social stimuli and rewards and equally adept at understanding the emotional reactions of others.)
2. *That girls are more suggestible than boys.*
3. *That girls have lower self-esteem than boys.* (Fact: Boys and girls are similar in overall confidence through adolescence. Girls rate themselves higher in confidence regarding social competence; boys more often see themselves as strong and powerful.)
4. *That girls lack the motivation to achieve.* (Fact: Although boys' achievement motivation appears to be more responsive than girls' to competitive arousal, there are no sex differences on the level of achievement motivation in general.)

5. *That the sexes differ in learning processes.* (Fact: Females and males are equally proficient on simple and high-level learning tasks.)
6. *That boys are more "analytic" than girls.*

Actual Differences

1. *Males are more aggressive than females* (boys are more aggressive physically and verbally).
2. *Girls have greater verbal ability than boys.*
3. *Boys excel in visual-spatial ability.*
4. *Boys excel in mathematical ability.*
   (Note: These ability differences usually do not first appear in early childhood but have their onset at adolescence and increase through the high school years.)

Obviously, these data do not support many common assumptions about differences between males and females. Several important points emerge. In those areas where sex differences do exist, we find considerable overlap in the distribution; for example, many boys have low-level visual-spatial skills and many girls demonstrate high levels of visual-spatial ability. Moreover, we cannot easily classify sex differential behavior as being either innate or learned. One sex may have a greater biological readiness to *learn* certain behaviors, or boys and girls may adapt themselves through learning to social stereotypes that have some biological basis. Further, it is probable that children learn sex-typed behavior through identifying with others of the same sex and through adopting sex-typed behaviors consistent with developing concepts of "masculinity or femininity."[3]

Considering the implications of their findings for social and educational changes, Maccoby and Jacklin write:

We suggest that societies have the option of minimizing, rather than maximizing, sex differences through their socialization practices. . . . In our view, social institutions and social practices are not merely reflections of the biologically inevitable. A variety of social institutions are viable within the framework set by biology. It is up to human beings to select those that foster the lifestyles they most value.[4]

SEX DIFFERENCES AND SEX-ROLE SOCIALIZATION

Additional research indicates, however, that our socialization practices maximize sex differences. Girls and boys are channeled into sex-typed behaviors and sex-differentiated roles that do not reflect the diversity of their individual abilities and the complexity of roles society requires of them. Although we must allow for differences across and within various cultural groups, we can draw some general conclusions:

- Sex-role behaviors are among children's first learnings.[5] In most cultures, behaviors considered desirable for boys include aggressiveness, suppression of emotion, well-developed reasoning ability and sexual initiative; for girls, passivity, dependence, conformity, nurturance and the inhibition of aggression.[6]
- By the time children reach preschool, they know their sex and the play preferences, behavior patterns and expectations adults hold for that sex.[7]
- As children grow older, their sex roles become more stereotyped and restrictive;[8] they tend to select fewer categories of behavior as sex appropriate and to indicate more polarized ratings of sex appropriateness.[9]
- Children of both sexes tend to see the male role as the more desirable one; male activities are accordingly given higher visibility and status.[10]
- Acceptance of traditional sex-role identity is related to positive psychological

adjustment for males and poor adjustment for females. Boys who identify with masculine roles show better psychological adjustment than do girls who identify with feminine roles. Females who display high IQ, creativity and originality are usually those who internalize cross-sex behavior; often they have exhibited tomboy behavior at some point in their lives.[11]

In our society, as children learn their biological identity and reproductive roles as females and males, they also learn that other roles open to them are influenced thereby. We need therefore to examine outcomes of our traditional sex-role socialization patterns and to reevaluate the restrictions and limitations they impose.

EDUCATION AND SEX-ROLE SOCIALIZATION

Recent data published by the National Assessment of Educational Progress indicate male-female differences in educational achievement that cannot be satisfactorily explained by our current understanding of basic sex differences in ability.

Results from NAEP assessments in eight learning areas show that males generally do better than females in four major subjects: mathematics, science, social studies and citizenship.

In the four other learning areas females consistently outperform males to any large degree in only one (writing); maintain a slight advantage in one (music); and in the remaining two subjects (reading and literature) are above male achievement levels at age 9, then drop to lag behind males by the young adult ages 26–35.[12]

Although the superior performance of males on the mathematics section of the Assessment is consistent with the differences in mathematical ability reported by Maccoby and Jacklin, it is difficult to attribute the performance deficits of females on non-

mathematical portions of the Assessment to their superior verbal abilities. More plausibly, many of these differences in performance may be the result of sex-differentiated patterns of educational socialization that perpetuate traditional male and female stereotypes.

We can also see effects of sex-role stereotyping in academic and career aspirations. Although girls average better grades in high school, they are less likely to believe that they have the ability to do college work.[13] Indeed, for the brightest high school graduates who do not go on to college, 75–90 percent are women.[14] Decline in career commitment has also been found in girls of high school age, related possibly to their belief that male classmates disapprove of a woman's using her intelligence.[15]

These sex differences in scholastic achievement, in college entrance and in career commitment suggest that females are not being adequately prepared to function optimally in the work roles that are increasingly theirs. Such data call forth important questions: Are we assisting our pupils to develop fully their unique abilities and interests, or are we channeling them into prescribed roles on the basis of sex? Are we providing the educational experiences necessary to promote the total development of both girls and boys and to insure that they will be equipped to function successfully not only in traditional reproductive roles but also in changing roles as workers, family members and individuals?

EDUCATION AND THE PERPETUATION OF TRADITIONAL SEX ROLES

Faced with such questions, we move on to explore four major ways schools function to transmit traditional sex roles and maintain stereotyped role expectations and behaviors.

1. Physical Environment of the School

Environmental sex segregation (e.g., a preschool classroom with doll corner at one end and block area at the other or a secondary school with separate entrances and corridors for boys and girls) discourages both sexes from exploring the full range of options available to them.

Symbols placed within the schools may also communicate differential expectations. Corridor displays of athletic trophies of males and clothing made by females reinforce stereotyped notions of sex-appropriate behaviors. School bulletin boards and classroom pictures frequently exclude images of women or portray both sexes in stereotyped and limited roles.

2. School Curriculum

Examples of sex-role stereotyping recur throughout the learning activities and materials that prescribe children's learnings:

In textbooks. Instructional materials often indoctrinate children in socially prescribed behaviors. Particularly for a young reader, these materials frame the child's range of experience and define the reality of his or her world.[16] Studies of the images of females and males in textbooks and other instructional materials used from preschool through college document both the relative omission of girls and women and the assignment of both sexes to stereotyped or limited life-roles. Females, when they appear, tend to be portrayed as passive and defined primarily by their relationships with males. They are usually seen at home, functioning in nurturant or supportive roles; when shown outside the home, they consistently assume traditional female roles of nurse, teacher, sales clerk or secretary. Boys and men tend to be depicted in different but also limiting stereotypes. Seldom do we see them expressing emotions or in nurturant roles; almost universally they are declared to be competent, achieving or career-oriented.[17]

In career and vocational education. The interest patterns, abilities and values that determine career goals begin to develop early. Materials and activities used to help children gain images of the nature of work and of the roles of adults in the community seldom present boys and girls with the range of options available to them. As children move up in educational level, materials and activities employed in formal career education programs are similarly stereotyped; so are those in most programs in vocational education.[18]

Through instructional groupings and course assignments. In both the preschool and the elementary school classroom, teachers frequently form instructional or classroom activity groups on the basis of sex. Although we may be able to justify some predominantly single-sex groupings on the basis of ability or skill levels, to categorize children solely in terms of gender demonstrates expectations that may function as self-fulfilling prophecies and limit the exposure of both girls and boys to unfamiliar subjects or activities.

Through physical education and competitive sports. Recent research suggests that development of physical, intellectual and social skills is inextricably related.[19] Although we should be encouraging all individuals to develop healthy bodies and body images and the commitment and skills for their maintenance, our physical education and athletic programs from preschool through college operate to minimize the importance of physical development for females. Such programs become increasingly sex-differentiated as students progress through school, and opportunities for females in competitive athletics become more and more restricted. As the emphasis on competition increases, greater and greater proportions of males are also excluded.[20]

Through counseling and guidance services. At the preschool and elementary school levels, our counseling and guidance services function primarily to help us identify and handle pupil behavioral or emotional problems. While the aggressive behavior of young boys is frequently treated as a counseling concern, we find relatively little attention is paid to excessive passivity in young girls.

At the middle and secondary school levels, counseling and guidance focus increasingly upon course selection and career planning. Stereotypical assumptions regarding sex-appropriate academic and career roles, as reflected both in the counseling process and in counseling instruments and materials, shape many choices.[21]

3. Structure and Organization of the School

In defining the parameters for provision of services, curricular and extracurricular programs, our school administrative practices and structures often transmit sex-role stereotypes. Policies influencing selection of instructional materials and course-content or those mandating different graduation requirements for males and females often reinforce stereotypes that limit options.

Allocation of staff roles is another source of sex-role stereotyping. In elementary schools, 83 percent of the instructional staff are females, yet women comprise only 14 percent of all elementary principals. At the secondary level, these figures are 49 percent and 2 percent respectively.[22] The relative

scarcity of men in preschool and elementary classrooms and of women in administrative positions clearly transmits traditional sex-role expectations to children.

4. Behavior of School Personnel

The attitudes and behavior of adults working in the schools (bus driver, custodian, teacher, principal, counselor, instructional aide, school volunteer) provide children with critical messages about how they are valued, what they can become, and what roles are envisioned for them by society. Research indicates that both counselors and teachers hold sex-differentiated expectations for girls and boys, women and men; further, that they may behave in ways that shape and reinforce pupils for conformity with these expectations.[23] Differential interactions of teachers with males and females in every category of teaching behavior has been clearly documented.[24]

TOWARD A NONSEXIST EDUCATION

Current Progress

What can we do to change these patterns? The beginnings of change have taken many forms and come from a variety of sources.

At least one school district (Berkeley, California) has supported a project for multiethnic nonsexist education which—through materials development, teacher training, and curriculum implementation in grades 4–6—aims to provide boys and girls from various racial-ethnic groups with opportunities and reinforcement to explore nontraditional emotional, physical, interpersonal and career roles.[25] Many other school districts have provided inservice training to help teachers identify and develop skills for alleviating sex-role stereotyping in schools.[26]

Especial attention has been given to modifying curriculum and instructional methodology. Selma Greenberg and Lucy Peck of Hofstra University have developed a "Basic Human Needs Curriculum" for preschoolers. It is designed to help children (1) to understand that all human beings—regardless of sex, race or class—share basic needs for food, clothing, shelter, love and affection, health and recreation, and sense of community; (2) to respect the diversity of vocations organized to satisfy these needs; and (3) to aspire to full participation in the adult world of work and leisure.[27]

Contributing to the change process for more equal and meaningful education for both sexes are (1) community groups that increase public awareness; (2) teachers who implement change in their classrooms; (3) administrators who provide supportive policies, programs and training opportunities; (4) professional associations that provide training or publication support; and (5) publishers, women's groups, teachers and students who develop curriculum and supplementary materials.[28]

But despite such significant beginnings, we have much yet to do to assure full sexual equality in the United States. Title IX of the Education Amendments of 1972 provides a comprehensive federal prohibition of sex discrimination in education. State legislatures (in such states as Massachusetts and Washington) have enacted similar laws. Such legislation can do much to increase public and educator awareness of the problem. We must all work to contribute to the development and support of meaningful efforts for its solution.

Goals and Actions or Future Growth

One good way to move toward effective nonsexist education is by evaluating our own schools and classrooms. As previously noted, our conclusions and responses will be shaped by our individual perceptions, experiences and values. Review several of the following educational goals and change-strategies to determine which may be most appropriate to your own situation and priorities.

Goal 1: The school's physical environment should be organized to encourage all children to explore the range of learning opportunities available and to provide symbols that affirm the contributions, values and potentials of females and males of all racial, ethnic and social class groups.

Action steps:

Examine your school and its classrooms to determine whether children are segregated by sex in activity areas, desk or work areas, storage areas for personal belongings, and recreation areas.

Examine bulletin boards, classroom exhibits, hall displays and office decorations for their:

- inclusion of males and females from all racial, ethnic and social class groups
- portrayal of males and females in both traditional and nontraditional roles in family, home, school, workplace and community.

Talk over your findings with pupils, teachers and administrators; determine steps each of you can take to accomplish necessary changes.

Goal 2: The school curriculum should prepare boys and girls for the full range of intellectual, economic, psychological, physical and social roles required for their healthy functioning as adults. It should not only transmit past experience and knowledge but also anticipate future needs—expanding rather than limiting the range of options available to all.

Action steps:

Review your textbooks and other instructional materials.

• Are males and females from all racial, ethnic and social class groups included?
• Are males and females portrayed in both nontraditional and traditional roles in family, home, school, workplace and society?
• Are the unique experiences, roles, histories and contributions of racial-ethnic minorities and women reflected?
• How will these materials affect self-images and aspirations?

Discuss your findings with pupils. Encourage them to develop critical evaluation skills that can help them to identify stereotypes or bias in materials.

Obtain supplementary materials that can be used to correct omissions or inaccuracies you identify. Involve pupils and teachers in creating such materials.

Review career education materials and vocational education programs. Do they reflect a full range of options for male and female students of every racial-ethnic group and social class?

Discuss with your pupils the range of options available to them and the relationships between themselves, their work, their families and their leisure activities.

Obtain supplementary materials that portray a diversity of career options for males and females. Expose all pupils to both traditional and nontraditional role models.

Review your vocational education programs. Are all courses open equally to males and females?

Review your counseling programs. Do they:

• reflect an awareness of behavioral and emotional problems experienced by both girls and boys?

• encourage all to explore the full range of academic and career options available to them?
• utilize instruments and materials that are free from sex-differentiation and bias?

Discuss your conclusions with counselors, teachers and administrators. Develop program goals and practices that can assist you in meeting the needs you identify.

Consider your assignment of classroom activities or classroom groupings. Are they made on the basis of sex?

Review your physical education and athletics programs.

• Are both boys and girls permitted and encouraged to participate in all activities and sports?
• Do athletic programs accommodate the interests and abilities of both sexes?

Review your total curriculum. Does it deal with both affective and cognitive needs? Do you feel it prepares both sexes for economic, psychological, physical and social roles and functioning?

Discuss your conclusions with pupils, parents and school personnel. Develop plans to begin modifications you find necessary.

Goal 3: Administrative policies and practices and the structural organization of the school should define the parameters of nonsexist education and support the development of programs for its achievement. Allocation of staff roles within the institution should model nonsexist practices and criteria.

Action steps:

Review student policies and practices of your institution. Do they differentiate between boys and girls in disciplinary, behavioral or dress requirements?

Review the staffing profile of your school or district. Do you see sex-stereotyping in the assignment of administrative positions? Classroom positions at the various educational levels from preschool through secondary? Classified staff positions?

Obtain a copy of the regulation promulgated by the U.S. Department of Health, Education, and Welfare under Title IX of the 1972 Education Amendments. Review the policies and practices of your school or district together with the federal requirements for nondiscrimination on the basis of sex in educational programs.

Goal 4: All school personnel should be able to respect and affirm the dignity and worth of all children, regardless of sex, racial-ethnic group or social class. School personnel should function to support and reinforce the development of children based on their potentials, values and abilities rather than on preconceived role-expectations.

Action steps:

Examine your own assumptions and values regarding appropriate roles and behaviors of females and males.

Read three articles pertaining to sex-role stereotyping in school and society.

Consider the ways your own sex-role assumptions and values influence your classroom or school behavior and shape the behavior and experiences of your pupils.

Review values clarification techniques and apply them in your school or classroom to explore with boys and girls their unique values and potentials.

Nonsexist education is quality education. Working toward its achievement provides each of us with opportunities not only for personal growth, but also for contributing to the reform of our schools and for developing a society in which every child and adult is freer to achieve his or her full potential.

NOTES

1. Karen Hapgood & Judith Getzels, "Historical Perspectives: Trends in Lives of Women," *Planning Advisory Service Report No. 301* (Chicago: American Society of Planning Officials, Apr. 1974), pp. 3–14.

2. Eleanor Maccoby & Carol Jacklin, *The Psychology of Sex Differences* (Stanford, CA: Stanford University Press, 1974).

3. *Ibid.*

4. *Ibid.*, p. 374. Reprinted by permission.

5. Jerome Kagan, "Check One: ☐ Male ☐ Female," *Psychology Today* 3, 2 (1969): 39–41.

6. Jerome Kagan, "Acquisition and Significance of Sex Typing and Sex-Role Identity," *Review of Child Development Research*, Vol. 1 (New York: Russell Sage, 1964).

7. Daniel G. Brown, "Sex-Role Development in a Changing Culture," *Psychological Bulletin* 55 (1958): 232–42. William Ward, "Process of Sex Role Development," *Developmental Psychology* 1, 2 (1969): 163–68.

8. *Ibid.*

9. W. W. Hartrupt & S. G. Moore, "Avoidance of Inappropriate Sex Typing by Young Children," *Journal of Consulting Psychology* 27 (1963): 467–73.

10. Roberta Oetzel, "Annotated Bibliography," in *The Development of Sex Differences*, Eleanor Maccoby, ed. (Stanford: Stanford University Press, 1966), pp. 223–322.

11. Eleanor Maccoby, "Women's Intellect," in *The Potential of Women*, Farber & Wilson, eds. (New York: McGraw-Hill Book Co., 1963).

12. National Assessment of Educational Progress, "Males Dominate in Educational Success," *NAEP Newsletter* (Oct. 1975). Reprinted by permission.

13. Patricia Cross, "College Women: A Research Description," *Journal of National Association of Women Deans and Counselors* 32, 1 (Autumn 1968): 12–21.

14. Women's Equity Action League, "Facts About Women in Education," (Washington, DC 20024: WEAL, 1253 4th St., S.W.).

15. Peggy Hawley, "What Women Think Men Think," *Journal of Counseling Psychology* 18, 3 (Autumn 1971): 193–94.

16. Sara Zimet, ed., *What Children Read in School: Critical Analysis of Primary Textbooks* (New York: Grune & Stratton, 1972).

17. Lenore Weitzman, "Images of Males and Females in Elementary School Textbooks in Five Subject Areas" (Washington, DC: Resource Center on Sex Roles in Education, 1975).

18. *Summary Data—Vocational Education, Fiscal*

Year, 1972 (Washington, DC: Office of Education, U.S. Dept. of Health, Education, and Welfare).

19. Robert Carkhuff, "Human Resource Development," unpublished paper, 1974.

20. *Summary Data.*

21. Arthur Thomas & Norman Stewart, "Counselor Response to Female Clients with Deviate and Conforming Career Goals," *Journal of Counseling Psychology* 18, 4 (1971): 353–57.

22. National Education Association, Research Division, *Research Bulletin* 49, 3 (Oct. 1971).

23. T. E. Levitan & J. C. Chananie, "Responses of Female Primary School Teachers to Sex-Typed Behaviors in Male and Female Children," *Child Development* 43 (1972): 1309–16.

24. Robert Spaulding, "Achievement, Creativity, and Self-Concept Correlates of Teacher-Pupil Transactions in Elementary School," Cooperative Research Project, No. 1352 (Washington, DC: Office of Education, U.S. Dept. of Health, Education, and Welfare, 1963). William J. Meyer & George S. Thompson, "Teacher Interactions with Boys as Contrasted with Girls," in *Psychological Studies of Human Development* (New York: Appleton-Century-Crofts, 1963). Phil Jackson & Henriette Lahaderne, "Inequalities of Teacher-Pupil Contacts," in *The Experience of Schooling*, Melvin Silberman, ed. (New York: Holt, Rinehart & Winston, 1971), pp. 123–34.

25. "Women's Studies Program" (Berkeley, CA 94709: Berkeley Unified School District, 1414 Walnut St.).

26. Based on requests for training assistance and materials received by the Resource Center on Sex Roles in Education.

27. Selma Greenberg & Lucy Peck, "An Experimental Curriculum Designed To Modify Children's Sex-Role Perceptions and Aspiration Levels," AERA Convention, New Orleans, 1973.

28. Myra & David Sadker, "Values Clarification Strategies for Confronting Sexism in the Classroom," 1972.

Index